D1321280

SECOND U-BOAT FLOTILLA

by the same Author
First U-Boat Flotilla
(Leo Cooper, 2002)

SECOND
U–BOAT FLOTILLA

by

LAWRENCE PATERSON

LEO COOPER

Dedicated to Bruce Shaw and Beam,
two of New Zealand's finest

First Published in Great Britain 2003 by
LEO COOPER
an imprint of Pen & Sword Books Ltd
47 Church Street
Barnsley, S. Yorkshire, S70 2AS

ISBN 0 85052 917 4

A CIP record for this book is available from The British Library

Typeset in 10/12pt Bembo by
Phoenix Typesetting, Burley-in-Wharfedale, West Yorkshire.

Printed by CPI UK.

CONTENTS

ACKNOWLEDGEMENTS

Many people have helped me while writing this book and I would like to begin by thanking Sarah Paterson - not least for hours of note-taking in Germany - as well as Audrey, Shane, Megan, James and Ray Paterson.

Among the varied people and organizations who have provided valuable information are John Vanzo, Wolfgang Ockert, Marc Haldimann, Hans Mair, Günther Ott, Chris Goss, Bob Cox, Lieutenant Goh RMAF, Walter Godinho, Russel Lemp, Mac McGowen, Oliver Meise, Jak Mallmann Showell, Frank James and the staff at the Lorient Naval Library. Thierry Nicolo helped enormously with his extensive knowledge of the U-boats in France. Ralf Bublitz put up with endless German translations without the slightest grumble, as did Robert Strauss. In the United States Tonya Allen aided a great deal with her meticulous proofreading, for which I am deeply grateful. From the Royal Navy Submarine Museum at Gosport, Maggie Bidmead (Head of Archives) and Debbie Corner (Head of Photographic Department) were, as always, extremely helpful with both reference material and photographs. My special thanks go to Jürgen Weber and the rest of the *München U-Boot Kameradschaft* for their help and patience with inexhaustible and often strange questions.

I would also like to mention Horst Bredow and Horst Schwenk of Altenbruch's priceless U-Boot Archiv. I strongly urge not only a visit to this remarkable museum, but also as much support as possible for its work.

Very special gratitude goes to the U-boat veterans who took the time to answer queries of mine in the course of writing this book, in particular Hans-Rudolf Rösing (*U35* and *U48*), Wolfgang Hirschfeld (*U109*), Bernard Geissman (*U107*), Fritz Weinrich (*U501*), Volkmaar König (*U99*) Ernst Göthling (*U26*), Georg Högel (*U30* and *U110*) and Jürgen Oesten (*U61, U106, U861*).

Photographic Acknowledgements.
Hans Mair (http://www.u35.com) Plate 1; Thierry Nicolo, 30; Wolfgang Ockert, Plates, 7, 10; Royal Navy Submarine Museum, Plates 4, 5, 8, 9, 11, 21, 22, 23, 26, 27, 28, 31, 32, 33, 34; ECP Armées, 12, 16, 17, 25; Don Presley, Plate 15; Personal Collection, Plates 2, 3, 6, 13, 14, 18, 19, 20, 24, 29.

FOREWORD

The fierce war for domination of the Atlantic Ocean between 1939 and 1945 remains one of history's greatest and most terrible naval campaigns. German U-boats, mainstay of the assault on British merchant lifelines strung between the New World and the Old, continue to elicit an emotional response from both those who participated in the action and those who study and remember the bitter convoy war.

Experiences of the various U-boat flotillas involved in this battle varied widely. Combat for the 2nd U-Flotilla 'Saltzwedel' began with an active, though covert, role in Spain's brutal civil war. It was also a U-boat of the 'Saltzwedel' Flotilla that opened Germany's naval attack against Britain on 3 September 1939. Thereafter 'Saltzwedel' was continually involved in front-line operations. While most combat units concentrated on the crucial onslaught within the Atlantic, the 2nd U-boat Flotilla was the first to use high-endurance U-cruisers to widen the boundaries of the struggle, ranging as far as Malaya. It was this unit that launched the devastating attack on America in 1942, 'Operation *Paukenschlag*', and the extremely successful assault against rich Caribbean oil and raw material arteries only months later. Long-distance boats of the 2nd U-Flotilla were also the first to cross three oceans to the Far East and form an uneasy alliance with Japanese naval forces. Indeed, among the top ten highest scoring U-boats of the Second World War, six belonged to the 2nd U-Flotilla.

Ultimately, as Germany's fortunes faded, so too did the composition of the flotilla until it was reduced to an infantry war in trenches around the ruined shell of Lorient, France, holding out until May 1945 and the general German surrender. Any seaworthy boats had long since transferred to Norway, where, although the flotilla still existed on paper, they were distributed among other units to join the struggle for survival in seas that no longer held any sanctuary for Germany's 'Grey Wolves'.

This book is not a day-to-day breakdown of flotilla actions, but, with extracts from War Diaries, veterans' recollections and records from Germany, Great Britain, France and the United States, to name but a few, it paints a dramatic picture of the war as experienced by the 2nd U-boat Flotilla 'Saltzwedel'.

GLOSSARY

Rank table

German	(medical)	British/American
Grossadmiral		Admiral of the Fleet/ Fleet Admiral
Admiral		Admiral
Vizeadmiral	(Admiralstabsarzt)	Vice Admiral
Konteradmiral (KA)	(Admiralarzt)	Rear Admiral
Kommodore		Commodore
Kapitän zur See (KzS)	(Flottenarzt)	Captain
Fregattenkapitän (FK)	(Geschwaderarzt)	Commander
Korvettenkapitän (KK)	(Marineoberstabsarzt)	Commander
Kapitänleutnant (Kptlt)	(Marinestabsarzt)	Lt Commander
Oberleutnant zur See (Oblt.z.S.)	(Marineoberassistenzarzt)	Lieutenant
Leutnant zur See (L.z.S.)	(Marineassistenzarzt)	Sub Lieutenant/ Lieutenant (jg)
Fähnrich zur See		Midshipman
Oberbootman		Chief Petty Officer
Obermaat		Petty Officer
Matrosenobergefreiter		Leading Seaman
Matrosengefreiter		Able Seaman
Matrose		Ordinary Seaman

(Note: In this book German naval reserve ranks are not indicated; i.e. Oblt.d.R. is referred to as Oblt.z.S.)

Aphrodite – (German) radar decoy comprising metal foil strips suspended from a helium balloon.

ASDIC – term applied to the snoar equipment used for locating submarines. A powerful and effective weapon, it emitted a distinct "ping" when locating the target. The word ASDIC is apparently an acronym for "Anti-Submarine Detection Committee", the organization that began research into this device in 1917, although some historians dispute this.

BdU – (German) *Befehlshaber der Unterseeboote*; Commander of all U-boats.

BdU.Ops – (German) *Befehlshaber der Unterseeboote Operationsabteilung*; Commander (Operations) of all U-Boats, responsible for the planning and execution of U-boat front-line activity.

BdU. Org – (German) *Befehlshaber der Unterseeboote Organisationsabteilung*; Commander of all aspects of logistical organization for U-boats while not at sea.

BETASOM – (Italian) Italian submarine command for operations in the Atlantic. Established in Bordeaux during 1940, becoming operational in September that year and totalling 32 submarines before Italy's surrender in September 1943. The name was a simple derivative of two words: B for Bordeaux and SOM as an abbreviation for *Sommergibile*, submarine in Italian. Within the Italian military, the letter B was indicated as "Beta", thus the combination of the two created the name BETASOM.

Bold – (German) Short for *Kobold* (goblin), an acoustic decoy, known also as the "submarine bubble target", it comprised a small cylindrical mesh container filled with calcium hydride. When ejected from a submerged U-boat the compound reacted with seawater to give off hydrogen bubbles and thus a false echo to ASDIC operators. Simple but effective.

Degaussing – Method of reducing the magnetic polarity inherently present around iron-hulled ships, thereby eliminating the threat of magnetic mines. This involved electrical cables carrying a strong electrical charge stretched around a ship's hull that reduced or even reversed the hull's magnetic field. Merchant vessels were given temporary degaussing treatment at naval degaussing stations rather than the permanent equipment installed aboard military ships.

DF – Direction Finding, homing on radio transmission.

Eel – (German) *aal* – Slang expression for torpedo.

Enigma – (German) German armed forces' coding machine.

FAT – (German) *Feder-Apparat-Torpedo*; Zigzagging torpedo head that followed a preset course. The warhead could be attached to both G7a and G7e torpedoes.

FdU – (German) *Führer der Unterseeboote*; Originally the title of C-in-C Submarines, later Flag Officer for submarines responsible for a particular geographical region.

Fido – Air-launched Allied acoustically homing torpedo – correct designation the "Mark 24 mine" – first used by VLR Liberators, May 1943.

Heer – (German) Army.

(Ing.) – (German) *Ingenieur*, engineering grade, eg. Kaptlt. (Ing.).

Kriegsmarine – (German) Navy of the Third Reich.

LI – (German) *Leitender Ingenieur*, Chief Engineer.

Luftwaffe – (German) Air Force.

OKH – (German) *Oberkommando der Heer*; Supreme Army Command.

OKL – (German) *Oberkommando der Luftwaffe*; Supreme Airforce Command.

OKM – (German) *Oberkommando der Kriegsmarine*; Supreme Navy Command.

OKW – (German) *Oberkommando der Wehrmacht*; Supreme Armed Forces Command.

Ritterkreuz – (German) Knight's Cross of the Iron Cross.

Sperrbrecher – (German) Barrage breaker, a specialized mine destructor vessel.

Torpedoboot – (German) Torpedo boat, designation given to light destroyers.

U-Boot Jäger – (German) Submarine hunter, usually a converted trawler.

UZO – (German) *überwasserzieloptik* – surface targeting device.

VLR – (British) Very Long Range, used in conjunction with aircraft, often Liberators.

Vorpostenboot – (German) Coastal Defence Ship.

Wabos – (German) *Wasserbomben* – depth charges.

Wacheoffizier – (German) Watch Officer. There were three separate U-boat watch crews, each consisting of an officer, Petty Officer and two ratings. The ship's First Watch Officer (IWO) would be the Executive Officer (second in command), the Second Watch Officer (IIWO) the ship's designated Second Officer, and the Third Watch Officer (IIIWO) often the *Obersteuermann* (Navigation Officer). Their duties were typically divided into the following time frames: 0800–1200 (1st Watch) 1200–1500 (2nd Watch), 1500–1700 (3rd Watch); then 1700–2000 (1st Watch), 2000–2400 (2nd Watch), 2400–0400 (3rd Watch); ending with 0400–0800 (1st Watch).

The duties of the IWO included torpedo and firing system care and maintenance as well as control of surface attacks; the IIWO handled administration regarding food and supplies as well as the operation of deck and flak weapons.

Wintergarten – (German) Nickname given to the open railed extension astern of the conning tower, built to accommodate increased flak weaponry. Known to the Allies as a "bandstand".

Zaunkönig – (German) 'Wren', title given to German T5 torpedo, acoustically guided and used particularly against escort ships, tuned to the pitch of their propellers. Known to Allies as 'Gnat'.

INTRODUCTION

'SALTZWEDEL'

"The faces of the men shine again.
These are the young recruits of the German U-boat arm."
Kurt Schulze, Propaganda Kompanie reporter.

By September 1936 Germany's second generation of submariners celebrated one year of existence for their premier flotilla 'Weddigen'. Unharnessed from the Great War's legacy of guilt by Adolf Hitler's formal renunciation of armament limitations imposed by the Treaty of Versailles, the 'Weddigen' Flotilla's small Type II U-boats had flourished in North Germany's Baltic ports.

The newly renamed Kriegsmarine held plans for a balanced and powerful fleet that could once again challenge the mightiest of navies on the High Sea. *Führer der Unterseeboote* (Flag Officer Submarines) *Fregattenkapitän* Karl Dönitz was determined that his callow U-boat service would take pride of place, their *Hakenkreuz* (hooked cross, or swastika) ensign on its red backing a symbol of resurgent national pride.

In that year he also realized that the small coastal boats that made up the 'Weddigen' ranks were not enough to carry his strategies into the Atlantic Ocean, scene of a bitter convoy battle between 1914 and 1918 and likely key to any future struggles that Germany may face. Their radius of action and weapon load would be unable to sustain a high-seas offensive. Larger prototypes had been developed during the previous decade in covert foreign design projects, yielding the disappointing heavy Type I, based on a large ocean-going Spanish design named *E1*, and the more versatile medium size Type VII, developed from three 500-ton Finnish submarines, *Vesihiisi*, *Kiu-Turso* and *Vetehinen*, whose lineage could in turn be traced back to the successful wartime UBIII model.

By August 1936 both Type Is had been commissioned, *U25* and *U26*, as well as *U33*, the first Type VII,[1] and a second U-boat flotilla was to be created for these new submarines. Like 'Weddigen', it too would receive the name of a U-boat hero of the Great War and so on 1 September 1936 the 'Saltzwedel' flotilla was officially raised under the command of FK Werner Scheer in the placid waters of Kiel's military harbour.

Oberleutnant zur See Reinhold Saltzwedel had been wartime commander of five U-boats, in the course of twenty-two patrols sinking a staggering 111 ships and winning the coveted "Blue Max" (*Pour le Mérite*) on 8 August 1917. But Saltzwedel's luck eventually deserted him on 2 December 1917 when his final command, *UB81*, sailed into an

---

[1] Often erroneously called the "Type VIIA".

uncharted minefield near the Isle of Wight and Saltzwedel and twenty-seven of his men were drowned.

Fregattenkapitän Scheer was also a veteran of the First World War U-boat service, Watch Officer aboard both *U30* and *UB85* during the final two years of that conflict. In the newly raised Kriegsmarine U-boat arm he had spent six months in command of *U10* before transfer as Senior Officer of the 'Saltzwedel' Flotilla.

The first generation Type VII was a single-hulled and single-ruddered medium-sized submarine, with four bow torpedo tubes and a distinctive externally mounted, thus not reloadable, stern tube. The deck weapon was a quick-firing 8.8cm naval cannon (not to be confused with the more famous '88' of the Army and Luftwaffe with which ammunition was not interchangeable). Saddle tanks slung outboard of each flank provided external fuel bunkerage and gave the submarine its characteristic bulges, while above the pressure hull a substantial deck casing had been built, tapering at each end and punctured by numerous flooding and drainage holes.

By December 1936 'Saltzwedel' comprised nine Type VII submarines numbered consecutively *U27* to *U35*. *U26*, one of the two unstable and heavy Type I designs, commanded by Kaptlt. Werner Hartmann, was also attached, ostensibly for training purposes. Both models were deficient in their mediocre turning circles, having only a single rudder between the prop wash of dual screws, but the Type I showed itself the weakest. Its diving time was extremely poor; at full speed with six tons of negative buoyancy in her diving tanks it took forty seconds to reach ten metres. The fuel bunkers' vent system was soon found to be defective as well, air bubbles running forward and aft and changing volume with ambient water pressure found at different depths. Ordinarily a nightmare to keep at stable depth, it was nearly impossible to control with this trapped air dancing back and forth. Combined with an inherent wobble while submerged brought on by the inefficient ruddering, *U26* bordered on unmanageable. Nor were the problems over when she surfaced. With the centre of gravity forward of the central control room the boat was bow heavy and difficult to handle, often taking so long to recover from pitching that the diesel engines' efficiency was severely impaired, props flailing wildly in thin air as they lifted out of the water.

The problems of stability in the Type IA and the lack of space for a stern torpedo tube below the waterline in the Type VII – both caused by the single rudder – were not lost on German designers and the later Type VIIB and Type IXA would both incorporate twin rudders, one directly behind each screw, allowing for internal mounting of the stern torpedo tubes and better handling for both.

The 'Saltzwedel' flotilla was soon joined by catch/escort ship (*Fang und Sicherheitsboot*) *T158* and newly recommissioned U-boat tender ship *Weichsel*, formerly the merchant ship SS *Syra*. The entire flotilla soon transferred to the estuary bay of Wilhelmshaven where before long two of its boats tasted action on a genuine war footing.

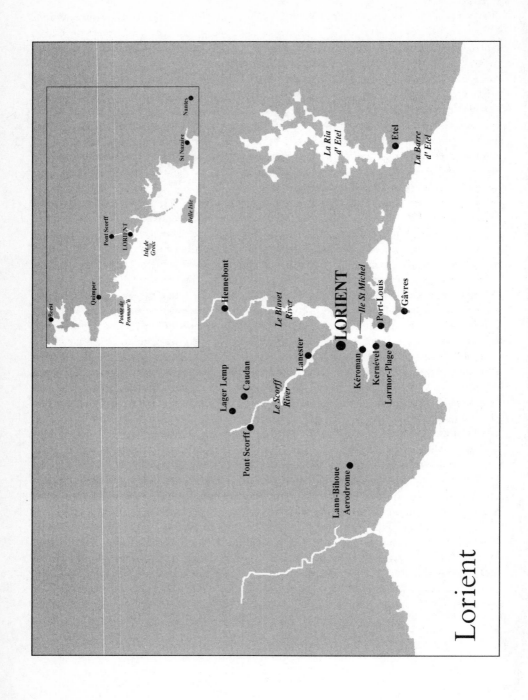

Lorient

The Atlantic Battleground

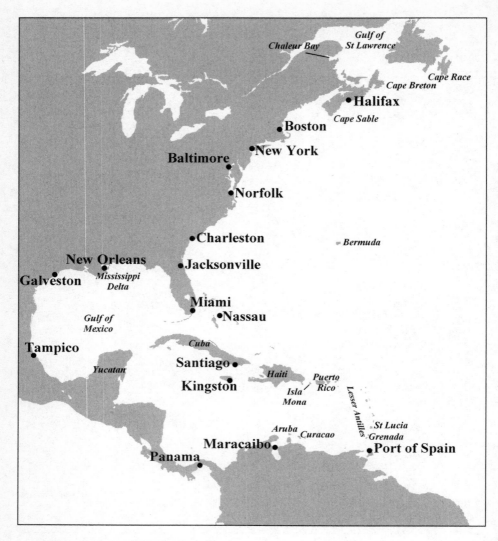

North America & Caribbean Sea

1

THE SPANISH ADVENTURE

Spanish politics had polarized into bitter opposition between left and right wing parties by the mid-1930s and, after the left wing were narrowly voted into power during February 1936, General Francisco Franco Bahamonde, commander of Spanish troops in the North African colony of Morocco, declared his opposition to Spain's ruling government, thus setting off what was to become the Spanish Civil War. Later, on 1 October, he was named Commander in Chief of the Nationalist Army and Chief of the Spanish State by the Nationalist rebels. The Spanish Naval Attaché in Paris, Lieutenant Commander (*Capitán de Corbeta*) Arturo Génova, resigned his post and joined Franco's Nationalist cause as naval adviser. With him he took a long and trusting relationship with Admiral Wilhelm Canaris, of the German Intelligence Service. Canaris lobbied in Berlin on behalf of Génova for armed assistance to be given to the Nationalists, who possessed no submarine force, as opposed to a flotilla of twelve belonging to their Republican opponents. Génova believed that one of the most urgent matters facing Franco was the breaking of the stranglehold that Republican naval patrolling around Gibraltar placed on Franco's troops trapped in Spanish Morocco.

However, Canaris' request was refused by the head of OKM, *Konteradmiral* Günther Gruss, as Hitler vacillated over whether to commit more support to the Nationalist cause. Italy displayed no such qualms and pledged immediate military aid, transferring two submarines and their crews to Spanish waters during October 1936. On 24 October Italian Foreign Minister Count Ciano met Hitler to sign the declaration that formed the Rome-Berlin Axis – "in the interests of peace and reconstruction" – and also to announce to the German dictator Italy's new Spanish naval commitment.

This was perhaps the spark that Germany had been waiting for and the Luftwaffe's 'Condor Legion' was moved to Spain. Shortly afterwards OKM decided to detach two new Type VII U-boats from 'Saltzwedel' to the Nationalist cause. *U33* and *U34* would operate covertly and independently of further operational orders. Under the codename 'Training Exercise Ursula' (named after Karl Dönitz's only daughter) both submarines slipped quietly from Wilhelmshaven on 20 November 1936, two days after Germany and Italy formally recognized the Franco regime as Spain's legitimate government. The two young regular commanders were replaced by more experienced men, *U33*'s Ottoheinrich Junker replaced by Kurt Freiwald, while aboard *U34* Ernst Sobe handed over command to veteran Harald Grosse, the latter having navigated in Spanish waters during the 1931 trials of *E1*. The man delegated in Berlin to supervise the operation and be the link between the boats and OKM was *Konteradmiral* Hermann Boehme, Admiral Commanding the Fleet (*Flottenchef*). As the boats prepared for their secret 'war' their crews were sworn to life-long silence regarding their forthcoming experience 'on pain of death' in an 'Exercise Order' (*Ubungsbefehl*) issued by OKM on 6 November 1936.

Once at sea the two U-boats painted out any identification markings before separately passing through the English Channel to Biscay. Both penetrated the Mediterranean during the night of 27 November, easing past patrolling Republican warships while remaining surfaced on a still and moonless night. Their brief stated that, should they be challenged, they were to declare themselves British and hoist the Royal Navy ensign. Fortunately, they were never compelled to attempt such a subterfuge. Once through the Straits of Gibraltar they waited for Italian submarine operations to cease in order to prevent any 'friendly fire' incidents. On 30 November German patrolling began, the two U-boats separated by an imaginary line drawn along the 0° 44" west longitude, *U34* to operate west of this line around Cartagena, *U33* to the east. In the case of an emergency that required one of the German boats to enter port they were instructed to use the Italian naval base at La Maddelena, flying an Italian ensign as they put in.

Clandestine patrolling by Kriegsmarine U-boats caused great anxiety among the upper echelons of Hitler's Admiralty. Eight days before the two German submarines had begun their missions Italian submarine *Torricelli* claimed the first victim of the undersea battle. After German surface ships engaged on an overt international 'peace-keeping' mission had seen and reported heavy units of the Republican fleet anchored outside of Cartagena, *Torricelli* crept cautiously towards the Republicans, the large warships sheltering from possible air attack, safe in the knowledge that their Nationalist enemy possessed no submarines. Two Italian torpedoes streaked from the darkness and ploughed through the machinery spaces of cruiser *Miguel de Cervantes*, disabling the ship for the duration of the Civil War. Republicans immediately blamed "foreign submarines", their allegation proved by the recovery of warhead fragments of Italian manufacture. Italian security regarding their submarine activity was in any case virtually non-existent, their involvement an open secret within Italy. German military leaders had a very different attitude, fearing immediate and far-reaching political complications if their level of involvement in Spain became known. Initially, it also appeared as if General Franco was not going to win his war, Republican forces more than holding their own in combat, albeit with Soviet assistance.

Worse still, both *U33* and *U34* were operating in an ever-increasing pool of confusion. Slow and laborious communications with OKM, often worded in extremely ambiguous language to foil any attempt at enemy code-breaking, conspired to sow uncertainty amid the men at sea. Boehme felt further hamstrung as time passed, his two U-boats under strict orders to engage only Republican warships. When OKM learned that he had requested Nationalist naval authorities not to sail warships within the German operational zone, they forbade any further communication of this kind in fear of a possible security breach. Questions as to which targets were legitimate passed from Freiwald and Grosse to Boehme, transmitted at night as the two U-boats lay twenty miles off the coast to recharge batteries and use their radios. Boehme in turn passed the query to Berlin, who inevitably denied them freedom of action against any but the most clearly identified target.

During the evening of 1 December L.z.S. Grosse engaged a Republican destroyer near Cartagena, but missed, his single torpedo impacting on nearby rocks. On 5 December, and again three days later, he tried further attacks against similar targets, also missing with his single shots. Perplexed by consistent failure, the spectre of possible torpedo malfunction appeared to Grosse and his officers as the most likely explanation for their lack of success. Fortunately, no betraying fragments from the stray torpedoes were searched for or found by the Republicans. Likewise, L.z.S. Freiwald in *U33* was experiencing no success. Several attempts at closing merchant and military shipping had been frustrated, either by an absence of firm target identification – as was the case on the night of 5 December when the Republican cruiser *Méndez Núñez* passed before his tubes with darkened destroyer escorts

– or defensive manoeuvring by the target vessels. OKM issued a strict edict to Boehme for transmission to his commanders that:

> "The lack of visible success must not lead to such determined action that camouflage and preventing compromising Germany are not considered the highest priority."

Finally German willpower gave out and the War Ministry issued orders that clandestine U-boat operations were to be discontinued as of 10 December. Plans to send further 'Saltzwedel' boats on a war footing to the Mediterranean theatre were scrapped and the two submarines were scheduled to begin their trek home the following night. Italy had willingly taken over the task of Spanish Nationalist naval operations.

Ironically it was at this point that *U34* scored Ursula's sole success. On 11 December while passing Málaga en route for the Straits of Gibraltar, lookouts aboard Grosse's boat sighted the low silhouette of Republican submarine *C3* patrolling four miles from the coast. It was a little past 1400hrs and the Spanish crew, commanded by *Alférez de Navío* Antonio Arbona Pastor, had just finished their midday meal. Swiftly submerging, *U34* approached its unwitting quarry. Grosse ordered a single torpedo fired, worried that the trail of bubbles left by the G7a torpedo may give warning to his target and identify from where the attack was launched. He had no cause for concern. The "eel" struck *C3* broadside eight metres from her bow at 1419hrs, tearing the hull in two and sending her straight to the bottom in seventy metres of Mediterranean water. Of forty men aboard only three survived, two being crew members flung clear by the blast while they were engaged in throwing food scraps overboard, while the third was a passenger on board, Merchant Marine Captain (*Capitán de la Marina Mercante*) Agustín García Viñas who had been in the conning tower talking to the submarine's commander. Fortunately for Germany the Republican disaster was eventually attributed to an internal explosion, despite initial fears of foreign submarine attack. Eyewitnesses from nearby anchovy fishing boats reported either little or no explosion but instead a huge cloud of "white steam or smoke", pointing at the possibility that the German warhead did not detonate on impact but sheared through the submarine's iron skin, seawater flooding rapidly onboard to cause an explosion within the battery compartment. It was the fourth German torpedo launched in Spanish waters and the only one to have hit its target. By the end of December both boats were back in Wilhelmshaven and returned to the control of their original commanders. The German naval covert war in Spain was over.

Of course the departure of *U33* and *U34* from Ursula was not the end of U-boat and Kriegsmarine presence off the shores of Spain. German naval power ironically, and somewhat absurdly, became participants in duties undertaken by the 'Non-Interventionist Committee' that comprised Britain, France, Italy and Germany, all guilty of meddling in Spain's affairs. During this period fifteen U-boats, including the entire 'Saltzwedel' Flotilla, were legitimately deployed at various stages, a constant U-boat presence that continued until May 1939.[2]

The majority of 'non-interventionist' naval activity was restricted to the Atlantic and U-boats were frequent visitors to Spanish ports for rest and replenishment, their conning towers resplendent with Germany's national colours. This politically acceptable Spanish

---

[2] *U14* ('Weddigen'), *U19* ('Weddigen'), *U23*, *U25*, *U26*, *U27*, *U28*, *U29*, *U30*, *U31*, *U32*, *U33*, *U34*, *U35* and *U36* (all 'Saltzwedel').

operation still provided valuable training in near warlike conditions as U-boats played cat-and-mouse with ships of the French and English navies.

Meanwhile the 'Saltzwedel' Flotilla had lost its commander, Werner Scheer, accidentally injured during July 1937 and forced into a period of convalescence. It took three months for an official successor to take his place: thirty-eight-year-old KK Hans Ibbeken, ex-commander of *U27* and veteran of a single Spanish patrol. In the intervening period the exhausting training schedule continued, Dönitz throwing his boats into gruelling 'wolf-pack' exercises, the tactics of which he had long been an advocate.

The flotilla's tenders provided targets for attempted interception and simulated attacks, but the Baltic proved too small to fully test Dönitz's theories on group operations. However, despite repeated appeals for permission to stage Atlantic exercises, Hitler and *Grossadmiral* Raeder refused to allow U-boats to operate in any strength in the Atlantic while the war in Spain continued, their presence *en masse* possibly open to misinterpretation by the British. On the other hand approval was granted for small-scale test cruises in the Atlantic. In Wilhelmshaven Kaptlt. Wilhelm Ambrosius of *U28* was temporarily replaced by the veteran Kaptlt. Hans-Günther Looff, while Looff's brother-in-law Kaptlt. Hans Rudolf Rösing, also a veteran submariner and naval officer since 1925, was placed in temporary command of *U35* for a planned joint voyage into the Bay of Biscay.

> "This was to be the first time that the boats had been into the Atlantic. I took over from Michahelles, as Dönitz was of the opinion that Michahelles had not enough experience, therefore one of the 'old horses' was put in. At that time there was the Spanish Civil War and our two submarines were initially to be sent to the Spanish Civil War, but when we were equipped and fully ready the Spanish war was practically over and so we were sent to the Azores."

The two U-boats sailed from Wilhelmshaven on 11 January 1937; their trip later deemed a success by both commanders and by Dönitz.

> "We made the first experiences in really heavy weather. We had a Force 11 to 12 and then we found out what excellent seagoing ships these submarines were. And when it was too wet we could go down and relax.
>
> "Of course, as usual, I was seasick. I used to be seasick for the first two days in the cruise. But later on I was okay. Normally I never did anything about it, in the war of course I took medicine."

After their return to Germany both temporary commanders were removed and the U-boats reverted to Baltic training, the realistic nature of their exercises leading to several near-fatal accidents.[3] By November 1938 four more U-boat flotillas had been established: 'Lohs' and 'Emsmann', composed of Type II U-boats, 'Hundius' comprising large Type IX U-boats; and 'Wegener' carrying the second generation of Type VII, the VIIB.

Korvettenkapitän Hans Ibbeken was to lead 'Saltzwedel' through the Sudetenland and Czechoslovakian crises when Germany seemed on the brink of war and U-boats put to sea on 'exercises', waiting to see if politics dissolved into combat. While international tension mounted in mid-1939, Hitler stoked the simmering embers further by renouncing any intention of abiding by the Anglo-German Naval Treaty. He stated before a full and

---

[3] Indeed *U35* received the unwelcome sobriquet of the flotilla's *Unglücksboot* (bad luck boat) due to its apparent penchant for accidental ramming.

enthusiastic *Reichstag* that Britain and France's declaration of support for Poland, with whom Germany was exchanging belligerent words, reflected their aggressive attitude towards Germany, thus removing the friendly basis on which the treaty had been founded. In May Dönitz finally got the Atlantic exercises that he had coveted and 'Saltzwedel' took to the ocean, the exhaustive drills proving highly successful and, despite the U-boats having some measure of favour granted them, were taken as a vindication of the 'wolf-pack' theory. However, the exercise also made starkly apparent how woefully inadequate Dönitz's submarine force would be in the face of an all-out commerce war.

But as late as August 1939 Hitler was still reassuring his naval commanders that war with Great Britain was impossible. During that month U-boat exercises were held around Hitler's yacht *Grille* in preparation for a demonstration of power before the King of Italy. After preparatory exercises had been satisfactorily completed, officers of the U-boats involved were invited to lunch with Dönitz and Raeder aboard the *Grille* in Swinemünde Bay. *U35*'s commander Kaptlt. Werner Lott remembered:

> "After lunch a most unusual thing happened: Raeder rose, made a few compli-
> mentary remarks and then said, 'Have you any questions?' I knew him personally
> well and shot without a second's hesitation the question at him: 'We cannot help
> feeling that we are drifting towards war – is that really unavoidable?' And he also
> answered without hesitation: 'Hitler has so far achieved so much in his six years in
> power that I do not think he will risk all the positive achievements in a hazardous
> war' ".[4]

But as Dönitz later wrote:

> "Our anxieties nevertheless were not wholly allayed."[5]

Little did the assembled officers know that 'Case White', the occupation of Poland, had already been planned to the smallest detail. As feared, at midday on 15 August 1939 coded orders reached FdU Karl Dönitz on leave with his wife and young family that read:

> "An officers' party for U-boats is to take place on Saturday 19 August and as many
> as possible are to be present."

The innocuous message threatened war – Atlantic U-boats to be prepared for departure. 'Saltzwedel' was in a high state of readiness and morale, seven of the ten boats having returned from Spain as recently as May. By 1300hrs 'Saltzwedel's deputy senior officer L.z.S. Johannes Franz had informed FdU that *U28*, *U29*, *U33* and *U34* could be ready to sail by Saturday 19 August.

Should hostilities with Poland begin, U-boats were charged with three main tasks. The first was minelaying and offensive torpedo patrols by sixteen Type II and VII U-boats within the Baltic to cut off any Polish attempt to break out of the Kattegat. Meanwhile seven Type IIs were to prepare for North Sea minelaying, while the third duty left all remaining Type I, VII and IX U-boats heading west of England to await the probable onset of operations against merchant shipping.

However, the alert highlighted the need for an intermediate regional command level for the U-boat service. As FdU, Dönitz exercised overall command of his small force, but

---

[4] Letter from Lott to Earl Mountbatten, 9 September 1974.
[5] *Ten Years and Twenty Days*, Karl Dönitz, p. 42.

two offices were created on 18 August after consultation with OKM to handle immediate and localized organizational concerns, including transits to and from German coastal waters and the allocation of provisions and stores. Local control of U-boats operating in the North Sea and Atlantic was placed in the hands of Kaptlt. Ibbeken, based at his 'Saltzwedel' head-quarters of Wilhelmshaven. Under the title 'FdU West', Ibbeken began his new role on 23 August alongside his acting Chief of Staff, 'Weddigen' commander, Kaptlt. Looff.[6] A second regional command, FdU East, was also established to oversee Baltic operations. In Wilhelmshaven Ibbeken was aware that, should England and France declare war in support of Poland, Dönitz himself would take control of all western U-boat deployment and oper-ations aboard his command ship *Erwin Wassner*.

During August the number of operational 'Saltzwedel' boats was raised to eleven with the inclusion of *U36* transferred from Neustadt's training unit and on 19 August, four days after Dönitz had opened entries within his War Diary (*Kriegstagebuch*), the first four 'Saltzwedel' boats left Wilhelmshaven for the waters west of England, followed days later by four more. Three boats had been ordered to Kiel for the Monday afternoon to receive orders directly from Dönitz himself.

By the end of August all of 'Saltzwedel' was at sea awaiting orders. Three were grouped in the Baltic lying in wait for the expected breakout of Poland's tiny navy. *U31*, *U32* and *U35* had all sailed from Neustadt to Memel on 24 August, augmenting the watch held by smaller Type IIs. After one day in Memel they put to sea again, patrolling north of Hela as part of the so-called 'Swedish U-boat group'. Their wait was too brief and uneventful.

At 1300hrs on 31 August Dönitz and his staff disembarked from their temporary accom-modation aboard the U-boat tender *Hecht* and boarded the large command ship *Erwin Wassner* in preparation for sailing to Swinemünde. On the eve of war Germany's Naval High Command became aware that the three priority Polish Navy targets, destroyers *Grom*, *Blyskawica* and *Burza*, had already escaped the Baltic trap and were free in the North Sea, slipping through the German blockade by a mixture of stealth and audacity. Further to that, on 23 August Hitler and Stalin's representatives had signed the German-Soviet non-aggression pact, removing the potential of hostile Russian forces in the Baltic. The three 'Saltzwedel' boats were transferred to the North Sea command, sailing into port over the next two days, forming a small reserve. Indeed Dönitz had already queried the wisdom of all boats immediately sailing for war stations as opposed to holding back an operational reserve, but OKM's reply had been unequivocal – all boats must sail. Dönitz was aware that they would 'dribble back' to base by the middle of September and the unexpected bonus of the three Baltic 'Saltzwedel' boats in port was a more than welcome development.

At 1553hrs on 24 August all Atlantic U-boats received notification of the Russo-German pact and that Poland and Great Britain were mobilizing. Dönitz was rebuked by Kaptlt. Hans-Jürgen Reinicke, advisor to Chief of Naval Operations (*Operationsabteilung 1/SKL*) *Vizeadmiral* Kurt Fricke, for being too informative to his officers, a criticism Dönitz brushed aside, stating that he must be able to give his men general information rather than the 'dry-bones' of orders. On 26 August the FdU War Diary recorded:

> "The moment of surprise is lost this year. Well-trained anti-submarine forces must be expected to be in action already when U-boats arrive at the position where mines are to be laid.

---

[6] This post of 'FdU West' was short-lived and bore little resemblance to the office of FdU West established in July 1942 under Kapitän zur See Hans-Rudolf Rösing.

"[Nonetheless] the very confident attitude of the crews deserves special mention. In my opinion it is a sign that the broad masses of the people have great faith in the government."

While Saltzwedel's three Baltic boats began to return to port the remaining eight flotilla boats were allocated different tasks, should war with England become a reality. They all lay to the Atlantic side of Britain, apart from the clumsy Type I *U26*. On 26 August *U26* had gone into the shipyards to repair a torn fuel bunker and complete final fitting out. Aboard this unwieldy machine was its new commander, Kaptlt. Klaus Ewerth, the man who had been in command of *U1*, the first U-boat launched by a rearming Germany in 1935. The thirty-two-year-old East Prussian commander, veteran of three patrols around Spain, was given the odious and difficult prospect of minelaying by OKM. Ewerth's final target orders would arrive while at sea, *U26* and its expectant crew sailing from Wilhelmshaven on 29 August.

Another important factor lay in Germany's favour. Between 1935 and 1939 Germany's code-breakers, B-Dienst, had penetrated Royal Navy signal traffic, the large volume generated by deployment during the Spanish Civil War, the Italian invasion of Abyssinia and the Munich crisis providing ample material for the diligent cipher staff. By September 1939 nearly all British naval signals could be decoded with relatively small delay, a valuable addition to an otherwise impoverished arsenal.

Dönitz had no illusions about his submarine strength. He reasoned that by the end of August he would have only forty-three boats at sea, the remainder either in dockyard, on training or experimental use. He felt that in order to plug some of the more gaping gaps in Germany's U-boat front line he would need forty-three more operational U-boats, plus an additional forty-three in dock undergoing overhaul. "Thus," he wrote, "for war of any length, 130 U-boats should be necessary. Even then I would have no reserves. . . . Therefore the minimum requirement to be aimed at is 300 U-boats."[7] Germany went to war with a total of fifty-seven.

---

[7] BdU KTB 21/8/39.

2

LOS! 1 SEPTEMBER TO 31 DECEMBER 1939

1 September 1939: At 0445hrs Poland's western border erupted in flame as Germany struck in what transpired to be a bitterly fought six-week invasion. Despite the heavy cruiser *Schleswig Holstein* opening the attack with a devastating artillery barrage, the Kriegsmarine had little part to play in the fighting that followed. All Polish submarines bar one had departed for war patrols as part of 'Operation Worek', Poland's naval defence plan, and within days had successfully evaded their enemy and raced for England. Of the returned 'Saltzwedel' Baltic boats both *U31* and *U35* would require slightly less than a week before they were ready to sail again. All eyes were on England as the world waited to see if the policy of appeasement had met its end. In case it had, and despite more protest from Dönitz, *U35* was also prepared for minelaying in the English Channel, hoping to clog ports that would likely become involved in ferrying British troops to France with TMB mines.

3 September: *"Kriegsausbruche mit England"*
At a little after 1100hrs Great Britain and the Commonwealth declared war on Germany. France followed suit four hours later and Europe was at war again. Aboard *U28*, crewman Herbert Lange remembered the declaration of war:

> "We didn't shout, 'Hooray'; we said, 'Hm!' If that's the way it has to be, we told ourselves, then roll up your sleeves and get on with it. We weren't actually pleased about it. We knew that our adversary, England, was a hard adversary. . . . We had all volunteered, the U-boats were somehow something special. But we knew it wasn't going to be easy."[8]

Orders that embraced the constraints of the Hague Convention, particularly the Prize Laws, were immediately sent out to all Kriegsmarine units at sea. However, with the meagre number of U-boats available for Atlantic operations at the outbreak of war, OKW ordered concentration on targets considered acceptable to be sunk without warning, i.e. vessels under warship or aircraft escort, troopships or ships transmitting information to the British.

But Dönitz hoped to bring his Atlantic boats closer to England's shoreline. Realizing the inevitability of convoy defence, Dönitz hoped to force Britain into adopting the convoy system before sufficient warship numbers could protect them, deploying his 'wolf packs' against the defenceless conglomeration of enemy shipping. But Berlin hesitated to sanction submarine use in shallow water, fearing severe reprisal from ASW warships. This hesitation became doubt, swiftly transforming into orders to move the U-boats to the outer coastal areas. The one 'Saltzwedel' exception remained Ewerth's *U26* and its minelaying

---

[8] *Servants of Evil*, Bob Carruthers, p. 70.

mission. Ewerth's jeopardy deepened when orders arrived to lay his twenty-four TMB mines in the approaches to Portland harbour, the homeport of HMS *Osprey*, the Royal Navy Anti-Submarine Warfare School. Immediately after the completion of its task Dönitz intended to recall Ewerth's boat to join *U31* and *U32* in Germany as relief for those Atlantic U-boats scheduled to return with fuel bunkers low by middle September.

Elsewhere, *U30* had been at sea for thirteen days when the broadcast of war with England reached the boat. Immediately, Oblt.z.S. Fritz-Julius Lemp and crew prepared to begin hunting south of the rock that thrust out of the Atlantic Ocean north-west of Ireland named Rockall. Lemp was well aware of the Hague Convention and the constraints that he would be acting under. There were also specific targeting instructions from his superiors – French shipping to be spared on orders from Hitler, following assertions from *Grossadmiral* Raeder that it was possible France would yet come to peace terms. All passenger ships were also out of bounds, again by order of Hitler who greatly feared a repeat of the 1915 *Lusitania* sinking that could again swing international opinion, particularly that of Americans, against Germany.

Lemp waited with his boat firmly astride Great Britain's northern merchant shipping lane, his lookouts scouring the horizon for potential targets. At a little after 1930hrs on 3 September the smudge of approaching smoke heralded one such steamer. Lemp ordered his boat dived and observed a "darkened steamer" steering a zigzag course – sure sign of a guilty conscience. The young commander could make out a passenger liner silhouette but took her to be either an auxiliary cruiser or a troopship heading toward the dominion of Canada. Whichever was correct, he reasoned that this was a legitimate target crossing his path, and an interception course was plotted, dynamos quietly whining as the electric motors reached full power. It was the first of two tragic and far-reaching errors that Lemp was to make during his wartime career. The ship that he was observing through crosshairs was in fact the passenger steamer SS *Athenia*, 13,580-ton three-decked liner of the Donaldson Atlantic Line Ltd. bound for Canada with 1,103 civilian refugees, including 311 Americans.

Within the bow torpedo room aboard *U30* two 'eels' were selected and lay ready to be pushed from the tubes, propellers engaging once the torpedoes were free of the boat to propel the weapons toward their target. The submerged U-boat swiftly attained a near-perfect firing position as the *Athenia* blundered towards it, and at 1934hrs Lemp gave the order to launch. Chaos ensued.

Nobody aboard SS *Athenia* saw the telltale streaks of bubbles from the single G7a torpedo as it sped toward the steamer's flank. An enormous explosion against the ship's port side slightly abaft of her bridge from the warhead's 280kg of '*Schiesswolle* 36' destroyed the forward engine room's watertight bulkhead and ripped an enormous hole in her side. The nineteen-year-old ship was doomed. As *Athenia* took on a 30° list she immediately began to settle into the water while her crew struggled to staunch the flooding.

Simultaneously, aboard *U30*, there were also frantic efforts being made by sailors to save their ship. Lemp's first torpedo had arced on a straight and true course towards *Athenia*, but his second was a 'hot runner' and had hung up inside the torpedo tube, propeller running and warhead armed. In desperation the torpedo room 'Lords' worked to free the weapon from its trap, finally succeeding in releasing it from the tube. Fearing the possibility of the unpredictable and possibly slightly damaged torpedo circling, Lemp crash-dived away from the dangerous 'eel' and it exploded nearby, but harmlessly. Unfortunately for Lemp and in subsequent written histories of his attack, this explosion was taken to be gunfire as *U30* surfaced nearby immediately after the explosion, thought by eyewitnesses aboard the listing *Athenia* to be closing distance to its target to begin shelling her. Georg Högel, junior radioman aboard *U30*, states that the two flashes later reported by British survivors to be U-boat artillery were (a) the detonator and (b) the high explosive of the errant torpedo exploding. He asserts vigorously that *U30* did not open fire with its deck weapon, although the gun crew manned their action station on deck. In several other accounts Lemp is said to have attempted to halt the ship's distress signals with artillery fire before ordering his 8.8cm cannon to cease shelling as the identity of the ship became horrifyingly clear. It was also Högel who intercepted *Athenia*'s SSS ('attacked by submarine') transmissions, promptly informing his commander on the bridge after the U-boat had surfaced. Lemp, who had indeed been preparing to fire artillery, ordered his gun crew to stand down. He had realized his tragic error, but compounded his mistake by suddenly leaving the area, thereby once again contravening the rules of war by offering no assistance. He knew that there would be a storm following his attack, but kept radio silence as *U30* cruised quickly away from the sinking ship.

In Berlin there was no inkling of what had happened off Rockall. British and Irish rescue ships had raced to the scene of the sinking to save the survivors clustered together in lifeboats. Of the people aboard, 118 died, twenty-eight of them Americans. The British Admiralty had been handed a propaganda coup within ten hours of the declaration of war, and used it to their maximum advantage. They raced to alert the media of all nations that a German U-boat in direct breach of the accepted rules of war had sunk *Athenia*, evoking the memory of the *Lusitania* – exactly what the German High Command had feared. German propaganda immediately refuted British claims, clumsily stating that Churchill himself had ordered the ship sunk to turn public opinion against Germany. Dönitz and his staff were adamant that no U-boat had been responsible, although fears that there may have been a tragic error steadily grew. On 4 September Dönitz's War Diary matter-of-factly recorded:

> "1035hrs: From the B.Dienst and radio reports we have learned of the sinking of the English steamer *Athenia*. (B-Leitstelle 0409). Exact statements about this sinking are not available."

Dönitz began to face the possibility that it had been a mistake by the only U-boat in that area, Lemp's *U30*. In the absence of any communication regarding the event Dönitz could only keep his silence and speculate, hoping that he was wrong.

4 September: Wilhelmshaven became the target for the first British bombing raid on Germany. Unfortunately for the British the results were spectacularly unsuccessful, seven Blenheim bombers shot down with only minor damage inflicted to the aging cruiser *Emden* by flaming British wreckage crashing on her aft deck. The shipyard, docks and 'Saltzwedel' garrison buildings were unaffected.

As Dönitz prepared to fling every available boat against England, 'Saltzwedel' was reinforced. The second large Type I, *U25*, was transferred from Neustadt's training flotilla, although it would not be freed from shipyard refit until October. 'Saltzwedel' commander Kaptlt. Hans Ibbeken recorded the arrival of *U25*'s new captain in the flotilla War Diary, 33-year-old Viktor Schütze, a man who would later play an important part in the unit's history. Schütze had been in the navy since April 1925, serving initially aboard Torpedo boats before transfer to the fledgling U-boat arm during 1935. After seventeen months in command of the 'Weddigen' flotilla's *U19*, including a 1937 tour of duty in Spanish waters, he then spent ten months training for destroyer service before returning once more to the

Unterseebootwaffe in August 1938 for a year aboard school boat *U11*. His insight into destroyer operations would later place him in good stead in the Atlantic.

'Saltzwedel' now had a strength of twelve U-boats, all Type VIIs apart from the two cumbersome Type I boats. Hans Ibbeken, however, was finished with the post of flotilla commander. He left in September 1939 to command the U-boat school (*Unterseebootschule*) at Neustadt before becoming commandant of the larger U-boat Training Division (*Unterseebootslehrdivision*) in June 1940.[9]

5 September: While the political flames of the *Athenia* sinking continued to grow, at 1700hrs Wilhelmshaven bade farewell to another 'Saltzwedel' boat. Kaptlt. Paul Büchel took *U32* to sea and to war, carrying eight mines and five torpedoes. Büchel and his crew had been added to the small list of boats intended for Channel minelaying, relieving *U35* and heading for Portsmouth. Just hours after sailing Büchel was signalled by Dönitz's staff to change his direct route through the Straits of Dover due to radio intelligence reports of a new British mine barrier being laid. Unsure of the scale of the mining, Dönitz diverted *U32*, allowing 'Weddigen' boat *U17*, already en route for the Dover Straits, to continue and report progress before a decision was to be made on redirecting *U35* and *U31* as well, both soon to put out from port.

8 September: By the fifth day of war Dönitz was feeling the acute lack of submarine strength with which he was expected to strangle Great Britain. To prepare for a second wave of boats sailing in a cohesive onslaught during October, when he expected the British to introduce convoying, he ordered the withdrawal of ten of the eighteen 'Hundius' and 'Wegener' U-boats then in the Atlantic. All that would remain in action were seven of the 'Saltzwedel' Flotilla's type VII boats. It was also time to pitch his small reserve into the fray and Kaptlt. Werner Lott slipped from Wilhelmshaven with his boat *U35*. Lott, now tasked with making a torpedo patrol and not minelaying, had received orders to make all possible haste toward the eastern Atlantic, preferably by the most direct route, the English Channel. The attempt failed as British aircraft spotted Lott's boat and harassed it as soon as *U35* had cleared German waters. Lott had already narrowly escaped destruction when at 1932hrs on 9 September British U-Class submarine HMS *Ursula* on patrol near the Elbe estuary fired five torpedoes at the surfaced *U35* as it departed Wilhelmshaven alongside *U21*, missing both boats but managing to rattle their crews into retreating northward.[10] Adopting the prudent northern route, Lott followed *U32* and passed between Scotland and the Faeroes to then head south again along Britain's west coast. *U31*, on the other hand, persisted, managing to penetrate the English Channel and slip through to safety at the western end.

14 September: A technical error of potentially disastrous consequences had reached Dönitz's notice. During a conference at BdU's command post on the *Toten Weg* in Wilhelmshaven's outskirts with *Oberwerftdirektor* Admiral Willy von Nordeck on the

---

[9] Ibbeken later achieved fame aboard the long range cruiser *U178*, sailing to the Far East and back as part of the 12th U-Flotilla.

[10] This is considered the first British submarine attack of the war. Five days later Lt Cdr G.C. Phillips sighted the German 'Köln' class cruiser *Leipzig* with six escorting destroyers. In a brave and devastating attack Phillips torpedoed and sank the cruiser, managing to escape retaliation and return in triumph to Gosport.

subject of torpedoes it was disclosed that all G7e torpedoes had been issued only partially adapted for angle shots. While gyro-angling gear had been fitted to the torpedo, the necessary adaptation of the weapons' tail fins had not been undertaken; thus the torpedoes were completely useless for angled shooting. Furious, he radioed this information to his men at sea, forbidding oblique shots with the G7e.

The older G7a steam torpedoes were unaffected by this particular problem and west of the northern tip of Ireland *U30* continued to add victims to its grim harvest. Two days previously Lemp had sunk the British steamer SS *Blairlogie*, laden with scrap iron, this time assisting the shipwrecked survivors with food, water and sailing directions. Now a third solo sailing freighter appeared. Lemp stopped SS *Fanad Head* with gunfire, a merchant ship en route from Suva to the British Isles laden with cereals. Despite her bridge and wheelhouse being protected with heavy sandbags, the German shells tore through the fragile structure and the crew abandoned ship at 1323hrs after a brief 'SSS' signal. Letting them pull free of the ship, Lemp opted to save valuable torpedoes and send a four-man demolition team led by First Watch Officer Oblt.z.S. Hans-Peter Hinsch by dinghy to search the British steamer for provisions and then destroy the ship with explosives. An error in loading aboard *U30* had caused much dismay among the crew and they saw the cargo of the *Fanad Head* as a possible answer to their woes. After the crew had finished their fresh bread supplies they graduated to canned bread, unpacking the carefully stored tins to discover that it was powdered milk, not as much as a mouldy bread crust to be found.

Meanwhile, 180 miles to the north-east, HMS *Ark Royal* was engaged on antisubmarine patrolling when it picked up the hurried distress call and despatched three Skua dive-bombers to search for *U30*. The aircraft arrived at the scene approximately half an hour later and observed a "patch of oil on the steamer's port bow", *U30* still surfaced nearby and apparently (but erroneously) thought to be firing shells. They immediately began attacking, forcing Lemp to dive while his men were still aboard the *Fanad Head*. One luckless crew member, *Oberbootsmaat* Hanisch, was also trapped above decks as the U-boat submerged, standing too far toward the stern to make it to the conning tower before the hatch slammed shut. As *U30* disappeared beneath him Hanisch swam to safety aboard the British steamer. Unbeknown to Lemp, a dinghy that was to have been used by Hanisch in ferrying provisions from the British steamer to *U30* was still tethered to the U-boat's stern, marking its exact location for the oncoming aircraft. Two Skuas dropped 100lb bombs on the dinghy, but at such a shallow angle that they bounced back off the water and exploded in mid-air bringing both aircraft down, each crashing at nearly 300 mph. Luckily for Lemp, the attack had cut the rope tethering the dinghy to *U30* and it drifted free. Aboard the steamer one of the demolition team, *Maschinenobergefreiter* Otto Ohse, witnessed the crash of the two RAF aircraft and leapt into the water, swimming toward a British pilot, obviously severely injured. Meanwhile, despite the presence of the third Skua above him, Lemp resurfaced, collected his men from the *Fanad Head* and the two wounded pilots, while anti-aircraft gunners attempted to keep their tormentor at bay. The remaining British fighter dived continuously toward *U30*, strafing her with machine-gun fire, causing light damage and injuring several of the German sailors on deck.

Finally *U30* was able to dive to comparative safety, the remaining Skua having fired a total of 1,150 rounds. Eventually, after the aircraft had gone, *U30* surfaced once more and Lemp decided to torpedo the crippled steamer and finish her off. One by one he fired all four bow tubes at near point blank range, every one of his shots missing the stationary target. In exasperation he then fired the stern G7a and finally sank the stubborn ship. Unfortunately for Lemp, Fleet Air Arm Swordfish from *Ark Royal* soon arrived on the scene and attacked the U-boat. Amid punishing explosives and gunfire *U30* suffered a 30° list and a bent periscope as it slipped underwater once more. Lemp dived to eighty metres to take stock of his situation. A member of Hinsch's boarding party, *Maschinenmaat* Adolf Schmidt, had received severe injuries, splinters from the bombing having severed the artery of his forearm, and soon the decking beneath him was slippery with blood while his comrades attempted to staunch the flow. Both Hinsch and Ohse had suffered splinter wounds to their heads, arms and backs, although not to such an extent as Schmidt, while the two British prisoners were also wounded. Lieutenant Thursden had suffered severe burns and laceration during his crash, before being rescued by Ohse, despite a large splinter embedded in the German's back. The second pilot, Lieutenant (Royal Marines) Guy Griffith, had escaped serious injury, swimming first to the *Fanad Head* where he received treatment for his minor wounds from Hinsch. Both air-gunners were killed in the crash. The U-boat glided slowly away, but the peace aboard *U30* was not to last for long.

Supporting destroyers from the *Ark Royal*'s group hunted *U30* for seven hours. Under attack by what Lemp perceived to be two destroyers and three aircraft the ordeal resulted in heavy depth charge damage before *U30* slipped through the attackers' cordon to safety. The U-boat was in chaos, thick showers of paint fragments mixed with dead cockroaches covering all surfaces, while traces of chlorine gas from cracked battery cells drifted through the boat.[11] Forward progress was difficult as the onboard pumps had ceased to operate and *U30* crawled to shelter, stern heavy with flooding. Furthermore, two torpedo tubes were found to be unserviceable, as was one of the temperamental diesels.

Eventually *U30* was free and able to surface, by which time Schmidt was suffering from severe blood loss. Lemp, fearing for the young man's life, broke radio silence to request permission from SKL to proceed towards neutral Iceland and hand the wounded man over to medical personnel. Permission was immediately granted and *U30* made way towards Reykjavik. While this drama was being played out at sea Berlin was able to study the balance sheet thus far, the reported sinking of *Fanad Head* raising the U-boat service's total to 100,000 tons of enemy shipping sunk.

At 1000hrs on 19 September *U30* arrived at Reykjavik where the German consul Dr Gerlach, a well-known and respected surgeon, boarded her to tend to Schmidt's and the two prisoners' injuries. The sailor, deemed too ill to return with *U30*, was transferred by local customs launch to the German steamer *Hamm*, also in harbour. Before his departure Lemp swore Schmidt to silence, ensuring that he would not divulge any information on the sinking of the *Athenia*, which, true to his oath, he never did. Later Schmidt was taken to Reykjavik's Saint Josefs-Spital Hospital where he remained for several weeks. The third officer from the *Hamm* was transferred aboard *U30* as a replacement for Schmidt and, after taking provisions from the steamer, *U30* left harbour at 1400hrs and sailed for Wilhelmshaven, limping on one diesel. Among the food provided by *Hamm* was a live turkey, promptly adopted by the crew and named 'Alfons', spending the voyage within the electro-motor room. On 27 September as *U30* approached its home port under minesweeper escort, Lemp proudly, but politely, refused offers of assistance for his battered boat and entered the harbour with available crew and both prisoners on deck as well as a flustered Alfons tethered to the deck gun. After *U30* had tied up, the two British

---

[11] In more peaceful moments pest control aboard *U30* was normally the domain of the large jovial Chief Engineering Officer Hans-Joachim Eichelborn who annihilated any sighted cockroaches using a chorus girl's elastic garter.

prisoners bade farewell to their captors before being offloaded into a waiting Gestapo car for incarceration.[12]

Later, behind closed doors, Dönitz accepted Lemp's patrol report, including confirmation of the *Athenia* sinking. However, his insistence that he had mistaken the target for an Armed Merchant Cruiser was accepted by Dönitz and, in the first of only three known cases of this happening during the Second World War, Dönitz ordered *U30*'s log book changed, eliminating the *Athenia*. Lemp was then flown to Berlin and ordered to report his actions to OKM, who concurred with Dönitz, they too content that Lemp had acted in "good faith". It was also felt that if Lemp, a respected, skilful and aggressive commander, had been punished it may well have sent the wrong signal to other commanders, urging what could be perceived as undue caution. Although not censured for the sinking, Lemp was, however, confined to barracks during his next leave period and made to study foreign shipping silhouettes as a form of reprimand. He was also promoted to *Kapitänleutnant* on 1 October.

In Wilhelmshaven there was one further alteration to be seen aboard *U30*, one which was to start a new trend within the *U-Bootwaffe*. Within the first week of war Lemp had asked Georg Högel to paint a picture on the conning tower sides of the Captain's fox terrier 'Schnurzl'. The dog had become a familiar sight at Wilhelmshaven as it waited for its master to return from sea, always faithfully accompanying Lemp during his time ashore. Högel complied and the image of Schnurzl graced the conning tower on both sides as the boat's chosen emblem, the first to be painted on any Kriegsmarine U-boat.

Success reports began to filter through to Dönitz at Wilhelmshaven, the most spectacular being achieved by Kaptlt. Otto Schuhart of the 'Saltzwedel' Flotilla's *U29* on 17 September. His triumph was achieved three days after Germany lost the first of its wartime submarine casualties, *U39*, a Type IX of the 'Hundius' Flotilla destroyed by escort destroyers of the 8th Destroyer Group following an unsuccessful attempt at torpedoing the ultimate prize, HMS *Ark Royal*. Despite the location and destruction of the attacking U-boat, only detected after premature detonation of the torpedo spread fired at *Ark Royal*, the lesson of the inherent vulnerability of aircraft carriers to submarine attack was one that the British failed to heed.

By the middle of September *U29* had already accounted for three ships during its patrol, sinking them with a combination of torpedoes and gunfire. But it had not all been good news from Schuhart. He too had experienced several premature torpedo detonations and broke radio silence to report this worrying trend to Dönitz.

However, Schuhart's greatest victory came about by a combination of German skill and a flawed British battle plan. With the potential for U-boat operations against Britain's ports and coastal traffic in the forefront of Royal Navy awareness (even if underrated), the Home Fleet's carriers, HMS *Ark Royal*, *Hermes* and *Courageous*, were employed as a stop-gap measure during the first weeks of the war, patrolling for U-boats and escorting the myriad unprotected, disorganized merchant ships heading toward the United Kingdom. Indeed it had been the *Ark Royal*'s aircraft engaged on such a mission that had damaged *U30* after

---

[12] Guy Griffith – the first Royal Marine to become a pilot – became the second longest serving British POW of World War Two at 5 years and 10 months. Schmidt, in Iceland, was subsequently captured on 23 May 1940 after Allied occupation of the island, taken first to Liverpool and thence on to Canada. The fate of Alfons remains unknown, although the crew of *U30* was treated to turkey stew the day after their return.

its attack on *Fanad Head*. Purpose-built anti-submarine flotillas were still in the process of forming, as was the overall strategy of merchant convoys. Therefore, in an attempt to shepherd far-flung ships into safe harbours, aircraft of HMS *Courageous* conducted what in reality were aimless and badly coordinated air patrols at a range of up to fifteen miles from their carrier which was left under the protection of four destroyers.

HMS *Courageous*, commissioned in 1917, had served as a battlecruiser during the First World War, conversion work to aircraft carrier being completed in 1930. Due to her not being a purpose-built carrier, *Courageous* was only able to transport forty-eight aircraft, as opposed to the seventy-two aircraft capacity of HMS *Ark Royal*, but she remained a valuable addition to Royal Navy airpower. Unfortunately she was not initially used in a role designed for such a warship. While aircraft are valuable for locating and attacking enemy submarines, aircraft carriers themselves are at risk to U-boat attack unless properly protected.

Courageous sailed from Plymouth on mission Anti-Submarine 3 at 1139hrs on 16 September to rendezvous with her four escorts from the 3rd Destroyer Flotilla. Meeting in the Bristol Channel, the four destroyers adopted the positions for anti-submarine screen No. 3 – one astern, one ahead and one on either beam.

At dusk on 17 September 1939 two of the four escorting destroyers had sheered away to follow a suspected ASDIC contact, the Type VIIB *U53* of the 'Wegener' Flotilla that had earlier that afternoon sunk a British steamer west of *Courageous*. Swordfish aircraft were also involved in the hunt for *U53*, several having already attacked the U-boat while it had been assisting survivors from a second victim. Schuhart had observed one of the Swordfish through his navigation periscope at 1617hrs, reasoning correctly that the short-range aircraft could only have originated from a parent ship. Intensifying his hunt, he found at last what appeared to be a large zigzagging steamer. Schuhart levelled his boat out at 20 metres and prepared to fire at the obviously hostile target. Only moments later, however, the ship altered course and the firing angle became too wide for an attack to be made. Undeterred, *U29* continued to run underwater rather than risk exposure on the surface. At approximately 1800hrs Schuhart's patience was rewarded with a glimpse through his periscope of what he at first took to be a square-shaped cloud on the distant horizon. Seconds later he saw the unmistakeable bulk of a British aircraft carrier, believed initially to be *Ark Royal*. An hour of underwater stalking ensued, the thin attack periscope periodically breaking surface to keep a check on progress. However, the carrier was drawing no closer and, with a severely curtailed underwater speed, Schuhart appeared to have little chance of closing to a potentially successful attack range. Every ounce of power was squeezed from the AEG electric motors but still only providing a fraction over four knots. Schuhart decided to attack anyway, firing a fan of three *Etos* set to run at six-metre depth. He now distrusted the magnetic pistols entirely, following his recent experiences. In the distance two aircraft could be seen flying in circles over the destroyers.

> "I am running at periscope depth constantly watching the carrier zigzagging. Having seen the zigzagging of the British, I do not yet need to give up the hope of getting him. . . . I have nothing to use as a reference for distance because of the enormous height of freeboard of the carrier, plus I have to look into the sun . . . The periscope is from time to time just beneath the surface as I am running at right angles to the swell."[13]

[13] KTB *U29*.

Just as it appeared that his quarry would probably elude him the carrier turned into the wind to allow one of her aircraft to land, bringing it directly toward *U29*. Outer bow caps were opened and, firing by guesswork, Schuhart loosed off a three-torpedo spread at *Courageous* – one ahead, one amidships and one astern – and then dived quickly to fifty metres to avoid destroyer detection.

> "At the time it looked like a hopeless operation. Because of the aircraft I could not surface and my underwater speed was less than eight knots while the carrier could do twenty-six. But we were told during our training to always stay close and that is exactly what I did, following him submerged until I was close enough to fire. . . . Then, without being able to see, we could hear the explosions."[14]

White trails streaked through the water toward *Courageous* before, after a run of two minutes and fifteen seconds, two dull blasts reverberated through *U29*, followed by "an enormous detonation and then a few smaller ones". The carrier, massive holes ripped in her port side, went down in only twenty minutes and 518 of her 1,200 complement went with her, including her commander Captain W.T. Makeig-Jones. The two escort destroyers swiftly obtained an ASDIC fix on *U29* and punished the U-boat for four hours with depth charge salvoes. *U29* was gradually taken deeper until she lay at a depth of 105 metres, electric motors humming gently on creep speed as she switched to silent running. The hull shook beneath the British attack, but, as was the saviour of many U-boats early in the war, the British charges were set too shallow, exploding some sixty metres overhead. Schuhart eventually evaded the escorting destroyers and, after retreating a safe distance, surfaced at 0135hrs on 18 September to report his success to BdU. The only damage suffered by *U29* was to her attack periscope. The slender steel neck had leaked, allowing water to flood the interior, coating the delicate Zeiss optics in a layer of grease and dirt even after twenty-four hours of drying out. Schuhart was unsure of what to do. He had not had a chance to observe the effect of his attack and considered returning to finish off what could be a damaged ship. However, with only two torpedoes left, low on fuel and a damaged periscope, he decided to set course for home. As he wrote in the boat's War Diary:

> "[Anyway] the conviction is that the ship was destroyed. The explosions were so loud that the ship must either have disintegrated or exploded."[15]

By midday he had confirmation when a British radio bulletin relating the sinking of HMS *Courageous* and subsequent destruction of the attacking U-boat was intercepted in Germany and relayed to Kriegsmarine forces at sea. Schuhart and his crew celebrated the premature news of their demise alongside their success, the destruction of an aircraft carrier being the pinnacle of warship targets. The victory was trumpeted later that day through German radio and newspapers, eclipsing news of a U-boat sunk by Allied destroyers three days later. Seven destroyers of the same flotilla that had accounted for the end of *U39* sank the second U-boat of the Second World War: first loss from the 'Saltzwedel' ranks.

Leutnant zur See Johannes Franz's *U27* had been at sea since 23 August, patrolling between Scotland and Northern Ireland. The search for enemy shipping had been relatively fruitless, two small British trawlers sunk by a combination of gunfire and scuttling

---

[14] *The Battle of the Atlantic*, John Costello & Terry Hughes; p. 17.
[15] KTB *U29*

charges. Franz and his crew, operating under strict Prize Law instructions, had stopped eleven large freighters, but all had been allowed to continue unmolested. Particularly galling for U-boat commanders at this stage was the order to spare all ships carrying wood to Britain – 'non-military supplies' destined for pit props in the coal mines of Wales and Northern England. A more treacherous event had occurred on 17 September when Franz made a submerged attack on an unsuspecting British freighter. Launching two G7a torpedoes from the U-boat's forward tubes, *U27* had been violently rocked by both eels exploding only a matter of metres from the boat, causing minor damage. Franz, shaken by the experience, broke radio silence to report the event to Dönitz.

By 19 September *U27* was low on fuel and provisions and en route for Wilhelmshaven. Half an hour before midnight the bridge watch reported the squat silhouettes of six warships on the horizon, believed to be British cruisers. Franz acted without hesitation – plotting an intercept course, turning the surfaced U-boat towards the targets for a charging attack, three torpedoes loaded and ready to fire. The eels were soon launched, but only seconds after hammering down on the firing levers two violent detonations were heard, too quickly to have been hits. Again, two of the three torpedoes had detonated prematurely, alerting the British ships to the danger, while the third corkscrewed off course.

In fact the target ships were a more dangerous proposition than cruisers. During the afternoon of 19 September seven ships of the Home Fleet's 8th Destroyer Flotilla were carrying out anti-submarine patrolling east of the Butt of Lewis following a reported U-boat sighting. The warships scoured the area until late in the evening, before forming two single-file columns for their return to their home port.[16]

At 2333hrs that night two distant explosions drew the attention of lookouts aboard lead ship HMS *Fortune*, and in the gloom they immediately spotted the unmistakeable silhouette of a surfaced U-boat on their ship's starboard beam. Without delay Commander E.A. Gibbs ordered his ship to increase speed and turn towards their foe in order to close the distance. Depth charges were readied and lamp signals made to the accompanying destroyers that they were preparing to engage the enemy.

Aboard *U27* there was momentary shock as the exploding torpedoes shook the boat, at the same moment that lookouts correctly identified their alerted adversaries as destroyers. Franz bellowed for a crash dive and the heavy sea boots of the bridge watch hurtled downwards to the control room decking as *U27* plunged under water. Above them *Fortune* charged into the attack, passing overhead and hurling five preliminary deep-set depth charges onto the U-boat's swirl before slowing to concentrate on a methodical ASDIC search. Obtaining a firm sonar trace of Franz's boat, *Fortune* dropped five more charges, set to explode slightly shallower this time, and waited for the disturbed water to settle.

Hammered by the accurate depth-charging, *U27* began to leak. One propeller and its shaft were heavily damaged and water sprayed into the pressure hull through the thick packing around the shaft. Crewmen struggled to contain the flooding, eventually managing to slow the inrushing water. Franz was faced with two possibilities: attempt to creep away submerged, crippled by flooding and a damaged propeller shaft while at the mercy of ASDIC, or surface and run on a single diesel for the safety of darkness. Above them *Fortune* had lost contact with its target in the swirling sea left behind by the explosions, and all seven destroyers began to sweep southwards in line abreast in hope of

---

[16] One column comprised HMS *Faulkener*, *Fearless* and *Fury*, the other HMS *Tartar*, *Eskimo*, *Forester* with *Fortune* leading.

regaining the U-boat. To foil any attempt at a surface escape searchlights crackled into life, scouring the surface for reflections. Rising to periscope depth, Franz straightaway saw the probing fingers of light and ordered an immediate dive to 120 metres – his option for a surface escape had been removed. At 0127hrs HMS *Forester* gained what was felt to be a tenuous contact and dropped several charges, shaking *U27* but inflicting no damage before the ASDIC pulse was again lost. However, a little over half an hour later at 0212hrs, *Fortune* ASDIC operators received a substantial sonar trace four miles from the first reported sighting position. With a combination of rack and thrower-mounted depth charges *Fortune* savagely pummelled *U27*, this time inflicting further serious damage on Franz's boat. Severe flooding was reported from all stations and *U27* began to sink into the depths. Periodic explosions and the sound of strong ASDIC impulses against the outer hull weakened the will of those aboard *U27*. The boat was nearly completely flooded in the stern compartments and she stumbled through the water with a 30° list to port while flooding continued from all areas, even around the conning tower directly into the control room. There was only enough compressed air left in the storage cylinders for one last attempt at surfacing and Franz realized that they had only two choices left – live in captivity or die. At 0241hrs the battered superstructure broke surface and crewmen began to tumble from the conning tower as Franz ordered the U-boat abandoned. The British destroyers did not at first see *U27* until lookouts aboard HMS *Fortune* spotted her lying stationary, her stern low in the water. Commander Gibbs ordered the helm swung over and his ship prepared to ram. Fortunately for Franz and his crew they were seen in the nick of time to be congregating on deck and *Fortune* veered away at the last moment. Megaphone instructions ordered the Germans to abandon their ship, while the destroyer's Chief Engineer Lieutenant (Eng) R. Mack and a small boarding crew readied a boat to investigate their still buoyant prize for possible salvage. While German crewmen were being pulled from the water Mack and his little group boarded the sinking U-boat, the first British seamen to do so in the Second World War. Courageously lowering himself into the flooding U-boat, Mack quickly realized that there was no chance of saving the boat and any loose documents found were hastily scooped up and passed to men outside for later scrutiny. The U-boat's LI, Oblt. (Ing.) Hans Steig, had ensured the boat's scuttling and despite Mack's best efforts there was no way to halt the deluge that was filling *U27*. Also, despite the bravery of *Fortune*'s engineer, there was little of real intelligence value to be had. Franz had ordered his Enigma machine destroyed with secret material and it was not long before the Royal Navy boarders pulled away in their dory and *U27* gradually tipped vertically and slid beneath the waves stern first into 1,500 metres of water.[17]

The remaining boats of the 'Saltzwedel' Flotilla that had sailed before the outbreak of war were heading home, low on fuel and in some cases ammunition. As the diesel bunkers of boats stationed to the west of Ireland began to run down they received instructions from Dönitz in Wilhelmshaven to use the return path north of the Shetlands, with the possibility of attacking Royal Navy warships while en route.

On 26 September *U26*, *U29* and *U34* all returned to Wilhelmshaven. The lumbering Type I *U26* had successfully laid mines off Shambles Light in Portland Harbour on the

---

[17] BdU learned of the reason for *U27*'s loss (detection after torpedo malfunction, the same as 'Hundius' boat *U39*) by a coded message from Franz within a POW post-card. The message read "Three torpedoes fired – two premature detonations – then enemy depth charges" and allowed Dönitz to confirm the U-boat's loss on 13 November.

night of 8 September after two abortive attempts. Retreating from the heavily guarded harbour, Ewerth then ordered all six torpedo tubes loaded while the U-boat rested on the Channel bottom. Strong British warship presence in his vicinity forced Ewerth to creep cautiously this way and that, unable to report his minelaying mission completed. Fears were raised in Wilhelmshaven on 10 September after OKM had passed on intercepted British and French broadcasts that [incorrectly] claimed the successful destruction of a U-boat laying mines inshore of England. When Ewerth, engaged in his deadly and drawn-out cat and mouse game with British destroyers, failed to report on time, Dönitz feared that *U26*, complete with Enigma machine and highly confidential documents, may have been sunk in shallow waters. When at 0007hrs on 13 September Ewerth finally radioed success at planting his minefield he received the brief but heartfelt "Well Done!" from FdU. *U26*'s minefield would later claim the destruction of three merchant ships in addition to severely damaging the British corvette HMS *Kittiwake*. While given complete freedom of action after belatedly radioing success to Dönitz, Ewerth sighted no torpedo targets.

As the three boats sailed inbound from the Jade River into the calm waters of Wilhelmshaven's outer harbour Schuhart's *U29*, with four confirmed sinkings, including the destruction of HMS *Courageous* and merchant tonnage accurately estimated at around 19,507-tons, led the flotilla's score. Kaptlt. Wilhelm Rollmann's *U34* claimed the successful sinking of two merchant ships by combined torpedoes and gunfire west of the English Channel and the capture intact of Estonian SS *Hanonia* near Norway during the U-boat's return transit. Taken by prize crew to Germany, she later joined the Kriegsmarine as minelayer *Schiff II*.

Two days later *U33* also returned to Wilhelmshaven. Her captain, Kaptlt. Hans-Wilhelm von Dresky, had accounted for three ships during his five weeks at sea. The first victim, British merchant SS *Olivegrove*, had fallen to a single torpedo west of the English Channel in mid-afternoon on 7 September, the seventh ship sunk of the Second World War and the third by 'Saltzwedel' boats. As the crew had abandoned *Olivegrove* von Dresky approached the lifeboats and took its captain aboard for questioning. Later, after depositing the captain back in his lifeboat, *U33* signalled nearby American liner *Washington* to come and rescue the survivors, circling the small boats for nine hours until help finally arrived. The final two ships added to von Dresky's tally were both sunk by gunfire from the boat's 8.8cm cannon, SS *Arkleside* west of Brittany on the morning of 16 September and fishing boat *Caldew* south of the Faeroes eight days later as *U33* circled north to return to Wilhelmshaven.

On 28 September as von Dresky returned, his entrance to port and disembarkation were witnessed by Germany's Führer, Adolf Hitler, visiting Wilhelmshaven in the company of Karl Dönitz, Wilhelm Keitel and Erich Raeder, to inspect the two local U-boat flotillas. As well as meeting officers, Hitler had come to decorate the entire crew of *U29*. Schuhart received the Iron Cross First and Second class while each of his men was awarded the EKII. Later Hitler spent an hour meeting his submariners, saying in a brief morale-boosting speech to the assembled Kriegsmarine men:

> "The real and psychological pressure that U-boats spread over wide areas is huge and superior to that from the world war. . . . It is not true that England has the technical means to neutralize the U-boats. Their experience so far confirms that the English anti-submarine apparatus is not as effective as they claim it to be.'

Unfortunately for Germany, he was wrong. While anti-submarine warfare had indeed been relegated to the back of Admiralty thinking, the British had still managed to develop

ASDIC to a level where it would prove one of the U-boats' deadliest foes. There were enough men among the Admiralty's upper echelons who quickly appreciated the potential U-boat threat. Though the initial days of the war were spent with both sides sparring, probing for weaknesses, the time was not wasted. Within weeks the first clear reports of convoying by the British had reached Dönitz. *U31* confirmed that it had passed through the Straits of Dover successfully by radioing the sighting of convoy OB4 in the Bristol Channel on 15 September. In fact the Admiralty had begun to institute coastal convoys on 6 September, ocean-going convoys being sanctioned two days later as a direct result of the *Athenia* sinking and Britain's perception that Dönitz had immediately instigated 'unrestricted submarine warfare'.[18] Overseas convoys left Britain initially via the South Western Approaches, escort ships provided to a limit 200 miles west of Ireland (15° west) and to the middle of the Bay of Biscay, cruisers and armed merchant cruisers occasionally escorting ocean convoys. On the opposite side of the Atlantic the Royal Canadian Navy escorted within a few hundred miles of Halifax.

Impotently caged within FdU Headquarters, all Dönitz could do was hope that the aggressive spirit of his commanders would shine through and OB4 suffer under sustained torpedo attack.

> "Perhaps they have a chance. I have hammered it into commanders again and again that they must not let such chances pass. If only more boats were out there!"[19]

Indeed *U31* did rise to the occasion and, after calculating its mean course, shadowed the convoy as it sailed west. The day after his report to FdU, Kaptlt. Johannes Habekost forged ahead of the predicted convoy path and submerged in readiness for a surprise attack. Later, as Habekost trained his periscope on the distant cloud that formed first into smoke, then lumbering merchant ships, he prepared to fire two torpedoes at the nearest target. Minutes later SS *Aviemore* reeled under the double impact and immediately began to sink, taking twenty-three men with her. Dönitz had meanwhile vectored nearby *U34*, *U29* and *U53* towards Habekost in hopes of annihilating the entire convoy and proving his theory on group attacks in the field of actual combat, but none of the three made proper contact. Interestingly, Admiralty statistics state that the nine ships of OB4 dispersed that same day, *before* Habekost's attack; therefore *Aviemore* not really considered a convoy loss.[20]

Dönitz had also risen in stature within the Kriegsmarine, although his demands for increased U-boat production continued to fall on barren ground. On 19 September he received promotion to the rank of *Konteradmiral* and the new title of *Befelshaber der U-Boote* (BdU, Commander-in-Chief of U-boats).

29 September: *U28* returned to Wilhelmshaven, claiming no merchant shipping but the presumed sinking of an auxiliary cruiser under heavy escort. South-east of Cork on the morning of 14 September *U28* had chanced upon what was thought to be an escorted Armed Merchant Cruiser. Manoeuvring slowly into an advantageous submerged firing

---

[18] The first British convoy – AB1, comprising eight tankers – actually departed Gibraltar for the Persian Gulf on 2 September.

[19] FdU KTB, 15 September 1939.

[20] It was practice for the OB traffic to disperse after four days or so at sea at a point to the west of the British Isles beyond what the Admiralty considered U-boat range. This dispersal point moved further and further west until 1941 when mid-Atlantic escort ships were available and the convoys remained largely intact.

position, within an hour Kuhnke was ready to fire, the first torpedo impact registering at 1109hrs as *U28* dived away from escorting destroyers, thus unable to verify the effect of the torpedoes. However, the sound of distant explosions followed by groaning steel and the bursting of bulkheads indicated success. In fact the ship that slowly went under with five of her crew was MV *Vancouver City*, a merchant bound for the UK from Suva, holds filled with sugar.

Kuhnke's report of shipping activity and strong escorts in the Bristol Channel also served to confirm Dönitz's theory that the region was being used as a 'merchant gathering point' for convoy assemblage. Meanwhile, after return to Germany, Kuhnke's boat was consigned to the repair yards, the rigours of intense active patrolling showing deficiencies in the U-boat's engine mountings and even body work. The first generation of Type VIIs were suffering considerable strain and damage.

30 September: The loss of *U27* was assumed in Wilhelmshaven as Dönitz noted in his War Diary:

> "*U27* has failed to report . . . English radio spoke some days ago of captured U-boat sailors."[21]

With the return of *U32* (claiming 5,738 tons of enemy shipping sunk) and *U36* (2,840 tons) during the course of the day almost all of Dönitz's operational U-boats were now home in their German ports. *U36* had brushed with a British submarine offensive aimed at U-boats in the North Sea as they sailed to and from their home ports. A little after midday on 17 September as Kaptlt. Wilhelm Fröhlich lay alongside a Danish steamer in the process of examining the ship's papers for signs of contraband, four torpedoes streaked past, fired from the bow of S-Class submarine HMS *Seahorse*. All four missed and the shaken *U36* rapidly departed the area after crash-diving to comparative safety. Although the German crew were unaware of it at the time, the event held a certain portent for their future.

Both commanders had received the Iron Cross Second Class for their patrols and, worryingly, both boats required intensive maintenance for myriad mechanical problems, *U32* for example requiring work on her torpedo tubes, leaking exhaust vents and twelve new cylinder blocks for her diesels. During this enforced stay in dock, the boat's First Watch Officer, Oblt.z.S. Hans Jenisch, was ordered to Warnemünde to take his commander's course, also using the time to get married.

All the Type VIIs that had returned to port had suffered damage. While enemy destroyers inflicted some, much was also due to faulty design and a lack of mechanical reliability in the submarines' machinery. Dönitz decided that they would be unable to return to torpedo patrols without extensive modification. The bulk of 'Saltzwedel' was to be assigned unpopular and dangerous mine-laying duties. Dönitz was also aware that shortening daylight and harsh winter weather favoured the task of minelaying, torpedo patrols judged unfavourable for boats not up to the strain of the natural elements.

By 9 October, when the only 'Saltzwedel' boat still at sea was *U35*, BdU had reckoned on five boats being ready to return to action within twelve days, four from 'Saltzwedel': *U25*, *U26*, *U31* and *U32*. The latter two Type VIIs possessed only a limited radius of action and Dönitz consequently ordered both of them to sow mines where they could be most effective. For military targets Loch Ewe was chosen, this Scottish anchorage having become the Royal Navy's second major harbour after Scapa Flow. The responsibility for

[21] BdU KTB 39/9/39

mining tightly defended Scapa had been handed to the Luftwaffe, although as time would show Dönitz had other plans for the Orkney harbour. As well as attacks on warships, TMB mines were to be laid in the transport lanes of the English Channel and those harbours used to control and coordinate convoys – Milford Haven, Bristol and Liverpool.

While U-boats had begun the war under strict orders to fight according to Prize regulations, as it became increasingly clear that England and France were unwilling to come to peace terms with Hitler, the latter began to relax restrictions. On 23 September Raeder convinced Hitler to allow all merchant ships which began using their wireless after being stopped by a U-boat to be sunk. Of course the reporting of U-boat attack was included in Admiralty instructions for merchant skippers so there was a strong likelihood of this happening. The next day the ban on attacks against French vessels was also removed. Gradually Hitler loosened the reins on his submariners as observance of Prize Regulations was removed, first within the North Sea, then steadily outwards until by 17 October all ships "identified as hostile" were declared fair game and Germany issued warnings that the safety of neutral shipping in the seas around Britain and France could no longer be guaranteed. The final taboo was lifted on 17 November when U-boats were given freedom to attack any passenger liner if "clearly identified as hostile", reaching a state of "unrestricted submarine warfare", although explicitly ordered by OKW never to use that term officially.

12 October *Kapitänleutnant* Werner Lott brought *U35* into harbour at Kiel after a patrol during which he obeyed the Prize Laws meticulously. Lott had begun a successful action on 18 September with the sighting of British trawler *Alvis* in the North Atlantic. Approaching the small British vessel, Lott hailed the captain, demanding that he present the ship's papers to the U-boat while preparing to sink the ship with gunfire. However, realizing that the thirteen Britons stood little or no chance of reaching land in their small lifeboat, Lott allowed the trawler to return to her home port of Fleetwood after an officer and three ratings of *U35*'s crew had boarded the British trawler, destroying her fishing gear and dismantling its wireless. Once the four had returned to *U35* the *Alvis* set course for home. In exchange for this unforeseen act of humanity, the British captain advised Lott that HMS *Ark Royal* was hunting in the area.

Later the same day two other British trawlers were less fortunate. West-north-west of Saint Kilda *U35* encountered a small fishing fleet of three trawlers, firing warning shots to bring them to a halt and summoning the captains of all three ships to present their papers. After establishing the trawlers' identities, he allowed the crews of *Lord Minto* and *Arlita* to abandon ship before opening fire with the 8.8cm gun and sinking them both. The third trawler, *Nancy Harg*, remained unmolested, spared by Lott to rescue the other crews and return them to their home port.

Three days later, after scouring shipping lanes further south in heavy seas, *U35* mounted the second convoy attack of the war. Sighting and approaching OA7 south-west of the Scillies, Lott fired two torpedoes, missing one of the leading ships, SS *Inanda*, but damaging SS *Teakwood* at the convoy's rear. In limp retaliation an escort destroyer that had acquired what it considered "a doubtful contact" hurled a single depth charge at the retreating U-boat two hours later. Unfortunately for Lott and his crew this one lucky shot disabled the navigation periscope and the U-boat's high-pressure blowing system. Plummeting downwards, *U35* hit the sea bed at 120 metres, deeper than the Type VII hull was intended for. Despite heavy leaking from flooding valves, Oblt. (Ing.) Gerhard Stamer was able to use the comparative calm of a stationary boat with a well-disciplined crew to effect repairs.

The next two weeks saw Lott claim two more sinkings by torpedo and gunfire. On 30 September the blacked-out silhouette of passenger-liner *Aquitania* hove into view, crossing the U-boat's path at a range of only 500 metres. Lott, obeying the restrictions previously imposed upon him and other commanders, held his fire and the 45,000-ton ship steamed on her way unhindered. Unbeknown to Lott, the restrictions against attacking such a ship had already been lifted by Hitler, although no message to that effect had yet been received aboard *U35*.

Three days later *U35* was forty miles west of Skellig Rocks, Ireland, when its lookouts detected another steamer at 1300hrs. In weather that had turned from threatening grey skies to angry rain-lashed storm, Lott surfaced his boat and fired a warning shot across the steamer's bow, hailing the commander of Greek SS *Diamantis*, bound for Barrow in Furness with 4,000 tons of iron ore. The German gun crew stood on *U35*'s deck, safety harnesses holding them against the possibility of being pitched overboard. Lott again wished to determine that the freighter was carrying contraband before attacking it, but the sea was too rough to send a boarding party to examine the ship's papers, or to expect the Greeks to approach him. He therefore signalled by lamp for the *Diamantis* to follow him.

> "I wanted to go to the Irish coast where I knew there would not be such rough weather, [but] it did not follow me so I fired a shot from my gun at the bow of the ship. This had the result that the crew panicked and jumped into the small boats."[22]

Lott was now faced with the spectre of twenty-eight struggling Greeks abandoning their perfectly seaworthy ship in waves that continued to mount. The diminutive lifeboats began to founder and *U35* edged closer with deck crew at the ready, preparing to throw life-lines to the struggling Greeks. With great difficulty all twenty-eight crewmen from the *Diamantis* were rescued and brought aboard Lott's boat, offered beds and cigarettes and tea while their abandoned ship was sunk.

There was, however, no room for the captives to remain aboard the cramped submarine. Lott asked the captain, Panagos, where he and his crew wished to be landed, denying them their first choice of England and instead planning to take them to neutral Ireland where they could hand their captives over to local fishermen. After thirty-five hours of sailing the U-boat approached Dingle Harbour in waters calmed by the lee of the land. Lott eased his boat into harbour, coming within 100 yards of shore and attracting crowds of locals. Finding no local fishing boats available for the task, Lott ordered the U-boat's rubber dinghy broken out and crewman Walter Kalabuch to begin the arduous task of ferrying the Greeks ashore. Lott recalled:

> "When the Greek sailors said goodbye to me on the conning tower they went on their knees and kissed my wedding ring as if I was a bishop. I did not want this but they said, 'We owe our lives to you. You have treated us very nicely'."[23]

When the last Greeks had been rowed ashore Kalabuch climbed back aboard *U35* and the dinghy was deflated and stowed. At slow speed *U35* engaged her diesel engines astern and backed away.

On 12 October *U35* returned to Wilhelmshaven, claiming a total of five ships sunk for 16,839 tons. Gerhard Stamer received the Iron Cross First Class for his actions at repairing

[22] Courtesy of Hans Mair, http://www.u35.com
[23] Hans Mair.

U35 when she lay damaged in the Irish Channel, but Lott received a stern reprimand for "endangering his boat". Meanwhile, in America *U35* was immortalized by its mercy, emblazoned on the cover of *Life Magazine*.

17 October: Despite having suffered mechanical failure during its first patrol *U34* slipped from Wilhelmshaven in the early morning to begin the journey to the North Atlantic. Kaptlt. Rollmann's boat had been judged the sole Type VII immediately capable of mounting a torpedo patrol after extensive shipyard repair and conversion work. Later that day, far to the west, U-boats engaged the Anglo-French convoy KJF3 in the first 'wolf pack' attack, coordinated at sea by 'Hundius' commander Kaptlt. Werner Hartmann aboard *U37*. By early evening the Atlantic was disfigured by sinking shattered wrecks. Distressingly for Dönitz, during a second pack attack mounted by 'Hundius' and 'Wegener' boats, several torpedoes carrying magnetic warheads had prematurely exploded, leading an enraged BdU to place an immediate ban on use of the "unsafe" magnetic pistol. Worse was to come as fresh news of torpedo defects arrived, following the despatch of a small Mediterranean task force on *Grossadmiral* Raeder's orders.

On 18 September *U25*, commanded by Viktor Schütze, had sailed from Wilhelmshaven for what would transpire to be an abortive attempt at opening a new area of operations in the Mediterranean. Following the instructions of Operational Order No. 8, *U25* was to travel in company with sister ship *U26* and 'Wegener' Type VIIB *U53*.

While *U25* and *U53* were ordered to lay off the south-west tip of Ireland, Klaus Ewerth aboard *U26* was tasked to lay a TMB minefield across Gibraltar's harbour mouth. Once completed, the two waiting U-boats would sail to meet Ewerth, whereupon all three were to slip through the straits and attack Allied shipping.

On 31 October Viktor Schütze's *U25* sighted French convoy K20, running from Casablanca to Brest, and immediately opted to attack this target of convenience. In calm seas Schütze managed a textbook approach and fired four contact-pistol torpedoes, all failing to explode. With no escort concerns, Schütze in desperation ordered his deck gun to open fire on SS *Bauolé*, eventually sinking her. Schütze had meanwhile appraised BdU by radio of his torpedo problems, igniting further furore in Wilhelmshaven. Dönitz recorded within his War Diary that "at least 30% of all torpedoes are duds", either refusing to detonate at all or prematurely exploding. "Torpedo failure," he wrote, "is at present the most urgent problem for the *U-Bootwaffe*."

However, *U25*'s troubles were far from over. During the action the concussion of firing the 10.5cm gun had cracked the supporting crosspiece in the forward torpedo-loading hatch, rendering the boat unable to dive to any significant depth. Brief shallow submergence was deemed possible, but in the event of depth charges the hatch would undoubtedly give way and the boat flood. After four days of attempted repair Schütze was left with no alternative but aborting the mission and setting course for Germany, arriving on 13 November in Wilhelmshaven. But there had been one final disaster for Schütze's boat. On 5 November as *U25* battled through the Bay of Biscay en route for Germany *Bootsmaat* Wilhelm Lützeler was washed overboard and lost, dragged beneath the sea by the weight of his heavy leather gear.

Ewerth in *U26* reached Gibraltar after departing Wilhelmshaven on 22 October but, faced with bad weather, bright searchlights and roving anti-submarine patrols, aborted his mining attempt and ordered tubes reloaded with torpedoes. The constrictive Strait of Gibraltar was extremely challenging for any submarine to break through. Not only was the maximum depth only 300 metres due to a ridge running between Spain and Morocco, but the sea floor varied enormously with many submerged obstacles and rocky outcrop-pings. The narrowest portion, a thirty-mile-long 'choke point', was an easier proposition to guard than penetrate. However, Ewerth managed to coast through with the eastward-moving surface current adding as much as 4 knots to the boat's engine speed. But, unfortunately for Ewerth, his search for prey in the Mediterranean produced little. He reported the torpedoing of a single small ship but this was never confirmed and remains doubtful according to historians who have studied the subject.[24] After several fruitless days *U26* successfully escaped the Mediterranean bottleneck and began its return journey, the only U-boat ever to return from the Mediterranean Sea. The last of the three U-boats, *U53*, also achieved nothing, bumbling around aimlessly west of the Strait before returning to Germany where Kaptlt. Ernst-Günter Heinicke was relieved of his command and reassigned to the auxiliary cruiser *Widder*. The first German attempt at attacking Gibraltar and the Royal Navy's Mediterranean forces had ended in abject failure.

30 October: *U31* returned to Wilhelmshaven. During the course of a nine-day mission Kaptlt. Johannes Habekost fouled the entrance to Loch Ewe with TMB mines. Finding no picket ships at the Loch entrance, but prevented from penetrating deeply due to a thick net defence, Habekost successfully deposited his eighteen mines across the entry channel during 28 October. The field was later to damage HMS *Nelson* on 4 December and sink a pair of minesweeping trawlers two days before Christmas.

8 November: *U28* sailed from Wilhelmshaven to operate in the Bristol Channel east of Ireland, carrying twelve TMB magnetic mines and six torpedoes. Kaptlt. Günter Kuhnke experienced success in transit, on 17 November sinking the Dutch tanker MV *Sliedrecht* under the relaxed operational rules concerning neutral tankers and eight days later attacking northbound convoy SL8B, sinking SS *Royston Grange*.

Early the following month *U28* laid its mines off Swansea, sowing the small field during the night of 5 December. Initially, as there were no discernible effects from the minefield, it was considered a failure, but on 21 January 1940 the sinking of British SS *Protesilaus* was finally attributed to these mines, the damaged steamer beached in Swansea Bay before breaking in two. *U28* returned to its Wilhelmshaven base on 18 December 1939 and again had to be returned to the shipyard for extensive alterations and repairs, highlighting once again the inadequacy of the early Type VII boats.

12 November: *U34* entered the Jade Estuary with six victory pennants flying. Claiming 26,094 tons of enemy shipping destroyed, Kaptlt. Wilhelm Rollmann had actually sunk three during his second war patrol. Accompanying his confirmed sinkings was the arrival in Germany of Norwegian steamer SS *Snar*, captured by a small prize crew from *U34* near Norway on 9 November.

14 November: *U29* sailed, set for Milford Haven and more minelaying. It was to be an abject failure for Schuhart, returning with his full complement of twelve TMB mines and six torpedoes after judging bright moonlit conditions to have been unfavourable for any kind of successful operation. Dönitz was furious and Schuhart only narrowly missed being relieved of his command, past victories persuading Dönitz to give him a second chance.

Meanwhile, as Schuhart put to sea, newly appointed civilian *Torpedodiktator* Professor

---

[24] See Jürgen Rohwer's *Axis Submarine Successes* and Jak Showell's *U-boats under the Swastika*, p. 39.

Cornelius arrived in Wilhelmshaven to discuss the deepening ammunition crisis with BdU. Cornelius, who had helped design German torpedoes between the two world wars during his twenty years of service in Eckernförde's *Torpedoversuchsansalt* (TVA, or, Torpedo Experimental Institute), had been appointed by *Grossadmiral* Raeder to cut through all obstacles in an effort to solve the mysterious torpedo problems. Dönitz began by bitterly complaining that not only had he been forced to enter combat with an insufficient supply of torpedoes, but those available were of little or no use. Magnetic detonators were prone to premature detonation, while contact detonators either ran too deep or simply failed to explode. Dönitz was in large part correct when he stated that the majority of U-boat losses thus far in the war were caused by the attacking U-boat's presence being betrayed by a defective torpedo attack. Unfortunately Cornelius had no miracle cure. By January 1940 TVA's Director, KA Oskar Wehr, had performed fresh test firing against the target ship *T123*, finding that several shots taken in ideal conditions failed to fire upon supposed impact. Following further magnetic measurements and tests the only result was an open admission from the Torpedo Inspectorate that there was indeed a problem. Dismally short of a solution, BdU waited impatiently for Cornelius to provide one.

19 November: Kaptlt. Johannes Habekost, in *U31*, left Wilhelmshaven to begin his fourth war patrol. The boat's departure was delayed briefly while awaiting escorts from 2nd Minesweeping Flotilla before *U31* nosed into the North Sea. The day following Habekost's departure Kaptlt. Werner Lott took *U35* on electric motors from its berth and set course for the North Sea and a planned torpedo patrol of the Orkney Islands in search of Royal Navy targets. After an uneventful passage *U35* began prowling the waters of the Pentland Firth before moving north to Fair Isle Passage. Weather conditions were deteriorating and the U-boat pitched wildly as she bucked her way through mountainous seas, the bridge watch frequently submerged in a deluge of icy water. It was in these conditions sixty miles east of the Shetland Islands that lookouts spotted the unmistakeable outline of heavy cruiser HMS *Norfolk* ploughing her own way through the huge sea on 28 November. With no hope of chasing or catching the tempting target Lott broke radio silence to report the sighting for the benefit of any other U-boats nearby.

At dawn the next morning *U35* surfaced beneath a clearing sky. Unfortunately for Lott, as *U35* ploughed onwards it was sighted by patrolling destroyer HMS *Icarus*, herself remaining unseen with the blinding early morning sun at her back. Radioing for support from other destroyers operating within the area under the overall command of Captain Lord Louis Mountbatten, *Icarus* closed the distance rapidly at action stations and prepared to attack.

It was in the final minutes of its approach that *U35*'s startled lookouts saw their charging enemy, attempting an immediate crash dive as men tumbled into the control room. Tilting sharply downwards *U35* was put into an evasive corkscrew, churning propellers pushing her rapidly to a depth of nearly eighty metres. Above, ASDIC operators obtained a clear fix on the twisting boat and the first depth charge pattern was released from *Icarus*.

Meanwhile, British reinforcements had arrived in the shape of HMS *Kingston* and *Kashmir*, the former immediately dropping more charges, directed to the target by *Icarus*. This second pattern sealed Lott's fate. As *U35* reeled under the first impact of *Icarus*' charges the second pattern exploded nearby, throwing the boat's interior into confusion and jamming hydroplanes into a full upward angle. All available men were rushed to the bow compartment in an attempt at slowing the boat's ascent while control room crew wrestled with the wedged hydroplanes. Fuel and ballast tanks were also found to have suffered from the concussion, leaving a clearly visible slick behind the U-boat as her tormentors closed for another attack. With the boat refusing to come under control, Lott realized that *U35* was doomed and in order to save his men or attempt to flee he gave the command to blow all tanks and surface, gun crew standing by.

When the vessel surfaced Lott emerged from the conning tower hatch, followed by his gun crew. While diesels roared into life, he was able to take stock of his position, immediately seeing that not one but three destroyers were closing rapidly. HMS *Kashmir* opened fire at the stricken boat and Lott was forced to accept the inevitable, ordering *U35* abandoned and scuttled. The LI, Kaptlt. (Ing.) Gerhard Stamer, opened the seacocks and, as the men abandoned ship, *U35* began to go down by the stern. German sailors on deck raised their hands in surrender before plunging into the sea and swimming away from their sinking ship. The entire crew of forty-three men were rescued, Lott and eleven others pulled from the water by HMS *Kingston*. Lott later remembered:

> "I was picked up as the last but one and as my life preserver had been damaged when the U-boat sank under my feet I was already completely exhausted and stiff from the cold water. [Lt.Cdr. P] Somerville made a perfect manoeuvre and they threw me a rope which I could not hold in my stiff fingers. To my amazement they lowered a boat, hauled me into it and threw me like a bag onto the destroyer's deck because I had become too weak to jump on my own in the heavy sea. Under a doctor's supervision I was put into a hot bath and a bottle of Scotch held to my mouth which altogether gave all of us an astonishingly quick recovery."[25]

In fact relations between the British crew and German captives were extremely convivial. Warning that they would accept no trouble from their rescued enemy, the British sailors treated them with great kindness. On 3 December the destroyers landed their captives in Scotland, the incident reported the following day in the newspaper *The Scotsman*:

> "When the prisoners went down the gangway they were cheered by the sailors, who lined the decks and rails of the warships. One little fair-headed German was greeted by the British sailors as 'Blondie' and he was given a special cheer to himself.
>
> "The U-boat commander, a strongly built young man, was the last to go ashore, and as he stepped across the gangway there was clapping and cheering."

Indeed, as Lott took his leave of HMS *Kingston*, he was invited to sign the wardroom visitor's book in which he wrote: "Wishing you the best of luck except against German U-boats".

This story of chivalry in war did not end there. Put under guard by a Scottish battalion at Greenock, the Germans were placed on a London-bound night train where, in the early hours of 3 December, Gerhard Stamer passed out bottles of beer, provided by their escort, to the entire crew in celebration of Lott's thirty-second birthday. The Scotsmen taught the Germans to sing 'Happy Birthday' and tensions quickly relaxed under their arrival in London and transfer to the Tower of London, used as an interim prison camp. Here Lott, separated from his crew, was angered by being placed in a cold wet cell and immediately went on hunger strike as a protest. On 4 December Lord Louis Mountbatten visited him, arranging his transfer to new quarters and offering by way of apology to take Lott out to dinner in London. After giving his word that there would be no escape attempt and accepting on condition that First Watch Officer Oblt.z.S. Heinz Erchen could also

---

[25] Letter from Lott to Mountbatten, 9 September 1974.

accompany them, the two Germans were taken in civilian clothes to Scott's Restaurant by Admiralty limousine. There they were joined by two other British officers known to Lott and his IWO from their days spent in Gibraltar during the Spanish Civil War. Later that evening the Germans returned to their cells and the entire crew were moved shortly afterwards, officers and the ship's cook to the newly established POW camp at Grizedale Hall in the Lake District and the crew to Oldham. By 12 December BdU tentatively confirmed *U35*'s loss, the twelfth of Dönitz's U-boat force to be declared *Vermißt ein Stern*.[26]

At sea the death toll had risen. While Lott and Erchen enjoyed the mixed fortunes of war, *U35*'s sister ship, Kaptlt. Wilhelm Fröhlich's *U36*, was heading north for the Shetlands, having left Kiel on 2 December. Two days later the British submarine HMS *Salmon* sighted the surfaced boat south-west of Farsund, Norway. Her commander, Lt.Cdr. E.O. Bickford, ordered a full bow salvo of six torpedoes fired at a range of 5,000 yards before going deep to avoid detection. One of the torpedoes broke surface and continued on its way as a 'surface runner', but poor visibility hid the approaching menace from the U-boat's lookouts. Aboard the British submarine a single detonation was heard as *U36* was blown completely in half. Surfacing, *Salmon* cautiously approached, sighting a single mutilated corpse, the top half of a man's body suspended by its life jacket, in a sea stained with tons of spilt diesel. Fröhlich and his thirty-nine-man crew were dead.

Success for 'Saltzwedel' boats in other areas was also tinged with complications. On 26 November Kaptlt. von Dresky returned from nearly a month at sea engaged on his second war patrol. He had departed Wilhelmshaven bound for minelaying in the Bristol Channel. However, almost immediately on leaving harbour the boat was barely operable, both diesels breaking down and rendering it immobile except by electric motor power, with no way of charging the batteries.

Nearly three days were spent lying on the sandy bottom of the North Sea while the Kaptlt. (Ing.) Fritz Schillig and his engine room crew attempted repairs, the crew finally rewarded for their efforts and *U33* continuing on course. Twelve TMB mines were successfully laid off Foreland Point on 9 November, sinking the British merchant ship SS *Stanholme* on Christmas Day 1939 and the British tanker MV *Inverdargle* on 16 January 1940. In addition to these kills, the huge 13,467-ton tanker MV *Sussex* had been seriously damaged toward the end of November and for the second time in three months the port of Bristol was closed to shipping.

After sowing his deadly field von Dresky hunted for artillery and torpedo targets. During the afternoon of 20 November *U33* sighted a small British fishing fleet of three trawlers north of Tory Island, sinking all three with gunfire after their crews had abandoned ship. The following morning two more were sunk by gunfire north-west of Rathlin. Satisfied with his patrol von Dresky ordered *U33* to set course for Wilhelmshaven and it was while returning that the alert bridge lookouts spotted the German ship *Borkum* in sheets of rain and rolling seas north-west of the Orkneys on 24 November. She had been captured by the British seven days earlier, a Royal Navy prize crew taking her to Kirkwall. Opening fire with both the deck gun and torpedoes, *U33* crippled the captured merchant ship, forcing her new master to beach and abandon her in the bleak and windswept Papa Sound. Tragically, four captured German crewmen aboard *Borkum* were killed during the attack.

---

[26] *Vermißt Ein Stern* (missing one star) was used by BdU to denote a presumed sunk U-boat, confirmation raising the designation to 'two stars'. See *First U-boat Flotilla*, Lawrence Paterson, p. 31.

With diesels still providing trouble for the fatigued engineers, *U33* staggered back to Wilhelmshaven on 26 November. Although Dönitz congratulated von Dresky on a well-executed patrol, decorating the young commander and his officers and crew, *U33* was again consigned to the *Germaniawerft* shipyard for extensive overhauls, including the replacement of one of her diesels. To facilitate the removal of the MAN engine, the pressure hull had to be cut open, rewelded after work was completed and the boat's structural integrity tested again in Kiel's huge pressure dock.

Coupled with submarine design faults and unexpected levels of wear and tear, sabotage also reared its ugly head during December. Three U-boats, *U25*, *U51*, and *U52*, were all found to have had sand added to their lubricating oil during maintenance in Wilhelmshaven's dockyards. Particularly galling was the extra damage inflicted on Viktor Schütze's already bothersome Type I *U25*. To add a final humiliation to *U25*'s patchy career, an attempt at putting out for patrol was aborted during December due to an oil leak from the boat's fuel bunkers. On 20 December Dönitz wrote in exasperation:

> "*U25*, the boat that has only managed a short patrol since the war's beginning and spent the rest of its time in the shipyard, must again break off its trip and return to the yard.'

Elsewhere the degradation of other U-boats took a toll on operations. Kaptlt. Lemp left Wilhelmshaven on 9 December aboard *U30* for minelaying in British waters, but radioed BdU two days later that he would be forced to return, the diesel exhaust vents unable to be closed, rendering *U30* incapable of diving. Fortunately for Lemp, chafing at the enforced curtailment of his mission, the required repair lasted only days, *U30* putting to sea again on 23 December bound for Liverpool with a cargo of ground mines and torpedoes. With *U28*'s and *U29*'s return from Hamburg's *Westwerft* shipyard on 24 December, 'Saltzwedel' had three Type VII boats, including Büchel's *U32*, almost ready for renewed operations. Indeed, on Christmas Day 1939 there were only two U-boats actually in action: *U30* and Herbert Sohler's *U46* of the 'Wegener' Flotilla.

By the year's end *U32* had at last put to sea. *U25* also sailed once more, all lubricants changed and the external fuel tank leak apparently traced and repaired after a slightly extended shipyard stay. As the niggling *U25* was en route for the North Sea its sister ship, *U26*, continued refitting, having arrived in Germany on 5 December following the abortive Gibraltar mission. It was to be the end of Ewerth's command, the thirty-two-year-old commander due to transfer from the 'Saltzwedel' to a post as consultant to BdU Org. as chief of the Weapons Department's torpedo office.[27] The remaining Saltzwedel boats, *U31*, *U33* and *U34*, were all undergoing extensive repair and refitting in over-worked German shipyards as New Year's Eve came and went.

---

[27] Ewerth returned to operational U-boats in April 1943 as commander of *U850*, sunk with all hands on 20 December 1943 bound for the Indian Ocean.

3

ONSLAUGHT: 1 JANUARY TO 8 APRIL 1940

1 January 1940: BdU reorganized the six existing combat U-boat flotillas. Plans that took account of new construction envisaged a future strength of fourteen front-line flotillas, each of twenty-five U-boats. Before this grandiose scheme could become reality BdU focused the strength of available combat boats; several flotillas were combined and the 'new' units renamed. They would no longer be known by the names of First World War commanders but would only bear numerical designations. From the beginning of 1940 the Saltzwedel Flotilla became simply the 2nd *Unterseebootflottille*.

Into the ranks of the 2nd U-Flotilla went the 'Saltzwedel' men and machines, with the addition of all former members of the 'Hundius' Flotilla, equipped with large Type IXA ocean-going U-boats.[28] Accordingly *U37*, *U38*, *U41* and *U44*, the latter a brand new boat commissioned on 4 November 1939, arrived on 'Saltzwedel' strength. 'Hundius' had lost three boats during the first four months of the war and at first they were the least favourably viewed U-boat type in Dönitz's arsenal. While they were roomier inside, they were correspondingly slower to dive and manoeuvre, possessing a wider turning circle than the smaller Type VIIBs now being manufactured. The 'sea cow', as it had been nicknamed by their crews, also took nearly three times as long to build as its smaller cousins, hindering Dönitz's desire for an immediate increase in numbers for his U-boat arm.

As well as new boats the 2nd U-Flotilla also received a new senior officer. Thirty-seven-year-old Kaptlt. Werner Hartmann became flotilla chief after having successfully commanded the now defunct 'Hundius' Flotilla since October 1938. Hartmann was already a veteran U-boat officer with over sixteen years in the navy. He had begun his career as commander aboard the Torpedo boats *Seeadler* and *Albatross* before transferring to U-boats in 1935. Hartmann spent over two years in command of the unpopular Type I *U26*, including one Spanish patrol during the Civil War, before becoming senior 'Hundius' officer in October 1938, a post he held until the flotilla's disbandment. He had also taken command of the Type IX *U37* in September 1939. By January 1940 he had completed two war patrols aboard *U37*, sinking eight ships totalling 35,306 tons.

But things did not run smoothly from the year's outset, even the weather itself seeming to conspire against the U-boat men. That winter was one of the coldest experienced in Germany's recent history and problems were encountered with the icing up of the Kaiser Wilhelm Canal and the North Sea and Baltic harbours. All spare Kriegsmarine surface vessels were pressed into the task of ice-breaking for the U-boats, while wooden 'shoes' were bolted into place over the submarines; bows to protect their delicate forward

---

[28] Kaptlt. Paul Hundius had been commander of *UB16*, *UC47* and *UB103*. During the First World War he sank sixty-seven ships during twenty war patrols, totalling 95,280 tons. He was killed 16 September 1918 when *UB57* was sunk by depth charges from HMS *Young Crow*.

torpedo-tube caps. The Kriegsmarine's obsolete 1906-built battleship *Schlesien* was responsible for clearing ice from the Elbe, particularly the difficult area at Brunsbüttel, western mouth of the Kaiser Wilhelm Canal, while the Jade River and Baltic were left in the hands of naval dockyard tugs augmented with *Sperrbrecher* and minesweepers. Despite these measures, ice damage continued to be suffered by an already meagre submarine force as the temperature continued to fall. The first day of January also saw a radio report from Schütze's *U25* that, only twenty-four hours into its patrol, the oil leak had returned, forcing yet another aborted mission.

6 January: Kaptlt. Ludwig Mathes, former pre-war commander of the 'Weddigen' Type IIs *U6* and *U9*, took *U44* out of the Jade estuary for the Atlantic. It was the boat's maiden voyage and Mathes was bound for the Bay of Biscay west of Portugal in search of torpedo targets.

Two days later BdU received a radio message from Kaptlt. Paul Büchel aboard *U32*. The thirty-two-year-old commander reported that due to "fixed listening stations" and heavy anti-submarine patrols he had been unable to penetrate the Clyde in order to lay his mines. Büchel suggested instead that he lay the minefield inshore south of Ailsa Craig Island where he had observed British merchant traffic. Although agreeing to the request, Dönitz was displeased with Büchel's apparent lack of aggression:

> "Until I hear the commanding officer's verbal report I shall not be satisfied that the first operation was really impossible."[29]

Büchel was then ordered to hunt for torpedo targets in the Western Approaches before proceeding to the western coast of Spain to coincide with the expected arrival of Schütze's *U25*, the clumsy and obstinate boat hastily repaired and sailing once more on 13 January.

17 January: Lemp brought a triumphant *U30* into the Jade estuary. The patrol, begun on 23 December, had started well with the successful torpedoing of requisitioned auxiliary patrol boat HMT *Barbara Robertson* north-west of the Butt of Lewis, sent to its grave with an artillery *coup-de-grâce*. That same day Lemp sighted bigger game.

In late afternoon north-west of the Flannan Islands the U-boat's lookouts sighted the mastheads of two battleships, HMS *Repulse* and *Barham*, patrolling with a screen of five destroyers in anticipation of German battleships *Gneisenau* and *Scharnhorst* entering the North Sea. With the cool deliberation which his crew often remarked on, Lemp dived beneath the destroyer screen and fired four electric torpedoes tipped with magnetic pistols at the overlapping battleships. With two torpedoes streaking towards each ship, Lemp retreated and managed to evade any British counter-attack as the echo of a single detonation was heard aboard the deeply submerged boat. They had scored a single hit on *Barham*, flooding the forward magazine and causing damage enough to put the battleship out of commission for three months.

After this successful outward voyage Lemp carefully deposited his mines near Liverpool harbour's Bar Lightship during 6 January before retiring and beginning the return journey. The minefield was extremely successful and on the day that Lemp entered Wilhelmshaven harbour the British Admiralty was forced to close Liverpool port after the loss of two ships and a third damaged. By 9 February that total had been raised to four ships sunk by the TMB mines, totalling 22,472 tons. Dönitz wrote in his diary:

[29] BdU KTB.

"The minelaying off Liverpool . . . required a lot of dash, thought, ability and determination. It was carried out in shallow water strongly patrolled."

There was, however, tragedy for Lemp and his veteran crew after their return. The loyal terrier Schnurzl whose picture adorned the conning tower was nowhere to be found in Wilhelmshaven, normally waiting at the quay for U30 to tie up and the crew to disembark. An anxious Lemp and his men were unable to locate the small terrier. It was days later when they learned that the eager dog had leapt aboard a German destroyer sailing for North Sea patrol duty, identified afterwards as either the destroyer Z1 "Leberecht Maass" or Z3 "Max Schulz". Both ships were sunk in error by Luftwaffe bombers on 22 February. Schnurzl was no more.

On the same day that Lemp returned Kaptlt. Habekost's U31 sailed for Loch Ewe on another minelaying mission. The boat had undergone trials near Heligoland, the island bastion proving its worth to the German Navy now that ice had curtailed much training within the traditional Baltic and Jade grounds.

22 January: A subdued Kaptlt. Büchel brought U32 into Wilhelmshaven. The field that he had laid at Ailsa Craig yielded no results; probably the water was too deep for the delicate magnetic triggers. A single sinking while outward bound of the small Norwegian steamer SS Luna, carrying rubber hose, zinc plates and hessian cloth, was no compensation and Dönitz relieved Büchel of his command, U32's First Watch Officer, Oblt.z.S. Hans Jenisch, being promoted to captaincy. Dönitz wrote in the BdU War Diary:

> "The commanding officer's explanation of why he thought the minelay could not be carried out in the Clyde is not convincing. . . . He did not make another attempt on another day. The operation was a difficult one – too difficult for this commanding officer."[30]

Although Dönitz accepted that this particular mission was one of the thorniest, he chose to pass it on to a second boat to attempt – Kaptlt. Hans-Wilhelm von Dresky's U33.

The war appeared to have lost momentum. On land static German troops faced French and British soldiers through reams of barbed wire and strong concrete fortifications. While England was joined by its dominions, Canada, Australia and New Zealand, in declaring war, Hitler attempted to entice support from other European states. Nagged by Grossadmiral Raeder to close the Mediterranean to the British, Hitler repeatedly endeavoured to persuade General Franco into active participation in the war, but failed at every attempt, Franco avoiding any direct involvement.

Despite arrangements dating back to August 1939 for the provision of German naval supply bases at Cadiz, Vigo and El Ferrol, Franco's declaration of neutrality caused problems. By late autumn 1939 Madrid's veteran German Naval Attaché, KzS Kurt Meyer-Döhner, had accumulated enough stores to provide a healthy supply for U-boat replenishment. Since there was, at that stage, no chance of delivering these materials to U-boats at sea, it had been planned that they would call into Spain's harbours, but this became unacceptable under the laws of neutrality. Dönitz was faced with an impasse, but circumvented the problem by the strategic 'internment' of five German merchant ships,

---

[30] Büchel was transferred to command the 21st Unterseebootsschuleflottille in Neustadt. He later returned to operational U-boats for ten months as commander of 12th U-Flotilla's Type IXD-2 U860 in August 1943 and was captured when his boat was sunk en route to the Far East on 15 June 1944.

laden with supplies, in mainland Spain and the Canary Islands. There they secretly waited for orders from Meyer-Döhner's covert supply service (*Ettapendienst*). They were not long in coming.

German merchant tanker MV *Thalia*, owned by 'DG Neptun', was among the internees. In the 72-metre merchant ship lying in Cadiz harbour was a cargo of torpedoes, fresh food and diesel fuel earmarked solely for clandestine transfer to U-boats in need of replenishment. Four other U-boat supply ships soon joined *Thalia*: *Bessel* interned in Vigo; *Max Albrecht* in El Ferrol; *Corrientes* and *Charlotte Schliemann* in Las Palmas in the Canary Islands. A fifth supply ship, *Lipari*, stationed in Cartagena, was refitted for the task but never used.

To test the worthiness of this proposed system Dönitz instigated a covert undertaking, codenamed in Spanish 'Moro' (Moor), which directed the Biscay-bound *U44* to make the first attempt at secret resupply from *Thalia*.

But on 26 January there was frustration at BdU headquarters when it became apparent that *U44* would be unable to comply. This time, however, the nuisance was tinged with success as her commander, Mathes, had already sunk an impressive seven merchant ships totalling 27,688-tons while en route for Cadiz. The last two were French cargo ships from the northbound KS56 convoy, during which chase Mathes had used up much of his fuel. It was now obvious that if he were to attempt the 'Moro' refuelling and fail, he would have insufficient diesel for a return journey. Dönitz decided to allow Mathes to continue his patrol and instead ordered the Spanish-bound *U25* to attempt 'Moro'. Five days later news was received overland from Meyer-Döhner that Schütze had successfully refuelled from the *Thalia*, the first of six U-boats to do so. Arriving shortly before 2000hrs Schütze had silently entered the harbour with decks awash and only the squat conning tower visible to any onlookers. Despite taxing conditions of an offshore breeze and moderate swell, within six hours *U25* was easing its way from harbour, fresh food and fuel safely stowed in the boat. In fact Schütze was in the middle of what would transpire to be his most successful operational cruise aboard the lumbering boat.

Flushed with the apparent ease of 'Moro', Dönitz ordered Kaptlt. Gustav-Adolf Mugler aboard *U41* to follow suit and refuel from *Thalia* under the code-name 'Gata' (cat), which would designate *Thalia* from then on. Mugler, former IWO aboard the pre-war *U30* and already with three confirmed sinkings and two prize captures to his credit, had been prowling the waters west of Vigo, providing distant cover for an attempt by other trapped merchant ships to sail for Germany. Despite sighting no enemy, the operation was deemed successful by Dönitz as the convoy sailed without incident and, much to the relief of BdU, without need of its originally requested close U-boat escort.

The first week of February continued the trend of mixed success for 'Saltzwedel' boats with both the torpedo and the mine. *U31* returned empty-handed after attempting to mine Loch Ewe, while *U34* sank a single tanker after sowing eight powerful TMC ground mines off Falmouth, a torpedo kill en route for Wilhelmshaven raising his score slightly. Attempts by *U26* and *U37* to search the Western Approaches alongside the 7th U-Flotilla's *U48* for the expected return from West Africa of three Royal Navy capital ships, HMS *Ark Royal*, *Renown* and *Exeter*, were foiled by British radio direction finding locating the trap. However, on 9 February Kaptlt. Mathes brought *U44* into Wilhelmshaven to a rapturous welcome. Dönitz recorded the claimed sinking of eight ships for 38,266 tons, each 'kill' meticulously logged by Mathes: two ships stopped and found to be carrying contraband, three darkened and thus presumed hostile, one in convoy, one armed and the last without identifying markings. It was the most triumphant patrol for the 2nd U-Flotilla, indeed of any U-boats, thus far of the war, "perfectly executed and rewarded with well-earned success".

16 February: *U33 Vermißt ein Stern.*

> "It seems more and more likely that *U33* has been lost. Several radio intelligence reports show that she was in action with an English minesweeper and then surrendered."[31]

Kaptlt. Hans–Wilhelm von Dresky had left Wilhelmshaven with *U28* on 5 February, the two boats bound for Heligoland and trials of their recent shipyard repairs. *U33* had come close to disaster the previous night when in the course of loading ammunition she rapidly developed an unexpected 15° list to port, her bow slumping low into the water. Freezing water gushed over the boat's deck through the bow torpedo-loading hatch, flooding her bilges, and was only prevented from doing serious damage by a quick-witted crewman who blew all ballast tanks, raising the deck out of the water. *U33*'s LI, Kaptlt. (Ing.) Fritz Schilling, surveyed the flooding later that day, declaring it slight and the bilge pumps able to cope with it.

After emerging from harbour in the wake of an ice-breaker and an accompanying freighter the cause of the mysterious list became apparent with the discovery of a small hole in the port torpedo tube and another in a copper pipe within the torpedo room. The boat was forced to spend two days moored in Heligoland as its crew struggled with the small but significant defects. By 7 February von Dresky could wait no longer and *U33* sailed with repairs still incomplete and crew uneasy about the seaworthiness of their ship. The mood of discontent was further exacerbated by the fact that the introverted and serious von Dresky had never fully endeared himself to his men. While other commanders had engendered an unconditional loyalty from displays of daring skill in attack, tempered with a genuine concern for their crew's safety, von Dresky had always remained slightly aloof from his crew, a quiet and deliberate man who, although an extremely able U-boat commander, was not given to the displays of reckless courage that were the hallmarks of many of his comrades.

By 11 February von Dresky was preparing for the final leg of his journey to the British naval base at the Firth of Clyde. Bringing *U33* to a halt on the sea floor, torpedo men laboured at removing the four bow tubes' torpedoes and replacing them with TMC mines, loading two within each tube. As the boat rocked in the North Sea currents von Dresky and his *Obersteuermann* (navigator) checked and re-checked their course for the attack on the British harbour.

Late that night *U33*'s electric motors whirred into action to cover the final distance to target. By midnight the waters of the Clyde estuary were washing around the submerged U-boat as it nosed inshore preparing to launch the first mines.

At 0250hrs Lt Cdr H.P. Price, aboard British sloop HMS *Gleaner*, patrolling the outer reaches of the Clyde estuary, received reports of a strong hydrophone trace, submerged mechanical noise one mile on the starboard bow. Minutes later a firm ASDIC contact confirmed the contact as *U33* edged into the estuary. Running at periscope depth searching for landmarks, the sudden lance of *Gleaner*'s searchlight blinded von Dresky, the British crew sighting the slender tube and opening fire as Price ordered full speed toward

[31] BdU KTB

the U-boat. At 0353hrs, as *Gleaner* raced over the unmistakeable swirl of a shallow diving submarine, four depth charges rolled into the water. Contact with *U33* was lost as the disturbed water ruined all reception for the British sonar and hydrophones and *Gleaner* suddenly becoming a temporary victim of the explosions. While the first four charges had been devastating for *U33*, they had also disabled the British sloop, all auxiliary machinery failing for thirty minutes as frantic electricians attempted to coax aging generators back to life after the unexpected violence of the shock waves from below.

Von Dresky had initially believed his antagonist to be a heavy cruiser passing astern of the boat and chose to lie on the bottom in only sixty metres of water. The first four charges detonated only metres overhead, damaging delicate instruments and starting numerous small leaks throughout the boat, which was plunged into darkness as bulbs shattered every-where. As emergency lighting flickered on, the crew urged their commander to rise and flee to deeper water where they would stand a better chance against enemy assault. Von Dresky, however, seemed paralysed by the violence of the first attack. As a last resort, his crew argued, *U33* had at least a single torpedo in its stern tube with which to dissuade their pursuit if they turned tail and ran. Then *Gleaner*, by now back in action, dropped a further five charges on the regained ASDIC contact. These new explosions brought flooding to a critical level and von Dresky was galvanized into action. Believing the game was lost, he ordered all tanks blown and the boat prepared for scuttling.

At 0522hrs *U33* broke through the surface and German sailors began streaming on to the upper decks. Price ordered his main 4" gun to begin firing and primed his ship to ram. However, as it became obvious that the crew were not preparing for a gun action and had raised their arms in surrender, fire was checked after only five rounds and *Gleaner* altered course to come alongside, Price latching onto the possibility of boarding and capturing an intact U-boat. Below decks in *U33*, von Dresky had distributed Enigma rotors among three of his men, Rottmann, Lt. Karl Vietor and *Obermaschinist* Fritz Kumpf, ordering them to swim away from the U-boat and drop them into the water. A small explosive charge was placed among confidential documents and Kaptlt.(Ing.) Fritz Schilling prepared to destroy the ship by scuttling charges and opening the vents of torpedo tubes one and two. As the penultimate man climbed from the inside of the U-boat's hull, leaving the Chief Engineer alone, Schilling realized that his first attempt at flooding the boat was failing, the vent on tube two only partially open. Running through the boat to the control tower he shouted for von Dresky who scrambled back down the ladder and together they tried to open the jammed vent, but with no success; so the commander went back to the conning tower while Schilling made his way aft and opened outboard valves, emitting a steady gush of water that threatened to engulf the boat in no time. With the fuses for the scuttling charges crackling behind him Schilling began to follow his captain outside. But the charges exploded before Schilling could escape and his lifeless body was thrown through the air as *U33* plunged underwater.

Struggling in the frigid water von Dresky could be heard urging his men to stay together, but only seventeen men were pulled out alive, the remainder succumbing to exposure and shock. Von Dresky was one of the twenty corpses later recovered by HMS *Kingston* as she and two British trawlers arrived on the scene. The surviving Germans were stripped of their clothes and given hot baths and thick blankets to fend off hypothermia. From the clothes of one of the survivors, *Obermaschinist* Fritz Kumpf, three of the enigma rotors were recovered, although they yielded little of value to the British.[32] Likewise, attempts to dive to the wreck provided little, the scuttling charges having done their work well. Three radio messages from *Gleaner*, the first on initial contact with the surfaced U-boat, the last at 0545hrs requesting assistance in rescuing survivors, were intercepted by B-Dienst, telling Dönitz that the second attempt at mining the Clyde had probably failed.

19 February: Viktor Schütze docked *U25* in Wilhelmshaven after a long overdue successful patrol. Besides being the first boat to re-supply under the 'Moro' operation, Schütze claimed six ships sunk for an estimated 27,795 tons, only 495 tons higher than the true total. The bright red cap of a toadstool, painted on the tower's flanks while at sea, offset the boat's distinctive striped camouflage. The second unorthodox decoration hanging from the conning tower was a red and white life ring, inscribed with the name *Songa*, Schütze's fourth victim of the voyage sunk on 22 January within the Western Approaches.

24 February: *U32* sailed from port bound for her operational area, but was forced to return the same day due to a shimmering wake of leaking oil trailing behind the boat. The following day as *U26* reported itself beginning its homeward trek due to mechanical problems, BdU finally acknowledged the likelihood of the loss of *U41*. She was over three weeks late for communication regarding the planned 'Gata' refuelling operation in Cadiz. No word had been received either aboard the tanker or in Wilhelmshaven as to whether the boat had been prevented from reaching Spain. In fact the last action of Kaptlt. Gustav-Adolf Mugler's *U41* had been to attack two ships of convoy OB84 on 5 February west-south-west of the Scillies, damaging the Dutch tanker SS *Ceronia* and later sinking British SS *Beaverburn*. But the convoy's sole escort destroyer, HMS *Antelope*, immediately fixed the submerged boat with ASDIC and delivered an effective depth charge salvo, *U41* and her entire crew of forty-nine men never resurfacing. But it was not until 15 March that the file on Kaptlt. Gustav-Adolf Mugler was definitively closed by BdU:

> "*U41* declared missing with immediate effect."

27 February: Flotilla commander Werner Hartmann entered port aboard *U37*, claiming to have sunk seven merchant ships for 45,000 tons plus an unidentified patrol boat of unknown tonnage. The boat flew its victory pennants from a conning tower adorned with Hartmann's trademark 'Westward Ho!' emblem.

After leaving Wilhelmshaven amid drifting ice floes on 28 January, *U37* had been tasked with a dual-purpose patrol. Aboard the Type IX boat was an extra passenger, known to the crew as a war correspondent. In fact the elderly man who had arrived aboard with two large suitcases was Ernst Weber-Drohl, Abwehr agent tasked to make contact with the IRA in Northern Ireland. Once at sea Hartmann revealed to his men the passenger's identity and destination, swearing the crew to silence 'on pain of death'.

En route to the north-west reaches of Ireland, Hartmann attacked and sank two targets of convenience sighted by his alert bridge lookouts before, in the early hours of 8 February, *U37* finally came within sight of Sligo Bay. Forced to submerge by the arrival of a steamer, Hartmann scanned the coastline for a suitable landing site through his periscope, dismayed to find no stretch of water calm enough for the Abwehr agent and his flimsy Luftwaffe-

---

[32] Two of the three rotors (VI, VII, VIII) were newly issued, additional to those of the U-boat's cipher system after the outbreak of war. VI and VII were captured, leaving the internal wirings of VIII unknown. Although valuable finds for the British they were ultimately unable to assist in rapid code-breaking. See David Kahn *Seizing the Enigma*, pp. 112–126.

issue rubber dinghy. There was no choice but to reroute the landing further west to Killala Bay where conditions appeared more inviting. The landing itself was, however, to be anything but smooth.

As darkness fell the small inflatable was placed on the U-boat's upper deck and the Abwehr agent with his two bulky suitcases jammed aboard. Hartmann, observing from the conning tower, gently lowered his boat into the water, allowing the dinghy to float off once the decks were awash. It was then that it became obvious that not only was the rubber dinghy not going to bear the combined weight of the agent and his hardware but also that Weber-Drohl had never rowed a boat anywhere in his life. Hartmann's contingency plan was now brought into play and the U-boat's wooden dinghy broken out for the agent to use. Again, however, although the contents would fit, the frantic flailing of oars promised no method of propulsion to the little craft.

U37's second watch officer, L.z.S. Hans-Günther Kuhlmann, on his first patrol aboard the boat, requested permission to leave the boat and, without much more than non-committal noises from Hartmann, leapt aboard the wooden dinghy and rowed into the darkness. Although Dönitz had expressly forbidden U-boat crewmen to leave their vessels in support of such dangerous undertakings, no effort was made to stop him and it was with visible relief that Hartmann and his lookouts saw him reappear minutes later. He had successfully ferried Weber-Drohl to the beach, unloading his suitcases and even carrying him ashore. Hastily Hartmann accepted Kuhlmann's report and the boat glided away to deeper waters, a brief four-letter code word transmitted to signify success. The first agent delivery by U-boat of the Second World War had been a triumph.[33]

The boat then went in search of targets, sinking three ships by torpedo and gunfire by 15 February, among them a suspected patrol vessel, the British steam trawler *Togimo*, sunk by artillery attack at 0330hrs on 11 February. After taking part in the abortive hunt for the *Ark Royal*, alongside *U26* and *U48*, Hartmann received orders to proceed to the sea west of Porto to act as tactical coordinator of a six-boat 'wolf pack' planned for the Biscay. Although sinking three more steamers from two separate convoys over the following days, the idea of controlling a 'wolf pack' from a boat actually involved in the action was deemed a failure for the second time. Although one more attempt would be made, it appeared to Dönitz that the most effective form of leadership for congregating U-boats into a single group would have to originate from BdU headquarters where the 'big picture' was available.

After Hartmann's triumphant return, Dönitz added three brief words to his report: "An excellent patrol". Two days later a similar endorsement was given to Kaptlt. Scheringer as *U26* also returned from over a month at sea.

4 March: Strictly labelled as 'Top Secret', fresh orders for Dönitz arrived:

> "1. Further U-boat sailings are to be stopped. U-boats which have already sailed are not to operate off the Norwegian coast.
> "2. All naval forces to be ready for operations as quickly as possible. No special degree of readiness."

Planning for the invasion of Denmark and Norway had reached its final stages. In Wilhelmshaven Werner Hartmann received orders to prepare all 'Saltzwedel' boats for

---

[33] Ernst Weber-Drohl, an ex-circus strongman, was captured and interned in April 1940.

operations, cancelling proposed transfers to U-boat school of some of the older boats and also putting large-scale repair work on hold, the ailing Type VIIs patched up only enough to be functional. When the order reached BdU headquarters four boats were at sea in the Atlantic, all from the 2nd U-Flotilla: *U28*, *U29*, *U32*, each carrying out minelaying along England's coasts, and *U38* west of Ireland hunting for torpedo targets.

Germany's preparations for a Scandinavian invasion were being matched in Whitehall. First Lord of the Admiralty Winston Churchill had promoted the idea of the 'occupation' of Norway under cover of assistance to Finland, embroiled in a brave but flagging war against Russia. While this convenient conflict raged, Britain and France felt they could persuade domestic public opinion that this was indeed their reason for invading Norway, not the 'coincidental' benefit of occupying Sweden's Gallivore iron mines, thereby cutting Germany's iron-ore supply. The Germans, however, were by no means blind to Allied thinking. They were aware that Royal Navy forces were returning to their anchorage at Scapa Flow and areas of north-east Scotland were being declared off-limits to shipping as troops massed alongside docked transport ships. Similar scenes in France painted the picture of an Allied expeditionary force preparing to sail, the armistice between Finland and Russia on 13 March doing nothing to halt it.

All twenty-eight boats available for the Norwegian campaign were held at twelve-hour readiness while Dönitz chafed at not knowing when the undertaking, code-named 'Weserübung', would begin. U-boats' operational orders, code-named 'Operation Hartmut', were drawn up and placed into sealed envelopes ready for distribution. The operation entailed the use of all major components of the Kriegsmarine. Simultaneous landings were to take place in Narvik, Trondheim, Bergen, Egersund, Kristiansand and Oslo, the first four using naval forces as troop carriers, the latter two utilizing requisitioned merchant transport ships as well. The screening U-boats were to prevent Allied naval forces escorting troops to Norway from either attacking the German landings or establishing their own bases, submerging to remain a hidden menace by day and recharging on the surface during the brief Arctic night. Any opportunity to attack Allied warships was given priority. Dönitz was well aware of the two most critical areas for his U-boats: Narvik, with its access to the Swedish mines and remoteness, and the "Shetland–Norway narrows", where the Royal Navy could attempt a crippling blow against German communications and supply lines. He concluded that:

> "It will not be possible to prevent landings by disposing boats in deep formation off the possible landing places, because such places and the approaches to them are too numerous and there are not enough boats. One would only run the risk of being in the wrong place or having too few forces."

He reasoned that his scant U-boat strength would be best utilized in the open sea within easy striking distance of threatened areas and astride likely avenues of Allied attack. He concluded that he had twenty-eight boats with which to achieve his aims: twelve Atlantic boats, ten smaller attack boats and six school boats.[34] In the Baltic two 2nd U-Flotilla boats engaged in working-up trials after their commissioning, *U64* and *U65* (the latter the first Type IXB commissioned), were under direct orders to accelerate the process in order to join the operation.

[34] These numbers did not include three U-boats held back to be kept in hand for the future operation code-named '*Gelb*' – the first intimation within BdU records of the forthcoming attack on Western Europe.

11 March: As tension mounted over the start date for 'Weserübung', Dönitz received fresh instructions. U-boats standing at twelve-hour readiness for sea and destined to operate off Narvik and Trondheim were ordered to sail to prevent what were thought to be imminent Allied landings. Four other boats were to patrol between Bergen and Stavanger. The sole stipulation was for all boats within the proximity of Norway to remain unseen, outside the internationally prescribed three-mile territorial limit and to attack only if engaging Allied naval or troop-landing forces. At Wilhelmshaven *U30* and *U34* prepared to sail. Already at sea, *U38* was ordered from the North Atlantic to the area of Utvær and Kors Fjord to augment the patrolling U-boat cordon.

As if that were not enough for Dönitz and his small staff to contend with, at 1615hrs a telephone call received at BdU headquarters reported that disaster had struck another boat of the 2nd U-Flotilla, this time while in Schillig Roads, doorstep of Wilhelmshaven itself. Kaptlt. Johannes Habekost had taken *U31* to sea earlier in the day for trials with thirteen dockyard workers aboard, shaking down the boat after her recent repairs following its fifth war patrol. At 1200hrs *U31* had finished an underwater run to ensure that the pressure hull was watertight and was preparing to surface near the black No. 12 buoy in Schillig Roads. Habekost had completed a cursory sweep through the navigation periscope for nearby shipping, the propellers of German steamer *Stadt Rüstringen* 1,500 metres ahead to port clearly audible on hydrophones. Visibility was moderate to poor, sheets of drizzling rain occasionally drifting across the sea. *U31* was lying virtually stationary as Habekost ordered tanks blown and the boat began to rise to the surface. A sailor aboard the *Rüstringen*, Erwin Franz, later reported seeing the boat begin to surface:

> "Bearing about 135 degrees, about 1,000 metres away, there was a U-boat down by the stern. Bows and jumper wire could be clearly seen. The bows were about two metres above the water. . . . Her stern was under water. The sea around the boat was foamy and white."

At that moment Squadron Leader Miles Villiers Delap, on an armed reconnaissance flight, brought his 82 Squadron Blenheim bomber out of thick low-hanging cloud and approached the *Rüstringen* at a height of only twenty-five metres, engines feathered so as to make no sound. Aboard the steamer Seaman Karl Fellensiek saw the aircraft streaking toward his ship:

> "It approached us amidships at about mast height with its engines off. It approached from port. The mate thought it was English. When it was close to the ship it turned away and made for the periscope, which was now astern."

Aboard the Blenheim, Delap and his crew only saw the surfacing U-boat as they prepared to drop four 250lb bombs on the steamer, veering away at the last moment to attack the *U31* emerging from the water, periscope still extended. In seconds the aircraft flashed overhead and the bombs arced downwards towards their unsuspecting target, exploding slightly forward of the conning tower. The U-boat recoiled beneath the impact and as the Blenheim dashed away to safety *U31* began to sink, thick black oil staining the water around it. The British aircraft had been so low that the bombs' detonation had caused serious damage and it took all of Delap's considerable flying skill to keep the aircraft airborne as he ordered course set for the squadron's home airfield at Watton, Norfolk.

Nearby, another submerged U-boat, *U21* of the 1st U-Flotilla, was also undergoing trials after shipyard work. A little after midday her commander, Kaptlt. Wolf Stiebler, heard a dull explosion that he felt was somehow "different from the detonation of a depth

39

charge or torpedo". He instantly ordered tanks blown aboard the small Type II, rushing to the conning tower as soon as it had broken surface. As well as the *Rüstringen* slowly steaming along its course Stiebler observed:

> "a streak of foam about twenty degrees to port, 800 metres off. I observed that it was a U-boat periscope flying a red flag. . . . As I could not see anything unusual and the boat appeared to be calmly submerged, I turned away and entered port."

Indeed Stiebler, who had not seen or heard the aircraft, wrongly misinterpreted the 'feather' of white water curling around the periscope to mean that she was underway at high speed, keeping "very good depth". In fact the U-boat lay crippled on the bottom in only fifteen metres of water, the strong Jade current flowing past her still extended periscope. The captain of the *Rüstringen* had by that time received reports of the attack from his own crew, as well as a Luftwaffe *Feldwebel* and civilians on board who had all been startled by the aircraft's initial approach. However, he chose not to intervene:

> "I took no further action. The sea was also quite calm, so I thought that the second U-boat would manage alone. When I arrived at Wangerooge I did not make a report, because I assumed that the U-boat would already have requested assistance."

Unfortunately for Habekost and his crew this was not the case. Four hours later the first rumours of a possible sinking reached BdU, the Luftwaffe man, *Feldwebel* Hoffmann, having telephoned Wilhelmshaven himself to report the incident. When Dönitz returned Hoffmann's call to his fighter group headquarters at Jever, he was able to determine that all U-boats undergoing trials were accounted for except one. Immediately, two *U-Boot Jäger* of Wilhelmshaven's 12th UJ-Flotilla were sent to the area described by Hoffmann, along with several smaller Harbour Patrol vessels. In Heligoland the *Saar*, tender for the 2nd U-Flotilla, was ordered to sail with boats made ready to be swung out in search of survivors. Kaptlt. Lemp aboard *U30*, at that moment within the Wilhelmshaven Tirpitz lock preparing for patrol, was also sent to the scene, sailing at 1800hrs.

To take charge of the rescue and salvage mission Kaptlt. Ernst Sobe, Chief of the U-boat Tactical Training School (*U-Front-Ausbildungsflottille*, known as the *Agru-Front*), was transferred from Kiel, to be accompanied by the 2nd U-Flotilla's Chief Engineer, Lt (Ing.) Karl Scheel. By 1945hrs the two *U-Boot Jäger* were at the scene, radioing the discovery of rising oil and the solid echo of a sunken U-boat. By 2030hrs Lemp's hydrophone operator had added the grim noise of knocking to the reports, as trapped survivors attempted to communicate with their would-be rescuers. Two floating corpses were also recovered, evidence that the hull had been breached to some degree at least. Minesweepers arrived, as well as a further pair of *U-Boot Jäger*, to guard the scene and provide anti-aircraft defence while the *Saar* took charge of the area until Sobe's arrival.

During the early hours of the following morning two directors of U-boat construction arrived aboard the salvage tugs *Kraft* and *Willie* with Kaptlt. Sobe and two U-boat construction experts. As *U30* left the scene to continue her patrol, *Saar* sent Morse messages through the dense water ordering any trapped crew to leave *U31* via whatever escape hatches they could use, the tender's lifeboats being on hand to rescue survivors. There was no reply.

At midday the following day the head of the Kriegsmarine's Diving School arrived aboard the tug *Hermes*. In worsening weather he began to dive into the shallow murky water, stirred by the changing tide. By midnight he had surveyed the scene, fastening a buoy to the conning tower before surfacing. He reported the boat with a heavy list to starboard and no reply to any knocking on the outer hull. The fifty-eight crew and onboard shipyard workers were more than likely dead. Dönitz recorded:

> "It is particularly regrettable that a boat should have been lost by enemy action in the immediate vicinity of her own base. . . . We must have sufficient AA defence for the approach route on the Jade so that at least the enemy is prevented from flying low undisturbed."

In response, new regulations for minesweepers or *Vorpostenboote* to shepherd U-boats in and out of port were framed on 14 February. *U31*, the first U-boat sunk by aircraft of the Second World War, was deemed upon further inspection by divers to be repairable and later raised by salvagers. The grisly remains of much of her crew were found wedged within the boat's conning tower, perhaps the last area to flood. It was surmised that many had been killed instantly as a result of a sudden and excruciating increase of internal pressure when one of the detonating bombs ruptured an internal compressed air tank, its explosion in turn destroying valves and pipes linking the other bottles. The dead men were removed and buried at Wilhelmshaven within the *Heldenfriedhof* (Heroes' Cemetery), the boat taken into Bremen's AG Weser yard for a complete refit and eventual recommissioning.

12 March: *U29* returned to Wilhelmshaven claiming three ships sunk by torpedo and a successfully laid minefield. The following day both *U43* and *U44* of the 2nd U-Flotilla sailed to patrol the waters outside Bergen's three-mile limit. Both boats were ordered to proceed slowly, at nine knots, as the Norwegian situation seemed obscure and confusing to Dönitz. He was unsure whether the operation was to be postponed or accelerated, particularly after the next day's declaration of an armistice in the Russo-Finnish war. Dönitz then repealed the previous orders and both Type IXs were ordered to the Orkney and Shetland Islands to cruise in search of Royal Navy targets. The patrols were miserable ones, unsuccessful in fierce gales and long seas. On 31 March *U43* suffered an unexpected casualty when IWO, Oblt.z.S. Hans-Wilhelm Behrens, was swept away and lost before the U-boat could drag itself around to attempt rescue.

23 March: Both *U28* and *U32* returned to the Wilhelmshaven lock during the day, the former successfully having laid its mines outside Portsmouth Harbour. During the boat's slow return to Germany she engaged and sank two ships for an estimated 12,000 tons. Dönitz was pleased at Kuhnke's handling of the operation, but the obsolescent boat would be unavailable for any impending operations, needing a complete overhaul.

Oblt.z.S. Hans Jenisch's first patrol as commander was also considered successful by his commander in chief. En route to his difficult minelaying mission Jenisch sighted and attacked the Norwegian steamer SS *Belpamela* west of the Orkneys. Surfaced at 0112hrs on 2 March the U-boat's IWO, Kaptlt. Ernst Kammüller, fired a full spread of four torpedoes at the easy target wallowing before *U32*. One missed, while the other three detonated metres short of their target, which beat a hasty retreat. Later that morning Jenisch determined to make up for this unexpected failure, surfacing to attack and sink the Swedish SS *Lagaholm*, after ensuring it was indeed carrying contraband. But a further pair of premature detonations wasted valuable torpedoes before the Swede was destroyed. *U32* continued through the Irish Sea to lay twelve TMB mines on 7 March alongside Lemp's minefield in the entrance channels to Liverpool Harbour. British merchant SS *Counsellor* sank the following day, the only reward for this high-risk enterprise.

By 29 March all 2nd U-Flotilla boats had returned to port following instructions from

Dönitz to refit for what he felt was a likely Norwegian campaign in early April. *U38* was the only flotilla boat still at sea. Lemp brought *U30* into port with four Luftwaffe crewmen aboard, their Dornier Do78 shot down by British aircraft south-west of Stavanger. The rescue of the lucky crewmen was later immortalized in a painting featured in the German newspaper *Volkischer Beobachter*.

For the 2nd U-Flotilla the unsettling news that *U44* had failed to report her position, despite repeated requests to do so, filtered through. By 30 March she was overdue and feared lost. The fear was justified, the shattered remains of Kaptlt. Ludwig Mathes' *U44* lay deep in the Heligoland Bight, sunk by the sudden blast of a British mine laid on 13 March. The entire crew of forty-seven men died in what must have been terrifying minutes of uncontrolled flooding, sending their Type IX boat to its grave. During only two war patrols the aggressive and skilful Kaptlt. Mathes and *U44* had accounted for eight ships totalling 29,608 tons.

By the beginning of April the strength of the 2nd U-Flotilla was ten boats and Kaptlt. Werner Hartmann was departing aboard *U37*, ordered to escort the raider *Schiff 16/ Atlantis* towards the Atlantic. Invasion or no invasion, Dönitz could not allow his U-boats to remain idle.

Three days later OKM gave the long-awaited notification to BdU that 'Weserübung' would begin on 9 April. Those U-boats detailed to take part that were not yet at sea sailed soon after, opening sealed orders on 6 April, allowing three days to be in position before the German axe fell. In Wilhelmshaven Kaptlt. Georg-Wilhelm Schulz took *U64* from its berth for its first operational sortie. After nearly four months of difficult Baltic trials, *U64* was tasked with escort duties on its first patrol. Two days previously the raider *Schiff 36/Orion* had departed from Kiel for what would become a monumental 510-day raiding voyage. Schulz was ordered to escort the ship through the North Sea to the hunting grounds of the Atlantic where the 'ghost ship' could vanish into the ocean wastes and begin its predatory voyage.

Georg-Wilhelm Schulz was no stranger to the sea after years spent within the merchant navy. A handsome 34-year-old native of Köln, he came from a military background. His father had been a major in the Kaiser's artillery and his brother was now part of OKH's General Staff. Schulz's Kriegsmarine career had led to positions as IWO on *U33* for the duration of two patrols during the Spanish Civil War before he had been posted as commander of the training boat *U10* for most of 1939. At the end of the year he had taken over *U64* as she underwent trials, commissioned into the 2nd U-Flotilla on 16 December 1939. Schulz is often thought of as reserved and aloof by those who did not know him, cut from the traditional Prussian mould. However, his crew soon learned to respect and admire a man whom they regarded as an infallible leader and excellent seaman, a man who also took a keen interest in their well-being. They were soon to discover those qualities in abundance as the flotilla moved to the North Sea and the greatest gamble thus far of Hitler's war.

4

'SALTZWEDEL' AT NARVIK – NORWEGIAN FIASCO:
9 APRIL TO 31 JULY 1940

9 April: During early morning German troops began unloading in Norway's major ports while Luftwaffe aircraft ferried *Fallschirmjäger* into battle for the first time. Under 'Operation Hartmut' nine groups of U-boats were arrayed at strategic locations, screening the massive landings and lying in ambush for the likely Allied response. From 2nd U-Flotilla, *U25* was the furthest north, attached to the three-boat *Gruppe 1*, lying in deep formation and shielding the exposed destroyers and transports in Narvik harbour. *U64* was intended to be a fourth boat for *Gruppe 1* once *Orion* was far enough towards the Atlantic. The smallest group, *Gruppe 2*, patrolling between Trondheim and Namsos, was composed of Lemp's *U30* and Rollmann's *U34*, in deep formation. At sea in the shipping lanes between the Shetlands and Trondheim *Gruppe 5* lay in wait, two of the seven boats coming from 2nd U-Flotilla: Hartmann's *U37*, having completed its escort mission, in grid square AF7890 and Heinrich Liebe's *U38* in AN2810. The remainder of the flotilla, apart from *U28*, were in Wilhelmshaven, refitting after long patrols. Kaptlt. Günter Kuhnke's *U28*, however, had suffered such severe mechanical breakdown that the boat remained in Kiel's AG Weser shipyards until May.

Although Denmark fell to the Wehrmacht almost instantly, Norway proved a harder nut to crack. In Narvik ten destroyers under the command of KzS Friedrich Bonte (FdZ) successfully landed troops early on the morning of 9 April, the Vestfjord securely guarded by the three U-boats of *Gruppe 1*. The following morning during pre-dawn darkness the crew of *U25* noticed a sudden gentle roll as if in the wake of a passing ship. In drifting banks of snow Kaptlt. Viktor Schütze was unable to verify exactly who or what had swept past. It had in fact been five ships of the Royal Navy's 2nd Destroyer Flotilla that now entered the narrow fjord and attacked Bonte's destroyers. Within only thirty minutes, by 0430 hrs, two Kriegsmarine destroyers and several merchantmen including the valuable German supply ship *Rauenfels* had been sunk, another freighter completely disabled and Bonte himself killed. Although the British had also suffered losses, the position of the German invaders in Narvik, far from their supply base of Germany, became markedly more precarious.

As the three surviving Royal Navy assailants emerged from the fjord *U25* and *U51* located the retreating enemy. Aboard *U25* Viktor Schütze aimed two torpedoes at point blank range, unable to miss in such a calm sea. But Schütze was rewarded with complete silence as both magnetic warhead torpedoes vanished without trace. Germany's torpedo crisis had reached its peak.

The following day B-Dienst radio intercepts detected stirrings of powerful Royal Navy units again heading for Narvik and in Berlin Hitler frantically ordered all available U-boats rushed to the area. Dönitz reacted by reinforcing the Narvik screen with four U-boats from *Gruppe 5*, the fresh *U64* replaced by inbound *U37* as escort for *Orion* and also racing toward

Narvik. Sister ship *U65* was also committed, cutting short her trials as the potential of a complete German reversal loomed. In order to bolster the 2,000 ground troops faced with depleted supplies after the loss of the *Rauenfels*, BdU also ordered *U26*, *U29*, and *U43* (along with the 1st U-Flotilla's *U61*) to act as transports, each carrying fifty tons of small arms and anti-aircraft ammunition for Narvik.

By 12 April there were five boats stationed at Narvik and a further four en route. Additional torpedo failures had been reported to Dönitz and with no fresh ideas about either cause or solution to the problem, complicated instructions regarding the mixing of magnetic and contact pistols were transmitted to all boats. Four of the reinforcing U-boats were redirected to the Vaagsfjord north of Narvik as fears of Allied landings grew, while those at Narvik itself were also redeployed. Both *U25* and *U51* were told to submerge and wait in the outer Vestfjord, while *U46*, *U48* and *U64* were to enter the inner Ofotfjord. While there the U-boats took the opportunity to refuel from supply ships or damaged destroyers in order to keep their combat potential at its maximum.

Hitler's fears of an enemy troop landing were in fact amply justified and by 10 April a powerful Allied force was making its approach to the threatened city. At the head of nine destroyers was the battleship HMS *Warspite*, intent on the annihilation of all remaining German ships. Once their threat had been neutralized, Allied ground forces landed in Vaagsfjord would be free to attack the isolated German mountain troops and take Narvik back. This time, however, the Royal Navy strike force was immediately detected. First they were sighted and abortively attacked by *U65* en route to Vaagsfjord, two defective torpedoes achieving nothing, but swift depth-charge retribution from escorting destroyers causing some damage and shaking up Kaptlt. Hans-Gerrit von Stockhausen's green crew.

Schulz also narrowly avoided disaster in the West Fjord approaches to Narvik. Diving after lookouts sighted the unmistakeable outline of a prowling British destroyer, Schulz approached with two tubes prepared to fire. A heavy swell rolled the U-boat, making Oblt (Ing.) Ludwig Steinmutz's job of trim keeping at periscope depth extremely difficult. Suddenly Schulz at the attack periscope shouted for crash dive, a single destroyer's bow wave accelerating in his direction. They had been seen and salvation lay in escaping to the depths. At that crucial moment, as Steinmutz ordered tanks flooded, a rating mistakenly blew the port diving tank, sending the boat stern first to the surface. Immediately Steinmutz pushed his way to the complicated air distribution panel and reversed the fatal blunder, *U64* plummeting below and barely escaping depth charges dropping through the water above.

Later still, Schulz again sighted what appeared to be two cruisers with a strong destroyer screen at the end of the fjord. After moving away to surface and send a brief message to Dönitz – "Strong destroyer guard stands before the fjord. Narvik threatens to be a trap" – Schulz again approached submerged, this time successfully firing two torpedoes, both of which exploded only seconds from the tubes. *U64* again barely evaded retribution, passing deeper into the fjord.

On the morning of 13 April in Vestfjord Schütze's *U25* sighted the approaching juggernaut HMS *Warspite* and its shepherding destroyers, but yet again failed in attack as all torpedoes disappeared without trace. Schütze was compelled to dive in alarm as the battleship roared directly for his boat and on overhead, the British force churning into the inner fjord. Inside *U25* the noise was deafening, the thunder of huge screws churning the water above joined by the racket of throbbing engines.

As the British force ground its way up the narrow fjord, *Warspite* paused to launch one of its Swordfish aircraft. Observer Lt Comm W.L.M. 'Bruno' Brown had been briefed earlier that morning for a general reconnaissance, particularly searching for German warships, ground forces and shore batteries, while free to bomb any suitable targets found.

The Swordfish floatplane was rated to carry a maximum of 1,000lb bomb load, but pilot F.C. 'Ben' Rice had overloaded it slightly, persuading the Catapult Officer who weighed out the cordite launching charge to add a "soupçon more". The aged aircraft hurtled from the ship at 1152hrs, Rice taking it up to 1,000 feet. They soon sighted various German destroyers hugging the fjord sides as if for shelter and firing ineffectual anti-aircraft barrages, Brown radioing his observations back to *Warspite*.

Unfortunately for *U64*, the small aircraft then overflew Herjangsfjord and found the U-boat as she lay at anchor near shore at the fjord's northern end. Kaptlt. Schulz had been refuelling his boat near Bjerkvik and was caught completely unprepared. High above him, Rice's voice crackled over the intercom: "Let's have a go at the bastard!" Swooping steeply down he pressed the control yoke's firing button before streaking overhead dropping two 100lb bombs. Pulling out of his dive at less than 150 feet, airframe strained as gravity grudgingly released its grasp, returning machine-gun fire arced from *U64*, stitching a pattern of holes across the Swordfish's belly but causing no real damage.

> "Kesselheim [*Funkmaat*] had gone on watch in the radio room . . . just tuned in the war news report when he heard the commander's urgent order 'Stand by to dive!' Next he heard the barking of the 2cm flak gun. He tried to make out from men in the control room what was happening, but they were as confused as he was.
> "Then two explosions shook the boat, and the unexcited voice of the radio commentator announced the time. It was 1313hrs."[35]

The first bomb narrowly missed the stationary target but the second struck immediately behind the conning tower, ripping an enormous hole in the pressure hull. Aboard the U-boat there was pandemonium as seawater poured in.

> "Kesselheim had just reached the control tower when the hatch above him slammed shut and the boat began to sink. His hands gripped the cold steel of the ladder, and the terror he had felt was suddenly replaced with an overwhelming sadness that he was really going to die. It seemed such a pity, and he was sorry that he would not live to see his 21st birthday."[36]

The crippled ship plunged thirty-five metres to the fjord floor to lie with a 45° starboard list. Schulz had managed to leap from the sinking ship along with twelve others, but there were still thirty-three men trapped below. It was Schulz who had slammed the tower hatch shut, instinctively knowing that the boat was sinking too fast for men to climb out. They stood more chance of survival in a controlled escape from the seafloor as they had practices in Kiel's training tank. Before Schulz had sealed the hatch *Bootsmaat* Arthur Piepenhagen courageously climbed back into the sinking ship to shout his commander's instruction to the trapped crew. Inside their tomb men were alternating between despair, resignation and panic. Survivors remember the words of Hannes Wiegand, a torpedo mixer crouching on top of the port diesel as the water level rose relentlessly:

> "If I'd known that this was going to happen, I wouldn't have paid my bill at the canteen."

[35] *Grey Wolf*, Grey Sea, Elizabeth Gasaway, p. 28.
[36] Gasaway, p. 29.

Finally the air pressure inside the boat equalled that of the surrounding water and the hatch to the surface above could be opened. One after the other, machinist Rudi Dimmulich leading the way, and using their well-rehearsed escape procedures, twenty-five of them managed to reach the surface safely, the shattered wreck holding the bodies of eight less fortunate crewmen, some killed in the blast, others by the freezing water.[37]

Fortunately for Schulz and his men there had been spectators to the sinking and several German mountain troops immediately launched small wooden boats to go to the aid of the U-boat crew. Schulz, clad only in a blanket, was taken ashore where he convinced a sceptical *Gebirgsjäger Oberst* to send his men out again in their small boats to assist those due to make their ascent to the surface. Eventually the *Gebirgsjäger* rescued all the survivors.

Meanwhile the British ships had savaged the German destroyer force and after two hours of constant gunfire, all remaining Kriegsmarine destroyers had been sunk or forced to scuttle. The victorious Royal Navy withdrew next morning after unsuccessful Luftwaffe and U-boat attack, thousands of Reichsmarks worth of torpedoes wasted by faulty detonation mechanisms.

Schulz and his bedraggled crew were now in the infantry front-line as the anticipated Allied landing in Vaagsfjord went ahead without a hitch, again after several abortive U-boat attacks. Their initial attire of civilian clothes borrowed from the local population, including a skirt and shawl for *Maschinenmaat* Bösner, was soon replaced by combat dress borrowed from the mountain troops. It is possible that the U-boat men were briefly attached to an ad-hoc naval battalion of survivors from the shattered destroyer force, the *Marine-Bataillon Erdmenger*, thrown together to defend Narvik, the improvised naval troops known as the *Gebirgsmarine* (mountain navy), an honour bestowed on them by their army colleagues.

Trained submariners were, however, urgently needed in Germany and whatever tenure they may have held within the *Gebirgsmarine* was brief. The return to Germany for the remainder of *U64*'s crew, again in civilian clothes, was made through Sweden by railroad to a German passenger ship and ultimately Wilhelmshaven, where Schulz and his men arrived on 26 April. Their new boat had already hit the water the month before: the Type IXB *U124* launched from Bremen's AG Weser yards and now ready to receive the men of *U64*, their numbers bolstered by sailors fresh from training school. Two months of shakedown trials lay ahead of them before commissioning into the 2nd U-Flotilla.

The sole U-boat success on the day of *U64*'s sinking had occurred further south at Søtvika, near Trondheim. The Norwegian minelayer *Frøya*, beached and abandoned after being hit by *Gebirgsjäger* artillery, was torpedoed by Kaptlt. Wilhelm Rollmann's *U34*, blown in half and completely wrecked. Everywhere Germany's submariners pressed home desperate attacks on their enemy, but to no avail as torpedo after torpedo either detonated prematurely or disappeared without trace, the U-boat often receiving severe depth-charging for its pains. Matters came to a head for Germany's U-boats when the celebrated Günther Prien aboard *U47* missed with eight shots against stationary troop transports unloading crucial Allied troops and supplies in Vaagsfjord. It was the final straw. Telephoning Raeder at OKM in Berlin, Dönitz insisted that all northern U-boats be withdrawn rather than continue to fight with scandalously defective weaponry. Reluctantly, Raeder agreed and orders were transmitted to bring the boats back to base.

U25 was ordered to continue patrolling well offshore, ultimately heading south to the

---

[37] Three months later the corpse of Willi Buhl was found floating in the fjord, having drifted out of the wreck; the remainder stayed inside their iron tomb.

seas west of the Shetlands. *U38* and the *U65* were in turn ordered seaward of Vaagsfjord, impotently representing the Kriegsmarine's U-boat arm during the bitter infantry struggle at Narvik. All four U-boats heading for Narvik laden with small arms ammunition were redirected and docked in Trondheim instead.

On 26 April OKM officially released the U-boats service from Norwegian operations. That same day that *U34* headed north from the Minch Rollmann sighted at 0245hrs the large steamer *Franconia*, her course plotted from intercepted communications provided by the B-Dienst listening service. In this, his last throw of the dice in 'Operation Hartmut', Rollmann was unsuccessful again, the only result from his attempted torpedo attack an apparent 'end run detonation'. Out of torpedoes, *U34* headed home.

27 April: Back in Germany the shortage of available supply shipping was becoming acute and three U-boats were earmarked for special preparation to enable the transport of volatile aviation fuel and either small-arms ammunition or Luftwaffe bombs, destined for the forward airfields. *U32* was one of the three selected and she departed for Trondheim on 27 April alongside the large ex-Turkish *UA* also filled with aviation spirit. Coupled with hundreds of litres of high-octane fuel held within modified fuel tanks, Kaptlt. Jenisch's Type VII carried a 8.8cm gun alongside its ammunition within the cramped pressure hull.

Jenisch took *U32* close to the Norwegian coastline in a bid to outwit hunting destroyers. The U-boat was unsuccessfully attacked during 2 May, but their enemy failed to press home what at best they considered a tenuous ASDIC trace. However, the sudden depth-charging had caused small fissures in several storage canisters, allowing toxic fumes from the aviation fuel to enter the boat, very nearly overwhelming the crew as they struggled to creep away to safety. It was only after they had cleared the area that the boat could surface to properly ventilate its noxious interior. After reaching Trondheim and unloading on 5 May, Dönitz ordered the fuel shipments ceased following *U32*'s harrowing experience. Returning to Wilhelmshaven *U32* was attacked three more times by destroyers, damaging the boat to such an extent that on her arrival in port on 13 May she was directed to Kiel for three days of repairs, heading through the Kaiser Wilhelm Canal with an engine missing badly on one cylinder, the shipyards of Wilhelmshaven full of boats in sorry condition after the 'Operation Hartmut' débâcle.

The U-boats' role in the Norwegian campaign had been a fiasco and, to make matters worse, six U-boats had been lost during the operation, including the 2nd U-Flotilla's *U64* and *U44*. On 2 May BdU recorded Mathes' *U44* confirmed lost (*Vermißt zwei Stern*) after she was counted as being impossibly overdue. Dönitz's men were not the only ones to have suffered, the Kriegsmarine as a whole sustaining ruinous casualties. Allied naval forces or minefields had sunk the heavy cruiser *Blücher*, two light cruisers, a gunnery training ship, ten destroyers and a torpedo boat, and what remained of the surface fleet was under repair for damage sustained during the invasion.

Even the imperturbable BdU Chief of Operations, Eberhard Godt, had stated that by mid-April he would no longer take responsibility for sending U-boat crews into action armed with blunted weapons. Dönitz and his service laid the blame squarely on the shoulders of the Torpedo Inspectorate and faulty weaponry, undeniably the major factor for the U-boats' ineffectiveness. The torpedo problem had been a calamity waiting to happen after a catalogue of disasters dating back to the mid-thirties.

During 1936 torpedo test firings against suspended nets at Eckernförde's Torpedo Experimental Institute (TVA) had shown that both the air-driven G7a and newer electric G7e torpedoes had a tendency to run metres deeper than set. A remedy was provided in the shape of the 'depth spring' which altered results to an error of less than half a metre. This newer torpedo was intended for 'Top Priority' production, but was relegated to the backwaters of Kriegsmarine weapon production, none being ready by September 1939. TVA chief KA Oskar Wehr clung to the belief that even if torpedoes ran deep the newly developed MZ magnetic fuses would render this problem irrelevant. When it was found in October 1939 that the northern latitudes of 'Zone O' (including Norway) interfered with the magnetic firing mechanism, the use of these fuses was forbidden and U-boats were ordered to change to contact fuses. It was at this moment that the tendency to run deep became crucial. Also, new four-fingered fuses, passed for operational use after only two test shots in autumn 1937, had replaced the reliable contact fuses used by the *Kaiserliche Marine* in the First World War. In fact it was later discovered that the new fuse was so delicate that, should the torpedo strike the target at an oblique angle, the fuse rod would bend and not fire the charge. But that was not all and it was only during 1941 that yet another flaw with German torpedo design was discovered.

Leaking balance chambers that housed a hydrostatic valve controlling the torpedo's depth allowed ambient pressure to build up. During long periods of submersion frequent releases of compressed air were essential aboard a U-boat for trim or weapon use and, as many 'Hartmut' boats had remained submerged for up to twenty hours daily, their accrued internal pressure was passed into the torpedoes, sending them deep after firing. As the Germans entered what would later be remembered in history books as the 'Happy Time', they did so with a defective main armament.[38]

In hindsight the decision to take the U-boats away from the merchant war and direct them against military targets during 'Weserübung' had been a blunder. Although they could have had a devastating impact upon the Royal Navy and the deployment of Allied ground forces, they were patently unsuited for the pursuit of fast warships and, if discovered, trapped with only restricted room for manoeuvre within narrow confined fjords. The additional handicap of defective weaponry made their presence border on suicidal.

Morale slumped, the submariners' faith in their weapons severely shaken for no tangible result. Dockyards were also full of U-boats requiring repair for myriad technical problems; oil leaks and engine-head wear particularly prevalent. Dönitz later wrote:

> "The men were discouraged. I could not just leave them in their slough of despond. I had to do something to restore their spirits. As long as there was the slender prospect of success I felt that I must continue to commit my submarines to battle.
>
> "During the weeks that followed the end of the Norwegian operations I therefore went from one operational flotilla to another. . . . I spoke to the crews, all of whom I knew and all of whom had confidence in me. The crisis was overcome. With renewed courage the U-boats went forth again to battle."[39]

Part of Dönitz's method to rehabilitate his U-boats as offensive weapons was to send Kaptlt. Victor Oehrn, 1. *Admiralstabsoffizier* at BdU and overall planner of the U-boat's role in

---

[38] 7th U-Flotilla's Oblt.z.S. Otto Ites aboard *U94* discovered the problem during torpedo ventilation. Electric torpedoes need their batteries re-charged from time to time, which releases hydrogen gas that has to be evacuated out of mechanical spaces to prevent unwanted explosion through sparks from the e-motor once the weapon is launched. His unauthorized investigation of all torpedoes aboard *U94* finally solved the recurrent problem of 'deep-running fish'.

[39] Karl Dönitz, p. 90.

'Weserübung', into action as commander of *U37* at the spearhead of a fresh assault on Atlantic convoys. The staff officer and peacetime commander of the small Type IIB *U14* was given five days to prepare himself for his first combat patrol. His transfer to replace Werner Hartmann marked the end of Hartmann's term as 2nd U-Flotilla commander, departing for six months as Oehrn's replacement. Apparently Hartmann was less than pleased with his new appointment.

> "He 'cursed like a tugboat captain', wrote Peter Hansen [a U-boat man who spent the majority of his wartime service attached to Admiral Canaris' *Abwehr*] at being made a staff officer."[40]

On 9 May 1940 Kaptlt. Werner Hartmann received the Knight's Cross for his exceptional combat career in sinking nineteen ships for nearly 80,000 confirmed tons while in command of *U37*. Replacing Hartmann as temporary flotilla commander was KK Heinz Fischer, Hartmann's former second in command.[41] Also celebrating the award of the Knight's Cross was Otto Schuhart, one week later, the decoration considered overdue after *U29*'s blow against the carrier *Courageous*.

15 May: *U122* attempted to leave Kiel, its interior brimful with ammunition crates and an unassembled artillery piece. Despite Dönitz's desire to renew the war on merchant shipping there were still demands from Army Group XXI for several boats to ferry supplies to Norway. Eventually he persuaded OKM and ultimately Hitler to use only two 'Saltzwedel' boats, *U26* and *U122*, primarily for transporting airforce equipment. Kaptlt. Hans-Günther Looff was, however, forced to abandon his first attempt at leaving port after *U122* developed handling problems. It had recently been reconverted from its status as a projected fuel tanker after Jenisch's brush with disaster. Another day of reconfiguring the hefty load was required before Looff, former senior officer of the 'Weddigen' Flotilla and pre-war commander of *U9* and *U28*, would be able to take his boat on its maiden operational voyage.

Meanwhile Victor Oehrn took the 'Westward Ho!' U-boat *U37* from Wilhelmshaven in his bid to kick-start the Atlantic offensive. As the large submarine slipped its mooring lines there was the traditional brass band playing its distinctive Anglophobic battle songs, Dönitz himself standing on the quayside to wish his subordinate luck and good fortune on his first ever war patrol.

16 May: Kaptlt. Looff slipped *U122* out of Kiel, his boat laden with Luftwaffe supplies for Trondheim. One day after departing harbour Looff reported sighting a 'hostile submarine' in 'Way I', the U-boats' passage through the Kattegat. There was, however, no engagement and the two submarines continued on diverging courses. *U122* entered Trondheim on 19 May, its final supply mission successfully executed. Two days were spent in the recently conquered port before Looff began his return journey to Germany, calling first at Heligoland before sailing for Wilhelmshaven. Despite having a small number of

---

[40] *Wolf*, Jordan Vause, Appendix p. 228.

[41] Hartmann later received a combat posting as commander of the long distance *U198*. His other posts included command of 27th U-Flotilla and *FdU Mittelmeer* where he was awarded the Oak Leaves to his Knight's Cross on 5 November 1944. He ended the war in command of *Marine Grenadier Regiment 6* fighting in West Prussia against the Russians.

torpedoes aboard for opportunistic attacks on Royal Navy forces, no targets presented themselves.

The second of the 'Saltzwedel' supply boats departed for Trondheim on 23 May, this time the Type I *U26* under the temporary command of flotilla senior officer KK Heinz Fischer. The uneventful voyage ended in Trondheim four days later. Like Looff, Fischer spent two days having his boat unloaded of its Luftwaffe supplies and refuelled before heading back to Wilhelmshaven.

23 May: Eight days into his patrol, supposed to reinvigorate by example the flagging morale of the *Unterseebootwaffe*, Kaptlt. Oehrn delivered a bombshell by radio to BdU headquarters. His tour of duty had begun well, although he had quickly learned that many of the principles of operation held by BdU were impractical in reality. As a staff officer Oehrn had prompted operational commanders to traverse the dangerous 'Fair Island Gap' between the Orkney and Shetland Islands, an area of sea heavily patrolled by sea and air forces, but a considerably shorter route into the northern Atlantic than skirting wide of the region. The day after making his decision to follow his own advice *U37* was accurately attacked by a British bomber, persuading the narrowly escaping Oehrn that what appeared viable on paper was not always so in practise.

His first victory was had in early morning on 19 May when the Swedish MV *Erik Frisell* was sent to the bottom south-west of St. Kilda, shelled by the U-boat's deck gun. Unfortunately the artillery had been used as a last resort after two magnetic torpedoes fired at the Swede had failed to explode. Three days later another spread of torpedoes was fired from *U37*, this time at British merchant ship MV *Dunster Grange*, the attack failing when two of the temperamental eels exploded after only nineteen seconds' run, the third missing the target entirely. Attempting to sink the ship with artillery fire, the *Dunster Grange* suffered some damage before managing to elude its pursuit. The next day, 23 May, Oehrn reported his weapon failures to Dönitz who, predictably, exploded with rage.

Although Dönitz had held high hopes that magnetic warheads would behave properly outside of the 'Zone O' influence he now prohibited all use of them. Contacting Professor Cornelius he again demanded that contact detonators found aboard recently captured British submarine HMS *Seal* be scrutinized and immediately copied to provide at least some form of reliable torpedo.

> "The latest explanations and theories of the technical branches to account for these failures henceforth carried no weight with me at all. I refused any longer to burden U-boats with these wretched things, and forthwith forbade all use of magnetic pistols."[42]

26 May: *U122* eased its way from the Kaiser Wilhelm Canal and into Kiel's shipyard during the morning. Looff had brought his boat through the inland waterway overnight as *U122* was scheduled to undergo work on her diving bunkers, still in an unfinished state of conversation after carrying aviation fuel. Kiel, possessing the highest quality yards in Germany, was considered the best place for the alteration work as the U-boat was desperately needed to augment the 2nd U-Flotilla's strength for the fresh Atlantic offensive.

Elsewhere the older 2nd U-Flotilla U-boats were still encountering mechanical

---

[42] Karl Dönitz, p. 101.

problems. Kaptlt. Günter Kuhnke radioed engine trouble while en route for the narrows between Dover and Calais. His Type VII, *U28*, was virtually worn out by then, its use prolonged only by a desperate shortage of combat U-boats. The decision had been taken to phase the type out to training duties, 2nd U-Flotilla due to be equipped solely with the large ocean-going Type IX U-boats. Kuhnke was forced to divert to Trondheim where the Kriegsmarine could now undertake the necessary repair work.

Meanwhile, new boats continued to be commissioned directly into the flotilla. In Bremen's Deschimag shipyard the new Type IXB *U123* was formally commissioned into Kriegsmarine service on 30 May. With the flag of the *Kaiserliche Marine* tied to the wintergarten, Kaptlt. Karl-Heinz Moehle spoke slowly and clearly into a microphone as he accepted the boat into military service. She had been launched, partially completed, on 2 March by her builders AG Weser, finishing work undertaken over the following months in the presence of most of her new crew. Following the speech the crew and many of the attendant party climbed inside the hull for further celebrations aboard the cramped boat, her interior still smelling of fresh paint. During its period of working up within the Baltic the camouflaged *U123* was loaned to the German Ufa film studios for exterior shots to be used in its new production *U-Boote Westwärts*. Released in 1941 the film became a classic of naval propaganda and a wartime favourite in Germany. For its real war, it was not until September that *U123* would sail on her first combat patrol.

By the end of May the battle for Norway had been decided. Although a combined British, Polish and French force had finally pushed the outnumbered German defenders of Narvik out of the devastated town on 28 May, the decision had been taken four days previously to withdraw Allied forces in order to concentrate on the developing crisis in France and Belgium. On 10 June Norway surrendered unconditionally. By then the battle of France was also as good as lost.

On 8 June *U28* had rejoined the outgoing tide of Atlantic-bound 2nd U-Flotilla boats. As Kuhnke sailed from Trondheim after engine repairs, *U25*, *U30* and *U65* all put to sea from Wilhelmshaven to join Oehrn's offensive. Oehrn, however, was nearing the end of his twenty-six-day inaugural war patrol. *U37* docked in Wilhelmshaven on 9 June, claiming over 43,000 tons sunk. Despite faulty torpedoes plaguing the patrol's opening Oehrn had managed to sink nine ships – the last eight within a single week – by a combination of torpedo attack, scuttling charges and artillery fire (for an impressive confirmed 37,214 tons). The spell of despondency cast by the Norwegian failure was finally broken by *U37*'s success. It also marked the proper opening of Dönitz's onslaught against British trade routes; the 'Battle of the Atlantic' had begun.

9 June: Among the first wave of 2nd Flotilla boats heading for the North Atlantic *U65* suffered persistent mechanical problems. Outbound in the North Sea the diesels rapidly faltered. In urgent need of repairs that the machinists were unable to cope with, von Stockhausen was forced to abort and head for Bergen, arriving on 12 June for a twenty-four-hour layover.

As von Stockhausen arrived in Bergen, Kaptlt. Heinrich Liebe brought *U38* quietly into Brandon Bay on Ireland's south-west coast. Repeating Hartmann's February mission, Liebe was ordered to land agents in neutral Ireland. This time, however, there were two men, their mission to provide coded weather reports for Germany. The Abwehr had trained both men as meteorologists and they were delivered without mishap during the hours of darkness, rowing ashore in a small rubber dinghy. Neither lasted very long. Walter Simon, arrested years previously and deported from Britain, was picked up almost immediately, while Willy Preetz (alias Paddy Mitchell) was at large in Dublin for months, sending valuable data to Berlin before also being arrested.

After delivering the agents Liebe took *U38* south into the Western Approaches, diverted along with flotilla-mates *U43*, *U32*, *U28*, *U25* and *U30* to a futile attempt at intercepting convoy US3, six liners carrying 26,000 ANZACs to the Middle East. The troop convoy was alerted by Kaptlt. Heinz Beduhn's sinking of British auxiliary cruiser HMS *Scotstoun* in his new command *U25*, thus escaping the ambush.

13 June: *U122* finally emerged from Kiel after its refit, proceeding through the Kaiser Wilhelm Canal and into the North Sea. A brief stop in Heligoland allowed a final topping-up of fuel tanks before Looff set course for the North Atlantic.

Kaptlt. Hans Günther Looff, ordered to operate in grid square CF30 against expected enemy shipping, made his last position report from *U122* at 0035hrs on 21 June from position 56°03N, 07°55W (AM51) and then disappeared. There are myriad theories as to why *U122* vanished, including several ramming explanations. To this author the most likely cause of *U122*'s sinking is an accidental ramming in Looff's area when SS *San Felipe* reported a collision with an "underwater object" on 22 June. Whatever the truth, Looff and his entire crew were posted *Vermißt ein Stern*, effective from 22 June.

Meanwhile on the Continent Holland, Luxembourg and Belgium had fallen quickly to the Wehrmacht, northern France being reduced to chaos as the *Blitzkrieg* smashed all opposition. Most of the British Expeditionary Force and scattered French units soon found themselves with their backs to the English Channel, their evacuation from Dunkirk under the auspices of 'Operation Dynamo' successfully completed by Monday 3 June. The remainder of France was next.

With the virtual destruction of the BEF in the north, France crumbled rapidly. Paris was declared an 'Open City' and abandoned, escaping the inevitable bombing and occupied without a shot on 14 June. As the Allied evacuation of western France – 'Operation Aerial' – got underway, Admiral de Laborde (French Naval Commander Western Theatre) ordered the immediate departure of all seaworthy vessels on 18 June as tanks from the 5th Panzer Division passed Rennes heading west. Among the Germans' targets was the port of Lorient.

Lorient had begun life as the medieval hamlet of Blavet, taking the name Port Louis when, by command of Louis XIII, the noted French engineer Vauban built a citadel between 1610 and 1643. In 1664 the *Compagnie des Indes* was established on the site, which was renamed L'Orient in reference to the Eastern countries with which it traded. After France lost its possessions in India commerce declined and Louis XVI bought the entire port, establishing a Royal Arsenal, the first sign of military power at L'Orient. The anchorage offered a superb natural harbour, sheltered from the ferocity of westerly Atlantic weather by an easily defended entrance channel, the thick walls of Kernével on one bank facing the bastion of Port Louis.

At Lorient on 18 June all ships that could sail put to sea; a total of fifteen warships and thirty-five smaller vessels left the harbour, a single trawler being lost to a Luftwaffe minefield.[43] Smoke hung low over Lorient after Vice-Admiral Hervé de Penfentényo de

---

[43] *La Tanche* wandered off course into a known minefield laid by the Luftwaffe in Lorient's roadstead the day before, the resultant explosion sinking the trawler with all but twelve of her crowded passengers and crew.

Kervériguin, military governor of Lorient, ordered the destruction of the naval fuel oil reserves contained in huge underground storage tanks at Priatec on the south bank of the Scorff River. Flames from 90,000 tonnes of blazing fuel leapt high into the air and soon flooded over the banks of the Scorff, inching towards the arsenal where several small tugs and three fuelling pontoons began to burn.

By then there was no doubt as to the fate of Lorient itself. To the north Brest had already fallen; in Lorient there remained little to fight for. Thus the port was declared an 'Open City' later that day, as a German *Leutnant* arrived at Lorient's naval arsenal to demand the city's surrender or face aerial bombardment. Vice Admiral de Penfentén15yo complied and the Wehrmacht entered Lorient at 1800hrs on the evening of 21 June, the blaze along the Scorff still rampant, French firefighters unable to quell the flames. Over the ensuing hours the conflagration within the arsenal and on the Scorff River was extinguished, although flames raged on the river's south bank until 26 July. The village of Casquer was burnt to the ground, with twenty-five of its inhabitants killed before Wehrmacht engineers cut fire breaks and combined French and German firemen finally brought the fire under control. The following day French representatives signed their country's armistice at Compiègne, to take effect from 0135hrs on Tuesday 25 June.

Dönitz had followed the battle for France with keen interest, despatching BdU's Chief Engineering Officer and Chief of Staff, Kaptlt. (Ing.) Hans Looschen and KK (der Reserve) Helmut Brümmer-Patzig respectively, to scout for likely U-boat bases and a site for BdU headquarters. The Atlantic ports offered huge strategic advantages to Dönitz. First and foremost they would allow U-boats to penetrate further into the Atlantic, the *Schwerpunkt* of U-boat operations against Britain's trade lines. No longer would U-boats be forced to take the northern route round the British Isles. Also, by using the French ports as flotilla headquarters, routine repairs and refit could be done in yards outside of Germany, freeing those overworked shipyards of this work and allowing them to concentrate on the construction of new boats. For himself, Dönitz had long favoured a 'hands-on' approach to command and relied heavily on instant face-to-face communication with U-boat commanders and crews to establish not only what was really happening at sea but also a unique level of trust between subordinate and commander.

Immediately after Lorient's fall Dönitz arrived on the Biscay coast to see for himself the areas that his two scouts had selected. The ports of Brest, Lorient, Saint-Nazaire, La Pallice and Bordeaux were all found suitable for the establishment of U-boat bases, Lorient being earmarked as the destination for the 2nd U-Flotilla. On 22 June a train left Wilhelmshaven carrying the first twenty-four torpedoes for the new base and various skilled mechanics from the flotilla. Trucks augmented the flow of personnel and supplies, the entire transfer of men and equipment overseen by the *Torpedodirektor* of Wilhelmshaven's *Kriegsmarinewerft*, KzS von Trotha, himself in transit to Paris. German engineers of the M.A.N. *Maschinen Fabrik* also arrived in Lorient to work at reinforcing slipway facilities to cope with the submarine tonnage. Slightly upriver from the Gueydon bridge on the Scorff a degaussing range was constructed opposite disused French construction yards, allowing U-boats and smaller naval vessels to demagnetize in attempts to counter the omnipresent threat of British aerial and submarine laid mines. The *Unterseebootwaffe* began to move west.

Elsewhere, U-boats at sea continued to receive supplies from neutral Spanish harbours. During the night of 18/19 June *U43* refuelled from the German ship *Bessel* in Vigo (code-named 'Bernardo'), four tense hours resulting in the U-boat departing with fresh food, fuel and torpedoes. Schuhart's *U29* entered the same port during the night of 20 June to refuel from *Bessel*, slipping unseen from harbour during the early hours of the following day. For Lemp's *U30* orders were received to refuel in Spain as well, but this time at El Ferrol, under the code-name '*Arroz*' (rice). Despite Dönitz having originally planned for Lemp to enter Vigo as Schuhart had, the northern Spanish port of El Ferrol was chosen as an alternative destination, *U30* successfully resupplying on 24 June. However, the *Max Albrecht* in El Ferrol was becoming unviable due to the proximity of watching ships anchored nearby and '*Arroz*' was soon discontinued. With the fall of France and access to Biscay ports, Spain was no longer crucial for extended submarine operations. The regularity of resupply missions was decreased, but kept on hand for emergencies.

28 June The ever-troublesome *U26*, eight days out of Wilhelmshaven destined for Biscay, radioed BdU over a problem with one of the diesel's oil coolers. While the boat's overworked Lt (Ing.) Herbert Freund and his men began the laborious task of stripping the engine's lubrication system Kaptlt. Scheringer was compelled to go round the north of England with his speed seriously reduced, ploughing onward on one diesel and electric motor.

The boat was carrying four G7a and the same number of G7e electric torpedoes into the combat zone, the first of which were used on 30 June south-south-west of Fastnet. That day Scheringer sank three steamships before receiving notification from BdU that an enemy convoy was expected to pass his operational area some time during the next twenty-four hours. On schedule the following morning contact was made and *U26* began skirting surfaced around zigzagging OA175 bound from southern Ireland to North America, searching for the optimum attack position. At 2100hrs Scheringer was briefly spotted to the west by lookouts aboard the convoy commodore's ship at a range of approximately five miles. Aboard leading escort corvette HMS *Gladiolus* notification of the approaching threat was received and Lt-Cdr H.M.C. Sanders ordered full ahead to the U-boat's estimated position.

Aboard *U26* Scheringer and his officers were planning their approach for a surfaced night torpedo attack. They decided to target a 12,000-ton tanker at the convoy's rear outer column with the first shot, a second torpedo aimed at the next in line, the British steamer SS *Zarian*. At 2318hrs *U26* lurched as two air-driven torpedoes sped from the forward tubes. The first shot narrowly missed the tanker's stern, while the second impacted against *Zarian*, ripping a hole in the steamer's aft hull plates. The stern began to sink lower into the water and her captain ordered white Very lights fired, attracting HMS *Gladiolus* engaged in a nearby, and misplaced, search for the U-boat spotted earlier that evening. *Gladiolus* raced toward the sector that the attack had come from, Scheringer and his bridge watch distracted by the result of their attack until alert lookouts cried out as they spotted the charging British warship. Scheringer immediately ordered his boat dived, turning towards *Zarian* as he did so. He considered the chances of surface flight negligible, the boats' engines still causing trouble. Unfortunately so was the starboard electric motor. As the propellers bit sluggishly into the water Scheringer ordered the troublesome motor run at half-speed while the port electric was set at three-quarters ahead. To compound his problems the magnetic compass was also defective, making precise navigation impossible. Almost immediately ASDIC operators aboard *Gladiolus* made firm contact on the diving U-boat at a range of 1,200 yards. While *U26* plunged to eighty metres, depth charges set to explode at forty metres began drifting downwards from *Gladiolus*. Only ten minutes after Scheringer's torpedo attack the first explosions pounded the escaping U-boat.

Lights flickered and died aboard *U26*, the uncomfortable glow of emergency lighting and phosphorescent paint gloomily illuminating the boat's interior. A second pattern of charges exploded beneath the boat, too deep to destroy *U26*, but close enough to inflict further serious damage. Now the U-boat began to take on water as the aft torpedo compensating ballast tank filled, its drain tube left open during the hurried crash dive. The stern began to sink lower, reaching an incredible 230 metres, men being forced to vacate the boat's rear compartments and take shelter in the forward torpedo room, attempting to wedge themselves as far forward between the two banks of tubes as possible. The starboard electric motor was proving increasingly ineffective and as the batteries steadily depleted with the strain of underwater manoeuvre, Scheringer was informed by his Chief Engineer that one of the boat's two compressors was inoperative. There was little compressed air available either to keep the boat level or to blow tanks for a final attempt at emergency surfacing.

Above them contact was periodically lost and regained as *Gladiolus* continued to hurl charges below her. By the corvette's sixth depth-charge pattern there were only five explosive canisters left, but the scent of victory lay in the air, a strong smell of diesel from the water noticed by the men on deck. As daybreak crept into the eastern sky a vast oil patch was revealed around the corvette which lay silently in wait, sonar probing underwater for the crippled target. Sanders radioed for reinforcement as he continued to stalk the U-boat.

Aboard *U26* the German crew realized that the external diesel oil tank was ruptured, leaving the betraying wake of leaking fuel as the boat slowly moved away, her rudder no longer fully answering the helm. There were few options left after exhausting hours of depth-charging and at 0520hrs Scheringer ordered the last vestiges of compressed air used to blow tanks and bring his boat and crew to the surface. *U26* broke through the Atlantic swell minutes later, stunned Germans racing to the conning tower to see *Gladiolus* dead ahead, only 800 yards away. Turning slowly to port Scheringer ordered diesels fired and the boat began to creep away, miraculously unseen by the corvette whose operators reported the sudden loss of ASDIC contact.

Aboard *U26* lookouts sighted further trouble in the shape of a circling Sunderland belonging to the RAAF 10 Squadron, F/Lt W.N. Gibson's flying boat participating in the convoy's escort. With odds so heavily stacked against him, it was inevitable that Scheringer should be spotted. At 0605hrs the sloop HMS *Rochester*, arriving as long-awaited reinforcement for *Gladiolus*, sighted the U-boat, initially believing it to be a hull-down merchant ship. Simultaneously, lookouts aboard *Gladiolus* spotted the diesel smoke thrown out by the temperamental U-boat engines. Sanders immediately recognized *U26* and, after alerting both the approaching sloop and the Australian Sunderland, turned in pursuit. Scheringer, his boat's compressed air banks filling painfully slowly from their diesel-driven compressors, attempted one final crash dive, the Sunderland narrowly missing his boat with four 250lb anti-submarine bombs. Although they did not impact against the U-boat's hull, the concussion of the blast was enough to shatter any hopes of escaping submerged and *U26* broke surface again as her crew assembled in the control room and conning tower. Scheringer was preparing his men to abandon ship when four more bombs exploded within forty metres of the boat. The crew finally began to escape their doomed submarine as Chief Engineer Freund remained aboard to ensure scuttling. *U26* ploughed onwards at half-speed, hatches open and hydroplanes pointed downwards, Freund escaping from the tower only as it began to submerge. Aboard *Rochester* all available weapons had been blazing in a vain attempt to avoid the U-boat's scuttling, but, as the conning tower disappeared, the sloop ceased fire and closed the scene to pick up survivors, seven of the German crew having already been killed by the gunfire. In total the British rescued forty men, including Scheringer, noting their captives to be "highly disciplined". Scheringer himself was considered "polite and intelligent" during interrogation.[44] It was not until 23 July that the Red Cross in Berlin reported as definite that the missing crew of *U26* were in English captivity and she was declared by BdU to be *Vermißt zwei Stern*.

Unfortunately for those men of *U26* who survived the sinking their war was not yet over. After travelling to the 'London Cage' at Kensington Palace Gardens, the crewmen began their trek by rail northwards, finally arriving at Sandyhillock Camp at Craigellachie, Banff. Reserved for prisoners felt to be 'ardent Nazis', the camp housed the U-boat men alongside Luftwaffe officers captured during the recent air battles over Britain. Soon after their arrival a Heinkel He111H of KG26, engaged on an unproductive inshore anti-shipping sortie, began its return leg from Britain to its Norwegian base near Stavanger. Under instructions to jettison any remaining bombs the Heinkel unknowingly unloaded its cargo onto Sandyhillock Camp, killing six of Scheringer's crew and a British camp guard.

Sister ship to Scheringer's boat, *U25*, had meanwhile made its return to Wilhelmshaven on 29 June. Sailing into port, Kaptlt. Heinz Beduhn reported the sinking of the AMC *Scotstoun* as well as an unidentified tanker from a small coastal convoy torpedoed at close range during a submerged night attack west-south-west of Brest on 19 June. The tanker, hit a little after 0128hrs, was seen by Beduhn slewing to a halt and beginning to burn. As Beduhn observed his quarry, preparing a second shot, his boat was suddenly pitched sideways as the ship following the tanker unknowingly rammed the submerged *U25*, smashing her conning tower and wrecking both periscopes. Alarmed, Beduhn ordered his boat taken down in an emergency dive, his crew assessing their damage and rapidly concluding that, although severely hit, the pressure hull had not been breached. Less than an hour later *U25* surfaced, the damaged tanker nowhere to be seen and presumed sunk. The U-boat had suffered a severe blow, the conning tower crushed to the level of the spray deflector and the painted mushroom insignia. BdU was informed of the boat's situation and *U25* headed home. To celebrate their miraculous escape, after arrival in Germany Beduhn immediately ordered a second 'lucky mushroom' painted on his boat's conning tower as soon as repairs were complete.

2 July: Kaptlt. Liebe's *U38* returned to Wilhelmshaven, its confirmed sinking of six ships, including the tanker MV *Italia* from convoy HX47, further bolstering the flotilla's success. The seemingly incongruous symbol of Cupid on the conning tower, painted by the boat's then IIWO, Oblt.z.S. Hanschel, in honour of Liebe ('love') and the fact that Cupid's shots never miss, showed the wear and tear of salt spray and constant submergence as the crew assembled on the upper deck for their entrance to port.

The day following Liebe's entry to Wilhelmshaven Dönitz received notification that Lorient would be cleared for operations within the next three days. KK Helmut Brümmer-Patzig was already operating as *Leiter der U-Stützpunkt Lorient*, while Kaptlt. (Ing.) Hans Looschen coordinated the base's engineering needs. Mines and weapons for the U-boats had arrived and were being housed within dockside buildings on the southern bank,

---

[44] The damaged SS *Zarian* was able to reach port and was repaired. She would outlive *U26* by two and a half years, finally torpedoed and sunk by *U591* on 29 December 1942.

transferred by barge to U-boats sandwiched between dock and floating pontoon during loading. Crew accommodation within the shabby town was initially farmed out to small hotels; naval quarters recently vacated by French African troops were found to be in an uninhabitable condition, floors strewn with refuse and human waste, requiring an immense clean-up effort.

The centre of the budding U-boat base was nearly five kilometres past the narrow entrance channel stretching between the Port Louis citadel and Larmor Plage, upstream along the Scorff River. Once past the small fishing port at Kéroman that lay at the junction of the Scorff River and Le Ter waterway the military arsenal lay spread along the northern bank. Within the sprawling complex, two dry docks could each accommodate a pair of Type IX U-boats, although they lay dangerously exposed to air attack. Fortuitously for the Germans, there was little British effort to capitalize on that fact.

On 4 July Kaptlt. Lemp received orders to head to Lorient for resupply, U30 having been in the Western Approaches for nearly a month, six ships already claimed sunk. Three days later U30 arrived for nearly a week of minor repairs, the first German submarine to dock in a French port. While at Lorient Lemp's men enjoyed local hospitality so recently used by French and British servicemen, frequenting the bars, cafes and brothels. Among the benefits to be had were fresh uniforms from huge stocks of British battledress abandoned during 'Operation Aerial', German clothing supplies still being en route. Lemp's crew were billeted outside the naval dockyard, still in the early stages of its renovation and cleaning, staying in a small and friendly Breton hotel, *Le Pigeon Blanc*.

On 13 July Lemp sailed from Lorient for the waters north of the Spanish coast. Despite successfully torpedoing the small British tramp SS *Ellaroy* west of Vigo, finishing off the burning wreck with gunfire, Lemp was forced to break off his patrol and begin his return journey from Gibraltar to Lorient on 19 July with major machinery problems, one diesel completely refusing to function. The worn Type VII was no longer up to the rigours of Atlantic patrols, no matter how much shipyard patching it received.

Meanwhile other 2nd U-Flotilla boats were returning to Wilhelmshaven from patrols boasting major success against the Allies: U28 on 6 July claiming three steamers for 10,860 tons; U65 on 7 July claiming five steamers and a tanker sunk, totalling 56,500 tons; U29 on 11 July also claiming five steamers and a tanker for 29,184 tons, and U43 on 22 July after ten weeks at sea and four ships and a tanker claimed for a total of 38,509 tons.[45] The repair yards were also working constantly to keep Dönitz's small number of boats in operation.

A second U-boat also entered Lorient, U34 sailing into port on 18 July after claiming to have sunk seven steamers for 26,338 tons, as well as the destroyer HMS *Whirlwind* west-north-west of the Scillies on 6 July. Kaptlt. Wilhelm Rollmann scheduled his boat and crew for five days in which to replenish U34, the crew following Lemp's men in enjoying Lorient before returning to sea and patrolling the waters west of the British Isles.

During Rollmann's stay in port, Dönitz arrived to confer with his officers at the new base, and local Luftwaffe commanders to coordinate valuable reconnaissance for the Atlantic U-boats. In Lorient over several days Dönitz spoke both to Rollmann and Lemp,

---

[45] U65's (Kaptlt. von Stockhausen) claim included the torpedoing on 21 June of the wreck of the 28,124-ton French liner SS *Champlain* already settled on the bottom of La Pallice roads after striking a Luftwaffe mine in the course of 'Operation Aerial'. It was generously allowed to stand as a legitimate sinking by BdU.

who pointed out that the elderly Type VIIs were all but useless in the Atlantic. Plagued by constant mechanical problems, the abilities of these two talented commanders and others were severely hampered by labouring with obsolete machines. Thus the remaining original flotilla boats would patrol towards Germany on their next forays, where the Type VIIs could finally be handed over to training units. From then on the 2nd U-Flotilla was to be equipped with large Type IX cruiser submarines, the veterans about to undertake a new role in Dönitz's commerce war.

5

LORIENT – THE FRUITS OF VICTORY:
1 AUGUST TO 31 DECEMBER 1940

1 August: Three 2nd U-Flotilla boats sailed from Wilhelmshaven, *U25*, *U37* and *U38* all bound for the Atlantic. Kaptlt. Oehrn's successful *U37* was leaving Germany to transfer permanently to 2nd U-Flotilla's new home of Lorient, a protected dock being prepared in anticipation of the boat's scheduled arrival on 12 August. The day following Oehrn's departure the newly installed Kriegsmarine Arsenal at Lorient reported itself ready for operations under the command of KK (Ing.) Waldemar Seidel.[46]

Kaptlt. Heinz Beduhn headed west on *U25*'s separation from its minesweeper escort. It was while the lumbering Type I was proceeding surfaced north of Terschelling in the West Frisian Islands that the boat finally ended its difficult career. *U25* unwittingly blundered into a new minefield laid by British submarines and vanished without trace, her crew of forty-nine men presumed lost on 3 August. It wasn't until notes were found by German inspectors aboard the captured British submarine HMS *Seal* describing the new minefield, code-named 'Traffic', that BdU surmised it to be the cause of *U25*'s loss, as well as that of an R-boat and some other small coastal patrol boats. The 2nd U-Flotilla's last 'ugly duckling' submarine was no more.

3 August: Kaptlt. Rollmann's *U34* entered Wilhelmshaven claiming 48,000 tons of shipping sunk during its eleven-day patrol and carrying a prisoner from the boat's final kill, the submarine HMS *Spearfish*. At 1817hrs on 1 August, as *U34* was west of Stavanger, the bridge lookouts spotted a slim mast to starboard. Eying it through their powerful Zeiss binoculars the Germans soon identified it as an approaching submarine and two minutes later Rollmann ordered his boat dived and crew to action stations. Through *U34*'s slender periscope Rollmann could see that what had initially been taken for mastheads was the housing for the British submarine's periscopes. HMS *Spearfish*, one day into its patrol from England, was heading straight for *U34*, unaware of the German threat. By 1848hrs the entire conning tower was visible and Rollmann prepared his attack. With a final burst of speed on electric motors Rollmann fired his last remaining torpedo from its bow tube, a run of one minute and forty-six seconds ending in a savage detonation as the torpedo hit the target's bow, probably igniting its own stored ammunition in a sympathetic explosion. HMS *Spearfish* disappeared from view in three seconds and *U34* surfaced to search for survivors. Amid much splintered wooden wreckage only Australian Able Seaman William Victor Pester was rescued.

---

[46] Seidel's position as *Arsenalkommandant* was superceded in September 1940 by that of *Werftkommandant*, this post held until October 1940 by VA Stobwasser, and thereafter by VA Matthiae, who occupied the office from 21 October 1941 to the war's end.

This additional claimed tonnage (in fact only 29,320 tons sunk between Lorient and Germany) to Rollmann's previous successes elevated him to the highest scoring U-boat 'ace' thus far with twenty-four enemy ships sunk, including a destroyer, minelayer and submarine, for an actual total tonnage of 100,064 tons (believed by Dönitz to be higher at 121,900 tons). This achievement earned Rollmann the Knight's Cross, the fifth for the U-boat service and third for 2nd U-Flotilla. His crowning accolade was the notation of an "excellent and especially successful operation" written by Dönitz in the BdU War Diary. His new-found glory also marked the temporary removal of Rollmann from the front line as he went first into the 2nd U-Flotilla's reserve pool and then on to instructional duties. The aged *U34* was also finally put out to pasture, transferring to the 21st U-training Flotilla on 30 September after an extensive refit.

8 August: *U65* sailed from Wilhelmshaven carrying two extra passengers aboard. The first was General Sean Russell, Chief of Staff of the Irish Republican Army. In September 1939 Russell had been in the United States raising money from America's strong Irish community. Already under surveillance by both British and American intelligence agencies, he smuggled himself out of the country aboard a merchant ship bound for Genoa, Italy, where he walked into the German consulate. Transported to Germany under the request of the head of the Nazi Foreign Office's Irish Desk, Dr Veesenmeyer, Russell began training under Abwehr auspices.

The second of von Stockhausen's passengers was Frank Ryan, recently released from a Spanish prison and now an agent for the Abwehr's Office 1 (West). Ryan had joined the East Limerick IRA Brigade in 1922 and been elected to the IRA Army Council in 1929. In the unrest that followed between socialist and non-socialist republicans, Ryan firmly aligned with the former and subsequently co-founded the left-wing Republican Congress.

During the Civil War in Spain Ryan commanded the Irish Brigade that fought against Franco's Nationalists until 31 March 1938 when he was wounded and captured by Italian troops in the Ebro valley. Imprisoned at Calaceite, he was court-martialled and sentenced to death, dubiously found guilty of war crimes.

While Ryan languished in Burgos Prison various Irish newspapers called for his release, prompting the *Taoiseach* (Prime Minister) of Ireland, Eamon De Valera, to intervene. In January 1940 he finally secured the commuting of Ryan's death sentence to thirty years' penal servitude. Meanwhile the Abwehr had become interested in him and on 14 July, in conjunction with sympathetic Spanish government officials, they aided his escape from prison. The Abwehr, who were convinced that his strong IRA connections would make him useful to the German war effort, brought Ryan to Paris. However, years of confinement in barbarous, almost medieval, conditions had damaged his health. Nonetheless, Ryan was taken from Paris to Germany to be teamed with Sean Russell.

It was an unhappy match. The two men were ideologically opposed and by all accounts detested each other. Sixty years later Russell would be described as a provisional IRA man (i.e. military, Irish-centric, nationalist, non-revolutionary) as opposed to Ryan's communist revolutionary type who advocated the use of indiscriminate terrorism. But the Abwehr was keen to improve relations between the Wehrmacht and IRA and, code-named 'Operation *Taube*' (Dove), von Stockhausen was scheduled to land the two men by rubber dinghy in an area to be specified once the U-boat was at sea.

At midday on 13 August BdU radioed *U65* the all clear to proceed with '*Traub*', scheduled for two days later. Fate, however, would have it otherwise. As the U-boat battled through a Force 8 gale en route to Ireland, Russell began to complain of severe stomach cramps, at first thought to be no more than chronic constipation caused by enforced inactivity within the submarine's confined space. After attempting whatever remedies the U-boat's radio operator/medic could provide, Russell collapsed and died the next day from what was later diagnosed as a probable perforated stomach ulcer. There are (unlikely) rumours of a fist-fight between the two Irishmen, as well as suspicion that Ryan might have had more to do with Russell's death than appeared: he often placed communist interests above those of either the IRA or Ireland. More importantly for Ryan, there was now little that he could achieve, his mission unclear even to him.

Interestingly, much debate still surrounds the Irishmen's probable instructions. Certainly Ryan was not an ideal choice to kick-start the IRA into action against the British; indeed his presence may well have divided yet further an already factional para-military group. Historian Gwynne Thomas has surmised that Sean Russell was sent not by the Abwehr but by Ribbentrop's Foreign Office to make contact with the Southern Irish Government and ferment an armed uprising, backed with German paratroopers, against British authority. He further claims that Ryan was 'turned' by the Abwehr and sent to monitor Russell and his Republican ambitions.[47]

But none of these possibilities bothered von Stockhausen as he ordered Russell's body sewn into a bed sheet and buried at sea. Although he was willing to continue with the landing, Ryan, in a state of agitation, was not and the operation was cancelled. *U65* loaded all torpedo tubes and prepared to enter the North Atlantic convoy war. It was a short-lived attempt. Two days later von Stockhausen was compelled to break off his cruise after his U-boat developed a strong oil leak. The patrol was cut short and *U65* sailed for Lorient. While en route *U65* was informed that facilities were not yet ready to deal with the boat's problem and so von Stockhausen ordered course set for Brest, the nearest friendly port equipped with the necessary amenities. On 22 August she became the first German U-boat to dock in that harbour and was immediately placed into dry-dock beside the Penfeld River, draped in hastily prepared camouflage netting. After disembarking Frank Ryan, von Stockhausen and his crew were hosted by freshly installed Kriegsmarine units in the city, while deck plating was removed and Kriegsmarine officials and engineers inspected the boat in search of the persistent problem.[48] By the end of August *U65* was fit to sail again and slipped from harbour to patrol west of the British Isles for a month before returning to Lorient.

9 August: The fierce storms that had battered *U65* were also making life difficult for other boats of the 2nd U-Flotilla. Both *U30* and its larger cousin *U38* reported the weather severely restricting their operations. The small Type VII had already proved unable to deal with the harsh Atlantic conditions; now even the ocean-going Type IX boats wrestled with it. Some measure of comfort was, however, on the way for both commanders. On 14 August Fritz-Julius Lemp and Heinrich Liebe were awarded the Knight's Cross for their accumulated victories.

Meanwhile the remainder of August saw a procession of U-boats depart for action in the Atlantic. *U28* sailed from Wilhelmshaven on the 11th, while Jenisch followed aboard *U32* four days later. In Lorient too there was growing U-boat traffic, boats beginning to

---

[47] *King Pawn or Black Knight?*, Gwynne Thomas.
[48] Ryan returned to Berlin. In January 1943, while living in Dresden he suffered a stroke, his health never fully recovered after his Spanish prison ordeal, dying on 10 June 1944 aged 38.

arrive with some measure of regularity. Oehrn's *U37*, escorted into harbour by a minesweeping R-boat, docked against the hulk of the former French prison ship *Isère* on 12 August after transit from Germany and a single confirmed victory. The *Isère* would serve during the coming years as mooring point for most U-boats entering the port. She had been sunk by the French before their June evacuation but raised by the Germans for use as a floating pontoon. One day outbound from Wilhelmshaven, Oehrn himself had narrowly avoided being the victim of a torpedo after Dutch submarine *O22* missed with a two-shot bow torpedo spread only minutes after also unsuccessfully attacking the 1st U-Flotilla's *U62*. Oehrn was still committed to leading the Kriegsmarine's submarine assault against England and, after only five days in port, *U37* sailed again for the Atlantic. Oehrn despatched seven ships within ten days after Hitler had declared an extended zone of operations encircling the British Isles in which ships could be sunk on sight.

However, by 25 August Oehrn was forced to announce that *U37* was breaking off its action to return to Lorient suffering the effects of *Wabo* damage and on the last day of August *U37* entered the French harbour again, flying eight victory pennants from its extended periscope for a claimed 36,381 tons of merchant shipping and a single "destroyer" (actually the sloop HMS *Penzance*) before beginning four weeks of repairs.

20 August: *U124* left Wilhelmshaven on its inaugural patrol, trailing in the wake of a single minesweeper escort. The large Type IXB replaced *U64* that lay deep in Norwegian water. On board the new submarine alongside Kaptlt. Georg-Wilhelm Schulz were Watch Officers Oblt.z.S. Reinhard Hardegen and Oblt.z.S. Werner Henke as IIWO. Hardegen was new to the boat, replacing L.z.S. Heinz Hirsacker, who had broken his hand while in port.[49] Hardegen had begun his navel career in April 1933, transferring two and a half years later to the fledgling *Marineflieger* (naval air force) where he received observer training and later as a pilot. However, he suffered severe injuries after an air accident while passenger aboard a Junkers W-34 that crashed on take-off, being left with a shortened right leg and continually bleeding stomach ulcer. This would normally have disqualified him from operational U-boat service, but in November 1939 he joined Dönitz's submarine corps, successfully managing to keep his disabilities secret and living on an especially bland non-inflammatory diet. The IIWO, Werner Henke, was a veteran merchant marine sailor, enlisting in the navy during 1934. His introduction to the *Unterseebootewaffe* had been turbulent to say the least, a burgeoning list of disciplinary problems nearly ending his career. But aboard Schulz's boat in the company of men that he respected Henke soon found a comfortable niche.

U124's conning tower had received the addition of large Edelweiss flowers on its flanks, painted in memory of the *Gebirgsjäger* that had saved Schulz and his surviving crew. Within hours of leaving Germany, in what must have seemed an ominous repeat of history, hostile aircraft were sighted approaching the U-boat and its escort. This time, however, accurate and sustained anti-aircraft fire from both German vessels drove away their British attacker.

This aerial harassment served to reinforce in Dönitz's mind the necessity of guarding his boats from enemy aircraft. Coupled with the loss of the experienced crew of *U25* to British

---

[49] Heinz Hirsacker went on to command *U572* between May 1941 and December 1942. He was arrested and tried fore alleged 'cowardice in the face of the enemy' as reported by his crew during operations against the 'Torch' invasion. Found guilty, he was condemned to death. In order to avoid the firing squad Hirsacker's friends slipped a pistol into his cell and he shot himself on 24 April 1943.

mines, decisions were taken at BdU to not only increase the anti-aircraft escort for departing and returning U-boats but also to transfer the *Sperrbrecher* 'Rostock' to Lorient as the first vessel of a new flotilla of massive minesweeping ships. British aerial mining had even managed to close the entrance to Lorient harbour during the last week in August and Dönitz could not allow such enforced penalties in his already under-strength Atlantic force. Lurking British submarines were considered an additional serious threat and *U-Jäger* were immediately transferred to the region or converted from captured French vessels. The first two *U-Jägers* arrived in Lorient on 12 September, the Kriegsmarine workhorses immediately beginning patrolling south of Penmark, recently off limits to U-boats.

In Lorient itself KK Heinz Fischer and the staff of 2nd U-Flotilla had also finally installed themselves fully into dockside buildings within the arsenal, taking over the 3rd Depot that had previously housed apprentice engineers of *la Marine Français*, known now as the 'Saltzwedel Caserne'. Extra personnel were billeted out the arsenal, moving into ten barrack buildings near the Place Alsace-Lorraine.

27 August: The beleaguered *U30*, almost overcome with mechanical difficulties during its voyage to Germany, arrived at Heligoland before Lemp and his crew made their grand entrance to Wilhelmshaven the next day, sporting freshly bought French berets and flying pennants claiming another 17,373 tons of enemy shipping sunk (in fact 12,407 tons). Dönitz was on hand to welcome them home, also to drape the ribbon of the Knight's Cross around Lemp's neck. *U30* was to be retired, the obsolete boat scheduled for months of overhaul in Kiel before she would be fit for Baltic duty and induction into the ranks of the 24th U-training Flotilla. While many men from *U30* would be transferred elsewhere to provide veterans for new U-boats entering service, Lemp retained a hard core of his crew for his new boat. Bolstered by an influx of raw recruits, they prepared to take over the large Type IXB *U110*, launched at Bremen's AG Weser shipyard. It must have seemed a luxuriously spacious boat to those who had served aboard *U30* and promised to be a more reliable weapon of war.

3 September: On the first anniversary of war with England, as *U38* entered Lorient after sinking three ships during a month at sea, Dönitz reflected in the BdU War Diary on the overall state of his now fully-staffed and operational 2nd Flotilla base at Lorient:

> "1. The accommodation of the flotilla in Lorient needs improvement, although the necessary work is underway. It is to be expected that the *Stützpunkt* Lorient will be extremely suitable for the sailors, especially in connection with the recuperation home in Quiberon [formerly a French railways rest home].

> "2. Mines and danger to U-boats is extreme and requires more defensive strength.

> "3. Flak defence is still insufficient. During the last attack [the previous night – the first RAF raid on Lorient using thirty-five Hampden bombers] five English aircraft passed over the yards at 300 metres and dropped ten bombs. Luckily there was no damage to any boats. The English flew from the north and north-east and it is here that a third heavy flak battery is needed.

> "[The base at Lorient] is fully suitable and extraordinarily valuable when viewed as a whole, but it can be expected to have in the repair shops simultaneously more than approximately ten to fifteen boats, a very large and disadvantageous conglomeration as long as there is the risk of air-raid.'

The effects on British maritime trade of the fierce air battle between the RAF and the Luftwaffe raging over England accentuated the importance of the French bases. While the Battle of Britain moved towards its climax, British merchant shipping had been diverted from the southern coast and Western Approaches after suffering repeated anti-shipping airstrikes. Now the ponderous convoys were routed through northerly waters further away from French Luftwaffe bases. Because of this British diversion U-boats were forced to range west and north in search of convoy traffic, Atlantic bases facilitating the increased western patrol radius.

The first half of September saw three more 2nd U-Flotilla boats sail from Germany: *U29*, *U43* and the recommissioned *U31*, the latter after three weeks of Baltic trials. Kaptlt. Otto Schuhart, sailing in the tired old Type VII, *U29* was forced to divert to to Bergen on 4 September, two days into his patrol, with damage to the boat's attack periscope.

While traversing the dangerous waters of the Skagerrak Kaptlt. Ambrosius' *U43*, destined for the mundane task of radioing meteorological information for Luftwaffe use, had been the object of another unsuccessful British submarine attack, HMS *Sturgeon* missing the U-boat with a full but badly aimed bow salvo. Like Schuhart, Ambrosius was also forced to divert to Bergen after only three days at sea, docking on 12 September with leaks in the boat's air intakes and one torpedo tube. The aged Type IXA was showing the strain of operational duty. Ambrosius and his men were detained for three days in Norway while repairs were completed before sailing for the waters to the west of the British Isles. The weather reporting duty had been passed to another boat and now Ambrosius and his crew hoped for confrontation with incoming convoy traffic as targets for their torpedoes.

By mid-September four of the flotilla's boats were moored in Lorient – *U32*, *U37*, *U38*, and *U124* – all having added to their combat laurels during the preceding patrols. Once moored in their new home, commanders began the task of replacing unsatisfactory crewmen with others from the reserve pool of manpower now stationed in Lorient. Iron Crosses were distributed to those who had proved their merit and the coveted U-boat War Badge to men who had completed their second operational patrol.

Damage suffered by *U124* after an attack on convoy HX65 had resulted in the 'Edelweiss' boat being relegated to weather reporting west of the United Kingdom. But even here the nature of submarine operation was not without its hazards.

While *U124* cruised back and forth on meteorological duty Schulz decided that it was an opportune time for the crew to engage in minor maintenance, including on the boat's aft WC, located in the stern torpedo compartment and nicknamed 'Tube seven'. The toilet system of a U-boat was a difficult mechanism to master and one that could only be used with any degree of safety at shallow depths lest the outside water pressure be too great. If it were, the flushing ended with the opposite effect than that desired. Indeed officer candidates at U-boat school were requird to pump out the heads at a depth of about twenty meters as part of their 'training', more often than not emerging covered in the toilet's contents and earning the award of the '*W.C. Schein*' (W.C. Certificate) to mark their first act of heroism.

During the course of work on *U124*'s aft toilet a machinist unwittingly removed its stopcock, becoming soaked by the ensuing deluge and running towards the control room, stopcock in hand. As the man bolted through the electric motor room, E-machinist Karl Rode snatched the bung from him and raced to the small compartment, shoving it back into place after only minor flooding into the U-boat's bilges. Fortunately the boat had been surfaced; if submerged the water pressure would have prevented Rode from stemming the flow of seawater and *U124* could have been in jeopardy. Schulz's anger over the incident was expressed in "terms that were eloquent, forceful and 100 percent Navy".[50] Reporting the expenditure of nearly all fuel and supplies to BdU on 9 September, Schulz arrived in his new base at Lorient a week later to be awarded the Iron Cross First and Second class.

The following day, 17 September, Günter Kuhnke supervised the docking of U28 by his IWO, Oblt.z.S. Ernst-Ulrich Brüller, in Lorient's harbour. Claiming five ships sunk from convoys SC1, SC2 and OA210, Kuhnke calculated that he had destroyed 30,000 tons of enemy merchant shipping. In reality he had overclaimed by 20,055 tons, a considerable margin of error. However, since the beginning of August Dönitz had relaxed his previously stringent demands at confirmation of success and, reckoning that Kuhnke had sunk in excess of 100,000 tons, he awarded the Knight's Cross to him on 19 September, the fourth for the 2nd U-Flotilla.[51]

18 September: Hans Jenisch took U32 from Lorient bound for weather-reporting duties west of Great Britain. The obsolete boat trailed behind a single minesweeper as it sailed from France, eleven torpedoes carried by the U-boat in anticipation of its release from weather chores. The predictable redirection was not long in coming when Jenisch received instructions to join other boats concentrating on the search for inbound convoy HX72 on 21 September, making contact the following morning.

At 0550hrs Jenisch tried a submerged torpedo attack that went wide of the stern-on British steamer SS *Collegian*. Opting to stop the ship with surface fire, Jenisch gave the order for U32 to surface, gun crew ready to man their weapon. Suddenly, as the German gunners, encumbered with oilskins and safety harnesses, struggled to load the deck cannon the dark was punctured by flame from the steamer's stern cannon as U32 was sighted and fired at by the alert gun crew. U32 returned fire, twenty-five rounds of 8.8cm cannon fire sporadically striking the steamer in conjunction with 2cm anti-aircraft fire. The *Collegian*, however, was relatively unscathed and Jenisch was forced to dive in case a lucky shot hit the boat's pressure hull. From periscope depth Jenisch fired a single torpedo at the ship's stern, a difficult shot at best and one that went wide. Aboard the U-boat the radio operator was able to confirm the ship's name as the intercepted SOS call filled his headphones.

Escort destroyer HMS *Lowestoft*, fifteen miles distant, had already picked up the flashes of gunfire, the steamer's predicament confirmed by the SOS sent from the ship's wireless shack. *Lowestoft* swung out of position and raced to the scene as Jenisch's second torpedo missed. With reinforcements in the shape of HMS *Skate* and *Shikari* also headed toward the scene, *Lowestoft* began a slow methodical ASDIC search for the submerged attacker while SS *Collegian* sailed to safety. At 0919hrs Jenisch's boat was detected at a range of 1400 yards, the ASDIC trace briefly lost and regained while depth charges were made ready. *Lowestoft*'s first pattern of six charged exploded beneath U32, too deep to harm the shallow U-boat which hovered at only 60 metres. With the disturbed water hampering British attempts at regaining ASDIC contact, Jenisch seized the opportunity to escape westwards, unscathed by the attack.

Over the next two weeks U32 sank five ships with combined artillery and torpedo attack, most from the dispersed remains of convoy OB217, another from OB218 southwest of Rockall. After this last convoy attack Jenisch sighted a lone freighter south-east of

---

[50] Gasaway, p. 60.

[51] Kuhnke had in fact sunk thirteen ships for 56,272 tons – slightly more than half his total claims.

Cape Farewell. During late morning on the first day of October he missed once again with a torpedo attack on the Dutch steamer SS *Haulerwijk* and opted to follow the freighter as it sailed onwards. After pursuing his quarry for eight hours Jenisch again ordered the boat surfaced to engage the Dutch ship with gunfire. As round after round riddled the freighter's waterline its crew abandoned ship. Gradually the steamer began to go under and Jenisch ordered his men below as he prepared to submerge and retreat from the scene. At periscope depth he approached the sinking ship in order to read its name before it sank. Unfortunately the sun shining directly into the commander's periscope hindered his perception of distance and, misjudging the approach, Jenisch and his men were shaken by a sudden collision between hunter and victim, damaging the U-boat's bow, though not its crucial torpedo tubes. *U32* retreated northwards. One more ship fell to Jenisch before he was obliged to return to Lorient low on fuel and ammunition. After docking on 6 October claiming seven ships for 39,393 tons, Jenisch recommended his IIWO and two crewmen for the Iron Cross. Jenisch received the Knight's Cross on 7 October from Dönitz.

Other less successful Type VIIs of the original 'Saltzwedel' line-up had arrived in Lorient during Jenisch's patrol. Schuhart's *U29* entered harbour on 1 October after a voyage that witnessed only one sinking, Dönitz concluding that no fault lay with commander or crew but with the "bad mechanical condition of the boat". The recommissioned *U31* also arrived, her cruise cut short by a rip in her diving tanks.

After only mediocre success, Kaptlt. Wilfried Prellberg, former IWO of *U34*, was bringing *U31* on its final approach to France during early morning on 8 October when five torpedoes streaked by, startling the bridge watch out of their complacency. Unbeknown to the Germans they had been stalked by HMS *Trident* engaged on anti-submarine patrols in Lorient's roadstead. *Trident* had been hounded by two overworked *U-boot Jäger* from 14th *U-Jäger* Flotilla near the Ile de Groix but had managed to evade the German hunters, before detecting by hydrophone the sound of approaching diesel engines. At 0520 *Trident* surfaced to search for the source of this noise with binoculars, *U31*'s low silhouette emerging ten minutes later. In fact the approaching threat had been seen by the U-boat's lookouts, but they thought the British conning tower was nothing but a slim outcropping rock. The first bow salvo of five torpedoes was launched at a range of 1,500 yards as the British commander ordered all diesels full ahead to close the distance. Narrowly missing *U31*, *Trident* fired two more torpedoes after the distance had closed to 500 yards, a further one following as the two boats drew almost together. The last torpedo was seen to streak by the U-boat's stern as *Trident* charged into the attack, gun crew closed up for surface firing. The British submarine rounded *U31*'s stern and its gun fired a single round at point blank range. The flash momentarily blinded the gunlayer, but a second was also fired, striking *U31*'s conning tower in a shower of sparks. Prellberg meanwhile had ordered his boat crash-dived while the men within the bow torpedo room struggled to load empty tubes. As the boat plummeted downwards the LI, Oblt. (Ing.) Erich Handt, lost control of the trim and she smashed into the sandy bottom, Prellberg immediately shutting down his electric motors as the dazed crew regained their composure. Aboard *Trident*, now also submerged, the hydrophone effect ceased and, with all tubes needing reloading and no clear idea of where the silent enemy lay, the British submarine retreated from the area.

After anxious minutes spent on the bottom with the boat perceptibly shifting in the Breton currents, Prellberg ordered tanks blown and *U31* broke surface and recommenced its passage to Lorient, conning tower battered by the shell hit but the pressure hull still untouched. Entering harbour, *U31* docked on the 'town side' of the Scorff River opposite Jenisch's *U32*. Once the tedium of deprovisioning had been completed and engineering and maintenance reports submitted many of the crewmen were bussed to Quiberon for five days of relaxation.

The apparent inability to rid the approaches to Lorient of British submarines prompted Dönitz again to demand priority for the protection of U-boats departing or returning from patrol. Extensive minefields were necessary, as well as increased numbers of escort vessels. As if to underline his determination, Kaptlt. von Stockhausen also reported a narrow torpedo miss when *U65* left Lorient on 15 October, the first of what would later transpire to be many boats bound for the waters off the West African port of Freetown.

But the British attempt at blockading the French bases was to intensify during the following months, aircraft, submarines and mines applying increasing pressure on the enemy. In July 1941 the British announced that they would also attack all fishing vessels found outside immediately coastal waters, tightening the noose around Lorient.

18 October: An unhappy Kaptlt. Ambrosius docked *U43* after another narrow miss by torpedoes from a British submarine in the aproaches. Ambrosius scored only a single sinking during his patrol from dispersed convoy OB217. Failures during previous attacks on convoy HX72, a convoy massacred by other U-boats in a 'pack' operation, underlined doubts about Ambrosius' ability during this second "unsatisfactory patrol". BdU recorded:

> "The commander had undergone a good peacetime education [as commander of *U21* and *U28*], but is better at theory and so will be replaced. He had held a miserable hand on the previous undertaking also."

Thus Ambrosius departed the front line, later to command the 22nd U-training Flotilla (2ULD) at Gotenhafen until early 1944 and then transferred to minesweepers. Replacing Ambrosius was a young commander already with experience and a proven combat record, Kaptlt. Wolfgang Lüth transferred from the 1st U-Flotilla to Lorient.

19 October: Kaptlt. Viktor Schütze ended his first patrol as commander of the new Type IXB *U103* in Lorient, the U-boat entering harbour flying pennants claiming five steamers for 31,000 tons sunk during action against convoy SC6 and the dispersed OB227. The AG Weser boat had suffered numerous small mechanical problems during the month-long voyage, part of which was spent depositing weather buoys north-west of Ireland, but arrived having fired all torpedoes and was welcomed boisterously, jubilation made even more intense with news of the success of a pack of eight U-boats in action against North Atlantic convoys. By Dönitz's reckoning the eight boats – *U46, U47, U48, U99, U100* and *U101* from the 7th U-Flotilla with *U38* and *U123* from Fischer's 2nd U-Flotilla – had destroyed forty-seven ships for 310,000 tons in a running battle against two separate convoys SC7 and HX79. Taken as a whole the extended combat became christened the "Night of the Long Knives", described as a "colossal success" on German radio.

Although the combined tonnage sunk from both convoys actually amounted to thirty-three ships of a total 154,709 tons – far short of that claimed by BdU and his commanders – it was still a slaughter by British standards. Churchill was prompted immediately to convene a meeting of the British Defence Committee where he called for swift implementation of radar for air and sea escorts, airborne depth charges and more cohesive radio communications between convoys and their beleaguered escorts.

On 22 October Oehrn brought the elderly Type IXA *U37* into Lorient harbour, claiming six steamers sunk during his fourth war patrol as skipper.[52] After the boat was secured alongside the *Isère*, Oehrn disembarked with his men and prepared for inspection by BdU. Smiling, Dönitz placed the ribbon of the Knight's Cross around his neck and congratulated him on being the 38th man of the German Wehrmacht to receive the award. Coupled with Oehrn's award was a Knight's Cross for the LI, Oblt. (Ing.) Ger Suhren, who had nursed the aged boat's constant mechanical breakdowns during difficult weeks at sea. The skilled Suhren was the first Engineering Officer to be honoured with the medal.[53] Before the assembled crowd Dönitz unexpectedly announced Oehrn's transfer back to BdU staff and the immediate promotion of IWO Nicolai Clausen to commander. Oehrn's newfound contentment was over. He had succeeded in spearheading the U-boat's resurgence after Norway; now Dönitz required his considerable skill as a staff officer.

The next day Kaptlt. Karl-Heinze Moehle sailed into Lorient bereft of torpedoes at the conclusion of *U123*'s maiden voyage, claiming 44,500 tons of enemy shipping sunk. The continued success of the U-boats in the Atlantic provided Dönitz with much-needed ammunition in the bureaucratic war for resources in Germany. It was clear to Dönitz that he did not have enough U-boat strength to intensify the pressure against Britain's convoy traffic. Increased building would have to take place if the U-boats were not only to keep pace with numbers taken out of front-line service by retirement or destruction, but also to step up the rate of attrition against merchant shipping that Churchill so feared. By the beginning of October 1940 the U-boat service had shrunk to a mere twenty-seven front line boats, many of which were small coastal models unsuited to Atlantic convoy warfare. Only thirty-six new submarines had been commissioned since the war's beginning (ten of which were Type IIC and IID models), while thirty-two had been lost, others taken out of combat to act as much-needed training boats. Indeed the decision had at last been taken for the remaining archaic Type VIIs of the 2nd U-Flotilla to sail to Germany on their final operational patrols before transfer to training flotillas.

On 25 October Dönitz entered the Reich Chancellory to deliver a presentation to Hitler illustrating the successes recently achieved by his U-boats. He argued persuasively for more material and resources for construction, the rate of which was already twenty-eight boats in arrears. But Dönitz's pleas fell on deaf ears. Hitler never fully realized the potential for defeating England within the Atlantic, his eyes no longer directed across the Channel but eastwards to a future war against Russia. The defeat of Stalin, an uneasy bedfellow held at bay by frail alliances forged by convenience, was to be Hitler's crowning glory, a war in which he saw no place for the U-boat service.

26 October: B-Dienst radio intercepts picked up British messages concerning the sinking of the liner SS *Empress of Britain* in grid square AM5455 north-west of Ireland. Within two days it was confirmed by radio transmission from *U32* that Jenisch had sunk the large liner.

---

[52] It was his third sinking of the patrol that caused Oehrn the largest dilemma. During an artillery attack on SS *Severn Leigh* shellfire accidentally struck a lowering lifeboat. Reflexively fearing this propaganda gift to the Allies, Oehrn ordered guns trained on the remaining lifeboats, wrestling with his decision to erase witnesses. A testimonial to his own character, he ordered fire returned to finish off the wounded freighter, its survivors unharmed.

[53] By coincidence, his brother, Oblt.z.S. Reinhard 'Teddy' Suhren, who was serving as IWO on the famous '*Dreimal Schwarze Katte*' boat *U48*, was the first Watch Officer to receive the Knight's Cross, on 3 November 1940.

In his novelized wartime biography of Günther Prien, Wolfgang Frank, head of the naval propaganda company, recounted an evening spent in Berlin with Prien and Karl Dönitz the day before Prien was due to be invested with the Oak Leaves to his Knight's Cross. While the three men were sitting in the lobby of the Kaiserhof Hotel Dönitz was paged to receive a telephone call.

> "When he came back he was beaming all over his face. 'Jenisch has sunk the *Empress of Britain!*' This was something! The *Empress of Britain* was the 40,000-ton luxury liner which the Luftwaffe had had a whack at and whose concealment the British had made a matter of prestige. Good for Jenisch! So he had actually brought it off.
>
> "'I can just imagine my Jenisch creeping up on her with his tongue half out of his mouth,' said the Admiral."[54]

Jenisch had left Lorient on 24 October with all tubes loaded, four spare eels lying in the bilges and two wrapped in canvas below the forward decking. A passenger in the shape of Kaptlt. Friedrich Wentzel was also along for the ride, sent with the aggressive Jenisch in order to gain combat experience. Two days into his patrol Jenisch received a message from U-boat command to form a line with flotilla mates *U28* and *U31*, also travelling via the North Atlantic to German retirement, lying east to west within the North Channel. *Leutnant* B. Jope's KG40 Condor bomber had found and attacked the *Empress of Britain*, setting the huge liner on fire from the fore end of its bridge to the after funnel, but unable to deliver a fatal blow. To Dönitz it was an irresistible target and one that, unless his U-boats could find and sink it, the British could salvage and save from destruction. Jenisch at first did not respond to the message, believing Prellberg to be in the better position to carry out the attack, but after the urgent message was repeated Jenisch ordered full ahead and raced to intercept.

Nearing the reported location Jenisch surfaced beneath a pitch-black night in a heavy swell. He immediately saw the distant flames of the burning liner moving towards him. The great ship, under tow by the Polish destroyer *Burza*, had been evacuated of all her surviving passengers and a sizeable part of her crew after the Luftwaffe attack, a skeleton crew of only fifty-five remaining on board. In a display of sheer nerve *U32* remained surfaced ahead and slightly to port of the *Empress*'s path as other destroyers zigzagged on either beam and a Sunderland flying boat circled unseen overhead. Finally, at a range of only 600 metres, Jenisch's IWO Oblt.z.S. von Gulat-Wellenberg fired three torpedoes, the first striking to starboard abreast of the forward funnel, the second hitting the engine room, while the third prematured. It was the end for the massive ship. Her back broken by the blasts, she sank rapidly and Jenisch left the scene still surfaced, flak gunners ready to open fire on the Sunderland which swept blindly above, failing to notice *U32* as it sped to safety.[55]

Flushed with success at the sinking of what would remain the largest ship destroyed by U-boat during the Second World War, Jenisch headed west into heavy rain-squalls and high seas. The morning of 30 October saw no improvement in the weather and visibility was extremely poor for the lookouts as they swept the horizon for enemies. Through the intermittent walls of rain they glimpsed the outline of a steamer, SS *Balzac*, zigzagging and

---

[54] *Enemy Submarine*, Wolfgang Frank, p. 110.

[55] The Polish destroyer *Narvik* closed to pick up survivors and rescued the last surviving crew in what the Admiralty correctly termed a "magnificent way".

apparently alone. Jenisch ordered his boat put into pursuit while he pondered the target ship. Her behaviour aroused suspicion in the young commander and he drew the conclusion that it may well be a Q-ship – the submarine traps that had been invented during the First World War, a source of constant warning from Dönitz who had himself run afoul of one during the last war. Nonetheless it was too tempting a target to let slip and at 1240hrs, after reaching an advantageous submerged firing position, Jenisch let loose a single torpedo at *Balzac*. Unfortunately it exploded prematurely on the ship's starboard side fifty metres short. *Balzac*'s master believed that they were under shellfire and radioed immediately for help from any nearby naval vessels.

Forty-five miles to the south escort destroyers HMS *Harvester* and *Highlander* were engaged with incoming convoy SC8 when *Balzac*'s message was received. Once freed from his duties, *Highlander*'s captain Cdr. W.A. Dallmeyer, ordered course laid to meet the besieged steamer, the destroyer surging forward at 25 knots, while *Harvester* was retained as SC8's escort into the Clyde.

Some hours later Jenisch was still shadowing the steamer. While studying the ship through his attack periscope Jenisch periodically swept the horizon for danger and was startled to see the silhouette of HMS *Highlander* materialize from grey sheets of rain. He ordered his boat dived from periscope depth, electric motors on maximum revolutions as *U32* plunged deeper, the commander allowing time for the destroyer to pass by and continue on its way. The German radio operator reported strange hydrophone effect approaching to which Jenisch apparently replied: "Rot! That is our own noise, we are travelling at high speed." It was then that Jenisch made his mistake. Ordering periscope depth at 1812hrs, he again studied the steamer, while *Highlander* made ASDIC contact, swiftly followed by the sighting of two feet of extended periscope only 80 yards to port.

The sudden appearance of the terrifyingly close destroyer shocked Jenisch and he shouted for a crash dive. Dallmeyer immediately ordered *Highlander* full astern on port engines and full ahead starboard with the wheel hard over in an attempt to swing his ship around and ram *U32*. But the German was too close and instead depth charges were readied, set to explode deep while *Highlander* roared forward. The first six blasts failed to hinder Jenisch as *U32* turned hard to starboard away from its attacker and dropped to 110 metres. The U-boat's gyro-compass was turned off and power to hydroplanes and rudders shut down as the men went over to hand operation in an attempt to quieten any possible noise. But ASDIC had a firm hold of *U32* as the two vessels jockeyed for position. Jenisch came shallow and attempted to torpedo the destroyer, firing two wild shots at 1853 as fourteen more depth charges battered the boat. Dallmeyer swung *Highlander* towards the telltale trail of the two eels, combing the tracks of the incoming threat. *U32* had not been so fortunate. The barrage had caused havoc. At the moment of explosion Jenisch had thrown the boat into full reverse as he tried in vain to turn away from the ASDIC beam, but as the boat violently bucked beneath his feet he knew that the attack had finished his chances of escape. The main lighting failed, as did all electrical instruments, cables ruptured by the concussion, electric switch-gear dangling from damaged wiring. The crew clutched their heads in agony as the boat filled with high-pressure air from severed compressed air leads, all valves now inoperative. The boat's aft ballast tanks were crushed, releasing a massive air bubble which was visible to the British hunters above and even the depth gauge was found to be smashed as Jenisch realized he had no compressed air with which to fire torpedoes and little chance of reaching the surface. Most of the crew were ordered forward as the remaining ballast tanks were blown. At 1908, after darkness had fallen, *U32* broke surface, diesels spluttering into life as the stern-down boat vainly tried to flee. Jenisch flung open the boat's conning tower hatch and immediately saw *Highlander*, shouting for the boat to crash dive once more, but it was not to be. Oblt. (Ing.) Hans Wahl replied that there was neither power nor compressed air to allow the boat to submerge: the game was over. As *Highlander* opened fire with machine guns and 4.7" cannon fire Jenisch gave the order to abandon ship, a single shell hitting the conning tower and killing several men, including the boat's popular IIWO, Oblt.z.S. Günther Damm. The *Funkmaat* remembered Jenisch appearing as if he was "about to carry more ammunition to the outside deck" before he was forced to give up the fight and himself leap from the doomed submarine. British guns fell silent when it became obvious that the U-boat was going down and the shaft of the destroyer's searchlight framed *U32* as its bow lifted vertically before sliding under stern first. Nine men went down with their boat, most killed by gunfire, while HMS *Highlander* rescued Jenisch, Wentzel and thirty-two others.

There followed what is perhaps one of the most bizarre propaganda battles between England and Germany. The BBC trumpeted the sinking of *U32* and subsequent capture of a U-boat 'ace', the 'Killer of Giants', sinker of the *Empress of Britain* and holder of the Knight's Cross. These had been the first prisoners taken in months and their propaganda value was not lost on the British. Berlin, on the other hand, attempted to play down the entire event and went to the extraordinary lengths of staging a fake radio broadcast of the 'triumphant return of Hans Jenisch', the subject of so much recent media coverage.

While both *U28* and *U31* were at sea on their final patrols before retirement, the last remaining 2nd U-Flotilla Type VII in Lorient left France on 28 October. Schuhart had been ordered to take his boat, still plagued with machinery problems, west to rendezvous with the incoming raider *Schiff 21 'Widder'* returning from 180 days at sea and the sinking of nine ships. Her commander, KK Hellmuth von Ruckteschell, had reported to *Marinegruppenkommando* West in Paris that the raider was suffering engine problems after a suspected collision with an Italian submarine. Von Ruckteschell requested a U-boat escort and so *U29* rattled to sea once more. By 29 October Schuhart was expressing doubts as to whether he would be able to rendezvous with the raider that day, although at 2300hrs the converted merchant ship hove into view, falling in alongside the U-boat for the uneventful two-day transit to Brest.

Two days later Schuhart left France again, this time acting as weather boat west of Great Britain while travelling to Bergen where *U29* docked on 30 November. The final two-day transfer to retirement in Wilhelmshaven was completed by 3 December 1940, *U29*'s combat days over as she transferred to the 24th U-training Flotilla. Sister ship *U28* had already reached Germany on 15 November where she too was allocated to the 24th U-training Flotilla. Günter Kuhnke immediately transferred to oversee the building of his next combat command, *U125*, in Bremen's AG Weser yards, while Schuhart remained with his boat, leaving combat to begin a career within the U-boat training flotillas, eventually commanding Pillau's 21st U-training Flotilla.

The last Type VII belonging to the 2nd U-Flotilla also left the roster during November 1940, *U31 Vermißt ein Stern*. Like Jenisch and Kuhnke, Prellberg had been ordered to the patrol line, sweeping forwards in search of the *Empress of Britain*. Also, like Jenisch, Prellberg carried a passenger in training, Kaptlt. Hans Engel as *Kommandant Schüler*. Outbound from Lorient *U31* again narrowly missed being a victim of British submarine attack, diving for safety as the retreating screws of their adversary were tracked by hydrophone. Although beaten to the punch by Jenisch, *U31* managed a single sinking on 29 October when

Prellberg torpedoed the drifting and abandoned wreck of SS *Matina*, the British steamer damaged by *U28* during its transit to Germany.

Weather conditions during the cruise were vile and Prellberg opted to spend most of his passage west of Ireland submerged, both to rest his weary crew and provide an opportunity for the hydrophones to sweep for convoy noise, ships all but invisible to the bridge watch as they clung to the rolling conning tower amid sheets of blinding rain and sea spray. Days merged together as *U31* struggled northwards.

During the morning of 2 November *U31* rose from the depths, hatches thrown open as the boat was ventilated and diesels run to charge depleted batteries. The sea had calmed somewhat and visibility was rated at seven miles, a cloudy sky spilling intermittent showers on the boat, rolling in a mild force three south-easterly, although the heavier weather of previous days was shortly to return. At 1015hrs Prellberg and his off watch officers were just sitting down to breakfast when lookouts reported an enemy ship sighted in what were increasingly heavy seas. Prellberg raced to the bridge where he swept the indicated quarter with his binoculars before spotting the threat of an escort destroyer, distant merchant silhouettes behind it. *U31* crash-dived as men threw themselves down the ladder and the bow bit into the sea. Immediately, the hydrophone operator detected a strong effect of destroyer propellers as well as the distinctive noise of the ship's subsidiary machinery. *U31* sank deeper still as Prellberg ordered the boat silent at sixty metres.

Above the U-boat HMS *Antelope* had been engaged as escort for convoy OB237 inbound to Great Britain. At 1025hrs as the destroyer forged ahead on the convoy's starboard quarter a firm ASDIC contact was made on a submerged target 600 yards ahead and to starboard. Lt-Cdr T. White instantly ordered depth charges made ready and with five minutes the destroyer had raced over the confirmed ASDIC trace dropping six charges that blew *U31*'s main lighting, but failed to damage anything serious.

The tumbling water obscured *U31* from the ASDIC and Prellberg threw his boat into a zigzag, actually closing the distance to his attacker. At 1103hrs the destroyer regained contact and a second six-charge pattern was dropped, battering the submarine's hull. At first there appeared to be little damage until it was discovered that the stern hydroplanes had jammed and that internal machinery damage meant that the boat could no longer alter depth silently, a lethal vibration betraying the U-boat's position if she attempted to rise or fall. Prellberg tried to make a wide detour around his assailant, but the reinforcement of a second destroyer, HMS *Achates*, rendered his attempt futile. *Antelope* regained its temporarily disrupted ASDIC contact and prepared for a third attack, to be followed by *Achates* dropping still more charges on the first destroyer's spread. By then Prellberg had taken his only silent option and risen to 30 metres where the boat hung, altering course to dart under the oncoming *Antelope* where she was blind. In the confusion ASDIC contact was lost and, rather than waste ammunition, the depth-charge drop was held, *Achates* returning to the convoy in defence of any other predators lurking nearby.

By 1230hrs it appeared that *U31* had shaken off the British hunter, moving quietly away towards where the first contact had been made. Unfortunately for Prellberg, the same thought had occurred to Lt-Cdr White. As he circled in frustration he decided to start again with an ASDIC sweep originating where they had first gained contact. At 1320hrs contact was regained dead ahead at a range of 2,500 yards. The destroyer closed up for action and charged full ahead towards the shallow boat. Prellberg had managed to sink gradually to 50 metres without creating too much disturbance, but as *Antelope* raced overhead the distinctive sound of depth charges hitting the water presaged a devastating barrage.

As the explosives thundered around *U31* the boat reeled in agony, water gushing through wrecked valves and seals into the stern compartment, flooding it severely and causing the stern to slip 15° down. The boat was sinking. Prellberg, the inevitability of destruction making him conscious of his obligation to the crew, immediately wanted to surface but after a short and violent argument with Oblt. (Ing.) Erich Handt was dissuaded from doing so in the vague hope that the boat could creep far enough away to surface and escape. Above them the chances of hiding were nil as the boat leaked air and oil behind it. Large bubbles broke the surface and British hydrophone operators could hear the noise of constant gurgling from the damaged German ballast tanks. A third depth charge attack with deep settings was made ready and *U31* pulverized still further.

There was now no doubt about the boat's ability to escape. She had sunk to 95 metres, stern down and water flooding throughout the pressure hull. The exterior stern torpedo tube was flooded and useless, as was the diesel engine airshaft. High-pressure compressed air had leaked from ruptured bottles, raising the internal pressure and increasing the level of discomfort for crewmen struggling to staunch the flow of water into their boat. They were aware of the oil slick left by their shattered boat and Prellberg decided to give up his hopeless escape bid, ordering the remaining high pressure air to blow tanks and the crew to prepare to abandon ship. Codebooks and documents were thrown into the bilges where the water rendering them unreadable. The Enigma machine and its rotors were made ready to be ditched from the conning tower as soon as the boat had surfaced. At 1350hrs the battered grey tower broke through the surface as the British guns opened fire.

Men were seen to be leaping from their doomed boat and the fire was ordered stopped after twenty-three rounds. Instead Lt-Cdr White ordered a boarding party made ready and the whaler launched. To capture a U-boat, or at least board her and recover secret material, would be the pinnacle of achievement.

But the LI was still aboard *U31* where he left electric motors running and rudder hard to port. The U-boat circled slowly at four knots, too fast for the whaler to catch her. As *Antelope* drew alongside, the boat appeared to stop its forward movement and more British crewmen prepared to drop onto the floundering deck and attempt to get below, but at the last moment *U31* surged to port and rammed the destroyer, before being thrown into full astern. The destroyer had been holed in two fuel tanks and a boiler room and was forced to lose way as damage parties shored up the buckled hull plates. With the weight of its flooded interior pulling the U-boat down, she heeled over and water soon rushed over the conning tower, cascading through the hatch and sending *U31* to its grave 1000 fathoms below. Prellberg and forty-three others were rescued by the whaleboat, one man disappearing with the U-boat, another lapsing into a coma and dying aboard HMS *Antelope*. *U31*, given a second lease of life after its RAF attack in 1939, had earned the dubious distinction of being the only U-boat sunk twice by enemy action.

The end of November saw the 2nd U-Flotilla's combat strength at eight front-line boats (Type IXAs *U37*, *U38*, *U43*, Type IXBs *U65*, *U103*, *U104*, *U123* and *U124*) with a further four undergoing Baltic shakedown cruises after their recent commissioning (*U105*, *U106*, *U107* and *U110*). One of the Baltic boats had already brushed narrowly with death. Veteran commander Kaptlt. Jürgen Oesten, late of the 1st U-Flotilla's *U61*, had already undergone torpedo trials at Kiel and UAK testing at Danzig when on 19 October his *U106* rammed a submerged Type VIIC, *U136*, while undergoing UAK testing. Luckily the severe impact caused little damage to either boat and, after a brief stay in the yard, *U106* was soon ready to leave for front-line service, her conning tower sporting the intricate design of a pair of duelling sawfish, designed by the brother of IIWO Oblt.z.S. Werner Grüneberg, a Bremen architecht.

Kaptlt. Harald Jürst's *U104* was also late in reaching front-line status. Scheduled to have been ready by the end of October, she finally sailed on 12 November, slipping from Kiel through the Kaiser Wilhelm Canal bound ultimately for the Atlantic Ocean. Harald Jürst, former commander of the 1st U-Flotilla's *U59*, was forced to divert to Bergen with a faulty gyro-compass after only five days, resailing on 18 November. He sank a convoy straggler south-south-east of Rockall on 27 November, later damaging British tanker MV *Charles F. Meyer* in the same area. Then he disappeared, Jürst and his forty-eight crewmen lost to unknown causes sometime after 29 November.

11 November: At 0900hrs on Armistice Day Admiral Karl Dönitz's new headquarters at Kernével's Villa Kerillon was officially made operational. It was an inspired choice, the middle of three villas standing on the western bank of Le Ter waterway facing the fore-shore of Kéroman. The construction of the three villas had been completed during the second half of the nineteenth century, a testament to the success of shipowners involved in the Breton sardine fishing trade (hence the often-used title 'le Château des Sardines'). To left and right the remaining villas, Margaret and Kerozen, housed the officers who worked in Dönitz's tightly run command post. The 'Lion' would now be on hand to interact with his subordinates, able to obtain a personal feel for the fortunes of Germany's Atlantic war. The all-important communications centre within the BdU complex, commanded by Kaptlt. Hans Meckel as *4. Admiralstabsoffizier*, was one of the bomb-proof bunkers behind the villa, supplied with power by its own generator.[56] This communications nerve centre was reached via the château's kitchen and a narrow stone stairway that descended through armoured double doors into the huge wood-panelled bunkers, completed by the Organization Todt in 1941. The Kernével nerve centre, christened "Berlin" by those within, soon became a veritable fortress. To landward the defences included an anti-tank ditch, behind which were sited three 5cm anti-tank guns in their own bunkers. Another concrete shelter carried the armoured turret of a small French tank alongside a surveillance bunker with armoured machine-gun firing slots. Fringing the coastline were more anti-tank weapons, 10.5cm and smaller calibre AA guns, machine-gun bunkers and a searchlight in its own thick-walled concrete emplacement. Further defence from seaborne attack was provided by weapons on the small Île St. Michel sitting astride the entrance channel to the Scorff River.

13 November: Kaptlt. Georg-Wilhelm Schulz brought *U124* into the Scorff estuary at Lorient, pennants accounting for five steamers flying from the extended periscope of the 'Edelweiss boat'. The victory had been hard-won, *U124* detected and subjected to hours of ferocious depth-charging three times. The last battering had only ended after Schulz had fired a tube full of debris and oil to the surface, the ruse succeeding and their tormentor retreating. Once surfaced, crewmen noted the bizarre coincidence that each time chocolate pudding had been on the menu they were severely attacked. Schulz promptly banned the dessert from *U124*.

Their final ordeal took place while approaching their escort rendezvous point before Lorient. Travelling submerged due to the increasing threat of air attack, the terrifying

---

[56] Meckel held this post from November 1939 to June 1944, specializing in radio and radar.

sound of metal striking the outside hull froze men in their tracks. The thick cable of a moored mine grated slowly from bow to stern, minutes of terror as the wire rasped along the entire length of the boat before sliding free. They had survived.

In Lorient *U124*'s IWO, Reinhard Hardegen, left and a new officer came aboard. Johann 'Jochen' Mohr was a gifted and irrepressibly good humoured twenty-four-year-old veteran of operations aboard the cruiser *Deutschland* during the Spanish Civil War. Then he had been flag lieutenant under Admiral Wilhelm Marschall, entering the U-boat service during 1940.[57] *U124* was to be his first boat and one in which he would later achieve fame.

14 November: *U123* sailed from Lorient on its second war patrol. Kaptlt. Karl-Heinz Moehle's U-boat was bound for the North Atlantic. Three days into the tour tragedy overtook them when *Machanikergefreiter* Fritz Pfeifer was lost overboard in heavy weather.

On 22 November Moehle made contact with convoy OB244, being shadowed by flotilla-mate *U103*. Kaptlt. Viktor Schütze's boat had sailed from Lorient on 9 November and spent the previous two days doggedly pursuing the convoy, sinking two ships already, despite fierce counter-attacks. Moehle attacked in the face of determined escorts, sinking five ships as the convoy dispersed. This obstinate snapping at the enemy's heels ended abruptly when the submerged *U123* was shaken by underwater collision with an unknown object, possibly its last victim SS *Anten* on its way to the bottom. Both periscopes were destroyed and the conning tower heavily damaged, forcing a premature return to base. *U123* entered port proudly on 28 November due for fifty days of repairs, the crew granted home leave in Germany.

Schütze docked *U103* in Lorient on 12 December with a confirmed seven ships sunk. The day before he had received radio notification of his award of the Knight's Cross, presented in person by 'The Lion' after docking had been completed.

17 December: Despite Kaptlt. Wolfgang Lüth's command of *U43* starting inauspiciously during November when his first departure was curtailed by diving problems and a persistent oil leak, he finally ended his first patrol with three ships sunk and a damaged fourth. North-west of Ireland *U43* had attacked the dispersing convoy OB251, sinking British steamer *Pacific President* a little after 0900hrs. His second victory proved to be more problematic. After hitting SS *Victor Rose* with two torpedoes and managing only to slow her, Lüth brought his boat to a virtual stop, preparing a final shot to finish the ailing tanker off. Firing his third torpedo, Lüth was irritated to see if veer off course and go wide. Preparations for a fourth shot were made, but, as Lüth made ready to fire, the bows of the *Victor Rose* swung inexorably towards *U43* as her master attempted to ram. Lüth snapped his shot off and frantically ordered all tanks blown, the stationary U-boat dropping agonizingly slowly underwater as the tanker roared overhead, missing by mere metres. When the enraged Lüth rose to view his enemy he was gratified to see that his fourth shot had hit her and she was sinking rapidly by the stern. The jubilation was short-lived, however, as the U-boat's *Obersteuermann* was able to identify the ship by sight. He had sailed aboard her in peacetime as a merchant seaman. The destruction of shipping did not come easily to many sailors.

[57] Among his distinctions Mohr had taken part in a clandestine mission in civilian clothes in Spain during 1936 at the age of 19 when he had landed on Tenerife to spirit away a group of German diplomats caught there by the conflict.

The final 2nd U-Flotilla U-boats at sea at the end of 1940 were *U65*, having sailed during October and been replenished near the Cape Verde Islands by German supply ship *Nordmark*, disguised as the neutral American tanker *Prairie*, and *U124* leaving Lorient on 17 December. Aboard Schulz's *U124* two *Konfirmand* trainee commanders soon to be assigned their own boat were included in the crew: Kaptlt. Gero Zimmermann and Kaptlt. Wilhelm Kleinschmidt, accompanying the veteran crew to gain valuable experience.

Although international opinion had been staggered by the apparent success of the small U-boat force in the Atlantic, the facts belie the image. During 1940 twenty-four U-boats had been lost to enemy action. While fifty-five had been commissioned, many were small coastal boats unsuited to open ocean warfare, while older obsolete Type VIIs had been pulled off the front line and transferred to training units. Boats and crews were worn to the point of exhaustion by punishing voyages and were in desperate need of rest and refit. The myth of the 'Happy Time' persists even to this day, but it is somewhat inaccurate. German equipment was barely improving while the Allies were quick to realize several basic truths: radar was needed as was air power and improved anti-submarine weaponry.

By the end of 1940 Lorient was the most heavily bombed of the French Atlantic ports, the RAF dropping 220 tons of high explosive on to dockyard installations. With this in mind, on 25 October Dönitz reported to Hitler near Paris to update him on the U-boat situation. Among the items given attention was the need for protective U-boat shelters. Dönitz expressed the belief that only thick concrete covering moorings, dry docks and the various workshops would offer adequate safety from air attack. Hitler took Dönitz's words to heart and within days Dr Fritz Todt, head of the German labour organization to which he lent his name, visited Lorient with *Grossadmiral* Raeder to settle practicalities with the project.

Two huge, arched bunkers (named 'Cathedral Bunkers' or *Dombunkers*) had been constructed at Kéroman capable of handling two small Type II U-boats each, but they alone were obviously not sufficient, the bunkers too small and their slipway incapable of carrying larger boats. Lorient's Scorff River moorings and dry docks were extremely exposed. On the southern river bank a small tidal shelter was to be built slightly down-river of the Gueydon Bridge. Measuring 145 metres wide, 51 metres long and 15 metres high it was divided into two separate open-mouthed pens, each able to shelter a pair of Type VII or IX U-boats beneath a 3.5-metre-thick roof. This also, however, was only a temporary solution. It was apparent even before construction began that, while useful both for U-boats and other small Kriegsmarine vessels, the bunkers' size was insufficient for Lorients' needs. Todt planned an ambitious project to build three separate submarine bunkers on the Kéroman foreland that jutted from Lorient towards Île St. Michel.

The three bunkers envisaged by Raeder, Dönitz and Todt were to be the most complex of all the Kriegsmarine's U-boat shelters. Two large bunkers were to be constructed as dry docks, fed by a sheltered slipway, and in November 1940 the Kriegsmarine's Work's Director, Alfred Eckhardt, appointed the *Marinebaudirektor* Walter Triebel to begin design work on the facility. Triebel had built the first U-boat bunker of the Third Reich on Heligoland and, after installing himself with the Lorient arsenal, he brought his consider-able engineering skill to bear. Initially envisaged as a completely subterranean complex, the hard rock at Kéroman prevented any kind of rapid construction of either this or above-ground wet-dock facilities. He decided to stay with a slipway/dry-dock system. Once boats were lifted from the river they would be moved by cradle to any of twelve concrete pens onshore.

The final bunker, Kéroman III, was begun after work on the previous two had progressed considerably. Rather than the complicated system of removing boats from the water and transporting them to dry berths, Kéroman III would be open to the River Ter. Once the boats had sailed inside and were secured, their berths could be sealed by submersible caissons and armoured blast doors, water pumped out to provide a dry dock. It was an ambitious building project, the results of which would remain long after the 'Thousand Year Reich' had vanished into history.

6

THE EAGLE'S CLAWS:
1 JANUARY TO 31 DECEMBER 1941

New Year in the Atlantic witnessed nature's uncontrolled fury. While the elements raged there was little opportunity for U-boat commanders to use any weapons against what few merchant targets they found. The combination of howling gales, blinding rain and short winter days made the job of locating targets difficult enough, let alone attempting combat. While his men struggled to come to grips with an elusive enemy, Dönitz scored a triumph in the shadowy world of interdepartmental wrangling when on 7 January Hitler transferred aircraft of 1/KG40 to BdU. After an impassioned plea from Dönitz, Raeder and Jodl supported his request to the Führer for aerial cooperation. Hermann Göring, who jealously guarded his air force from outside influence, was not present when Dönitz secured the use of the small Luftwaffe unit equipped with long-range Condor aircraft for the purpose of reconnaissance in the Atlantic.

In Lorient that same day Kaptlt. Nicolai Clausen brought *U37* in after his first free-ranging patrol, claiming six steamers sunk. However, three of his victims were highly problematic. The first was the 233-ton Spanish sailing vessel *San Carlos*, prompting a brief protest from Franco. But worse came on 19 December when *U37* sank a military tanker and a suspected enemy submarine: oiler *Rhône* and 1,500-ton ocean-going submarine *Sfax*, both operated by the Vichy French. Clausen had also been scheduled to refuel from *Corrientes*, code-named *Culebra* (Snake), in the Canary Islands but was denied access to Las Palmas by a virtual blockade of the port by British warships. Despite these setbacks, BdU noted that he had:

"Acted correctly on his first patrol and showed he had the right qualities."

10 January: *U65* put into Lorient after nearly three months at sea. Having sailed on 15 October, von Stockhausen had operated almost continuously off the Sierra Leone port of Freetown, claiming eight steamers and the tanker MV *British Zeal* heavily damaged.

The harbour of Freetown lay on the south side of the River Rokel estuary, five miles from the open sea. The most important colonial outpost between South Africa and England, Freetown was land-locked by heavily forested, humid, mosquito-ridden countryside. Founded by emancipated slaves, the harbour had become known as 'white man's death', but comprised a huge roadstead, capable of sheltering large fleets. As well as a seaplane landing, facilities enabled watering, coaling and minor repairs and the Battle of the Atlantic made Freetown an important assembly point and stopover for shipping bound both north and south. With North Atlantic convoys the focus, the Royal Navy was unable to give heavy protection to ships south of Dakar, leaving Freetown dangerously vulnerable.

After sinking his third victim on 16 November, von Stockhausen exercised his customary compassion and approached the ship to ensure the safety of those who had survived. A narrative of the encounter between the German commander and Captain Hocking, master of the SS *Fabian*, inbound from Liverpool, was later given to the Admiralty for inclusion within intelligence reports.

"The submarine then cruised slowly over to us and someone whom I assumed to be the officer in command, asked if the Captain was there. I replied, 'Yes,' and he asked me in very broken English to come on board.

"He was a fair man of about 35 to 40 years and had a clipped ginger beard of about a month's growth. He was quite a good-looking fellow with round features and blue eyes. . . . He was dressed in a brown shirt, brown shorts, and wore a uniform cap. I saw no decorations and there were no distinguishing marks about him apart from the fact that he gesticulated a lot when talking. The only man on board with any regular uniform was the man who acted as doctor. He was dressed in a navy blue suit and had two gold rings on the sleeves of his coat. . . . The remainder of the crew on board were all dressed alike – in brown shirts and shorts.

"[Stockhausen] asked if we had any injured, and I replied that he had killed six of my men and injured four. He immediately instructed the doctor to bathe and dress the wounded and said that he was sorry he had killed some of my crew and asked if they were married. I said, 'Yes, they're all married, with families,' and he again apologized and asked when I next saw their people to convey his sympathy, adding that he would not have torpedoed our ship but for the fact that we were armed, and it was his duty as there was a war on."

Von Stockhausen then went on to supply the shipwrecked British with water, lemon juice, biscuits, black bread, cigarettes, ham and a side of bacon. After conferring with Hocking regarding the best course for land, checking the Englishmen's compass and handing them a chart of the region, the U-boat commander wished his enemy well and gave Hocking and his surviving crew "the proper German naval salute – none of the Nazi stuff". Finally *U65* pushed away from the lifeboats and sailed from view, her crew waving as she disappeared over the horizon. Hocking and his men were rescued by SS *British Statesman* near midnight on 18 November and taken to Sierra Leone.

Von Stockhausen had been obliged to refuel twice from the disguised German supply ship *Nordmark* sailing near the Cape Verde Islands.[58] Despite the rewarding fact that four of the eight ships sunk had been valuable tankers en route for England, Dönitz was unable to decide if the results warranted three months at sea to achieve them. When added to time spent both in preparation for the patrol and subsequent repair work, the U-boat was occupied for nearly half a year. Dönitz was also displeased that von Stockhausen had failed to keep BdU Operational Staff fully apprised of his progress or lack thereof. SKL held no such reservations, their War Diary recording:

"The area around Freetown is specially profitable for us because there are very few anti-U-boat defences. The results of *U65*'s appearance have got to be of great value."[59]

Dönitz was soon persuaded that the West African theatre held promise, particularly while weather conditions in the North Atlantic were prohibitive. The next time, he decided, he

---

[58] *Nordmark* was on station to support the raider *Admiral Scheer*.
[59] SKL, KTB, 11 January 1941.

would send at least three of the 2nd U-Flotilla's long distance boats. For von Stockhausen there was a Knight's Cross, awarded on 14 January for what was believed to have his total sinking of more than 100,000 tons of shipping (in fact 87,278 tons). After an extended home leave for the commander and most of his crew, von Stockhausen departed the ranks of the 2nd U-Flotilla to begin his new post as commander of the 26th U-training flotilla.[60]

Meanwhile in the Atlantic the Condor aircraft of *Oberst-Leutnant* Harlinghausen's KG40 began flying two reconnaissance missions a day in efforts to make contact with the vanished convoy streams, but to no immediate effect. When on rare occasions the Luftwaffe pilots managed to sight targets, position reports radioed to BdU were often wildly inaccurate. Flying deep into the Atlantic with no fixed references played havoc with precise positioning. Ironically it appeared that U-boats, with their superb navigation, would be working as spotters for the aircraft.

At sea there was little more cause for optimism, a subdued *U105* crew docking in Lorient on 31 January with only two ships confirmed sunk. After reporting to Dönitz, freshly returned from leave, and undergoing the ritual of explaining every move and decision made during his patrol the BdU War Diary noted:

> "This new boat with an experienced Kommandant has completed its first patrol. After contact with the enemy, successes could have been higher."

While *U105* had been at sea two other 2nd U-Flotilla boats had also returned with meagre results due to bad weather conditions. On 22 January both *U38* and *U124* entered Lorient, crews and boats battered by the storms. The former, suffering severe damage from retaliatory depth-charge attacks, claimed two steamers, the latter a single merchant ship, the attack on which nearly destroyed *U124* after a torpedo suffered an internal gyroscopic defect, circling towards the U-boat and missing by a mere "few metres".

While the only 2nd U-Flotilla boats to depart Lorient in January were *U103* on the 21st and *U37* on the 30th, two new Type IXB boats had sailed from Germany, both under experienced officers. Kaptlt. Jürgen Oesten's *U106* and Kaptlt. Günter Hessler's *U107* sailed from Kiel towards the Atlantic and ultimately Lorient. Hessler had previously commanded the *Torpedoboot Falke* for a year beginning March 1939, although *U107* was his first U-boat command. The boat had already received its unofficial *Wappen* – four Aces painted on the conning tower sides, designed by IWO Oblt.z.S. Helmut Witte in honour of Hessler's addiction to poker.

To the west Kaptlt. Karl-Heinz Moehle's newly arrived *U123* ploughed backwards and forwards below Iceland sending the necessary weather reports expected from meteorological duty on behalf of the Luftwaffe after relieving Oesten's *U106*. However, even weather duty produced its dividend and after ten days at sea the diesels began to thrash as Moehle took up the chase of a steamer sighted by his bridge watch. As waves crashed against the conning tower *U123* surged forward until Norwegian SS *Vespasian* was close enough to be torpedoed and sunk. This marked an upturn in *U123*'s fortunes, sailing into the central Atlantic in search of prey. To their west Hessler's *U107* made contact with convoy OB279 bound from Liverpool to North America. Radioing his sighting report, Hessler was given clearance to attack the dispersing convoy immediately, while *U123*

---

[60] On 14 January 1943 Kaptlt. Hans-Gerrit von Stockhausen was hit and killed by a driver in Berlin while crossing the road. This incident has fuelled many "conspiracy theories" that there was more to the mission to Ireland with Frank Ryan and Sean Russell than met the eye – all the major participants dead or dying soon afterwards. There remains no evidence to support these ideas.

U103, *U96* and *U52* were ordered to make all speed to join the hunt. Moehle again threw his engines full ahead as *U123* battered its way toward the convoy. En route he came across and sank a straggler from SC21, but, like the other three boats directed to the action, never made contact with Hessler. Finally Moehle abandoned the attempt and returned eastwards, where he later destroyed two single ships near Rockall before forced home, fuel bunkers worryingly low.

Meanwhile Hessler had already attacked, torpedoed and sunk SS *Empire Citizen*. When night fell after a day spent stalking the scattering ships, *U107* sank SS *Crispin* under close destroyer escort. In the minutes that followed the remaining thirty-seven merchant ships managed to evade the tenacious German and *U107* lost contact, Hessler creeping away from the probing escort. Following *U123*'s hit on the straggler from SC21, Hessler directed his own boat towards the slow convoy, sinking the lagging SS *Maplecourt* on 6 February.

22 January: Amid drifting ice in Bremen the new Type IXC *U67* was commissioned into the 2nd U-Flotilla by Kaptlt. Heinrich 'Ajax' Bleichrodt, former commander of *U48*. *U67* was the second of the new type to be launched and commissioned, Richard Zapp's *U66* preceding Bleichrodt by twenty days. *U67* faced months of work-up before being engaged in trials of a newly developed rubber anti-sonar coating known as *Alberich*.

Alberich comprised textured synthetic rubber (Oppanol) panels, 4mm thick, coating the outer surface of a U-boat, thereby absorbing enemy sonar pulses. Experiments with this material had begun in 1940 when the Type IIB *U11* was used for Baltic trials. Results were somewhat disappointing, a reduction in sonar pulse strength of only 15% recorded when at periscope depth. *U67* was coated in the long metre-wide rubber strips over her conning tower and hull, repainted grey, rendering them unnoticeable to the casual observer. The new research produced no more encouraging result. It was found that the benefit was more than offset by loud vibrations as panels worked themselves free; during the boat's final test cruise from Wilhelmshaven to Lorient in August 1941 *U67* shed 60% of its coating. Adhesion problems halted the idea in its tracks. By this time Bleichrodt had been transferred to command another front-line boat, *U67* being taken over by Kaptlt. Günther Pfeffer, the boat's former IWO, in June.

2 February: Hundreds of workmen from a newly established camp near Hennebont converged on the Kéroman foreland to begin construction of the first U-bunker – Kéroman I. After demolition of the small boat-building and maintenance yards on the requisitioned foreland, work began in earnest. The start of its sister construction, Kéroman II, was scheduled to begin three months later, while elsewhere work on the small two-pen Scorff bunker was done in a matter of months during 1941, officially commissioned into naval service on 6 September. The final construction project of the year took place in Lann-Bihoué, north of Lorient, where a concrete airstrip was laid to allow bombers an airfield closer to the Atlantic U-boats' nerve centre.[61]

Meanwhile there was considerable activity in the dockyard. While *U37* prepared for sea, fitting out for operations off West Africa, the 2nd U-Flotilla suffered a most unexpected casualty. The old and weather-beaten Type IXA *U43* had been tied up at its berth fitting out for sea when it mysteriously sank during the early morning of 4 February.

[61] Between September 1942 and October 1943 the principal occupant of this airbase, known as Kerlin-Bastard, was 5/KG 40 with Ju 88C-6 long-range fighter-bombers for use over the Bay of Biscay.

Flotilla commander KK Fischer demanded to see Lüth, convening a court of enquiry with the full backing of an equally exasperated Dönitz.

The next day, after *U43* had been dragged from the muddy harbour bottom, Lüth and his crew paraded in Lorient's town square. BdU's black Mercedes swept to a halt and Dönitz stalked towards the crew of *U43*, Lüth standing rigidly at their head.

> "You through your own carelessness and neglect have lost a valuable boat. You have betrayed my trust and you have damaged the prospects of our war at sea. . . . There will be no leave and no liberty."[62]

While half of the men remained in Lorient to clean the thick mud from their boat, the remainder were posted to Germany for further training. The court of enquiry decided that the two senior watch officers, Oblt.z.S. Hinrich-Oskar Bernbeck and L.z.S. Erwin Witte, were to be held responsible. Apparently an aft ballast tank vent valve had been mistakenly left open, allowing a gradual seeping of water into the bilges over several hours. To compound this error, the stern torpedo-loading hatch was agape, contrary to standing orders. Thus, as the diesel and electric motor room bilges filled, weighing *U43* down, harbour water gradually crept over the boat's stern, suddenly flooding through the hatchway and sending it to the bottom. Both men were ordered to pay the cost of the three-month refit necessary to get *U43* back into fighting trim (estimated at 80,000RM). To make their disgrace complete Bernbeck was transferred from *U43* to take command of the Type IIA *U4*, the first of a continual string of training posts and administrative positions that stretched to the end of the war. Witte spent a year in Kiel, attached to the 5th U-training Flotilla before being sent to Flensburg where he oversaw the clearing of land destined to be the site of new barracks.

Repairs to the boat lasted five months and included the installation of new electric motors, although the banks of flooded batteries were not replaced, never again able to hold a complete charge.

8 February: In mid-Atlantic *U37* became embroiled in a prototypical event. Kaptlt. Nicolai Clausen had taken his boat from Lorient on 30 January bound for the south-central Atlantic. Eight days after leaving France Clausen galvanized BdU operations staff, reporting a convoy steaming north from Gibraltar. A BETASOM boat had initially found HG53, the Italian guiding Clausen toward it. Ordered to shadow the merchant ships, escorted by a woefully inadequate single destroyer and sloop, Clausen kept regular beacon signals flowing while awaiting permission to attack. His long-wave signals were not summoning U-boats to gather but instead KG40 Condors from the Bordeaux-Mérignac airbase.

He was soon cleared for combat. Approaching at speed in early morning darkness, *U37*'s IWO, L.z.S. Hans-Günther Kuhlmann, crouched behind the UZO on the boat's bridge and fired a spread of torpedoes, hitting and sinking what were believed to be three steamers, but in fact two. *U37* sped away from the escorts and later that day five Condors homed on the beacon and at the limit of their range launched their own attack, sinking five of the remaining eighteen ships. A single FW 200 aircraft was badly hit, damaged by accurate anti-aircraft fire raking the aircraft's belly and its vulnerable fuel lines, limping away to crash-land in Spain.

This was the first successful joint U-boat and aircraft operation, although Dönitz sensed even greater possibilities. Contacting OKM, Dönitz urged for the nearby cruiser *Admiral*

---

[62] *U-Boat Ace*, Jordan Vause, pp 84–85.

Hipper to divert towards *U37*'s signal. Despite initial reservations. OKM agreed and *Hipper* was ordered at all speed to engage HG53 as it ran north-east. The cruiser had already sunk seven ships, adding an eighth after catching a straggler from HG53 before having to turn away to Brest for engine maintenance. Dönitz was delighted with the landmark action, writing later:

> "The operation merits description because of its somewhat exceptional character. . . . This was the only combined air, surface ship and U-boat operation that ever took place in the Atlantic."[63]

Clausen had sunk another as well and, having expended all his torpedoes, began his return to Lorient, all thoughts of West Africa now erased.

Despite this success, the generally poor results obtained during the first months of 1941 began to worry Dönitz. He felt that the atrocious weather could be held accountable for such failures to only a certain degree, he and his staff beginning to wonder whether improved Allied direction-finding had allowed the British to re-route their convoys north of U-boat operational areas. While frequent radio signals of status, sightings and positions were essential to the very nature of coordinated attacks managed from distant Kernével, Dönitz took moves to limit unnecessary communications, gradually realizing how badly Germany had underestimated British advances in radio direction-finding.

10 February: Kaptlt. Jürgen Oesten brought *U106* into Lorient from its first operational voyage, the meagre showing of two victories fully illustrating Dönitz's concern, although the sinking of the large British liner MV *Zealandic* provided some consolation. The U-boat would spend little more than two weeks in France, much of it in Brest's spacious dry dock alongside *U124*, before it was ready to put to sea once more.

Kaptlt. Viktor Schütze made the most successful February return when *U103* docked in Lorient two weeks later. Schütze entered harbour having destroyed four confirmed ships for a total of 33,464 tons, nearly two-thirds of this figure coming from two straggling tankers of the Halifax convoy HX106, sunk off Iceland.

Elsewhere in Germany operational departures and training were severely hampered by weather conditions. A lack of minesweepers in home waters caused frequent delays to scheduled departures while thick Baltic ice damaged boats in training, forcing sporadic suspension of exercises. There were also the omnipresent accident statistics to add delay to the process. *U109*, commissioned on 5 December 1940 and still in training before scheduled transfer to 2nd U-Flotilla, was rammed during appalling visibility by the aged torpedo boat *T156* acting as both target ship and escort. Although the crew were unscathed, both periscopes had been sheared off and the boat consigned to repair yards.

4 March: The three boats of Dönitz's renewed offensive against Freetown convoy traffic had already sailed south for the Canary Islands. Between 4 and 6 March *U124*, *U105* and *U106* entered harbour individually at Las Palmas to refuel without hitch from German tanker *Corrientes* (*Culebra*), the Royal Navy conspicuous by their absence.

Schulz's 'Edelweiss boat', *U124*, soon made contact with the battleships *Scharnhorst* and *Gneisenau*, preparing to wreak havoc among central Atlantic convoy traffic. IIWO Henke spotted them, at first only distant unrecognizable shapes. Originally taken as British, Schulz harboured doubts that a pair of British battleships or cruisers would operate there without

---

[63] *Memoirs*, Dönitz, p. 141.

destroyer escort. Nevertheless *U124* prepared to attack while Schulz radioed BdU for notification of any German warships within the region. As Schulz made ready to fire, both targets abruptly began to zigzag, informed by SKL that a U-boat was stalking them following a rushed telephone call from Dönitz. Schulz and his crew stood down, later running alongside *Gneisenau* to exchange greetings.

It wasn't long before the ships' catapult aircraft sighted northbound convoy SL67, escorted by the battleship HMS *Malaya*. Hitler's paranoid standing orders forbade capital ships from engaging similar opposing vessels, thus *Gneisenau* alerted Schulz to the convoy's presence. An ambitious plan was devised whereby the West African U-boats would approach SL67 and try to torpedo *Malaya*, as well as any other targets of convenience, enabling the German ships to attack the remaining inferior escort and its precious charge. Only *U105* and *U124* were near enough to partake in the plan, the tardy *U106* considered well-placed further north to intercept any ships that may slip away from the combined assault.

The assault began under calm equatorial early morning darkness when Georg Schewe in *U105* torpedoed and sank SS *Harmodius* with its cargo of pig-iron, his only success against SL67. Schulz took *U124* unobserved into the heart of the convoy, firing all six tubes at various targets, claiming five sunk and a sixth 'heavily damaged and in a sinking condition' as he withdrew to reload. In fact four British freighters had gone down after his twenty-one minute assault. Kaptlt. Oesten's *U106* also found a straggler, sinking SS *Memnon* and raising the British casualty list higher.

Although the U-boats could fairly claim a triumph, they had failed to hit the prime target, HMS *Malaya*, and, with the large surface threat still intact, *Scharnhorst* and *Gneisenau* withdrew. The resulting analysis of this operation and the previous success of cooperation between *U37* and the *Admiral Hipper* led to meetings between Dönitz and the C-in-C Fleet during April to discuss possible future U-boat operations in support of battleships. The discussions, while deemed worthwhile, came at a time that in hindsight marks the beginning of the decline of German surface operations.

The submarine onslaught in West African waters continued when Oesten sighted north-bound SL68 on 11 March, summoning support from *U105*. The ensuing nights of carnage saw both U-boats claim the combined sinking of nine ships with another damaged (in fact sinking six). As well as the claimed freighters sunk in bad light on the night of 19/20 March, Oesten had also hit HMS *Malaya*, again on escort duty and herself lacking destroyer escort.

> "I was well aware that I had hit the *Malaya* as she played hell, firing star shells all over the horizon, disbanding the convoy. [But] my torpedoes were used, so I could not do anything more."[64]

The battleship was severely damaged and forced to limp across the Atlantic, first to Trinidad and then onwards to the United States for repairs, out of action for months. This, combined with a claimed total of over 80,000 tons of enemy shipping (a confirmed total of twelve ships for 58,723 tons), convinced Dönitz to award the Knight's Cross to Oesten via radio.

10 March: Dr Fritz Todt conferred again with Dönitz in Lorient about the progress of submarine pen construction. Only the previous day RAF's Bomber Command had

---

[64] Correspondence with Jürgen Oesten, 15 June 2002.

received a directive to lay emphasis of future bombing attacks against both the U-boat and Focke Wulf menace. However, Dönitz was concerned that facilities for refitting and repair could soon be overburdened.

"In addition to previous plans shelter berths are to be built in La Pallice . . . necessary because in the course of the summer the repair facilities in Saint Nazaire, Lorient and Brest will be absolutely exhausted. . . . I propose the fullest possible development of Lorient which according to experts has a capacity of thirty boats, Brest and Saint Nazaire twenty each."

Also, the deeply disturbing problem of torpedo failure again required investigation. *U37* reported nine unexplained failures over two days and *U107* three failures and one 'surface runner' during February. On 23 March Lemp added his weight to the escalating series of torpedo complaints. *U110* on its inaugural patrol had suffered repeated misses and 'surface runners' while heavily engaged against convoy HX112. Furious at his lack of success, Lemp was losing faith in his torpedoes. However, the cause of failure may have been error rather than faulty equipment. With the severe icing of the Baltic, *U110* had had no opportunity to practice either torpedo firing, pack tactics or gunnery, the crew as a whole neither cohesive nor well practiced. Despite this more prosaic reasoning, Lemp continued to believe that faulty weaponry denied him success.

Meanwhile, as he continued to shadow HX112, reinforcements pounded towards the battle. Flotilla-mate *U37* led the way, followed by the 7th U-Flotilla 'Aces' Schepke in *U100* and Kretschmer in *U99*, Lemp losing contact at about the same time as *U37* gained it. In his original report Lemp had estimated escort strength at two destroyers, Clausen aboard *U37* dismayed to find that Escort Group 5 comprised instead five destroyers and two corvettes.

Clausen tried an immediate surface attack amid random Allied star shells, but was detected by HMS *Walker* and rammed and depth-charged while attempting to dive. The destroyer's bow knifed through the conning tower destroying the periscope and Clausen was forced home to Kiel where the boat was scheduled for retirement. A battered though defiant *U37* entered harbour on 22 March for months of repair before relocating to the 26th U-training Flotilla, Clausen transferring to *U129*.

In the meantime Lemp failed to regain the initiative and *U110* was forced away to seek new targets. However, the ramifications of that convoy engagement would touch the entire U-boat service. In the course of that disastrous night both *U99* and *U100* were lost. Combined with the surmised disappearance of Günther Prien's *U47* some time after 7 March, the U-boat service's three leading commanders were suddenly gone.

The unexpected loss of these three 'Aces' in the Western Approaches, along with two other U-boats within the same fortnight, prompted Dönitz to take a step that can be acknowledged as the first Atlantic defeat for the U-boats. With an operational force of only twenty-seven seaworthy ocean-going boats, Dönitz decided to withdraw from the Western Approaches – the focus thus far of the convoy war. His boats were diverted north towards Iceland and south to the West African coast.

Lemp continued his patrol, stalking the waters west of Iceland. On 23 March he sighted a lone Norwegian freighter, tracking the ship before launching three single attacks, all of which missed. The normally composed commander was furious and immediately ordered the gun crew to prepare for surface action. As shells were passed up through the narrow conning tower the gun was laid on target and fired. Again the lack of Baltic training harvested a heavy price as the barrel exploded, watertight tampion still in place.

Miraculously, only three men suffered light injury, but shrapnel and pieces of steel had cut through the ballast and fuel tanks, causing severe damage and a thick oil slick. As the Norwegian steamer disappeared over the horizon Lemp ordered course set for Lorient. The holed trunking that ran through the boat's ballast tanks was patched as best as possible, helped by the fortunate onboard presence of a UAA (Submarine Acceptance Command) engineer, Ulrich Kruse, along for the experience.

1 April: Schütze's *U103* left Lorient, immediately re-entering harbour with recalcitrant diesels, forty-eight hours in dock sufficient to remedy the problem. When Schütze sailed again he did so alongside *U108* and the 7th U-Flotilla's *U52*.

Hundreds of miles away, his three flotilla mates who comprised the Sierra Leone task force, *U105*, *U106* and *U124*, all lay east of the 20°W meridian in wait for convoy traffic. Both Schewe's *U105* and Oesten's *U106* lay close inshore in grid square ET25, while *U124* cruised to the south-east. Schewe had rendezvoused with the raider *Schiff 41/Kormoran*, the largest of all German raiders, towards the month's end to transfer metal required for repair aboard the warship and taking torpedoes in return. Fuel was later provided for both Schewe and Oesten's *U106* by *Nordmark* on 29 March. *U124* had also rendezvoused with *Kormoran*, this time to transfer *Maschinenmaat* Toni Walbröl aboard for urgent surgery. Walbröl, a veteran of *U64*, had suffered an infected arm before sailing from Lorient but kept it secret lest he be confined to hospital and unable to sail with his boat. In weeks he was reduced to delirium and he and *U124*'s medical officer, MstA Dr Hubertus Goder, were taken on board the raider by dinghy. A replacement for Walbröl, *Obermaschinenmaat* Ackermann, was taken aboard as well as fuel and six torpedoes before the boat departed following Goder's return.

However, Dönitz's hope of a concentrated and sustained assault on West African commerce was dashed on 5 April when SKL requested two U-boats be sent to Rio as cover for the German minelayer *Lech*, lying in harbour loaded with valuable supplies for the Wehrmacht war machine. Dönitz had no choice but to comply, although he recorded that the task was "difficult and not certain to be successful". Both Schewe and Oesten were ordered to refuel from *Nordmark* and proceed south-west to South America.

On 11 April Schütze arrived in the region aboard *U103* and reported numerous small coasters and fishing vessels along the West African coast, hinting at heavily travelled shipping lanes ahead. Sure enough, as his two companions traversed the equatorial Atlantic, Schulz's *U124* soon reported heavy merchant traffic west of Freetown.

By 13 April *U105* and *U106* lay in the tropical heat east of Rio. They were expected to wait for a further two weeks before *Lech* began its clandestine sailing, the large ship employing every means at its disposal to prevent watching Allied agents reporting its departure. SKL also hinted that the two U-boats should stay well clear of the coastline, but be prepared for operations against merchant shipping escorted by increasingly hostile 'neutral' American ships if the German government lifted restrictions on attacks within the American neutrality zone. For twenty-four hours they waited in tense inactivity for confirmation of the ban being lifted, deflated when SKL informed Dönitz and he ordered only Oesten's *U106* to remain on station while Schewe returned to what was becoming a burgeoning battle off Freetown. An irritated entry by Dönitz recorded:

"[Oesten could not engage shipping] apparently because of fuel and lubricating oil [shortage]. The whole operation has miscarried. . . . This means a useless period of waiting for the boats, which they could have spent more profitably in the operational area off Freetown. In addition they cannot be given freedom to attack enemy ships outside the scope of their escort duty for *Lech*, although originally assurances were received from SKL that this would be allowed.

"They have therefore not only been withdrawn from a good area for several weeks, but they will have been a total loss to the war against merchant shipping during this time and their long passage will make demands on their engines which will eventually mean a longer period repairing when they return."

Meanwhile Schulz's *U124* was also forced to withdraw, out of torpedoes and left with only enough fuel for a return voyage to Lorient beginning on 14 April. Schulz had also passed over spare quartz crystals, disguised in a cigar box, to the cruiser *Admiral Scheer*, IIWO Werner Henke's old ship, for its radio gear, receiving fresh bread and thousands of fresh eggs captured by *Scheer* from the refrigerator ship *Duquesa* in return. After departing from *Scheer*, *U124* faced disaster as she suffered a complete failure in both engines, leaving her drifting and helpless near the African coast for hours as frenetic machinists made their repairs. A Highland class passenger liner flashed by at high speed while Schulz waited furiously. Eight bearings had been destroyed within the two engines and, with not enough spares aboard, compacted foil from cigarette packets were used as replacements by the resourceful LI ObH. (Ing.) Rolf Brinker.

Schulz had sunk a further six ships during the voyage thus far, by BdU reckoning putting him over the 100,000-ton mark and prompting Dönitz to award him the Knight's Cross on 4 April. Well aware of the skill and ingenuity of his LI, Schulz also recommended Brinker for the Knight's Cross; instead he was awarded the German Cross in Gold, the first man of the 2nd U-Flotilla and fourth of the entire navy to receive this decoration.

An episode from Schulz's patrol illustrates the enigmatic sense of inhumanity and humanity that marks submarine warfare. On 8 April *U124* sank its eighth ship of the patrol, British SS *Tweed*. At 1225hrs Schulz hit her in a submerged attack with a single torpedo, blowing the rudder off and holing her badly. *Tweed* immediately careered out of control, so much so that Schulz thought that she was a Q-ship intent on ramming *U124*. Diving deep at full speed, he waited for the seemingly inevitable impact, only to be rewarded with the sound of creaking bulkheads replacing that of the steady rhythmic thump of the steamer's screws. The U-boat slowed for a full hydrophone sweep that failed to show any trace of the attacker. Rising silently to periscope depth Schulz swept the horizon and saw only three small lifeboats.

U124 surfaced and approached. Two of the lifeboats had overturned following their rapid launch and *U124*'s crew pulled the men from the water, righting their boats and passing supplies to the British seamen. After interrogating the survivors, Schulz learned that the ship had gone under in less than four minutes as *U124* had been trying to escape attack. Several of *Tweed*'s crew were injured, including a man with a broken leg and dislocated shoulder. While lookouts scoured the sea and sky for enemies the wounded were laid beneath the blistering sun on the U-boat's wooden deck where Dr. Goder administered first aid, resetting the shoulder and splinting the smashed leg of the most severely injured. Returning them to their lifeboats, now fully provisioned and rigged with sails, *U124* left the scene.

While Schulz sailed homewards it wasn't until the end of April that Oesten radioed his successful rendezvous with *Lech*, finding the steamer in grid square GB38, the furthest west that any U-boat had so far ventured. The successful escort of this minelaying blockade-runner from Rio prompted SKL to request that *U106* then be diverted to escort the blockade-runner *Windhuk* from Santos, Brazil, a task soon called off when *Windhuk*'s sailing was delayed for an indefinite period.[65]

1 May: *U124* entered Lorient harbour to an enthusiastic dockside reception, pennants flying and several oil-stained life rings tied to the conning tower. Schulz was welcomed by Dönitz, accompanied, among others, by Eberhardt Godt and Heinz Fischer. Schulz, wearing his distinctive side cap and light grey tunic, received his *Ritterkreuz*, the new decoration replacing the version fashioned by his engineering crew off West Africa. The following day *U108* also returned, a single sinking of Armed Merchant Cruiser HMS *Rajputana* to its credit, the auxiliary warship torpedoed in the Denmark Strait.

By May four boats were stationed off West Africa, *U105*, *U107*, *U38* and *U103* astride the Freetown shipping lanes. Results were spectacular. Merchant vessels still sailing unescorted were sunk by the prowling U-boats as British naval power, thinly stretched across the Atlantic, struggled to provide any form of cohesive protection. While the attackers divided into two groups they alternated between closing the West African coast and replenishing from the tankers *Nordmark* and *Egerland*, allowing extended patrols in the unremitting heat.

While all four boats achieved great success, Hessler's *U107* made by far the most impressive patrol. Hessler sank fourteen ships for a total of 86,699 confirmed tons (claimed as 90,793 tons), the most successful single patrol of the Second World War. While this put him well above the 100,000 tons necessary for the award of a Knight's Cross, his decoration was delayed by Dönitz's discomfort at awarding the medal to his son-in-law, which he felt could be misconstrued as nepotism. It was not until Raeder himself intervened, saying that if Dönitz did not grant the award then he would, that Hessler received radio confirmation of his receipt of the Knight's Cross on 24 June while the boat was returning to Lorient. By that time tragedy had overcome the supply tanker network that had kept the West African boats at sea for patrols of nearly four months. Not only had eight of the nine tankers been intercepted and sunk, but the huge battleship that they had been originally designed to support had also paid the ultimate price.

The mightiest of all German battleships, *Bismarck*, had sailed alongside heavy cruiser *Prinz Eugen* from Gotenhafen on 18 May to begin a raiding voyage into the Atlantic. After the sinking of HMS *Hood*, *Bismarck* received a direct hit on her bow causing a large and revealing oil leak, doggedly trailed by ships intent on her destruction. *Bismarck* soon suffered another debilitating hit in her steering mechanism from Swordfish torpedo bombers, leaving her unmanoeuvrable and vulnerable while *Prinz Eugen* dashed for the comparative safety of Brest.

There were two new 2nd U-Flotilla boats at sea in the North Atlantic when *Bismarck* was disabled, *U109* and *U111*, with a third, *U108*, sailing from Lorient on 25 May. Kaptlt. Hans-Georg Fischer's *U109* was embarking on its first war patrol and one in which it had already narrowly cheated death several times. Fischer had proved reckless in his thirst for action, the boat narrowly missed by bombs while running surfaced for the Atlantic.

In the North Atlantic the weather worsened as towering waves battered the conning tower, but the patrol had been relatively uneventful until, on 19 May, *U94* of the 7th U-Flotilla sighted convoy HX126 and began to shadow, *U109* among the boats vectored to intercept. Fischer drove his boat onward until at 1600hrs the following day smoke was

---

[65] On 28 May, after *U106* had left the blockade runner, *Lech* was surprised and forced to scuttle by Royal Navy ships.

sighted on the horizon. After thirty minutes of pursuit the watch came tumbling through the conning tower hatch after destroyers emerged from a squall to starboard, *U109* plummeting downward as the inept Chief Engineer *Leutnant* (Ing.) Martin Weber struggled to maintain trim.[66] A perfunctory depth-charge salvo rattled the crew but inflicted no damage. Fischer was not to be dissuaded, however, and after surfacing and racing along a planned intercept course *U109* was positioned ahead of the steamer and submerged at 2230hrs to attack. Within an hour two torpedoes sped from the bow tubes and SS *Marconi* exploded, going under with forty-one of her eighty passengers and crew.

Following the distant sound of other boats attacking the main convoy, Fischer surfaced and battled through a long heavy swell, blundering headlong into two of HX126's destroyer escorts. As Fischer shouted for a crash dive a third destroyer was heard by *Oberfunkmaat* (Senior Petty Officer) Wolfgang Hirschfeld in the hydrophone cabin and *U109* again plummeted below.

Propellers of a fourth and then fifth destroyer were detected, Fischer shouting at Hirschfeld to stop feeding him 'rubbish'. But soon all aboard could hear the telltale screws as their attackers closed in. Depth charges hammered the boat from above, but again failed to inflict a crippling blow. In courageous desperation Fischer ordered the boat semi-surfaced, so that the conning tower was clear of the water, before climbing up alone to observe through the darkness what their chances of escape were. He quietly confirmed that there were indeed five destroyers ringing the boat and, remaining alone on the bridge, conned his boat silently through the cordon of steel to safety.

As dawn crept into the sky *U109* surfaced fully and continued the convoy chase. IIWO L.z.S. Keller warned Fischer that they were dangerously exposed, but Fischer ignored the advice until two destroyers were sighted and again forced a hurried dive, *U109* suddenly illuminated by flames from an exploding tanker. This time there was no 'easy' escape. ASDIC impulses scoured the steel hull as *U109* was punished for its temerity with rigorous depth-charging. The world inside *U109* turned upside down. She was flung wildly about while the main lighting flickered and died, water jetting inside the pressure hull through the starboard propeller shaft seals, diesel exhaust caps and one of the two stern tubes. The boat gradually flooded as Fischer again attempted to creep away.

Filling with water, *U109* was in serious trouble and Fischer had no alternative but to allow the main bilge pump used to keep them afloat. The pump's noise seemed deafening and heralded fresh attacks almost immediately. Explosions smashed the hull and the pumps were silenced as Dräger escape gear was handed out and the crew prepared for a long, gruelling wait.

Hours later destroyers continued to circle above, sporadically dropping charges as the water rose within *U109*. Men lay in a stupor of oxygen starvation, mental exhaustion and fatigue while the propeller gave barely enough revolutions to stay buoyant. It was nearly sixteen hours later that *Maschinenmaat* Kaufmann in the bow compartment discovered that the boat had sunk to a depth in excess of 280 metres. At first the control room, whose depth gauge registered only 70 metres, refused to believe him until confirmation came from the stern gauge. Lt (Ing.) Weber panicked, immediately tilting hydroplanes sharply upwards and throwing both motors on full ahead. *U109*'s bow rose almost to the vertical and water streamed to the stern which dropped to nearly 300 metres, a sudden fire in the electric motor room adding to the confusion. Weber gave up in despair after attempting to blow the stern tanks and it was *Obermaat* Otto Peters who, on his own initiative, blasted

---

[66] See also Lawrence Paterson, *First U-Boat Flotilla*, p. 39.

what little compressed air remained into the bow ballast tanks. Slowly *U109* began to rise to the surface.

Now she was in an uncontrollable ascent, lancing upwards and breaching like a whale before falling back into the sea with a tremendous crash. The boat's interior was in chaos as Fischer ordered *U109* abandoned, expecting any second to come under fire from the British and be rammed. Documents were destroyed and men raced for the outside with their lifejackets ready. As they reached the conning tower and freedom they were surprised by what they saw; the sea was empty, their enemy had gone.

In this crippled state *U109* began to slog its way home to Lorient when messages concerning *Bismarck*'s predicament arrived. After radioing the battleship's plight Dönitz followed with a message to any Biscay boats still carrying torpedoes to go to the aid of the crippled giant. Fischer, despite protests from his LI, ordered *U109* out to sea again in a futile attempt at helping *Bismarck*. Despite sighting destroyers and aircraft in the driving rain and tumbling seas, *U109* could do nothing for her and *Bismarck* radioed her last message on 27 May as she went under, pummelled by British shellfire.

U109 re-entered French coastal waters two days later. But her woes were not over. As Fischer followed his *Vorpostenboot* escort into Lorient harbour *Bootsmann* Walter Gross on watch duty reported an English periscope to starboard at a range of only 100 metres. With no other confirmation, Fischer decided not to report the incident. Within half an hour *U74* following behind and carrying survivors from *Bismarck* reported itself narrowly missed by a spread of English torpedoes. It was the final blot on Fischer's combat record.

Later that day the crew of *U109* paraded before Dönitz who addressed them in no uncertain terms:

> "Your patrol was shit. You know that. And when you go deep, there's no need to break the world record. Your 7,000 tons wasn't much. You'll have to do better. But at least you brought the boat back, I suppose that's worth something."[67]

After his brief speech he awarded Fischer an EKII before listening to the young commander's report. It was the end of Fischer's U-boat career. While Otto Peters received a richly deserved EKI for saving the boat from destruction, Fischer was relieved of his command. The BdU War Diary recorded that:

> "The general impression made by the commander was one of uncertainty and worry. The boat sank to a great depth during a depth charge hunt and was only just saved by the presence of mind of an experienced Petty officer who blew tanks of his own accord. . . . There were already considerable doubts about the suitability of this commander during his training. . . . I have therefore found it necessary to relieve him at once."

In his place arrived Kaplt Heinrich 'Ajax' Bleichrodt, Knight's Cross holder and veteran of the celebrated *U48*, fresh from six months in command of *U67*.

The second of the new flotilla boats to have been caught up in the *Bismarck* tragedy was *U111* on its maiden war patrol. Commissioned on 19 December 1940, *U111* had been one of those whose training had been severely hampered by Baltic ice and the commander, 34-year-old Kaptlt. Wilhelm Kleinschmidt, while a calm and careful man, was considered by his crew 'too old' for U-boat command.

After passing north of the Faeroes surfaced by night and submerged by day, *U111*

---

[67] *Hirschfeld: The Secret Diary of a U-boat*, Wolfgang Hirschfeld p. 54.

entered the North Atlantic and found and sank its first victim after eight days at sea, SS *Somersby* straggling from SC30 sent under with two torpedoes. Kleinschmidt then became involved in the battle for convoy HX126, homing on *U94*'s contact reports, hitting SS *Cockaponset*, leaving it floundering and burning. Although claimed as a probable, the ship broke and sank after *U111* had departed the scene. A third solo sailing ship was added to *U111*'s victories two days later east of Cape Farewell after which the boat was detailed to transmit dummy radio traffic, disguising the paucity of U-boats at sea.

It was on 24 May that *U111* and six other boats received orders to form a patrol line as *Bismarck* attempted to draw its pursuit across it, but to no avail. Following the final message from the doomed ship *U111* searched for survivors, but found nothing but men lashed to small rafts and killed by exposure, floating amongst a sea of empty liferings.

On 25 May *U111* refuelled from the tanker *Belchen* before joining the fifteen-boat *West* group, encountering only heavy seas, rain and freezing fog. Pack ice proved a further hazard as miserable lookouts attempted to keep the boat away from the silent danger. Kleinschmidt had been ordered to explore the waters around Newfoundland in an effort to detect the elusive Halifax convoys. This marked the first U-boat incursion into Canadian waters and Kleinschmidt recorded in his boat's KTB how unprepared for the venture he was. To his dismay he discovered that he had not a single nautical chart, List of Light Signals or Sailing Directions for Canadian or American waters. Instead he was forced to rely on the G1870 large scale (1:8,000,000) Kriegsmarine grid chart for his navigation. Further operational handicaps due to his boat being so close to the United States were direct and explicit warnings relayed from Hitler not to shoot at anything except "especially valuable ships" that could be identified beyond any doubt. It transpired to be an unnecessary order. An iceberg, nearly invisible against the grey horizon, nudged the boat, knocking two torpedo doors off and Kleinschmidt withdrew to the east, reporting to Lorient the absence of sightings and his damage. The lack of traffic near Newfoundland solved Dönitz's question as to whether Allied merchant traffic had routed close to the North Canadian coast or the Belle Isle Strait. *U111* was then directed by combined contact reports from KG40 Condors and the newly sailed *U108* towards convoy OG66 south-west of Ireland, again to no avail as the boat cruised through thick swirling fog. In a two-week period during June Kleinschmidt reported only 100 hours of decent visibility.

On 7 July *U111* docked in Lorient where the boat was placed in dry dock. While the crew received leave in either Carnac or Germany four upper-deck torpedo-storage canisters damaged by the storms were replaced. The chilling discovery of a sack filled with sand dumped inside one of the boat's diving tanks raised the ugly spectre of sabotage, all the more disturbing because it had originated in Germany.

12 May: The 2nd U-Flotilla received a new Type IXC commissioned directly into the flotilla. Kaptlt. Ulrich Heyse's *U128* transferred from Bremen's AG Weser yard to the Kriegsmarine, forty-eight hours later proceeding east to Kiel to begin trials for the U-boat Acceptance command. Heyse was regarded by his crew as an extremely competent and approachable man, on occasion sitting down with ratings on kitchen detail, whipping out his pocketknife and, while peeling potatoes, discussing any subject that interested them. But his first foreign journey as commander was fraught with problems. Proceeding surfaced at slow speed toward Oslofjord, Norway, *U128* ran aground on uncharted rocks, ripping the hull open. Unable to free herself, help was summoned from Horten, and after two uncomfortable days the depot-ship *Odin* and two steam tugs, assisted by the light cruiser *Nürnburg*, successfully released the trapped boat. After five days of local repair *U128* put to sea again to return to Kiel for extensive renovation within *Deutschewerke* shipyards.

17 May: "*U65* ordered to give weather report. Again no reply. There is grave concern."

The veteran boat had left Lorient with its new commander, Kaptlt. Joachim-Hoppe, the former IWO, on 12 April bound for the Atlantic. Less than a week after putting to sea Hoppe had been ordered to join four other boats south of Iceland where, on 28 April, Kaptlt. Heinz Moehle aboard *U123* sighted eastbound HX121 and summoned his comrades with homing signals. *U65* raced to the scene but was swiftly located by the escort destroyer HMS *Douglas* which dropped a devastatingly accurate depth-charge pattern. There were no survivors.

For his part, Moehle had no luck in attack. Although the convoy would eventually lose four ships, *U123* was kept at bay by effective escort work. He returned to Lorient on 11 May with only the sinking of Swedish SS *Venezuela* to his credit. It was his final patrol. Dönitz, judging by Moehle's poor performance that he was suffering from 'health problems', relieved him of his command, transferring him as Senior Officer to the 5th U-training Flotilla and Kiel's U-boat base. His replacement aboard *U123* was Reinhard Hardegen, former IWO aboard *U124*.

Meanwhile another 2nd U-Flotilla boat had been sunk, one that would have far-reaching consequences for the U-boat war. Kaptlt. Friz-Julius Lemp had left Lorient aboard *U110* at 1932hrs on 15 April, the customary brass band playing while well-wishers waved the crew from harbour. Aboard was an extra passenger, L.z.S. (temporary) Helmut Ecke of the naval branch of the *Propaganda Kompanie*. The western-based naval PK service, commanded by KK Karl Hinsch, frequently assigned war correspondents to the U-boats, wreathed in the glamour of an elite service. The officer directly commanding those correspondents was noted journalist Wolfgang Frank, now famous for his books on the U-boat war in general and Günther Prien in particular. Ecke had taken part in both the invasions of Poland and France attached to Panzer units, racing around on a motorcycle before transferring to the naval branch in late 1940. After being attached to *Vorpostenboote* based in Boulogne he volunteered for service at Lorient, becoming one of fourteen permanently stationed PK men under the command of Herbert Kuehn. Lemp was no stranger to reporters and apparently Ecke melded well with boat and crew, even taking part in watch duties, although not officially a crew member.

Lemp cruised west of Ireland, sinking a single ship before days of inactivity in rolling Atlantic swells. But aircraft reports of "fifty ships and fifteen destroyers" forming near the Hebrides and *U94*'s sighting of OB318 south-west of Iceland invigorated Lemp's crew. Two days later aircraft forced *U110* under while a destroyer prowled on the edge of periscope visibility before Lemp was finally rewarded with convoy smoke on the port bow at 1815hrs. In increasingly bad weather *U110* surfaced to close the gap, dissuaded from attacking immediately by bright moonlight.

Soon Oblt.z.S. Adalbert Schnee's 1st U-Flotilla *U201* joined *U110*, the two commanders conferring by megaphone. They agreed that Lemp would attack first before separating, *U201* submerging immediately. Lemp's *Obersteuermann* urged him to delay, feeling that the escort was due to depart at the limit of their range. But Lemp ordered tubes made ready and at 1237hrs *U110* dived to begin its final approach. At his periscope in the conning tower Lemp selected three targets, unleashing a torpedo for each, two steamers soon hit and burning, a third erroneously also believed to be sinking. Choosing what appeared to be a 15,000-ton whale factory ship as his fourth target Lemp ordered the last bow tube fired, but the torpedo suffered a misfire, provoking a brief argument between the LI Hans-Joachim Eichelborn and IWO Dietrich Löwe, Lemp's cousin but a man disliked by the crew as overbearing and arrogant. It was during this confusion that the startled commander swung his periscope to starboard and saw the bow wave of a destroyer thundering directly for them. HMS *Aubretia* had detected by hydrophone the torpedoes before they impacted, making brief contact with *U110* before sighting and bearing down on the small attack periscope only 800 yards away.

Lemp immediately bellowed for the boat to dive. Caught shallow by the sudden attack, *U110* was bracketed by a salvo of six well-placed depth charges. The concussion flung men to the deck as *U110* clawed its way under, main lights flickering and dying, replaced by the glow of emergency lighting as the DC current auxiliary circuit kicked in. Dials and gauges had been smashed and the boat continued to drop, Lemp himself with a thin trickle of blood running down his face after smashing his forehead into the steel decking.

Two other destroyers, HMS *Bulldog* and *Broadway*, raced to the scene and added their own depth charges to the attack. As water gushed through multiple fractures, the stern began to sink lower. Survivors reported hydroplanes and rudder inoperative, electric motors out of commission and chlorine gas beginning to seep from seawater entering cracked battery cells. The wheels controlling the high-pressure air for blowing tanks were sheared off and lay on the disarrayed decking.

There was no reliable way of telling how deep the boat had sunk, but Lemp knew that there was no option but to surface as the single unreliable gauge that remained intact showed the boat at 95 metres and sinking. As he ordered all tanks emergency blown and the crew to abandon ship a sudden and distinctive rocking motion betrayed the fact that the boat had already surfaced, either blown upwards by the final depth-charge blasts or surfacing after damage to the pressurised air distribution panel. Lemp rushed to the bridge and was confronted with the chilling sight of *Broadway* and *Bulldog* charging at full ramming speed while the remaining destroyers opened fire with all available weapons. Lemp yelled for Eichelborn to open the vents. Meanwhile the crew raced for the outside, radio operator Georg Högel and his small team neglecting to destroy the Enigma or its precious code books in their haste to escape. PK man Ecke also raced for the open air, leaving his cameras behind in the shambles. HMS *Bulldog*'s captain, Commander A.J. Baker-Cresswell, seeing men beginning to jump from the U-boat and noticing that *U110*, although down by the stern, did not appear to be sinking, ordered all attacks broken off and a boarding party made ready. *Broadway*'s commander also realized the chance of getting aboard and cancelled the ramming, although his destroyer brushed past the U-boat, snagging the bow hydroplane and dropping two shallow set depth charges in order to frighten the Germans and hasten their departure. It appeared to have the desired effect and the water was soon full of struggling sailors as the U-boat wallowed abandoned.

What happened next remains unclear to this day. Lemp had remained on the boat's bridge until all his men were clear before throwing himself into the water. Both the IWO and LI recorded him as asking after the junior Watch Officer who had recently recovered from a prolonged period of illness. Löwe said that he and Lemp both saw the tower of the boat lift high out of the water, obviously not sinking. Lemp apparently shouted that he was returning to the U-boat to open the vents or set off demolition charges when he was shot by a British sailor as the boarding party rowed for *U110*, Ecke also remembering being shot at in the water by British sailors. Other accounts of the event say that Lemp, realizing the disaster unfolding before him, raised his hands in the air and allowed himself to drown, possibly also suffering mild concussion as a result of the blow to his head.

Interestingly, twenty-year-old Sub-Lieutenant David E. Balme who led the British boarding party wrote years later in answer to the frequent speculation:

> "Neither I nor any of my party saw or shot Kaptlt. Lemp. No shots were fired by the boarding party. . . . The feeling of *U110* prisoners who were interrogated in *Bulldog* was that Lemp committed suicide in the water."[68]
>
> "I have always thought that Lemp committed suicide when he realized *U110* was not sinking and saw us rowing over to board."[69]

The surviving Germans were hauled from the water by HMS *Aubretia* and hustled below decks. Balme and eight men, all armed with rifles or pistols, brought their whaler alongside *U110* and climbed aboard, rushing for the conning tower. Bizarrely for a boat that was scuttling, the conning tower hatch was shut and Balme gingerly opened it, half-expecting to find German crewmen still aboard. As he and six men lowered themselves inside they found lights on and no discernible sign of flooding or chlorine gas, a single large splinter from the conning tower lying on deck. Panic appeared to have gripped the boat's crew during the depth-charge attack. Gear and books were strewn everywhere, although Balme's account that the boat looked "just as if one had arrived at someone's house after breakfast, before they had time to make the beds" is somewhat at odds with the version given by German survivors of smashed glass, flakes of paint and noxious fumes. Balme signalled *Bulldog* that *U110* appeared seaworthy and towable, requesting an engineer to be sent over to operate the U-boat's machinery, the port engine still running at slow ahead. He then set about salvaging anything that may have been of value, especially books other than those that were obviously novels. The boat's stern slowly slumped lower with a port list, hastening the human chain as men passed everything that they could find to the outside. Balme himself found Ecke's cameras and they were passed along with officer's gear, wallets and sheafs of paper, Balme unable to comprehend any of it, as he could not read German. Using Ecke's abandoned cine camera he photographed the radio and hydrophone rooms, before discovering it set to the wrong aperture. As he correctly stated in his after-action report, "I doubt if they will come out at all". But meanwhile Telegraphist A. Long, one of Balme's boarding party, went to the radio room and recovered many books marked *Geheime* (secret) and what he took to be an unusual typewriter. Therein lay the true value of the capture of *U110*. Among the papers recovered were code books for the *Heimisch* (Home Waters) code, known to the Allies as 'Dolphin', keys to the double-enciphered *Offiziere* (Officers-Only) code, the *Kurzsignale* (Short Signal) code, Kriegsmarine grid charts and a working naval Enigma with all its rotors. Also complete technical plans for the Type IX B were found, as well as charts of the latest German North Sea and French minefields. Kriegsmarine security would never be complete again. Why a man of Lemp' capabilities and experience would allow even the vague possibility of such an enormous mistake remains a mystery, perhaps explained somewhat by his concussion sustained during the depth-charging. However, Lemp and fourteen crewmen had paid the ultimate price for the momentous loss of *U110*.

U110's surviving thirty-two crewmen remained unaware their ship's capture, although Löwe harboured suspicions that the boat had been boarded. *U110* itself was placed under tow by *Bulldog* but floundered and sank in gale conditions at 1100hrs on 10 May while heading to Iceland. By then, however, the boat itself was largely irrelevant, having been

[68] Letter to the *Telegraph* Newspaper, 11 February
[69] Letter to Mac MacGowan from David Balme.

stripped of anything of value, including Lemp's Knight's Cross, found in the commanders' desk.[70] Intelligence officer Allum Bacon met *Bulldog* as it entered Scapa and raced to Bletchley Park with the priceless haul.

Penetration of Germany's supposedly impregnable Enigma code led swiftly to a concerted British attack opened on 3 June against the network of ten supply ships established to supply *Bismarck* but also extending U-boat operations in areas such as the West African coast. Another 2nd U-Flotilla boat was soon able to confirm the scale of the supply disaster now facing them.

During 7 June *U38* had been scheduled to replenish for a second time from the tanker *Egerland*. As the U-boat neared the rendezvous, *Egerland* was pounced upon by British warships and forced to scuttle. While Liebe hunted, unsuccessfully, for survivors he radioed the catastrophe to BdU who in turn learnt of the destruction of three other supply ships and a fourth captured. By 23 June the calamity had worsened with four more of the raider supply ships lost and, with refuelling no longer possible, West African operations were curtailed and the boats headed home. The precise targeting of the tankers aroused Dönitz's suspicions, but he blamed increasingly effective British direction-finding and even espionage before he would consider the possibility of a breach in the Enigma codes. Admiral Kurt Fricke, Chief of Staff at SKL made a thorough investigation of the matter, concluding that there were several theories: coincidence, spying, direction-finding or penetration of the Enigma coding system. Of the possibilities put forward, Fricke favoured the first.

11 June: Kaptlt. Richard Zapp brought the new *U66* into Lorient after nearly a month at sea on his maiden patrol. Zapp, a former naval artillery officer, had achieved no success, the voyage arrested when *U66* lost her bow torpedo caps to ice damage near Newfoundland, suffering minor flooding. After twelve days in port spent on repairs and fitting out, *U66* sailed for Freetown.

The West African theatre had yielded the most successful patrols of the war. Between May and June *U107*, *U105*, *U103*, *U124*, *U38*, *U106* and 7th U-Flotilla's *U69* had destroyed seventy-two ships for a massive 387,671 tons, plus damage to the battleship HMS *Malaya*.

Georg Schewe was the first to arrive home, *U105* welcomed by an enthusiastic crowd on 13 June. After the boat had been secured Schewe strode ashore to receive the Knight's Cross from Dönitz, notified of the award by radio on 23 May.

> "Schewe, who has been on operations since the beginning of the war but has had little success up to the last trip, proved by the well conducted operation that the trust which had been placed in him was justified. He has sunk 13 ships – 89,273 tons in 112 days at sea."[71]

Jürgen Oesten, bringing *U106* into Lorient four days later flying pennants for a claimed eleven ships, also received the esteemed Knight's Cross. On 26 June Kaptlt. Heinrich Liebe docked *U38* after sinking a confirmed eight ships in nearly three months at sea, arriving on little more than diesel fumes. His final victim south-west of the Cape Verde Islands was destroyed in a peculiar fashion to say the least. IIWO Oblt.z.S. Reimar Ziesmar remembered:

---

[70] It was later returned by Baker-Cresswell to Lemp's sister in Germany.
[71] BdU KTB, 13/6/41

"*U38* had only two torpedoes, both with uncertain functional value. One had no ignition pistol in its explosive head [damaged while transferring from *Egerland* during resupply in May] and the other showed some irregularities in its steering apparatus. Thirdly, after the attack on SS *Japan* [4 May] there was no artillery ammunition left.

"After some argument Kaptlt. Liebe decided to release the second torpedo. It developed a circular course and we were forced to run away from it at full speed until its running capability was exhausted.

"By doing this *U38* generated an enormous shimmering [phosphorescent] wake that stirred the [enemy] vessel's crew. We saw electric torches speeding aft where we supposed their deck gun was. *U38* stopped abruptly.

"I urged Kaptlt. Liebe to try the torpedo without ignition pistol and, if it were placed right, it could stop the ship and flood it eventually. So it happened. The ship stopped and one or one and a half hours after the impact . . . began to sink."

By BdU calculations Liebe had passed 200,000 tons, earning him the coveted Oak Leaves for his Knight's Cross, made by radio on 11 June.[72] Liebe travelled to Berlin to receive the honour from Hitler, his the Wehrmacht's thirteenth Oak Leaves to be awarded. Liebe then left his operational command, transferred to the staff of OKM.

By 2 July Hessler's *U107* had also returned from her record-breaking patrol, two tankers and British Q-ship SS *Alfred Jones* among the fourteen victories. The Q-ship's crew, spotted by Hessler through his periscope dressed in crisp white uniforms, had betrayed the *Alfred Jones*. Torpedoed three times, the ship succumbed slowly, Hessler's suspicions confirmed as the listing deck uncovered hidden cannon, depth charges and other weaponry. The cleanly attired crew had been at Sunday muster when the first torpedo hit, mistakenly ordered to abandon ship instead of hiding and allowing the usual oily group of engineers used as the decoy 'panic party' to lull an assailant into surfacing.

Ten days later the last of the West African boats arrived, Schütze's *U103* having sunk thirteen ships. Unfortunately his final victory that he thought was a Dutch vessel en route for England was in fact the Italian blockade-runner *Ernani* sailing under Dutch disguise from Las Palmas to France.

Due to the sudden dearth of supply ships at sea, Schütze refuelled under cover of darkness from *Corrientes* (*Culebra*) moored in Las Palmas, before completing the home leg of his voyage. Again, by BdU reckoning Schütze had accumulated over 200,000 tons of enemy shipping, earning the Oak Leaves to his Knight's Cross, crowning his operational career.[73] Promoted to *Korvettenkapitän* he was posted to command of a Baltic training flotilla. However, before the order was implemented he exchanged with KK Heinz Fischer who left to become senior officer of the 4th U-training flotilla and Schütze assumed command of the 2nd U-Flotilla. He was considered a fair and easy-going superior,

---

[72] Liebe had in fact sunk thirty-two ships, totalling 168,506 tons.
[73] Schütze's score was in fact a respectable thirty-six ships for 187,179 tons. His was the final boat to refuel in Las Palmas. The British War Cabinet, increasingly dismayed at the brazen covert supply within the Canary Islands, had authorized an invasion, code-named 'Operation Puma' in April 1941. Although later cancelled, the planned British move alarmed Franco who had been allowed to learn of it, and, bowing to pressure from Churchill, he obligingly barred U-boats from entering the Canary Islands on 16 July. The Spanish authorities went so far as to place guards aboard the 'interned' German ships, nullifying their ability to refuel.

unflatteringly nicknamed 'Fatty' by ordinary seamen. Meanwhile, former BdU Staff Officer Kaptlt. Werner Winter arrived in August to take command of *U103*.

The flotilla headquarters in Lorient had grown substantially. The buildings themselves were named after First World War U-boat heroes or the name of commanders lost during the last two years of war. The harbourside 'Saltzwedel Barracks' within the old French Arsenal housed the flotilla's Petty Officers and Ratings, its north wing named 'Haus Habekost', east wing 'Haus von Dresky' and south wing 'Haus Fröhlich'. Nearby, the former French School of Music had been requisitioned as 'Hundius Barracks', it too holding the lower ranks of the 2nd U-Flotilla until transferred to the 10th U-flotilla in January 1942. Its three wings were titled 'Haus Beduhn', 'Haus Barten' and 'Haus Mugler'. Chief Petty Officers were billeted within two large buildings, 'Haus Looff' and 'Haus Jürst', near Lorient's train station, while officers were either quartered in the Hotel Beauséjour, Hotel Centrale or the large yellow 'Haus Mathes', also near the station. A fortunate few occupied houses along Larmor Plage, the seaside retreat previously the domain of wealthy Breton families. The medieval village of Hennebont, seven miles to the north-east, housed Lorient's naval guard company, the military prison and U-boat clothing depot. For relaxation between patrols a Naval Convalescent Centre was established at Carnac, south of Lorient, consisting of twenty large four-story buildings along the oceanfront, luxuriously appointed with full recreational facilities and even a Bavarian *bierkeller*. Relations with the local Bretons were remarkably good. Twenty-three-year-old *Oberfunkmaat* Bernhard Geismann, radio operator on Hessler's *U107*, later commented:

> "We were treated very kindly by the French civilian population. At the same time, we soldiers were relied on to also behave well regarding the French population."

21 July: *U109* crept by night into Cadiz harbour to replenish from '*Moro*' (supply ship *Thalia*). By 0500hrs spare parts, fresh food and three torpedoes had been taken aboard and *U109* headed again for the open sea, narrowly avoiding two marauding British patrol vessels. An apparently neutral Spanish trawler appeared to trail *U109* as it departed Cadiz and, after several wild course changes failed to rid *U109* of its persistent follower, Bleichrodt ordered a burst of flak fired over the fishing boat's bow. This seemed to have the desired effect and it departed, although Bleichrodt was left with the lingering suspicion that the British had known of his presence.[74]

By this stage new flotilla boats had sailed from Germany to join the front line. Kaptlt. Karl-Friedrich Merten had put to sea from Kiel aboard *U68* at the end of June, while on 12 July KK Hugo Förster's Type IXC *U501*, commissioned in Hamburg's *Deutsche Werft* on 30 April, sailed from Horten bound for the North Atlantic.

The first type IXC keel to be laid down, *U501* had originally been intended for Günther Prien's command, but his loss with all hands aboard *U47* prevented this. Förster approached Dönitz and "formally, on bended knee" begged for transfer to the vacant commander's post. He had a good personal relationship with Dönitz and his request was approved. Although Förster had joined the navy in 1923, he and the majority of his officers

---

[74] Indeed the chain of Spanish refuelling bases for U-boats was partially known to the Royal Navy. While the British Admiralty had managed to shut down the valuable Canary Islands refuelling stations mainland Spain's secret supply system would last until the end of 1942. The British obtained concrete evidence of the breach of neutrality after interrogation of prisoners from the 1st U-Flotilla's *U574*, sunk after such a refuelling stop in Cadiz.

and crew were untried in submarine warfare. The East Prussian LI, Oblt. (Ing.) Gerhard Schiemann, and IIIWO, *Stabsobersteuermann* Lembke, were among the few possessing U-boat experience. In the diesel room *Obermaschinenmaat* Fritz Weinrich, another of the few veterans aboard, remembered:

> "*U501*, after a short stay in Kiel, went again into the Baltic Sea. There, some inconsequential practices were executed, that didn't contribute to the qualification of the crew in my opinion.
>
> "In June 1941, we put in at Kiel and equipped *U501* for the combat voyage. As this was completed, we ran out into the Baltic Sea at the end of June, headed shortly for the island Bornholm (Rönne) and then reached Horten. In Horten Bay, the crash dive was practiced under supervision of an experienced U-boat *Kommandant*. This was all, in my opinion, too little too late."[75]

Another new addition to the flotilla, Kaptlt. Ernst Bauer's *U126*, had already been at sea for a week as Förster slipped his mooring lines, Kaptlt. Günter Kuhnke's *U125* following soon after. Kuhnke's was an uneventful transit voyage, docking in Lorient on 28 July unharmed by large numbers of drifting mines encountered.

Meanwhile veterans had also been putting to sea. Kaptlt. Reinhard Hardegen's *U123* had tried to sail on 8 June for Freetown but was forced to turn back with a fault in the attack periscope's lifting gear. He sailed again on 15 June for the central Atlantic, his old boat, Georg Schulz's *U124*, following a month later. *U124* had temporarily lost its IWO, Johann Mohr undergoing commander training to replace Schulz in the near future. The boat had originally left on 10 July, forced back for five days of repair to troublesome engines.

U124 and *U109*, in company with *U93* and *U94*, were directed to sweep southwards from Spain towards the Canaries in a vain convoy search. Only Hardegen's *U123* remained near Freetown as the line of U-boats fruitlessly searched an empty sea, ordered at the end of the month to head northwards again towards Gibraltar. Meanwhile a Condor sighting confirmed previous B-Dienst intelligence that now placed the elusive OG69 west of the English Channel. Both *U68* and *U126* were immediately sent in pursuit, alongside six smaller U-boats. Kaptlt. Ernst Bauer's *U126* was the first to arrive at the appointed area but sighted nothing, a second Condor reporting the convoy 215 miles from its previously stated position. Merten's *U68* finally spotted distant mastheads and, once other boats had begun to arrive, he struck. As he prepared to fire his first shots in anger Merten was startled by a corvette's sudden appearance, throwing off his aim and sending the torpedoes wide. As *U68* dived deep to evade ramming, HMS *Sunflower* and *Pimpernel* steamed overhead and shook the boat with accurate depth charges.

Still the Germans continued to stalk at a distance and the following evening Bauer's turn came to initiate his combat career. During the day, as other boats converged on OG69, Dönitz broadcast to the assembled pack:

> "*U126* freedom of attack from fall of darkness. . . . All boats . . . split up escorts. Bring other boats up, attack yourselves. Press on!"

After carefully positioning his surfaced boat, Bauer fired all six tubes a little after midnight on 28 July, four explosions reverberating through *U126*'s steel hull prompting Bauer to claim a ship sunk with each. He had actually hit two as the merchant ships began to spread out. Merten attempted another unsuccessful attack before disengaging, OG69 slipping

[75] http://www.greywolf.de

away as *U68* made for Lorient. Bauer's *U126* would sink two more vessels during its patrol before docking in Lorient on 24 August, its first voyage inauspicious but satisfactory.

Meanwhile *U109* and *U124* prepared to intercept a freshly reported convoy bound from Gibraltar to Britain. In mounting seas they ploughed onwards, strung out in a line stretching west from Casablanca. On 10 August *U79* reported the expected convoy in grid square CG8661 and both Schulz and Bleichrodt powered towards the grid coordinates. Over the following days escort ships repeatedly drove away U-boats shadowing HG69, inflicting serious damage on *U124* and forcing Schulz to break off for Lorient. Bleichrodt also failed to make decisive contact, retreating to Lorient with no successes to boast of after radioing to BdU:

> "Returning to base. Thick trails of oil and, when submerged, air bubbles, increasing daily. Individual tanks H.P. blow valves eight and one and exhaust conduit not working. Both hydrophones out of action. 70 cubic metres, all torpedoes [remaining]."[76]

By the operation's end eight U-boats and three Italian submarines had attempted to attack HG69, only a KG40 Condor and the Italian boat *Marconi* claiming success. Escorts beat off even the aggressive Reinhard Hardegen after he added his weight to the attack. Mockingly, as Hardegen was homed onto the convoy by a Condor, *U123* suffered temporary but catastrophic failures in both diesels, lubricating oil leaking from the damaged engines and spoiling Hardegen's approach.

While Schulz and Bleichrodt had suffered humiliating failures (*U109* was nicknamed the flotilla's 'Torpedo Carrier') Hardegen had at least sunk four ships during his voyage, all from the boat's southbound voyage and three from convoy SL76.[77] The sole exception was the neutral Portuguese steamer SS *Ganda*, sent under by gunfire west of Casablanca on 20 June. The sinking of this vessel caused considerable concern within Dönitz's headquarters. The Portuguese were naturally outraged but decided that it had probably been a British submarine responsible. In order to keep the affair secret, Dönitz swore Hardegen to silence after *U123*'s return to Lorient on 23 August and instructed his War Diary altered to erase any mention of the attack, the second time that Dönitz had made such an order. Hardegen complied but failed to remove the shooting report which remained in *U123*'s War Diary and the files of the *Torpedokommando* where copies of all such reports were kept. Nevertheless, the affair remained secret.

Hardegen had refuelled from the German tanker *Corrientes* in Las Palmas en route to Sierra Leone, joined by Richard Zapp's *U66* outside the once target-rich Freetown for weeks of chafing inactivity. Zapp had also sunk two stragglers from SL76 while en route for Freetown, attacking the sinking a third with combined gunfire and torpedo attack. After departing Sierra Leone and sailing towards Lorient Zapp destroyed another British steamer before docking in Lorient on 5 August, problems with the outboard vents that had nagged the boat during its last days at sea requiring a lengthy overhaul.

---

[76] Bleichrodt wrongly reported his hydrophones out of commission. The conflict between Bleichrodt and *U109*'s hydrophone operator Wolfgang Hirschfeld is well documented in Hirschfeld's book *Secret Diary of a U-boat*, pp 64–82.

[77] Hardegen wrongly claimed one of the latter as an Armed Merchant Cruiser. After being shelled by the ship SS *Río Azúl* during his first attack on SL76 he assumed that it was an auxiliary cruiser. The 4,088-ton British steamer was in fact a Defensively Armed Merchant ship. Hardegen sank her two nights later.

Kaptlt. Schulz would not put into Lorient until 24 August, the commander's active service ending with disappointing results. The sole recorded sinking of Schulz's final patrol had been made shortly after leaving France. En route to the Gibraltar area the boat had chanced upon a buoy broken loose from its mooring and drifting dangerously in shipping lanes. Ordering his gun-crew to sink the obstacle Schulz reported by radio to BdU:

"Versenkte eine Tonne (sunk one buoy)".

There was, however, some confusion in Lorient as the German word for 'buoy' and 'ton' are the same. Dönitz may well have wondered what tiny craft U124 had attacked.

A potentially more serious problem developed on the boat's final submerged run towards the French coast. *Oberleutnant* (Ing.) Rolf Brinker had ordered U124 held steady at thirty metres while he played chess in the officers' mess with Schulz. A sudden rocking motion bought Brinker racing to the control room, demanding to know why the hell they had surfaced. But the helmsman's manometer still showed a depth of thirty metres. It was faulty and they had sailed surfaced in the worst area for British air attack, in broad daylight, with a deserted bridge and no way of spotting aerial threats.

On 25 August Schulz, Bauer and Hardegen were all at 'Berlin', Dönitz's Kernével headquarters, to report their experiences. Dönitz noted that all three had acted correctly, albeit with different results. Only U123's success warranted comment in the BdU War Dairy:

"Hardegen behaved very skilfully throughout the operation and used his opportunities to attack to the utmost."

Once U124 was in dry dock the transfer of command to Johann Mohr was completed, following Mohr's promotion to *Kapitänleutnant*, Werner Henke taking Mohr's old place as IWO. Schulz then left to take command of Danzig's 6th U-training Flotilla.

1 August: The 2nd U-Flotilla staff were on hand to welcome U68, its conning tower emblazoned with the Ace of Spades, as it arrived for the first time in France, a *Fähnrich* aboard dangerously ill with pneumonia. Kaptlt. Merten's sole 'success' remained the mystery corvette attacked during the clash with convoy OG69 and, as U68 tied up at its berth, Merten catalogued a list of woes to flotilla engineers. The Type IXC arrived with damage to the boat's main bilge pump that had curtailed their diving ability during the patrol's final days. Also, the starboard diesel had broken down, prematurely worn by the exertions of North Atlantic combat.

As U68 underwent repair work, Kéroman I's slipway lifted its first submarine into the massive shelter nearing final completion; U123 was hauled from the water on 25 August. While Hardegen's boat underwent treatment by the engineering staff, U67's transfer voyage from Germany to France was nearing its end. The boat was now commanded by Kaptlt. Günther Müller-Stockheim, a popular man with considerable engineering prowess, designing a mechanical toy for Oblt. (Ing.) Heinrich Eckert's five-year-old son and having engine room ratings construct it for him. U67 entered its new home on 29 August where she was swiftly 'adopted' by KK (Ing.) Walter Holland's *Kriegsmarinewerft* repair shops, the patronage of the *Reichskriegerbund* from Bleichrodt's days as captain now redundant.

7 August: The first week of August had seen five 2nd U-Flotilla boats put to sea: Kaptlt. Wolfgang Lüth's U43, the new Type IXC U129, commanded by Nicolai Clausen, Kaptlt. Georg Schewe's veteran U105, Kaptlt. Schuch's U38 and, finally, the new boat U501 sailing from Trondheim for the North Atlantic. Clausen was forced to abort his mission after a fruitless journey of just over three weeks when BdU ordered his return at 'full speed ahead', a suspected outbreak of infectious diphtheria aboard the submarine.

Following recent stagnation near Freetown and Gibraltar, BdU decided to reopen operations in the North Atlantic. For additional security, although unaware of Enigma's compromise, Dönitz ordered several further measures to protect U-boat codes. All boats were no longer to be addressed by number but by its commanders' surname. Grid references were double enciphered as of 9 September, using a complicated system involving a double letter code table which seemed to baffle as many U-boat commanders as potential eavesdroppers. Also, the introduction of a four-rotor U-boat Enigma was slated for late September. The machine would use a new Enigma net, separate from other Kriegsmarine coded traffic. Designed for four rotors, it was called 'Triton', known to the Allies as 'Shark'. The new net was scheduled to begin operating during October, although not in full use until 1 February 1942, and would begin an extended 'blackout' of German signal traffic for Bletchley Park codebreakers that lasted nearly uninterrupted during 1942.

U501 was part of Dönitz's new initiative against the convoy routes south of Iceland, but it was an unhappy crew that entered the Atlantic. Almost immediately after leaving Norway, while traversing the Loofjord, KK Förster submerged his boat to test repair work that had been carried out in Trondheim. At a depth of only sixty metres the groaning pressure hull led him to cut the dive; *U501* levelled out with orders to proceed no deeper. He refused to go deeper despite heated arguments with Oblt. (Ing.) Gerhard Schiemann. The integrity of the hull was paramount, particularly if attacked. Adding to their woes, as *U501* sailed west the main Junkers compressor malfunctioned, working only at reduced efficiency after hours of repair.

Dönitz assembled the *Markgraf* patrol line south of Greenland to intercept the main body of Allied convoy traffic between the New World and the Old. En route to the assembly area *U501* chanced upon westbound ON5 south of Iceland. Although not given freedom to attack, Förster provided homing signals that allowed the 3rd U-Flotilla's *U568* successfully to assault the convoy on 12 August. Unable to mount his own attack, Förster picked up his old course and headed west.

Markgraf, which included flotilla-mates *U38*, *U43* and *U105*, was originally tasked with searching for HX145, but the convoy eluded their trap. During the wait *Markgraf* boat *U652* made the first (inconclusive) attack on an American warship after being hunted by USS *Greer* south of Iceland. As political repercussions shook Washington, London and Berlin, the remaining *Markgraf* boats were shifted 150 miles west, trailing the scent of merchant traffic picked up by B-Dienst. Still nothing was found, although Förster managed to sight and attack a solitary ship on 5 September. It took six torpedoes and forty cannon shells to sink SS *Einvik*, a Norwegian straggler from SC41, probably once again due more to curtailed training shoots than any defect in the temperamental torpedoes; a scarcity of torpedo recovery vessels in the German training ranges had reduced by half the number of practice shots allowed. Following Förster's attack, convoys ON12 and HX148 were alerted to the threat and managed to divert southwards, avoiding the *Markgraf* boats. But a third, SC42, was not so lucky. On 9 September *U85* of the 3rd U-Flotilla stumbled upon the sixty-five ships of this slow convoy, a mass of densely packed freighters that brought the remainder of the *Markgraf* boats at full speed as *U85* fired once, missed and began to shadow. SC42 had set sail from Sydney, Nova Scotia, on 30 August, formed initially into twelve columns under the local escort of three Royal Canadian Navy corvettes, a thirteenth column of five more ships joining from St John's on 2 September. At that time the

Canadian 24th Escort Group, comprising HMCS *Skeena*, *Alberni*, *Kenogami* and *Orillia*, took charge for the ocean passage.

For four days after the convoy had rounded Cape Race easterly gales and heavy seas buffeted the deeply laden freighters and by 5 September they were hove-to, barely keeping steerage for two days before the wind at last began to ease. On 9 September SC42 altered course to 43° North, trying to skirt the *Markgraf* group until at 2237hrs the first torpedoes from *U85* flashed by.

Meanwhile two Canadian corvettes were racing towards the unfolding drama. HMCS *Chambly* and *Moose Jaw* had not long been in commission and were undergoing a period of intensive training. Scheduled to sail for another exercise, a study of predicted U-boat dispositions had convinced *Chambly*'s Commander J.D. Prentice of SC42's peril. His education, he reasoned, might therefore be given a more practical slant if he took his ships in support. Permission was sought and obtained and at noon *Chambly* and *Moose Jaw* left harbour and steered north-east.

During that first night SC42 lost seven ships. In the confusion of parachute flares and flames, artillery and depth charges merged in the cacophony of combat until dawn when the U-boats drew away to regroup and reload. They soon returned and by mid-morning torpedoes sped towards the convoy again. However, boats of the 2nd U-Flotilla had been totally unsuccessful. Kaptlt. Wolfgang Lüth in *U43* had fired six torpedoes, four porpoising, the rest missing their intended targets completely, so Lüth withdrew. Schewe's *U105* achieved similar results, while Förster did not even manage to fire during the mêlée.

It was after midnight by the time that *Chambly* and *Moose Jaw* finally neared from ahead of the convoy. *Chambly*'s lookouts sighted two distant white distress rockets from SS *Gypsum Queen*, heading to the bottom fatally holed. *Chambly* increased speed with *Moose Jaw* on her starboard beam, within minutes more rockets signalling further disaster for SC42. At that moment *Chambly* made ASDIC contact, the echo confirmed as a submarine, ahead and only 700 yards distant. Despite being well inside the 1,200 yards prescribed by depth-charge doctrine, Prentice decided to attack at once. Altering helm to bring the contact dead ahead, he ordered speed reduced, his target on a reciprocal course and closing rapidly. Prentice ordered a five-charge pattern be laid early, releasing them at 0138hrs. But the attack went awry, misfire and mishandling causing slight delay in firing the first and second charge.

Nevertheless Förster's *U501* was pounded by the badly laid attack. The sudden tapping against the hull of the Canadian's ASDIC had taken the Germans by surprise, rapidly followed by the grinding of propellers above. Ironically it was the misfired depth charges that sealed the boat's fate. With both charges exploding above the boat, which was at a depth of only forty-three metres, the concussion blew off the stern port hydroplane.

"The lights went out and *U501* lay with a strong bow-up tilt under water. I immediately went into the control room [where] the depth gauge had broken and the water indicator of the regulator tanks, which consisted of glass, had burst, releasing high pressure water. . . . To the Kommandant it seemed to mean that we were flooding. The *E-Maschinen* ran at low rpms . . . and the LI ordered: 'All men to Battle Stations!'

"Meanwhile, the seacocks to the gauges were closed and the LI's question to all areas: 'Is water entering?' was answered with 'No!' During this time, that lasted only seconds, the Kommandant had not spoken a single word. Suddenly, he stood at the foot of the ladder by the tower and screamed: 'Surface! Surface! We are flooding!'

"I stood opposite him at the ladder and looked into a face disfigured by fear.

I shouted to him: 'We must go down to 90 metres!' . . . However, the Kommandant had only one thought: 'Surface!' Since the LI didn't know what the Kommandant intended, and he still had sole command, he gave me the order: 'Blow!' . . . but the hand wheel was missing at the blowing panel. It had fallen off and was on the deck plates at my feet. *Obermaschinist* Moritz showed me the reserve valve and I blew the boat's ballast tanks with it. After surfacing the Kommandant went up, with the IWO, IIWO as well as the *Obersteuermann*, to the tower."

Chambly swung away to regain contact amidst the disturbed water, *Moose Jaw* already preparing its own attack when *U501* surfaced close by her port bow. The Canadian's searchlight came on and settled on the conning tower, a single shell slamming into it while the U-boat applied hard rudder to port. *Moose Jaw* ran quickly alongside *U501*, steel hulls grinding together as the two ships buffeted one another. They were close enough for the Canadian crew to be confronted with the bizarre spectacle of Förster suddenly appearing in the conning tower and stepping from his boat to the corvette's fo'c's'le without getting his feet wet. His bewildered men remained below, as their pitching boat lay helpless alongside *Moose Jaw*. Fortunately *U501* still possessed two competent officers and between the IWO Oblt.z.S. Werner Albring and Oblt. (Ing.) Gerhard Schiemann preparations were made to scuttle. Two *Fähnrich*, Wolfgang Horn and Theodor Mehlgarten, helped to complete the scuttling before ordered to abandon ship as Weinrich checked that the stern was empty, pausing to help Schiemann destroy the torpedo computer.

Fearing further boarding from less compliant crewmen, *Moose Jaw* withdrew, giving the U-boat the opportunity to get under way again. As *U501* passed slowly across the corvette's bows, *Moose Jaw* rammed her, firing weapons to discourage any attempt to man the U-boat's deck gun. Gradually the *U501* lost way and as the stern settled Albring ordered the boat abandoned. *Chambly* eased alongside and Prentice ordered away a nine-man boarding party led by Lt Edward Simmons.

Oblt. (Ing.) Schiemann ordered Weinrich, the only other man still below decks, to go to the tower and alert him to any attempt at boarding the U-boat. Weinrich was aghast at what he saw.

"Heavily armed Canadian personnel were climbing aboard. I called: 'Herr *Oberleutnant*, the enemy are on board!' A crew member of the cutter fastened their bowline to the rail of *U501*. As later was established, this was the stoker W.I. Brown. The cutter's crew herded the comrades of *U501*, situated on the upper deck, to the stern already flooded by water.

"I watched all of this from the tower, where three Canadians had begun to climb up carrying handguns. I wanted to climb from the tower, but was prevented. Instead I was asked to go into the boat. However, I didn't want to."[*]

After failing to force Weinrich and Schiemann, who had arrived above deck, to return below at gunpoint, Simmons and his small party attempted to enter the submarine alone but were prevented by the U-boat's rapid sinking. They had opened the stern torpedo-loading hatch and discovered the compartment below completely flooded. After clambering on to the conning tower Simmons was about to climb down the iron ladder when the control room lights suddenly went out and the sound of rushing water was plainly heard. With frightening speed *U501* flooded and went under, Stoker Brown of the boarding party lost during the Canadian's hurried abandonment. Eleven Germans were

[*] http//www.greywolf.de Interview with Fritz Weinrich

also missing, the boat's officers and two *Fähnriche* among the forty-six rescued. It was the first Royal Canadian Navy U-boat kill of the war.

The unfortunate Förster then began to face the consequences of the bizarre abandonment. He claimed to have left *U501* to negotiate his crew's surrender, a statement believed by neither the Canadians nor his own men, who harboured barely concealed bitterness towards him. Förster was segregated for his own safety.

Förster's initial incaraceration in England was to be at Grizedale Hall, but the hall had just witnessed the unsettling drama surrounding Kaptlt. Rahmlow and the officers of *U570*, which had surrendered to the Royal Navy at sea, *U570*'s IWO had died in an attempt to escape after being found guilty of cowardice by an illegal POW Court of Honour. Rahmlow arrived in the camp as the IWO's body was being interred with reinstated honour, but was hastily moved to a separate camp housing Luftwaffe officers when British authorities got wind of another Court of Honour to be convened. The same day that Rahmlow was transferred, Förster arrived and was promptly informed that he too would have to undergo court martial for abandoning his command in battle. Förster agreed that this would be the proper course of action and placed himself at the Council's disposal until the British transferred him to another camp as well. However, he remained ostracized by fellow officers while still a prisoner, paying a heavy price for what may have been a temporary loss of control – a luxury not allowed in wartime. Later, Förster returned to Germany as part of a prisoner exchange through Sweden. After his arrival in Stettin he was immediately placed under arrest to face court martial for cowardice in the face of the enemy. In February 1945 he committed suicide with a pistol smuggled to his cell. *U501*, listed missing in action as of 10 September 1941, had lost its twelfth crewman.

The battle of SC42 dragged on until 14 September, although no more ships were lost in its last three days, when Dönitz suspended attacks in the face of Allied reinforcement. Nineteen merchant ships had been sunk, although none by the three boats of the 2nd U-Flotilla. Dönitz, fuelled by inflated claims from many commanders, believed the battle to have been a decisive victory and it was to remain the second worst convoy loss for the Allies. Two U-boats (*U501* and *U207*) had been sunk and damage inflicted on others, but, bearing in mind that Dönitz believed the actual number of merchant sinkings to be nearly double, there was jubilation in Lorient.

Far from the Atlantic front the 2nd U-Flotilla received a share of the spoils of victory from 1940. *UD3* was transferred from the 5th U-training Flotilla to begin service as a training boat for Schütze's men. The boat had begun life as an 'O' class submarine of the Royal Netherlands Navy, *O25*, commissioned by the Rotterdam Dry Dock Company on 1 May 1940 in what can only be described as bad timing. During the lightning invasion of the Netherlands less than two weeks later the submarine was scuttled where she lay. In June 1940 she was raised by the Kriegsmarine, completed and later commissioned into the German Navy on 8 June 1941. Her tenure within the 2nd U-Flotilla lasted for over a year, all of it spent in Germany as a training and sometimes weather boat, until transferred in September 1942 to Lorient's 10th U-Flotilla and finally seeing front-line action primarily as a torpedo supply U-boat.

6 September: Elsewhere two flotilla boats had been the first Kriegsmarine submarines to cross the equator. Richard Zapp's *U66* and Kleinschmidt's *U111* had sailed in the latter half of August for Brazil, crossing the Atlantic in search of shipping using the American coast as cover. *U111* had expected to take part in Arctic operations before departure, thus the rather incongruous addition of a painted polar bear to the conning tower.

By 21 September Kleinschmidt had sunk two ships near the mouth of the Amazon and, with fuel low, was ordered back to Lorient. Meanwhile flotilla-mates *U67, U68, U103* and *U107* had sailed for West Africa, tasting action against convoy SL87 spotted by Hessler in the vanguard south-west of the Canary Islands. Over three days seven ships of the 'Hessler convoy' were sunk before the action was broken off, *U103* and *U107* proceeding south to what would transpire to be monotonous and futile patrolling, joined later off Freetown by *U125*.

However, *U67* and *U68* were ordered to Tarafal Bay near Santo Antão Island in the Cape Verdes to rendezvous with the returning *U111*. Müller-Stöckheim's *U67* carried a man suffering from gonorrhoea and the doctor aboard Merten's *U68*, MstA Dr Ziemke, planned to give what help he could. *U111* was added to the mix in case Dr Ziemke could provide no immediate cure, Kleinschmidt able to take the man aboard and transport him home, his injury eliciting no sympathy from crewmates irritated at their boat's unwelcome detour from operations. While in company, Merten also planned to obtain spare torpedoes from *U111*, illustrating his well-known penchant for obtaining and hoarding supplies wherever and whenever possible.

Merten brought *U68* into the seemingly deserted bay during the night of 27 September, followed shortly afterwards by *U111*. As Merten eased to a stop IWO Lauzemis pointed out distant figures, some in brown Portuguese uniforms, beside a ramshackle beachside hut. Kleinschmidt was nervous at their vulnerable position, anxious to complete their business and depart.

The two boats lay side by side as Kleinschmidt's crew began the difficult task of transferring four torpedoes from their upper deck storage containers to Merten's boat. The commanders had dinner together while machine guns were manned and lookouts scoured the nearby coastline for any sign of danger. The presence of the watching Portuguese could well mean that the meeting had been compromised and it was soon obvious that the clandestine rendezvous had indeed been blown.

A little before midnight the transfer was complete and as the two boats were leaving the bay HMS *Clyde* arrived, slipping into the bay surfaced. The 'River' Class submarine had been en route from Gibraltar to West Africa when she received orders to proceed to the U-boat gathering. ULTRA had deciphered Dönitz's coded instructions and a rather careless reply from Kleinschmidt that mentioned Tarafal Bay and, despite the risk of letting the Germans know that their codes were no longer secure, the chance of sinking two U-boats was deemed too good to miss. Faulty shooting was all that saved the Germans from the surprise attack. Sighting *U68* first, *Clyde*'s commander David Ingram turned to fire a full bow-salvo at Merten. At that moment British lookouts sighted *U111* approaching nose-on, incorrectly believing the boat to be on a collision course intent on ramming. Ingram switched his attention to the impending threat while Kleinschmidt, alarmed at the sudden appearance of an enemy submarine, elected to crash-dive rather than ram, passing beneath *Clyde* with only inches to spare. Now Ingram returned his attention to *U68*, firing six torpedoes that were at last spotted by lookouts, enabling Merten to 'comb the tracks' of the racing eels. *U68* also crash-dived as two British torpedoes exploded on the distant beach. Ingram now faced a pair of hidden adversaries and elected to take his boat underwater to reload and hunt his enemy by hydrophone.

While *U68* and *U111* retreated, Kaptlt. Günther Müller-Stöckheim's *U67* entered the bay ahead of schedule. His puzzlement turned to alarm at the detonating British torpedoes and, submerging, *U67*'s hydrophone operators detected propellers. But as there was no sign of anything through the boat's periscope Stockheim elected to surface and retreat in order to assess the situation. Suddenly, directly ahead, lookouts sighted the unmistakable silhouette of HMS *Clyde*, also surfaced and with tubes reloaded and deck gun manned. Ingram saw *U67* at about the same instant and ordered engines full ahead as he attempted to ram, *U67* in turn throwing engines into reverse and putting her rudder hard over to avoid the impact. *Clyde* swept by, narrowly missing its objective while Müller-Stöckheim unintentionally rammed the stern of the British submarine, which crash-dived lightly damaged. Ingram abandoned his attempt at attack and HMS *Clyde* set course for Gibraltar. Aboard *U67* the crew struggled with multiple leaks caused by the collision. The bow was twisted to almost ninety degrees and water poured from a multitude of small holes in the damaged torpedo tubes.

Confusion followed as all three U-boats surfaced independently to relay details of the attack to BdU. *U111* initially reported the probable loss of Merten's boat, causing Merten to retort to his own radioman:

> "That's how it goes. One morning you wake up a dead man and don't even know it."

Eventually BdU managed to clarify the situation and ordered *U67* to abort, ironically taking the sick (and sheepish) crewman who had caused their redirection home. Merten asked for a second meeting to take aboard whatever fuel and torpedoes could be spared from *U67*, this time the transfer taking place uneventfully in Vichy Mauritania. *U111* was also ordered to continue its homeward trek.

While his Commander-in-Chief in Lorient began to consider the odds against a British submarine arriving at the exact moment of such an unusual rendezvous, Kleinschmidt set course for Lorient. Intercepted radio traffic indicated that along *U111*'s return path west of Las Palmas lay the damaged British MV *Silverbelle*, hit by *U68* on 22 September. Kleinschmidt chose to try and sink the derelict with his remaining torpedoes rather than carry the useless ammunition home. However, unbeknown to both Allies and Germans, *Silverbelle* had already sunk.

Unaware of this, the British despatched ASW trawler HMT *Lady Shirley* to search for the ship. Departing from Gibraltar, the trawler was 220 miles west-south-west of Tenerife when masthead lookouts reported an object bearing 30° to starboard on the distant horizon. Identifying it as a probable submarine, *Lady Shirley* altered course.

Kleinschmidt dived *U111* after sighting *Lady Shirley* and began to plot a torpedo attack. Expecting a large merchant ship, he believed the approaching trawler to be *Silverbelle* and thus at a far greater distance than she really was and no amount of argument from either IIWO Oblt.z.S. Wilhelm Rösing or the hydrophone operator could shake Kleinschmidt's belief.[78] Exasperated, Kleinschmidt had a fresh look through his periscope, still believing it a large freighter at 3,300 yards. In fact *Lady Shirley* was less than a quarter that distance and preparing to drop six depth charges. Kleinschmidt was in the process of berating both Rösing and the hydrophone operator when the first explosions battered *U111*.

The charges' minimum settings had been 150 feet and, although there was only minor damage to the boat, Kleinschmidt ordered tanks blown and all deck weapons ready to fire. Water leaked into the diesel room, causing engine misfire before they failed completely, billowing dense white smoke. In near panic, Kleinschmidt changed his mind and ordered the boat to crash-dive, but it was too late. *U111* lay surfaced, dead in the water and under

---

[78] Oblt.z.S. Wilhelm Rösing was FdU West Hans-Rudolf Rösing's younger brother.

fire. *Lady Shirley* had wheeled to port in preparation to ram and brought all weapons to bear on the surfacing boat.

Kleinschmidt threw open the conning tower hatch and leapt on to the bridge, followed by Rösing, IWO OlzS Helmut Fuchs and frantic gun crews. The men tasked with operating the 3.7cm stern cannon remained below, later bitterly reproached for staying in shelter. Opening fire, the 2cm flak gun traced its shells over *Lady Shirley*'s main gun, killing the gunlayer and wounding several British sailors. But the trawler's artillery hardly faltered, new men taking the places of wounded colleagues. After several near misses had sprayed the U-boat with seawater one shell hit the conning tower, ricocheting off the attack periscope housing. Ammunition was now passed to the U-boat's forward gun crew through this new hole, but unfortunately the first shell jammed and as the crew struggled to free it they were sprayed with machine-gun fire, two falling dead and the remaining three running for cover.

A momentary burst of low revolution movement from *U111*'s crippled diesels ended with more dense smoke and complete seizure. Kleinschmidt was still on the bridge handling ammunition when another direct hit killed him, as well as Rösing and Fuchs. Kleinschmidt's body was thrown down the conning tower to lay across the hatch above the control room, blood pouring onto the deck plating below. The boat was ordered abandoned as Oblt (Ing.) Günther Wulf opened vents to scuttle her.

As men tumbled on to the upper deck and threw themselves overboard, *U111* began to sink, disappearing stern first. *Lady Shirley*, which had suffered one man killed, four severely wounded and relatively light damage, closed to pull forty-five prisoners from the water. Seven Germans had been killed during the battle, an eighth dying of severe wounds later that night. A brief attempt at redeeming the failure to man the aft deck gun was launched during the ship's voyage to Gibraltar when the gun crew's leader hatched a plot to overwhelm the outnumbered Royal Navy crew and seize the ship. Only one man agreed and so the idea was abandoned. Four days later, on 8 September, the survivors of *U111*, guarded by the only nine uninjured men from the trawler's original complement, were unloaded at Gibraltar. After confirmation via the International Red Cross that the surviving crew were held prisoner, Kleinschmidt received the honour of a barracks wing named after him in Lorient, added to the pantheon of fallen U-boat commanders.

11 September: *U106* put into Lorient after a month at sea. It had been Jürgen Oesten's final patrol, one in which he made no sinkings but successfully escorted the blockade-runner *Anneliese Essberger* for four days in September before the cargo ship was safely shepherded the remainder of the way to Bordeaux by aircraft. The blockade-runner's Second Officer Otto Giese remembered their rendezvous with *U106*:

> "It was exciting to see this long narrow tube of steel and iron pitching and rolling in the long swell. . . . The U-boat arm of the German navy brought much pride and glory to our military forces. I stared at the *U106* in awe.
>
> "The commandant, Kaptlt. Jüurgen Oesten, was a blunt, dashing fellow. As he talked with our captain his manner made a deep impression on all of us."[79]

After reaching Lorient Oesten trod ashore to be greeted by Dönitz with the news that he was to be transferred to command the 9th U-Flotilla forming in Brest. *U106*

---

[79] *Shooting the War*, Otto Giese. Giese later joined the U-Bootwaffe and served aboard *U405* and *U181*.

would have a new commander, her IWO Hermann Rasch promoted to *Kapitänleutnant*.

Three days later the aged *U38* also arrived in the Scorff River moorings, KK Heinrich Schuch flying a single victory pennant from his period with *Markgraf*, while the final returning flotilla boat for September entered harbour on the 20th, *U105* having also taken unimpressive part in the *Markgraf* assault on SC42, achieving a single sinking.

16 September: *U124* sailed from Lorient with her new commander, Kaptlt. Johann Mohr, on the bridge. Recently married, and at that point the youngest *Kapitänleutnant* in the Kriegsmarine at twenty-five, Mohr was an exceptional commander. Sailing alongside Adalbert 'Adi' Schnee's 1st U-Flotilla *U201*, he was bound for the shipping lanes between Gibraltar and Great Britain. *U124* also sported a new IWO, Oblt.z.S. Peter Zschech, soon to also carve a name for himself in history – albeit one of tragedy.

21 September: Kaptlt. Heinrich Bleichrodt, standing in his conning tower in his oldest sea gear and barely showing the effect of quantities of alcohol consumed only hours before with fellow officers, took *U109* for its third war patrol out of Lorient for the North Atlantic. Aboard *U109* was officer aspirant Eberhard Hoffmann, along to gain experience before taking his own command.

The boat had recently undergone trials outside of Lorient with the 2nd U-Flotilla's Chief Engineering Officer, Kaptlt. (Ing.) Karl Scheel, to judge whether the troublesome leakage of air bubbles had been eradicated by dockyard work. Scheel chose to observe from the surface, sitting in the U-boat's dinghy while *U109* submerged beneath him. Unfortunately *U109*'s *Bootsmann* Walter Gross had failed to notice the loss of the dinghy's bung and replaced it at the last moment with a hastily bundled set of rags. As Scheel waited patiently and *U109* sank beneath him the metal craft flooded, Scheel clinging to the boat's sky-periscope, shaking his fist angrily at Bleichrodt who observed the whole episode with much amusement through the attack periscope. The test was deemed successful.

Hours after leaving Lorient Bleichrodt took the boat down to 200 metres to test its worthiness for action. Abruptly, water burst through the direction-finder seals, soaking men in the control room. The hydrophone boxes in the bow compartment also gushed water, high-pressure spray dangerously close to men attempting to effect repairs. After surfacing and choosing to return to Lorient *U109*'s short-wave transmitter also flooded. Escorted by minesweepers *U109* sailed ignominiously back into port where she was put in dry dock. Much to the alarm of the crew and flotilla engineers, it was found that several watertight covers for the boat's hydrophones had been unscrewed in what could only be a deliberate act of sabotage.

27 September: Kaptlt. Nicolai Clausen took *U129* from Lorient for his boat's second war patrol. Instead of heading west into the Bay of Biscay Clausen went south to Bordeaux where he met the commander of supply ship *Kota Pinang*, one of two vessels rushed out as replacement U-boat supply ships for South Atlantic operations.

Following the disastrous June massacre of the *Bismarck* supply chain, OKM ordered two tankers modified to operate purely for U-boats. *Kota Pinang* and *Python* had been active during the sortie by *Bismarck* and *Prinz Eugen* but had survived after being recalled to port before the British offensive. *Kota Pinang* had been a 7,277-ton Dutch ship captured during the German invasion of Holland. After conversion to her Kriegsmarine role she served as a raider supply vessel until June 1941 when she began her U-boat conversion work, code-named 'Conrad'.

Clausen met her commander in Bordeaux, the two men confirming their respective orders. *U129* was detailed to escort the supply ship into southern waters, meeting a second U-boat escort, *U79*, bound ultimately for Gibraltar's narrow strait and operating on a tight deadline. *Kota Pinang* and *U129* sailed from Bordeaux at 0730hrs on 29 September, *Kota Pinang* leading the way disguised as a Sperrbrecher, with three small minesweepers in escort. By early afternoon engine problems had begun to dog *U129* and, lagging badly behind schedule, a last attempt at rendezvous with *U79* was cancelled by BdU on 1 October. Clausen was notified of this on 2 October and he and *Kota Pinang* continued alone, his mechanical problems over.

On 3 October, in patchy rain, disaster overtook them. At 1718hrs *U129*'s lookouts were alarmed by sudden acceleration from *Kota Pinang* accompanied by hurried Morse flashing from the ship's bridge:

"Ship in sight behind us."

The supply ship's own lookouts spotted what they took to be a British cruiser signalling from a rain squall to starboard. A biplane approached, forcing Clausen to dive to periscope depth. At 1625hrs *Kota Pinang*'s lamp flashed the call sign of an 8,432-ton English freighter in an attempt to disguise itself, trying to lure the attacking ship across Clausen's field of fire. Unfortunately, rain closed in and at that moment *U129* lost sight of *Kota Pinang*. At 1728hrs HMS *Kenya*, sent from Gibraltar to search for the tanker, betrayed by Bletchley Park's decryption service, opened fire at the same moment that 'Conrad' hove into Clausen's view.

"Visibility about 100m, artillery fire and some hits. . . . For a very short time I managed to see flashes from gun fire and a cruiser of type Belfast moving at high speed. . . . Moving too fast and far away for us to attack."

The supply ship immediately took devastating hits and her captain ordered the crew into the ship's boats two minutes later, scuttling charges prepared to go off at 1745hrs, exploding within the engine room as the only man left aboard, the Captain, ensured the ship's destruction. A small British catapult plane began to strafe the crippled ship as she slumped low in the water. Finally the Captain abandoned ship as *Kenya* fired a *coup-de-grâce* torpedo. Again Clausen caught sight of the unequal struggle.

"1808hrs. Heavy detonation. I saw tall flames and black smoke rising from the patch of very bad visibility. 'Conrad' is sinking. . . . The cruiser takes no notice of life boats. We can hear him move southwards at high speed. I saw him only once."

As the British propellers died away Clausen surfaced and approached the four lifeboats, floating on a large patch of oil that was all that remained of *Kota Pinang*. Despite shrapnel wounds to some, the entire crew had survived and Clausen embarked them all, firing three torpedoes and dumping his artillery ammunition to make extra space. Building a second layer of decking in the bow compartment created additional lying space as the cramped U-boat now contained 170 men. Every man was allotted his area in which to remain motionless while the LI attempted to trim the overloaded boat underwater. Clausen radioed his plight to BdU and, after receiving orders first to proceed to Western France, was then directed to the closer port of El Ferrol, Spain.

Urgent instructions were sent from Dönitz to KzS Meyer-Döhner, Madrid's Naval Attaché, before he radioed SKL:

"A Spanish naval tug is waiting for the U-boat in La Caruna Bay in the approaches to El Ferrol . . . to take on board the shipwrecked crew. Transfer is to take place only during the hours of darkness. The men will be accommodated aboard the German tanker *Max Albrecht* berthed in El Ferrol. The Spanish are under the impression that these men come from a civilian blockade breaker therefore it is essential to ensure that military badges and uniforms are removed before the transfer takes place. Transport in small groups to Germany will then be arranged."

On 6 October Clausen approached the Spanish coast, diving frequently and precariously to avoid Allied aircraft and Spanish trawlers. Finally at 1854hrs Clausen sighted the Spanish tug, tying alongside and transferring the crew of *Kota Pinang*. Two days later Clausen was also home, *U129* tying up in Lorient to high praise from BdU. Eberhard Godt recorded in the BdU KTB:

"His brave decision to take on board the entire crew has been rewarded by the saving of 119 seamen. The decisions taken for this rescue operation were good and correct."

While *U129* was transferred to the yard in Lorient for overhaul and preparation for fresh patrolling Clausen and a good portion of his crew went on leave to the Austrian Alps town of Pörtschach, the *Patenschaft* town of *U129*, enjoying the hospitality and freedom of the small community that had adopted their boat.

The loss of the *Kota Pinang* crippled West African operations once more and Dönitz was forced to recall three of the remaining four 2nd U-Flotilla on station, *U66*, *U103* and *U107* trekking homeward from Freetown, all bar *U66* diverted to the futile *Stoertebecker* pack off Gibraltar which battled fierce weather and mechanical problems while sighting no ships. Only Merten's *U68* was left to stalk the empty seas off Freetown. By mid-October Merten had been joined by Bauer's *U126*, the only German presence in the South Atlantic.

Far to the north *U502* sailed from Kiel on 29 September to join the *Mordbrenner* group forming in the North Atlantic. The boat was undertaking its first operational sortie from the North German coast, her commander twenty-eight-year-old Kaptlt. Jürgen von Rosenstiel, a veteran of Watch Officer duties aboard *U38*. The commissioning of *U502* into the 2nd U-Flotilla raised the unit's strength from thirteen at the year's beginning to twenty-one boats: two elderly Type IXAs, nine Type IXBs, nine Type IXCs and the captured Dutch submarine *UD3*. During the length of *U502*'s arduous shakedown within the Baltic that number had risen with the addition of the first of *Germaniawerft*'s Type XB minelayers, *U116* and three new Type IXCs – two transferred from the 4th U-training flotilla (*U129* and *U130*) and *U503* commissioned in July.

1 October: Kaptlt. Johann Mohr docked after his first patrol as commander, six pennants fluttering from the periscope as *U124* eased into the Scorff River. Mohr's patrol had begun well, both *U124* and *U201* ordered south to find Gibraltar traffic and clashing with OG74. Summoning Schnee, Mohr attacked on the evening of 20 September, IWO Zschech sending three torpedoes streaking from the tubes to sink a pair of merchants.

Mohr was frustrated by persistent escorts running surfaced before the speeding destroyers as he conned the U-boat alone in the sea-swept tower, his watch crew sent below in case of a rapid dive. Exhorting his overworked LI Rolf Brinker to give him 'maximum revolutions plus thirty' from the straining diesels, Mohr gradually drew ahead to escape unseen. The following night as *U124* pounded through the Atlantic to deliver a second attack, Zschech's target ships exploded. In frustration Mohr dived away from the conflagration, his boat starkly outlined by the leaping flames. Responding to a signal from Dönitz urging him to attack, Mohr replied that he was in contact with the convoy but added:

"*Schnee schuss schneller.* (Schnee shot faster)."

The following day OG74 wriggled free and *U124* and *U201* were ordered to a new hunt. 'Adi' Schnee made first contact on 25 September, sending beacon signals for Mohr. In constant squalls and a sea grown heavy with menace *U124* battled toward the target, bridge watch secured by strong harness. During the night Mohr finally made contact and over the next three days *U124* criss-crossed the convoy, adding four more ships to the total. He evaded the aggressive destroyer escort with pure nerve, once remaining surfaced only 30 metres from the starboard bow of one as it swept by, lookouts focused on the horizon, not the sea beneath them.

By 28 September all torpedoes were expended and *U124* was ordered home, arriving on 1 October, Dönitz's brief signal saying:

"*Der Mohr hat seiner Schuldigkeit getan; der Mohr kann gehen.* (Mohr has done his duty; Mohr can go)."[80]

Two days after docking in Lorient the crew of *U124* paraded before Dönitz where Zschech received the EKI for his marksmanship and other crewmen the EKII and coveted U-boat badge. For IIWO Werner Henke it ended a long period of probation and also his time with *U124*. While the boat was in the yards for overhaul he received orders to report to the 24th U-training Flotilla in Danzig to begin commander training.

Meanwhile the *Mordbrenner* boats had begun to assemble. ULTRA codebreakers had deduced that *Mordbrenner* lay in wait south of Greenland and rerouted convoys further south to avoid the waiting trap. But at that moment they suffered a temporary 'blackout' of decrypted naval Enigma traffic and SC48 blundered into the 7th U-Flotilla's *U553*, which immediately began to follow, seven new boats bound for *Mordbrenner* being redirected to the fresh sighting, including *U502*. Named *Reisswolf*, this fresh group was given freedom to attack, which they did with dogged determination until BdU ended the battle on the morning of the 18th in the face of strengthening escorts. Nine merchant ships, a corvette and a destroyer had been sunk – *U502* had had no success.[81]

The four remaining northern *Mordbrenner* boats, including *U109*, searched empty sea south of Greenland. Dönitz had come to believe that convoys were sailing north between Labrador and Newfoundland and around the great northern circle and the small group was ordered to make for the Belle Isle Strait. In force 11 gales and blinding sleet they battled onwards. There was no reward for Bleichrodt as *U109* powered through horrendous weather collecting thick layers of ice on her superstructure, requiring frequent dives to rest the crew and melt the ice before it rendered the boat dangerously unstable.

Finally it seemed as if Bleichrodt's patience was to be rewarded with the mid-afternoon sighting of two sets of mastheads on 30 October. The weather had calmed considerably

---

[80] This was a conscious word play. Before the outbreak of World War Two but after Mohr's escapade during the Spanish Civil War in which he aided the evacuation of German diplomats from Tenerife, Mohr was chosen for a similar undertaking until his commander aboard *Deutschland* answered "*Nein, der Mohr hat nicht seiner Schuldigkeit getan* (No, Mohr has not finished his duties)", unwilling to part with the enterprising young officer.

[81] See Lawrence Paterson *First U-boat Flotilla*, pp. 107–108.

and Bleichrodt was preparing his attack when the sudden appearance of an aircraft drove the boat under. As *U109*'s bow went under at a steep incline Bleichrodt realized to his horror that the boat's stern was still on the surface.

> " 'Damn! The plane's heading straight for us! Chief, our arse is still sticking up out of the water . . . Close all pressure doors!'
>
> "We were on the Newfoundland Banks, our bows in the mud and sand, and the stern projecting above the surface.
>
> "So this was how we would die, bombed by an aircraft on the Grand Banks. But it was only 150 feet here, I thought. If the bulkheads held, perhaps some of us might make it to the surface with a breathing set. And then I thought of the freezing water and realized that there was no prospect of survival at all."[82]

As the seconds dragged by, captain and crew waited for the bombs that would spell death to them all. To their astonishment they never came. Slowly, Bleichrodt opened the hatch to the conning tower and climbed in to use the periscope to search for their tormentor. His voice travelled to the men waiting below:

> "Machine is flying off. Strange. Open pressure doors. Chief, if you'd finally like to bring the stern under would you do so?"

Eventually the inept LI lowered the boat to the muddy seafloor before bringing *U109* to the surface in an empty sea, the two merchant ships having wasted no time in departing the scene. Bleichrodt did likewise and *U109* sailed south to the latitude of New York and warmer weather, enabling maintenance work on the diesel engines. This then was the first real penetration of American waters by U-boat.

By 3 November *U109* had begun its return journey, once more with no successes to boast of. Bleichrodt then received orders to divert to the east of Bermuda and rendezvous with the captured Norwegian ship *Silvaplana*, meeting on 10 November and the two ships making way for France. The following day *U109*'s LI caused Bleichrodt further embarrassment when he lost control of a trial dive, sending the boat hurtling down out of control before blowing tanks and shooting it stern first out of the water, much to the amusement of *Silvaplana*'s new master. On 16 November they parted company, *Silvaplana* entering harbour the next day. Bleichrodt returning to Lorient to congratulations on a "special mission well carried out".[83]

25 October: *U117*, the second of the huge Type XB minelayers, was commissioned. The Type XB minelaying U-boats were the largest built by Germany during the Second World War. Designed for laying distant mine barrages, the two Type XBs were not destined for operational use within the 2nd U-Flotilla, an embargo having been placed on the use of the TMC moored mines with which they were to be equipped. After extensive working up in the Baltic and conversion work to a temporary role as supply U-boats they would be transferred to Brest's 1st U-Flotilla in January 1942.

During the third week of October three 2nd U-Flotilla boats put to sea from Lorient: *U123*, the aged *U38* and *U106*, the latter's first patrol under her former IWO Kaptlt.

---

[82] Hirschfeld pp. 99–100.

[83] *Silvaplana* later became the *Irene* and was used as a blockade-runner under the umbrella of the Kriegsmarine's *Abteilung Marinesonderdienst*. She was sunk near Cape Finisterre on 10 April 1943, scuttled under attack by HMS *Adventure*.

Hermann Rasch. All three were destined for the North Atlantic. *U123* and *U38* were ordered to join the *Schlagetot* group lying south-east of Greenland while Rasch sailed independently for the same inhospitable waters.

Tragedy overtook *U106* two days from port while it battered northwards beneath a cloudless sunny sky. The sunshine crowned mounting swells and as the boat pitched its way into the Atlantic four men gulped down hot coffee before climbing the conning tower ladder to begin their watch. They were all experienced submariners and, after struggling into position atop the conning tower, began their four-hour watch while the wind rapidly increased from a stiff force 4 breeze to the howling gale of a force 8. Coupled with the increased turbulence was a following sea, dangerous to life and limb as it swept stern first over *U106*. Perhaps it was the unbroken blue skies that lulled the watch into inattention, or perhaps their desire to do without the heavy canvas webbing straps that slowed any attempt at getting below during an emergency dive. The reason for not using their harnesses can only be guessed at. The tower hatch had been closed for nearly an hour after towering swells had shipped through into the control room, adding tons of water to the boat's bilges. As the replacement watch threw open the hatch they were shocked to discover an empty bridge, all four men due for relief having been washed overboard. Oblt.z.S. Werner Grüneberg, *Fähnrich zur See* Herbert von Bruchhausen, *Oberbootsmaat* Karl Heemann and *Matrose* Ewald Brühl had disappeared, their cries for help lost in the noise of the Atlantic and pounding diesels. Rasch immediately reversed course to search for them for eight hours, but no trace was ever found. After a brief crew meeting they decided to press on, now short of an officer, Rasch himself being obliged to stand watches.

Meanwhile the two new *Schlagetot* boats had already seen action, diverted to the pursuit of 'four fast ships' sighted by the 1st U-Flotilla's *U84*. Considered by Dönitz a doubtful hunt at best, orders were issued cancelling the chase on 21 October after *U84* alerted the targets with a failed attack. The five armed merchant cruisers, escorted by a single British destroyer and two US Coast Guard cutters immediately increased speed, but, unfortunately for them, Kaptlt. Reinhard Hardegen, aboard *U123*, chose to ignore Dönitz's orders.

That day Hardegen made contact with the fast-moving group and fired three bow torpedoes at the third ship in line, a fourth stern shot at a separate target frustrated by the escort. While two torpedoes streaked harmlessly wide, the third struck the 14,000-ton converted White Star Liner HMS *Aurania*, causing considerable damage. *Aurania*'s captain ordered lifeboats swung out as a precaution, one of which accidentally launched and capsized on hitting the water. Hunted by the escort and believing his target doomed, Hardegen briefly changed course, vainly chasing the remaining liners which quickly outpaced him. Returning to the scene of *Aurania*'s torpedoing Hardegen found nothing except a single lifeboat carrying Leading Seaman Bertie E. Shaw who told Hardegen that he had seen an internal explosion in *Aurania*, after which she passed from view. Believing his story, Hardegen radioed success and was credited with the sinking by Dönitz who also forgave the breach of discipline. Unknown to Hardegen, however, *Aurania* had not sunk, making good her escape at reduced speed, three ratings, including Shaw, lost during the attack. Hardegen rejoined the other *Schlagetot* boats and resumed his course for Greenland.

Rasch meanwhile had restored spirits aboard *U106* after sinking the independently sailing SS *Rose Schiaffino* on 28 October. He then followed boats of the *Reisswolf* pack in their pursuit of ON28. Rasch, the only one to break through strong escort forces, mounted a solitary successful attack, torpedoing US Navy oiler SS *Salinas*. Reporting her 'disintegrating in violent explosions', Rasch claimed a kill, but in fact the badly damaged ship limped away to safety, reaching Argentina after a superb display of seamanship by her skipper Captain Harley Cope.

November began with all three of the 2nd U-Flotilla boats concentrated within the *Raubritter* group, *U123*, *U38* and *U106*, south-east of Cape Farewell. The trio had no success in subsequent attacks against SC52 and soon returned to Lorient. *U38*, arriving on 21 November and on to Stettin, Germany, where it left the roster of the 2nd U-Flotilla, transferred to training duties.

30 October: *U124* set out from Lorient, Mohr destined for an assault against the shipping capital of South Africa, lack of targets within the North Atlantic persuading BdU to attack Cape Town rather than the depleted Freetown area.

U124 had received a thorough overhaul during its time in port, including new paint on her 'Edelweiss', and a new on-board doctor, Dr. Gernot Ziemke, late of *U68*. A trainee LI, twenty-nine-year-old Oblt. (Ing.) Egon Subklew, transferred from *UC1*, accompanied the boat to learn from Brinker before eventually replacing him. Mohr joined Clausen's *U129* which had sailed nine days earlier, also tasked with the journey to South Africa. *U68* and the 7th U-Flotilla's *UA* rounded out the assault group, designated *Kapstadt* and scheduled for refuelling from the tanker *Python*. The *Kapstadt* boats were forbidden to attack shipping south of the equator to avoid nullifying the advantage of surprise required for success.

By 22 November both *U124* and *U129* had refuelled and received orders to head for their operational area. Nearby, Merten's *U68* had been at sea for over two months, having sunk only three ships, including the Royal Navy oiler SS *Darkdale* in the St Helena roads; the first British ship sunk by U-boat south of the equator.

On 24 November *U124* sighted the unmistakeable masts of a large ship on the horizon, slowly growing into the silhouette of British cruiser HMS *Dunedin*, unescorted and vulnerable, steaming a zigzag pattern at 18 knots. Mohr raced ahead of the ship's path and ordered his boat dived to lie in wait. As *U124* approached she suddenly broached and lurched to the surface for a brief but potentially fatal moment. Amazingly they remained unseen, Brinker having trouble controlling the boat's violent yaw as it plunged downwards, the forward hydroplanes jammed. Finally, Brinker brought the boat back under control, but when Mohr peered again through his scope there was no sign of the target. Then he spotted the ship at a range of over three miles, the cruiser having changed course at the most inopportune moment and now well past favourable attack range. Ever the optimist, Mohr ordered new calculations set into the torpedo computer and three eels fired at 1521hrs. As the dubious crew eyed their young commander standing nonchalantly next to the lowered periscope, minutes dragged by, Mohr seemingly unconcerned about the marginal attack that took three precious eels from their stocks. After five minutes and 23 seconds the distant rumble of two hits echoed through the water, *Dunedin* hit and rolling first to port then starboard before sinking stern first. Only seventy-two British sailors survived to face days of burning sun and prowling sharks before rescue by the American steamer SS *Nishmaha*.

Several 2nd U-Flotilla boats returned during November. Kaptlt. Günter Kuhnke brought *U125* to rest against the *Isére*, subdued after having no success as part of the Freetown hunting force, a disappointing way to end his front-line career. He was to be transferred ashore as commander of the 10th U-Flotilla, raising in Lorient. Taking Kuhnke's place aboard *U125* was Kaptlt. Ulrich Folkers, formerly of *U37*.

Four days later *U66* docked after an uneventful Freetown patrol, a single Panamanian tanker falling to Zapp's torpedoes at the end of September, taking six eels to destroy her.

1. *Kapitänleutnants* Lott and Büchel chat from the conning towers of *U35* and *U32* in Cadiz Harbour during the Spanish Civil War. Note the national colours.

2. The Saltzwedel Flotilla in pre-war Wilhelmshaven.

3. An early Type VII at sea. The small conning tower was soon extended with a *Wintergarten* to accommodate the flak weapon, its mounting visible here on the stern deck.

4. A Type VII moves toward its icebreaker escort, the obsolete battleship *Schlesien* in German home waters, early 1940.

5. The external stern tube of the Type VII can be plainly seen in this photograph taken during the harsh winter of 1939/40 in Wilhelmshaven. Note the cable supplying electricity to the moored U-boat and the absence of a firing pistol in the stored torpedo.

6. One of the two unstable Type Is in service with the Saltzwedel Flotilla. Neither lasted long in combat.

7. KK Werner Hartmann when commander of *U37*, soon to take charge of the 2nd U-Flotilla.

8. *U31* photographed from Squadron Leader M. Delap's attacking Blenheim bomber seconds before she was sunk by bombs in Schillig Roads, 11 March 1940.

9. Kaptlt Otto Schuhart (left in white cap) and Fritz-Julius Lemp (right in white cap) talk while *U29* and *U30* lie in the locks at Wilhelmshaven, 4 May 1940.

10. Kaptlt Victor Oehrn and the jubilant crew of *U37* on 9 June 1940 after their war patrol to kick-start the U-boat offensive. Oehrn is the central figure standing on the *Wintergarten* wearing the dark sweater. Immediately left of him, seated with one leg through the railing, is Oblt (Ing) Gerd Suhren.

11. *U30* enters Wilhelmshaven at the end of its final combat patrol, 27 August 1940. Kaptlt Lemp is at left on *U30's* bridge. Schnurzel's picture can be seen on the conning tower flank.

12. *Generalleutnant* Krazert tours *U65* with Kaptlt von Stockhausen, Brest, August 1940.

13. ObltzS Hans Jenisch's sinking on 28 October 1940 of the largest ship destroyed by U-boat during the Second World War is immortalized in the 'War Book for German Youth' "Empress of Britain, journey into death".

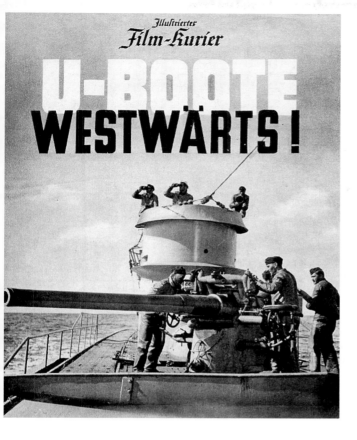

14. *U123* goes to
war – on the
silver screen.
An illustrated
film magazine
from 1941.

15. *U106* photographed
in Lorient before
departure,
February 1941.

16. The smallest of Lorient's U-boat bunkers, the so-called Scorff bunker, nears completion, 1941.

17. *U124* refuels from the German tanker *Python*, 20 November 1941, in the South Atlantic.

18. Operation *Paukenschlag* took the United States by surprise as the 2nd U-Flotilla opened the attacks on America in January 1942. Here a U-boat displays its trophies in Lorient.

19. Even aboard the spacious deck of a Type IXC, artillery crews suffered the effects of the weather.

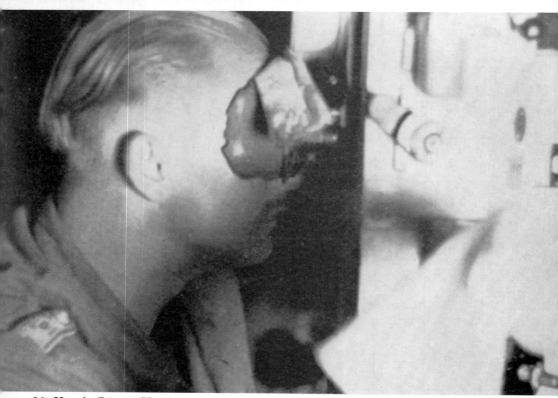

20. Kaptlt Günter Hessler at work.

21. KK Viktor Schütze, ex-commander of *U103*, senior officer of the 2nd U-Boat
   Flotilla between October 1940 and January 1943.

22. Kaptlt Werner Winter (right) atop the conning tower of *U103* in Lorient. The *Sigrune* symbol, originating from Schütze's time in command and incorporated into the 2nd U-Flotilla device, can be plainly seen.

23. Kaptlt Johann 'Jochen' Mohr on the *Wintergarten* of *U124*, Lorient April 1942.

24. Another Type IX returns to Lorient, triumphant if the sinking pennants are an accurate gauge.

25. *U124* – the 'Edelweiss boat' – successfully returned once more to Lorient.

26. July 1942: KK Werner Hartenstein and his crew arrive in Plauen, Hartenstein's birthplace and *Patenstadt* for *U156*. On the left of his jacket the large German Cross in Gold ('Hitler's Fried Egg') is above the Spanish Cross, awarded for service during the Spanish Civil War.

27. The crew of *U564* begin transferring fuel to *U162* (background),
1 September 1942. Two days later *U162* was sunk by Royal Navy
destroyers north-east of Trinidad.

28. Another photo of the resupply rendezvous between *U162* (right) and
U564.

29. *U518* under attack by an RAF Sunderland while outbound north of the Spanish coast, 27 June 1943. Kaptlt Friedrich-Wilhelm Wissmann managed to nurse his damaged boat back to Bordeaux.

30. Albrecht Achilles, the 'Ferret of Port of Spain'. Killed in action off Brazil on 27 September 1943.

31. The crew of *I29* are introduced to the European art of football at Lager Lemp, quarters for the 2nd U-Boat Flotilla, March 1944.

32. KK Ernst Kals comes to grips with Japanese cuisine on 20 March 1944 while guest of the crew of *I29* at Lager Lemp.

33. *Obersteuermann* Walter Kaeding (third from left) receives the Knight's Cross on 15 May 1944 in Lager Lemp. Second from left is Ernst Kals.

34. Part of *U1227's* crew arriving in Norway on Boxing Day 1944, the last boat to leave the roster of the 2nd U-Flotilla. Fifth from right (in peaked cap) is MstA Dr. Gerhard Pollakowski, the ship's doctor.

The day of Zapp's homecoming also saw *U502* back in Lorient, again claiming only a single success. Two days later it was Günter Hessler's turn at the end of his final voyage aboard *U107*. Futile patrolling of the Freetown and Gibraltar trade lines had added nothing to Hessler's score of three ships sunk in September west of the Canaries. After docking, Hessler began preparations to hand over command to Harald Gelhaus, former IWO of *U103*, before he himself took up his new post as *1. Admiralstabsoffizier* at BdU (Ops), replacing Victor Oehrn.

1 December: The third of four AG Weser additions to the 2nd U-Flotilla, KK Ernst Kals' *U130*, left Kiel for France. Both *U127* and *U131* had preceded him during November and *U128* would follow on 9 December. Dönitz, who wanted *U130* in Lorient to prepare for an ambitious forthcoming assault, curtailed Kals' journey, but *U130* still managed to account for three merchant ships from convoy SC57 west of Rockall before reaching France.

9 December: In Lorient, showing the effects of RAF bombing, KK Klaus Scholtz took *U108* out for its fifth war patrol, destined originally for the western Atlantic before diverted to join the *Seeräuber* group in action west of Gibraltar. En route Scholtz attacked and sank the Portuguese freighter SS *Cassequel* before joining *Seeräuber* lying in wait for HG76 due to sail for England. The day following Scholtz's departure the veteran *U107* sailed for the same region on her first patrol with Kaptlt. Harald Gelhaus in command.

Two days after Americans awoke to find their country at war with Imperial Japan, following the surprise attack on Pearl Harbor by the Imperial Japanese Navy at dawn on 7 December, *Grossadmiral* Karl Dönitz noted the removal of operational limits against American shipping in the BdU War Diary:

> "The lifting of all restrictions regarding USA ships and the so-called Pan-American safety zone has been ordered by the Führer. Therefore the whole area of the American coasts will become open for operations by U-boats, an area in which the assembly of ships takes place in single traffic at the few points of departure of Atlantic convoys."

There was satisfaction among many officers and men of Germany's U-boat service. The belligerence of American warships operating in close cooperation with the Royal Navy had brought the two countries into conflict before, in a virtual state of undeclared war. Now, however, Japan had lit the fuse with fortuitous timing for Dönitz, having virtually suspended Atlantic group operations in the face of diminishing success. The possibilities for success in fresh hunting grounds augured well.

That day Dönitz requested the release of twelve Type IX long-distance U-boats for an immediate attack against America's east coast. He knew that he needed to strike straight away at main points of convoy congregation and at that extreme range only the twenty commissioned Type IX U-boats would be suitable, in particular the eleven Type IXCs. Eight Type IX boats were unavailable – *U43*, sole-surviving Type IXA, preparing to return to Germany for an extensive overhaul, *U124*, *U126* and *U129* encountering problems in the South Atlantic and needing repair and mechanical overhaul, *U67*, *U107* and *U108* about to engage the enemy outside of Gibraltar. Nevertheless the chance remained for his twelve remaining long-range U-boats to achieve what Dönitz hoped would be a "spectacular success" on the American coast. But the following day it was with barely repressed anger that he recorded Berlin's decision regarding the attack on America:

"The Naval Staff has released only six large boats for operations off the American coast . . . It is only regrettable that there are <u>not</u> [original emphasis] sufficient boats available to strike a truly 'spectacular blow'."[84]

In Lorient *Korvettenkapitän* Viktor Schütze was informed that six of his flotilla's boats were to be prepared for sea, *U66*, *U109*, *U123*, *U125*, *U130* (still en route) and *U502*, although this last boat was not destined to make the voyage on schedule. As some small measure of support, ten smaller Type VII boats were to sail for North Canadian waters to operate off Newfoundland in the hope of tying vital Allied escort ships and anti-submarine units to the frigid northern waters. A second wave of Type IXs was also scheduled for a fortnight after the first, followed by more 2nd U-Flotilla boats directed to the far reaches of the West Indies. The following day, 11 December, in a public broadcast that vilified and ridiculed President Roosevelt, Hitler declared war on the United States.

13 December: Kaptlt. Schewe brought *U105* into Lorient after a month in the North Atlantic and Biscay. It was the last operational patrol for Georg Schewe, due to leave the boat for the staff of the new FdU Mediterranean. *U105*'s new commander, Kaptlt. Heinrich Schuch, arrived aboard during January 1942.

The more successful Kaptlt. Ernst Bauer brought *U126* into Lorient at the end of seven weeks at sea, mostly spent off Freetown. He sank an independent steamer while en route and after reaching the equator during mid-October began his lonely patrolling alongside Merten's *U68*. On 19 October Bauer sighted what he at first took to be a Greek ship running the familiar zigzag course of a guilty conscience.

"Because the steamer is zigzagging and is bound for Freetown undoubtedly, it is clear to me that he is an enemy."[85]

Unfortunately he was wrong. She was American SS *Lehigh* bound for Takoradi, on the Gold Coast. Bauer launched his torpedoes at a distance of nearly 3,000 metres, but it was only after they were on their way that he saw the large American flags painted on the ships's sides. However, the impartiality of the United States had long been such a sham that, after noting the ship's neutrality in his KTB, he wrote:

"Anyway, I hope the torpedo hits."

It did, the ship sinking in flames south-west of Freetown. The following morning he added a third ship to his tally, British SS *British Mariner*.

It was well into November before Bauer successfully attacked another target south-south-west of Monrovia, then following BdU instructions and taking his boat into the South Atlantic to refuel from the raider *Schiff 16/Atlantis*. Meeting as planned north-west of Ascension during the early morning of 22 November, the U-boat gulped diesel from hoses trailing behind Kaptlt. Bernhard Rogge's raider, Bauer and a few of his officers visiting *Atlantis* to breakfast with Rogge and his officers. Rogge had already refuelled Merten's *U68* south of Saint Helena in what transpired to be crowded shipping lanes between Freetown and Cape Town, but this time events took a sinister turn. The radio messages directing the two ships together had been intercepted by the British and, with the benefit of Enigma decryption, warships were sent to the likely area of the proposed

---

[84] BdU KTB, 10/12/41
[85] U126 KTB.

meeting. As Bauer enjoyed the rare delight of a hot bath after breakfast, the cruiser HMS *Devonshire* appeared on the horizon, immediately demanding identification from *Atlantis*. *U126* crewmen hastily spilled from the conning tower armed with axes to cut fuel lines as the boat dived under the orders of her IWO, Oblt.z.S. Hans Schweichel. Unfortunately they had already been seen by the cruiser's scout plane, negating any chance of a submerged surprise attack. Aboard the *Atlantis* attempts at bluff were made with a reply that she was the British freighter *Polyphemus*, but they were to no avail and the cruiser opened fire, staying outside the raider's artillery range and that of any underwater U-boat near the German ship.

Schweichel clung to *Atlantis'* side, expecting the cruiser to approach, but *Devonshire* did not oblige, pulverizing *Atlantis* until she was obviously sinking. Rogge scuttled what remained of his ship and *Devonshire* departed at high speed. Immediately the ship was gone *U126* surfaced and began to collect survivors, including the commander, irate at the lack of offensive tactics used by his subordinate. *Atlantis'* crew of 305 men were fished from the water, distributed above and below decks and in six lifeboats taken in tow by *U126*. Bauer radioed his predicament to BdU, adding that he did not have sufficient fuel for the return journey.

Instructions were sent to rendezvous with *Python* in the central Atlantic. As before, Bletchley Park was quick at breaking the coded messages and a second Royal Navy trap was set in motion. On 24 November *U126* found *Python* after homing on her beacon signals and transferred *Atlantis'* crew to the comparatively spacious tanker while taking fuel. As the two parted company *Python* sailed to its rendezvous with the *Kapstadt* U-boats awaiting resupply near Cape Town.

By 20 November *U124* and *U129* had successfully refuelled and returned to operations. On 1 December Merten's *U68* and the 7th U-Flotilla's unusual *UA* were in the act of refuelling when the cruiser HMS *Dorsetshire* appeared on the horizon and again a German tanker found itself under concentrated and accurate fire. Both U-boats dived to attack, but Merten's boat still had partially stored torpedoes aboard and trim was lost, sending the boat out of control, *UA* firing a wild spread of torpedoes that missed.

Aboard *Python* all hope was lost and the captain ordered his ship scuttled and men to the lifeboats. As the tanker settled the combined crew of *Python* and *Atlantis* pulled away from the dying ship while *Dorsetshire* retreated. Merten surfaced alongside *UA* and the two U-boats began collecting survivors. There were hundreds of men to be taken back to France and Dönitz ordered both nearby *U124* and *U129* to assist, men crammed into every available space as the bizarre flotilla headed for France, all plans for the *Kapstadt* assault on Cape Town abandoned. Mohr had added a final ship to his score on the way to the rescue. At 2146hrs on 3 December he torpedoed a darkened steamer, hitting her with all three eels fired. Unfortunately, the victim was the neutral American SS *Sagadhoc*, sunk while bound from New York to Durban with general cargo. Nevertheless Mohr and his crew lost little sleep over the destruction of the American and souvenirs of one of the ship's life rings and two tyres fished from the sea were hung from the U-boat's aerial jumper wire during their return to France after taking on board *Atlantis* and *Python* survivors. More practically, six drums of transmission oil, a drum of ball-bearing lubricant and eighteen canisters of oil were also retrieved from the scene of the American's demise. This in some way rectified problems that Oblt. (Ing.) Brinker was having with contaminated lubricant. Near the Cape Verde Islands four BETASOM boats arrived and the German raider crews were redistributed between the eight boats. The first to dock was Merten on 24 December, carrying, among others, a US medical officer POW as well as twenty-five German naval ratings, whom he took to St. Nazaire. Merten subsequently returned to Lorient where the remaining submarines arrived by the end of 1941 in what was the longest range German rescue operation of the war.

The safety of the U-boats' surface passage had been in no small part due to Mohr's actions as he sailed with his overloaded boat near Ascension Island. Cruising within sight of land Mohr could not resist the temptation of creeping into Georgetown harbour in search of stationary targets. He reasoned that even if *U124* were detected it would help convince the British that U-boats were still rampant in the South Atlantic, deflecting attention from their perilous homeward trek.

On 9 December, at 1200hrs, *U124* approached Ascension Island surfaced, intending either to close the island with time to submerge and sink shipping in the harbour or, at the very least, bombard Ascension's small cable station. Unfortunately for Mohr he was quickly spotted by British observers and shelled by the two 5.5" guns at Fort Bedford. These mighty weapons had arrived in Ascension during 1941 along with a small detachment of troops to man them. The guns themselves had a naval history, having been part of HMS *Hood*'s secondary armament, removed in 1934 during a refit in Malta. With artillery fire landing uncomfortably close, Mohr opted to retreat, diving away to safety as Brinker wrestled with the boat's trim, heavy with its unusual burden. However, the ruse had served its purpose and British authorities remained convinced of a U-boat presence around Ascension Island.

The sinking of the supply ships finally convinced Dönitz to abandon the use of surface vessels in support of extended U-boat missions. Fortuitously, during the previous November the first of the newly designed supply U-boats, the Type XIV *U459*, had been commissioned in Kiel into the 4th U-training Flotilla. Although she would not be ready for active service before March 1942, BdU expressed great confidence in the concept of the *Milch Kuh* supply submarine, replacing the vulnerable surface tankers. The planned sailing of *Charlotte Schliemann* from Las Palmas to the South Atlantic as an extra supply ship was cancelled and she remained penned in the Canary Islands port.

17 December: The six U-boat commanders who were to begin Germany's American offensive, now sporting the code name 'Operation *Paukenschlag*' (literally, 'beat on a kettle drum'), travelled from the 'Saltzwedel' Caserne across town to BdU's Kernével headquarters. There they were briefed on their destination and mode of operation. Heinrich Bleichrodt and Ernst Kals, aboard *U109* and *U130* respectively, were to patrol off Newfoundland with the Type VIIs, Richard Zapp, Reinhard Hardegen, Ulrich Folkers and Jürgen von Rosenstiel (*U66*, *U123*, *U125* and *U502* respectively) being ordered further south to attack shipping spread between New York and Cape Hatteras. Due to the shallow waters off the United States' east coast the captains were advised to attack at night, heading offshore for the shelter of deeper water during daylight. Even the Americans, Dönitz reasoned, would be capable of mounting an effective anti-submarine presence once the attacks had begun.

The use of deck guns was encouraged, although no attempt was to be made to tangle with naval escorts or other warships. The spreading of panic and confusion along the entire eastern seaboard was the overall ambition. All six Type IX boats were to lie in wait until 13 January 1942 when BdU would give the order for simultaneous attacks.

Early next morning the first boats sailed, *U125* and *U502* both slipping from Lorient in the wake of *Sperrbrecher* escort. Ominously von Rosenstiel lasted only four days at sea before a conspicuously large oil leak compelled a return to base for nearly a month of repairs.

Ulrich Folkers and his crew sailed west as *Paukenschlag*'s spearhead, ignoring a sighting of Gibraltar-bound shipping to continue towards America. By the months' end all fourteen remaining Type IX and Type VII boats were ploughing through deteriorating mid-Atlantic weather to the USA. Radio operator Wolfgang Hirschfeld recalled the departure of *U109* alongside *U130* from Lorient on 27 December:

> "The crew of *U109* paraded on the forecasing in their pirate outfits, hooped shirts from impounded French Navy stock and grey dyed RAF battledress, while Bleichrodt at our head, wore his oldest patched reefer jacket and trousers tucked into salt-streaked seaboots. . . . The Flotilla Chief, Schütze, was addressing the crew of *U130* and talking about the 'Music of the Depth Charges'. I wondered if he would subject us to this drivel again, but when he crossed our decks on the way back to the *Isére* he merely cast an eye over our seedy-looking crew, muttered a brief blessing and departed."[86]

Dönitz's American offensive ploughed steadily westward, sealed orders broken open once they had passed 20° west, commanders finally informing their crews of their objectives. All *Paukenschlag* boats were ordered not to engage enemy shipping before reaching their objectives unless the target could be identified by Gröner's book on merchant shipping as above 10,000 tons. Otherwise the loss of the element of surprise was deemed unwarranted. It was not until the second week of January that the three southernmost U-boats targeting the United States' east coast came within sight of their objective.

Meanwhile Kaptlt. Wolfgang Lüth returned to Lorient after over a month at sea. He (and the luckless *U105*) had made up part of the six-boat-strong *Steuben* group, operating in atrocious conditions near Newfoundland. After days spent scouring the deserted area Dönitz was forced under OKM pressure to redeploy the group west of Gibraltar in search of Allied supply convoys heading to the Mediterranean. Dönitz was adamant that those supply routes spanned the waters of West Africa and Cape Town but was overruled by Raeder who insisted on the relocation of available U-boat groups to the southern Biscay area, heavily patrolled by British sea and air forces.

U43 had begun the trek through heavy seas on 23 November, reaching the Azores within five days. It was there that lookouts spotted elements of the convoy OS12, amounting to about half of its original strength after scattering in severe weather. Approaching surfaced that night, Lüth's IWO fired torpedoes, hitting the ammunition carrier SS *Thornliebank*, which exploded in a welter of enormous cascading flames, flinging huge chunks of debris in all directions. Aboard *U43*'s conning tower, a thousand metres away, *Obersteuermann* Theodor Peterson was hit and severely bruised on his arm by an intact 105mm star shell hurled from the ship. Located by US Coast Guard cutters, *U43* was driven under and subjected to an intense depth charge barrage. Lüth, rattled but not unnerved, quietly slipped away.[87]

Over the next few days Lüth sank two more ships, the final victories of the patrol, *Steuben* then waiting to no avail west of Gibraltar, constantly crash-diving from the attention of enemy aircraft in a testing war of nerves. The old Type IXB boat was badly in need

---

[86] Hirschfield, p. 111.
[87] The unexploded star shell was later recovered from the boat's diesel exhaust and mounted on a wooden plinth by Lüth as a desk ornament.

of refurbishment and Lüth received instructions to take her back to Germany at the end of December for overhaul.

20 December: In Lorient, a brief ceremony passed the Kéroman I and II bunkers officially over to the Kriegsmarine. They were the most intricate and ambitious of all U-boat shelters. Kéroman I measured 120m long, 85m wide and 18.5m high, sufficient room for five dry-dock pens (designated K1 to K5), a slipway jutting alongside K1 into the water for lifting submarines. Kéroman II was built on dry land immediately before Kéroman I, the two separated by an 85m esplanade, KII also fed with submarines raised using the single slipway. This 'dry bunker' measured 138m long by 128m wide with a height of 18.5m, and held seven pens designated K6 to K12, each closed with a metre-thick armoured door like those of Kéroman I. There was also an eighth pen, designated K6A, that housed the two traversers which transported the submarines once on dry land.

Both bunkers had the same general internal layout and organization. Each pen interior was 15m wide, 10m high and able to house any U-boat exclusive of the Type XB and the later Type IXD2 long-range boats stationed at Bordeaux. At the rear of the pens was a five-metre-wide passageway which ran the bunker's entire length, separating each pen from the various workshops. Additionally, behind Kéroman I, was an 82m by 25m shelter housing electrical generators, a similar smaller bunker behind Kéroman II protecting transformers and fuel tanks. Feeding the voracious needs of repair and overhaul facilities, underground pipes delivered oil, gasoline, lubricants, fresh water and seawater into the bunkers.

A small addition built onto the south-western edge of the slipway during 1942 contained an eight-metre-high escape training tank for U-boat crews. The tank could take up to twenty sailors in a single session, standing bathed by the glow of four red lights as fresh water was pumped to chest level. At the sound of a hammer striking the upper rim, the men slipped below the water before entering a flooded hatchway where an instructor crouched, opening the hatch and swimming for safety through the full upper chamber.

The final touch for Kéroman II was in the upper levels of pen K6A (the traverser garage) where accommodation was built for 1,400 men, including a theatre, canteen, living quarters, cold storage and food lockers, mess facilities and scores of drafting and engineering offices. Other spaces contained fire-fighting, repair, supply and storage rooms, kitchens, bakeries as well as hospital and dental facilities. Along a winding road that stretched from the rear of Kéroman II toward the *Quartier d'artillerie Frébault* lay six large bunkers, named *Wolf*, *Tiger*, *Luchs*, *Leopard*, *Iltis* and *Jaguar*, which housed torpedo warheads or detonators.

The system for raising and moving U-boats from the sea into their pens was relatively complex. The first stage was for the U-boat to enter the slipway, a dock gate closed behind it and some water pumped out. The boat was guided onto a cradle by a huge overhead crane, the wheeled cradle in turn running on four rails on the bed of a wheeled trolley base. The trolley, 45m by 11m, was then winched up the mild gradient by a 220hp electric windlass. Once at the top the cradle moved off the trolley, running on its own wheels on to equivalent four-railed tracks set into the bed of the traverser, a thirty-two-wheel mobile platform measuring 48m by 13m. This traverser moved laterally along the esplanade, half its wheels powered by a 40hp electric motor. Once directly opposite the chosen pen it stopped and the cradle moved along feeder tracks into the pen, armoured doors closed and work began. The entire operation from water to the farthest pen of KII could be accomplished in an absolute minimum of one hour. The sole procedure that couldn't be undertaken within the bunkers themselves was the periscope removal, the ceiling height disallowing it. However, a mobile crane running on rails at the edge of the Kéroman II roof was used for this purpose. Meanwhile work continued on Kéroman III, having begun the previous October.

While the 2nd U-Flotilla teetered on the brink of their American onslaught, BdU recorded the possible loss of two flotilla boats elsewhere, both casualties underlining Dönitz's contention that slow-diving and heavy Type IX U-boats were unsuitable for operations around the North African coast.

Despite his request for greater *Paukenschlag* forces being rebuffed in Berlin, Dönitz had already despatched a second small wave of "drumbeaters" in a bid to reinforce his opening assault. *U107* and *U108* had begun their journey during the second week of December, but, to Dönitz's exasperation, they were first obliged by OKM to join the *Seeräuber* group lying west of Casablanca in wait for convoy HG76. Completing the pack were *U67*, *U131* and *U434*, the latter a 7th U-Flotilla Type VIIC. Guided by a Condor sighting, initial U-boat contact was made by Scholtz's *U108* at 1008hrs on the morning of 17 December, shadowing strongly defended convoy with "aircraft carrier, destroyers, corvettes and large motorboats", actually sixteen ships of Captain Frederick 'Johnny' Walker's Escort Group 36. By early afternoon *U107* had also made contact, holding it until 0051hrs on 18 December, whereupon Kaptlt. Harald Gelhaus reported the convoy within striking distance of the assembled *Seeräuber* pack. Dönitz gave the awaited order and battle commenced, becoming a German disaster.

The first to fall before Walker's force was KK Arend Baumann's brand new *U131*, fresh from Kiel and twelve days past its first victory, the sinking of British SS *Scottish Trader* south of Iceland. Baumann was sighted attempting to close HG76 by a Martlet aircraft from the flight deck of HMS *Audacity*. Gliding into a shallow dive, the small aircraft strafed *U131*, causing the startled bridge watch to tumble inside the control room as Baumann ordered a crash dive to escape. Five escort ships converged above *U131*, hurling depth charges below them, the corvette HMS *Penstemon*'s charges causing severe damage as the U-boat sank deeper into the Atlantic in an effort to shake off her pursuers.

Baumann succeeded in escaping, but was forced to surface two hours later to decide whether his boat could continue the chase after its beating. He rapidly concluded that this was not possible and opted to run for home on the surface. However, Baumann could not have emerged at a less unfortunate moment. The escorts had not left the scene and immediately spotted the cough of smoke from igniting diesels. Destroyers HMS *Blankney*, *Stanley* and *Exmoor*, the sloop *Stork* and corvette *Penstemon* again roared after *U131*. Joining the chase was another Martlet fighter, flown by Sub-Lieutenant G.R.P. Fletcher. As the fighter aircraft dived for a strafing run Baumann's men manned their flak weapons and responded with a devastating anti-aircraft barrage, hitting Fletcher and tearing the cockpit area to shreds, sending it wheeling into the sea. This was the first victory of a U-boat against an aircraft, and fatal for its pilot. Walker, watching from the *Stork*'s bridge, was now determined not to let his quarry escape.[88]

Baumann knew that to dive was probably fatal, not only because of the perilous state of his damaged boat but because he would be denied mobility by adept ASDIC operators. But his boat was losing the surface race. He ordered a rapid message transmitted to BdU that he was "unable to dive and chased by four destroyers" [sic] but the reply provided no comfort. The battle against HG76 was taking form elsewhere and Dönitz radioed "aid was not possible and that she should scuttle herself, if there was no other alternative". Almost

---

[88] Fletcher's body was later recovered and buried at sea with full military honours.

as the message was received, British shellfire began falling around *U131*, zeroing in on the steel hull. Shell splinters killed one man on the bridge as Baumann gave the order to abandon ship and scuttle. It was the end of a short U-boat career for KK Arend Baumann and the majority of his crew. At 1640hrs distant *U434* reported observing artillery flashes and at least three destroyers near *U131* and BdU recorded:

"No further reports have been received from *U131*, or regarding her."

The following day confirmation of a sort was had in Lorient's 2nd U-Flotilla headquarters as commander KK Schütze received a brief copy of an intercepted British message that reported the sinking of *U131* and "capture of forty-four men".[89] By then the full scale of the German débâcle against HG76 was beginning to be appreciated in the underground BdU command centre at Kernével as further boats ceased to respond to appeals for information, including a second from Viktor Schütze's flotilla. *U127* had stopped replying to position requests.

Kapitänleutnant Bruno Hansmann had taken *U127* from Kiel on 29 November 1941, traversing the Kaiser Wilhelm Canal before entering the open sea from Brunsbüttel. The U-boat crossed the stormy waters between the Faeroes and Iceland before striking south into the mid-Atlantic. This had initially been this new boat's destination, but alternative instructions from BdU diverted it east towards the North African traffic lanes. Hansmann had served on *U95* as a 'commander-in-training' during the same period the previous year, prowling from the North Channel to the Outer Hebrides for a month of uncomfortable and arduous patrolling. He may indeed have felt relief at being directed away from the Atlantic toward Spain, but such feelings were to be short-lived.

Hansmann was vectored toward the impending battle with HG76 as it was reported departing Gibraltar Roads on the afternoon of 14 December, the *Seeräuber* group already assembling in ambush. Unfortunately for Hansmann's inexperienced crew their very eagerness for battle proved their undoing and during the course of the day a Gibraltar-based Sunderland flying boat on a routine reconnaissance sweep sighted them, accurately reporting their position to the Royal Navy.

Meanwhile an erroneous report from German spies in Portugal stated that the British convoy had returned to Gibraltar for reasons unknown. Perhaps this lowered the level of vigilance aboard *U127*, which by now had arrived on station at the southern end of the *Seeräuber* line. Unbeknown to Hansmann and his men they lay directly in the path of a small hunter-killer group detached from the powerful "Force H" following the Sunderland's report and comprising the destroyers HMS *Croome*, *Foxhound* and *Gurkha II* and the Australian HMAS *Nestor*. It was Commander G.S. Stewart's *Nestor* that first sighted *U127* at approximately 2300hrs, the large U-boat visible at a distance of seven miles. The Australian ship immediately opened fire. Despite all shots falling wide, the sudden barrage succeeded in driving *U127* under as Hansmann made a fatal error and ordered the boat dived.

Sonar conditions were excellent and both *Nestor* and *Foxhound* were quickly able to find the U-boat and attack. Stewart ordered an initial spread of five shallow-set depth charges prepared for dropping, all five plummeting onto *U127*'s unmistakeable sonar trace. As the underwater detonations subsided HMS *Foxhound* was in turn preparing to engage Hansmann's U-boat when a sudden rumbling explosion deep beneath their keel heralded the complete destruction of *U127* and her crew. The victorious Allied destroyers were

---

[89] There were in fact 47 men captured, including the commander.

able to confirm their success by recovering pieces of splintered wooden debris and what was described in the after-action report as "human remains" from a sea stained with thick diesel oil.

Seeräuber's attacks on HG76 and the devastating British response were catastrophic for the Germans. While three merchant ships, the destroyer HMS *Stanley* and escort carrier HMS *Audacity* were sunk, five U-boats were destroyed. *U67*, *U107* and *U108* all returned to Lorient virtually empty-handed from the engagement, KK Klaus Scholtz's *U108* scoring the sole flotilla success by damaging British SS *Ruckinge*. Despite the poor performance, *U67*'s Kaptlt. Müller-Stöckheim travelled to Paris for the official presentation of the Knight's Cross, awarded by radio during November.

Two new boats were transferred to the 2nd U-Flotilla during the last week of December. *U161* and *U156*, the latter sailing for Lorient at 2200hrs on Christmas Eve under the command of Kaptlt. Werner Hartenstein. Former commander of torpedo boats *Seeadler* and *Jaguar*, as well as commander of the 6th *Torpedobootflottille*, Hartenstein was enjoying his first U-boat command, having transferred to Dönitz's service in March 1941. Those who served alongside him remembered the thirty-three-year-old native of Plauen as a quiet and private man when off duty.

> "I met him for the first time in a French bar. He sat by himself, oblivious to those around him. When I sat down next to him he said in an unfriendly voice, 'My name is Hartenstein. I don't care who you are.' He was a newcomer in the circle of well-known names. He did not hesitate to repulse intrusions into his reserved behaviour with some vehemence, an attitude grounded more in a sense of humility than a desire to hurt others. His experiences and the way he overcame challenges made him someone special."[90]

An oddity of *U156* was the installation of the fixed array FuMO 29 'Seetakt' radar mounted along the upper conning tower frontage. The firm Gema (*Gesellschaft für Elektroakustische Mechanische Apparate*) had developed the original version of 'Seetakt' in 1935 as one of the first operational German radars. Operating on an 82cm bandwidth, its antenna comprised an array of horizontal or vertical dipoles and after two abortive attempts Gema produced a version small enough to be installed into a U-boat during 1941. Two horizontal rows of vertical dipoles were arranged on the conning tower's outer shielding, installed in a half-circle, following the curve of the tower, while the transmitter was mounted internally next to the conning tower ladder; a location that guaranteed it would flood with water nearly every time the hatch was opened. With a maximum range of roughly seven kilometres and a field of view of 60 degrees, the 'Seetakt' proved to be relatively unsuccessful aboard U-boats.

[90] *Odyssey of a U-boat Commander*, Erich Topp, p. 84.

7

THE 'GOLDEN WEST': 1 JANUARY TO 30 JUNE 1942

1 January: The beginning of 1942 found the *U-Bootwaffe*'s strength at 248 boats, twenty-one commissioned during December. Although this figure closer approximates Dönitz's early desires, it includes forty Type II training boats, twenty-eight other training boats and one hundred engaged in either builder's trials or Baltic exercises. Ninety-one front-line boats were available for action at the year's beginning: seventy-one Type VIICs, nineteen Type IXs (all belonging to the 2nd U-Flotilla) and the oddity *UA*. Further statistical analyses showed that of these front-line boats fifty-four were in repair yards. Of the rest, once those returning from patrol or assigned by OKW to the Mediterranean and Arctic were excluded, nineteen U-boats remained active within the Atlantic, all but six sailing for operational areas.

> "The renewal of the U-boat war in the Atlantic will have to be considered on the following points . . .
> a. The number of combat boats which are to carry the load is smaller than before the Atlantic battle . . .
> b. The entrance of America into the war has provided the commanders with areas which are not hemmed in by defences and which offer much better chances of success."[91]

On New Year's Day the 2nd U-Flotilla numbered twenty-four boats, the two large Type XB minelayers still in Kiel's shipyards and due to transfer at the month's end to Brest's 1st U-Flotilla.

2 January: In the early morning B-Dienst radio interception picked up distress broadcasts from the Greek SS *Dimitrios Ingtenis*, separated from its parent convoy SC63 after breaking its rudder. Lying less than 200 miles east of Newfoundland BdU estimated it to be within possible range of Hardegen's *U123*, authorizing the young commander to search for the damaged ship providing it lay within 150 miles. Over twice that distance away, Hardegen nonetheless again chose to 'bend' his orders and chased after the lame duck. That night, after several hours at full speed, *U123* entered an eerie seascape of drifting fogbanks. The sound of a foghorn echoed through the gloom, soon joined by a second and then a third foghorn from separate quarters. Hardegen was perplexed and warily ordered both slow-running diesel engines shut down. The unmistakeable sound of the steamer's large slow propeller, an ocean tug and two higher-pitch screws could be heard – destroyers. Hardegen's lookouts then spotted a shadow ahead, at first taken to be the steamer, before the fog thinned and revealed an enemy warship flanking the Greek as she was towed by tug towards the mainland, a second destroyer lying only 500 yards to

[91] BdU KTB, January 1942.

starboard. Deciding that the risk outweighed the prize, Hardegen dived and retreated, berating himself for wasting valuable fuel on the abortive diversion and later for not immediately seizing the initiative and following his Admiral's advice – "Attack, pursue, sink!"

As the first wave of *Paukenschlag* boats battled westwards, a second group was setting out from Lorient in order to preserve the attack's momentum. Kaptlt. Werner Winer took *U103* from Lorient alongside Hermann Rasch's *U106* on 3 January, followed four days later by Harald Gelhaus and *U107*. On 8 January *U108* also sailed, although Scholtz was compelled to return to Lorient with damaged diesels, docking in Lorient three days later for twelve hours of repair before resailing. The fifth boat for the new wave was Ulrich Heyse's *U128*, putting to sea from Lorient in the company of a single *Sperrbrecher* and two *Vorpostenboote* on 8 January, the only Type IXC of the second group. But the boats' movements were not unseen. Their progress reports to BdU were picked up by Admiralty direction finders as they passed mid-Atlantic. This intelligence, added to Rodger Winn's Submarine Tracking Room's warnings of U-boats headed westwards, painted an indelible picture of German intentions for anybody who was inclined to look.

As *U128* slipped into the Bay of Biscay orders flashed from Kernével for the new 2nd U-Flotilla boat *U161*, in transit from Kiel, to put into Lorient at once in preparation for a separate assault across the Atlantic. This new group, '*Neuland*', was to journey to the Caribbean and attack shipping within the Aruba-Curaçao-Trinidad triangle in the aptly named 'Operation *Westindien*'.

9 January: The *Paukenschlag* boats finally received notification of their exact patrol areas. *U66* was ordered off Cape Hatteras, moving progressively south while *U123* was given the prize – a huge square before New York. *U125* was placed seawards of Hardegen, operating against offshore traffic. To the north, astride the Canadian-American sea lanes, Bleichrodt's *U109* was ordered to patrol south and south-east of Nova Scotia. Kals was also given the Canadian region, *U130* sailing between Nova Scotia and Newfoundland.

Hardegen provided intimation of what was to follow when he chanced upon the 9,076-ton British steamer SS *Cyclops* south-east of Nova Scotia. The thirty-six-year-old Ocean Steamship Company vessel, mastered by Captain Leslie Webber Kesley, lumbered into Hardegen's crosshairs on 11 January doing nine knots, her triple expansion steam engine hammering away below decks at three-quarter speed. A single torpedo streaked from *U123*'s number three bow tube at 0149hrs the following morning, striking the merchant ship slightly astern of her tall smokestack. *Cyclops* staggered under the impact and began settling in the water, her 'SSS' distress call prompting Hardegen to order deck gun manned as the MG34 machine gun mounted atop the conning tower opened fire, attempting, unsuccessfully, to hit the wireless shack. Seeing the British steamer refuse to go under and some crewmen possibly preparing to reboard their abandoned ship, Hardegen ordered stern tube number five fired as a *coup-de-grâce*. The torpedo cut through the body of one of the freighter's gunners who had been hurled overboard by the first explosion before crashing into *Cyclops*' iron hull. Five minutes later the bow of SS *Cyclops* rose skyward before disappearing underwater, taking two men, a gunner and the ship's doctor, down with her. Eventually only ninety-four survivors would be found of *Cyclops*' 181 crew and passengers. Meanwhile Hardegen continued on his way. The first drumbeat had begun to play in American waters.

Dönitz attempted to divert Allied attention away from the *Paukenschlag* boats by sending various Type VIIs into the North Atlantic to run sweeping patterns, broadcasting frequent signals in the hope of simulating a larger presence, in the traditional U-boat hunting ground. It failed, and Rodger Winn in the Admiralty's U-boat tracking room had pieced together enough information to deduce that 'five or six' U-boats were heading west towards Newfoundland and New York.

But to their amazement the Germans who closed America's coast discovered a country behaving as if in peacetime. Lights burned brightly at night along the entire seaboard and merchant shipping plied crowded waterways, silhouetted clearly against the American coast and displaying no discipline in their frequent radio chatter. The portent was of a German field day.

On 13 January, at 0118hrs, KK Ernst Kals made what he called an "attack on the first drumbeat" and torpedoed Norwegian SS *Frisco* at the mouth of the Gulf of Saint Lawrence, eight hours later sending a second ship to the bottom, using three torpedoes to destroy SS *Friar Rock* heading from Quebec to Sydney, Nova Scotia. Four days later seven survivors were rescued from a lifeboat along with the bodies of twelve others who had frozen to death during their ordeal. The survivors reported that Kals had closed their lifeboat and 'fired either torpedo or gun at them', an allegation never proved nor disproved.

Kals moved to the south-east to signal his opening attacks to BdU, then maintaining radio silence to avoid falling victim to what he suspected was accurate onshore direction-finding. Kals had also reported an unwelcome near miss from aircraft before being placed in great jeopardy off Halifax by a combination of aggressive defence and sub-zero temperatures. Five days after his first attacks Kals approached another steamer off Cape Breton, surfaced in the early morning darkness. As IWO, Oblt.z.S. Hans Möglich handled surface firing, Kals hovered on the bridge keeping an all-round view of the situation and passing navigational instructions to the helmsman below. Two torpedoes were fired with no discernible result, a waste of precious ammunition that merely hardened their determination to sink the unidentified ship. The morning was bitterly cold, frozen spray lashing the conning tower, thick ice forming on the upper hull as *U130* positioned for a third shot. At that moment Kals spotted a destroyer bursting from the darkness and racing toward *U130* at high speed, the "bone gripped firmly between its teeth". With no time to dive Kals bellowed for one engine to be thrown full ahead, the other full astern and *U130* pivoted on the spot, its attacker charging by at a distance of only ten metres.

> "I order 'Crash Dive!' As I enter the conning tower a second destroyer appears astern of the steamship. About eight tons of water enter the boat through the frozen diesel exhaust valves, causing us to hit bottom [at a mere 48 metres]. Here I remain, bumping uncomfortably on the rocks. . . . There is no sign of the destroyer; presumably her depth-charge dropping gear has frozen up."[92]

Miraculously, the same weather effects that had nearly spelt doom saved the men of *U130* as they crept away from Canadian destroyers, unable to launch their own weapons.

The following day Hardegen also began operations in earnest, sinking the first ship in American waters, Panamanian tanker SS *Norness* and its Liverpool-bound cargo of 12,222 tons of Admiralty fuel oil. The floundering tanker's crew took to their boats, leaving behind two dead crewmen and the body of the ship's mascot, Pete, a small white-haired mongrel killed by his owner rather than left to face death in an icy lifeboat. Hardegen watched the Norwegian-owned ship go down bow-first, her nose striking the seabed and breaking the wreck in two, before setting course for Ambrose Channel,

---

[92] *U130* KTB, Hessler Chapter IV, p. 4.

the entrance to New York harbour. The following day America woke to the fact that the war had arrived offshore, the *New York Times* headline: 'TANKER TORPEDOED 60 MILES OFF LONG ISLAND".

15 January: Kaptlt. Albrecht Achilles brought *U161* into Lorient's Scorff River after complying with Dönitz's request to cut short his transfer voyage from Kiel. The wiry and athletic Achilles, an ex-merchant mariner, had been a Watch Officer aboard the *Gneisenau* before transfer to the U-boat service and his first post as IWO for Zapp's *U66*. Captaincy of *U161* had come about purely by chance during December 1941. As the boat came out of its lengthy Baltic trials and prepared for sea, her commander Kaptlt. Hans-Ludwig Witt broke his leg in an onshore accident. Achilles, having recently come through his own commander's course, was next in line for a new commission and took charge of the boat as it prepared for action. Now as he entered Lorient he readied himself immediately for the anticipated briefing by Dönitz, alongside the other commanders due to take part in the *Neuland* group.

Dönitz had been taking advice from two ex-merchant navy captains of the Hamburg-Amerika Line who had plied the waters of the southern Caribbean before the war. Based on his own theories on Allied convoy traffic and the insight of the two men Dönitz was determined to at least have one boat each attack Aruba and Curaçao and a third astride the shipping lane from Maracaibo to Aruba. Kaptlt. Günther Müller-Stöckheim's *U67* leaving on 19 January was assigned Curaçao, Kaptlt. Werner Hartenstein's as yet untried *U156* Aruba, alongside Kaptlt. Rosenstiel's *U502*. Kaptlt. Achilles' new *U161* was planned to assault Port of Spain, Trinidad, while Kaptlt. Clausen's *U129* was given the task of general patrolling off the coast of Guiana.

Neuland's primary task was to interfere with the flow of oil and raw materials from South to North America. The two main points of origin for this crucial oil were the fields below Venezeula's Lake Maracaibo and Trinidad, the latter holding its own huge refineries. Trinidad also accommodated small ships carrying raw bauxite from South America, their cargoes transferred to larger freighters which moved the ore onwards to the United States and transformation into aluminium. Curaçao and Aruba also held valuable refineries where Venezuelan oil was transformed from crude to petroleum and gasoline. Aruba's was on the island's eastern tip, the largest in the world and capable of producing 7,100,000 barrels of oil a month. Oil shipped from Lake Maracaibo to Aruba passed through the shallow waters of the Gulf of Venezeula, necessitating the use of a small number of specialized shallow-draught tankers for the fifteen-mile journey.

The *Neuland* offensive was planned for 16 February with the new moon, but opinion sharply differed between Raeder and Dönitz as to how the attacks should begin. Raeder demanded that surfaced U-boats shelled land targets at the outset. Dönitz, on the other hand, refused to order this of his boats as he felt that the U-boats would not only be vulnerable to fire from shore batteries but also that the surprise shock value of an unheralded attack on tanker traffic was of greater importance. Dönitz thus ordered his men to begin their attack with torpedoes, surfacing for artillery attack on refineries and harbour installations only if events allowed. On 19 January *U67*, *U156* and *U502* put to sea, followed five days later by *U161* and *U129*, crawling westwards across the Atlantic on single engines to conserve fuel. The German attack on the Caribbean had begun.

22 January: Wolfgang Lüth brought *U43* from the locks of the Kaiser Wilhelm Canal into the familiar territory of the Kieler Fjord. Sailing past moored training ships Lüth conned his boat into Tirpitz Harbour, tying up alongside the Scheer Mole. During the transfer voyage to Germany he had managed to add a confirmed 21,307 tons to his accumulated victories.

Leaving port on 30 December, his crew refreshed after Christmas ashore, Lüth travelled north-east bound for the circuit around the tip of Scotland. Late on 11 January he surfaced to discover by visual sightings that he was some way off course. More disconcerting, he had surfaced in the midst of convoy HX168 some 500 miles south-west of Iceland. The weather was so atrocious that as *U43* plunged from wave crest to trough her propellers thrashed wildly as they came free of the sea. Then a destroyer escort was sighted behind *U43*, it also making obvious contact. But, after the destroyer nearly capsized while attempting to turn towards the German intruder, both protagonists were reduced to sailing bow-on to the enormous waves, fighting the sea instead of each other. Lüth, realizing the futility of a surfaced attack, dived. Hours spent submerged allowed the weary crew a chance to rest before *U43* resurfaced and began to trail the convoy. Finally, at 0802hrs the following day, Lüth succeeded in sinking a straggler, Swedish MV *Yngaren* hit and broken in half by two torpedoes before losing contact. Two days after this Lüth again chanced upon a convoy, sighting westbound ON55, the ships disorganized after heavy winter storms. During the early hours of 14 December Lüth torpedoed and sank three freighters, claiming a fourth also hit and destroyed, although never corroborated. It has been a successful voyage, and the last that Lüth undertook as part of the 2nd U-Flotilla. While *U43* lay in Kiel for its six-month refit his IWO Oblt.z.S. Hans-Joachim Schwantke replaced him as commander. Lüth, given the choice of subsequent assignment, elected to stay in combat and transferred during April 1942 to the Type IXD2 *U181*, then near commissioning.

25 January: Kaptlt. Fritz Poske took *U504* from Lorient bound for the east coast of the United States as the tail end of the second wave designed to keep the attack momentum begun by the *Paukenschlag* boats. Poske had spent two weeks sailing from Kiel to Lorient, arriving on 20 January for five days of fitting out before his ambitious war patrol. Joining Poske from the 2nd U-Flotilla would be *U105*, sailing the following day.

28 January: By the end of *Paukenschlag*'s second week merchant traffic along America's eastern seaboard had suffered losses exceeding even Dönitz's expectations for damage that could be inflicted by only five boats. Hardegen's *U123* flourished claiming ten ships for a total of 66,135 tons sunk (in fact nine ships sunk for 53,173 tons, with the American tanker SS *Malay* damaged), earning a Knight's Cross for its commander awarded by radio on 22 January. During his mission Hardegen kept arguably the most meticulous and colourful War Diary of the *Paukenschlag* boats. Other commanders heard his lively reports flashed across the Atlantic.

> "The distinguished Hardegen had the bright idea of reporting his successes in verse; Dönitz was not impressed. When I heard the radio-report go out in rhyme, I just thought – 'Oh dear, oh dear, oh dear, you've really put your foot in it now . . .' for the 'Lion' absolutely hated anything like that. The expected thunder held off, though it rumbled inaudibly. Such temptations are better resisted."[93]

---

[93] *Nasses Eichenlaub.*

Nonetheless, Hardegen and his men had been the first German servicemen to glimpse the lights of New York reflected in the night sky as they entered Ambrose Channel, car headlights plainly visible alongside Coney Island's funpark. At 0941hrs they torpedoed the British tanker *Coimbra* as she left New York. Hardegen, echoing Dönitz's sentiments, bemoaned the lack of U-boats with which to press home the offensive.

Elsewhere, *Paukenschlag* boats experienced mixed fortunes. Richard Zapp's *U66* had sunk five ships, having no trouble evading what minor ASW efforts the Americans provided, Zapp remarking later that US destroyer patrols along the east US coast were so regular you could "set your watch by them". But Ulrich Folkers' *U125* only succeeded in despatching a single freighter west of Cape Hatteras, losing several torpedoes in malfunctions or misses before reporting three of the four forward tubes 'out of order'. Low on fuel, Folkers was ordered home, stern tube loaded for opportune targets. None transpired.

Further to the north Kals in *U130* and Bleichrodt's *U109* experienced different conditions. In contrast to the brightly lit American coast where merchant shipping behaved as if still in peacetime, the Canadians had been at war for years and both U-boats were constantly frustrated by air and destroyer patrolling. There were small returns before they were eventually forced south into American waters where Kals went on to destroy six ships in total, Bleichrodt sinking four.

Hardegen's penultimate sinking of the *Paukenschlag* offensive was the British steamer *Culebra*, sunk on 25 January in grid square CC7927 laden with general cargo and aircraft parts bound for England. During mid-afternoon in a moderate sea the mast tips of the British ship were picked up by the bridge watch, Hadegen taking one look before ordering his boat dived and preparations made to engage the ship with artillery. All of *U123*'s torpedoes were gone and the only weapons left were the guns on the boat's deck and conning tower. As the ship approached unawares, Hardegen waited until he was within only 400 metres before ordering tanks blown and gun crews to their stations. The IIWO rushed to oversee the deck gun's action and within minutes shells were whistling toward their target, hitting their mark as *Culebra* began to return fire until its stern weapon was demolished by a direct hit. Atop his conning tower Hardegen had ordered flak fired to silence the British gun, but the 2cm's firing pin appeared to have broken and minutes passed before a replacement pin arrived on the aft *Wintergarten*. The PK reporter aboard *U123*, Alwin Tölle, received permission from Hardegen to come to the bridge and observe the battle with his camera. While fire ceased in order to allow the British crew to abandon ship, Tölle stood near the attack periscope housing in order to photograph the drama of the burning ship's final moments.

As gunnery was about to recommence the anti-aircraft gun crew succeeded in replacing their damaged pin, test-firing a single round. With a blinding flash the barrel exploded, flinging splinters around the conning tower. The gunner's mate, ship's cook Hannes, was wounded with a gash in the left thigh while Tölle collapsed bleeding profusely, a metal fragment protruding from the back of his head. Tölle was carried below, another crewman continuing to snap pictures of the attack. The battered *Culebra* finally succumbed to the heavy gunfire and sank stern first, a final blistering display of pyrotechynics coming from stored ammunition and flares. Approaching the crew's lifeboats Hardegen ordered bread, lard, sausages and canned food passed to them before resuming course for Lorient.

Now, however, there was Tölle's serious injury to be taken into consideration. While the onboard medic, *Funkmaat* Fritz Rafalski, ably treated Hannes, Tölle's wound leaked large amounts of blood and pus, immediately beginning to fester. As Tölle lapsed into a serious fever Hardegen radioed for emergency advice from BdU.

During the early morning of 8 January Hardegen was directed to rendezvous in mid-Atlantic with returning blockade-runner *Spreewald* en route from Manchuria to Bordeaux with a cargo of badly needed rubber, tin, tungsten, quinine and prisoners taken by the raider *Kormoran* in the Far East. The 5,083-ton Hamburg-Amerika Line steamer carried not only a surgeon aboard but also the facilities needed to conduct an emergency operation. *U123* pounded toward the meeting point, arriving a little before midday on 30 January. Hardegen expected to find the steamer as well as *U575*, its escort into Bordeaux, but found nothing but empty sea. By early evening contact with *U575* had been established but there was still no sign of *Spreewald*.

It was on 31 January that news was received from BdU in the form of a signal to all Atlantic U-boats.

"Report at once who torpedoed a ship in BE7140. Give details."

With ominous silence over the airwaves Dönitz repeated his question.

"German steamer *Spreewald* sending SOS. Torpedoed at 1700hrs German legal time. On fire and sinking."

Minutes later a reply from 3rd U-Flotilla's *U333* confirmed that it was she who had sunk a 'definitely enemy steamer' at that time, the ship on the outskirts of the so-called 'Anton' corridor for neutral shipping. *U123* and eight others were ordered to make haste to the scene in order to search for survivors.

Among the U-boats racing to the scene of *Spreewald*'s sinking was *U105*, six days from port, her new commander, Kaptlt. Heinrich Schuch, forced to break off his shadowing of convoy SL98. At 2331hrs Schuch had made a single sinking from the convoy on what he believed was probably an ammunition ship. After firing four torpedoes two large explosions were seen by Schuch and his watch, so huge that they could surely have only come from a sympathetic detonation of stored ammunition. In fact they had, but it had been the sloop USS *Culver* that had exploded. By a coincidence that would probably have pleased the U-boat commander had he known, *Culver* was the first ship fitted operationally with the newly developed advanced automatic HF/DF set, a short-wave direction finder that could track the source bearing of even very short radio communications, soon to cause the U-boat service fresh technological headaches.

During the afternoon of 2 February Schuch arrived at the location of the unfortunate *Spreewald*, finding six lifeboats and rafts carrying twenty-four of the sixty-strong crew and fifty-eight of her eighty-six British prisoners. With the bedraggled men taken aboard, Schuch set immediate course for Lorient, reporting the severe injuries of one survivor by radio to BdU and Dönitz arranging for a Dornier Do24 seaplane to rendezvous with *U105* and take the wounded man to emergency treatment in France. However, after successfully finding the U-boat, the Dornier snapped a wing while attempting to land in the rough sea, her crew added to the rescued men aboard *U105*. Schuch entered port on 8 February, his mercy mission successful.[94]

Hardegen, who had found no survivors, also set course for Lorient, sailing at the most economical speed to conserve his dwindling fuel. He paused to engage a second ship with

---

[94] Cremer, of *U333*, was immediately court-martialled on his return to Lorient for the sinking. He argued that the steamer was in the wrong place, miles from the area that it was supposed to have been in. His evidence was accepted and he was acquitted.

gunfire, sinking the Norwegian SS *Pan Norway* in mid-Atlantic on 26 January, summoning assistance from a Greek freighter for the shipwrecked Norwegian survivors. When the U-boat docked on 9 February she was down to only 80 litres of diesel, tying up to the *Isère* before the gaze of hundreds of well-wishers, photographers, newsreel cameramen and of course Dönitz and the 2nd U-Flotilla staff. The crew posed for cameras before the deck gunk painted with white tonnage scores of the two artillery sinkings. While commander and crew were congratulated, Tölle was lifted gently out of the forward torpedo hatch and taken ashore for emergency surgery.[95] However, despite the success of the *Paukenschlag* boats, Eberhard Godt (BdU. Ops) lamented in the BdU war diary:

> "The commander's report [Hardegen] showed clearly that the initial attack could have been much stronger if instead of only six it had been possible at the time to release to BdU the twelve large boats he had requested."

By then *Paukenschlag* had ended, Bleichrodt's *U109* sinking its final ship on 6 February with artillery, the Panamanian SS *Halcyon* going down at 0300hrs. Bleichrodt had attempted to hit the ship with his last two torpedoes, but both had missed, running under the target and failing to explode. He was inclined to let the target go, fearing that it was a Q-ship, but his IWO persisted in requests to attack the ship with gunfire. Bleichrodt's violent reaction betrayed signs of the neurosis beginning to affect the veteran commander.

> " 'You're all mad!' he screamed . . . 'Very well if that's what you want. Control room! Prepare for gun engagement! . . . Our blood be on your head First Lieutenant!' "[96]

Wissmann gave no ground and ordered all guns manned, even going so far as to bring machine guns to the conning tower. At 0130hrs *U109* opened fire with every available weapon at *Halcyon*, so many different calibres striking the ship that the distress signal sent indicated that she was under attack from a German surface raider. Once *U109*'s ammunition was exhausted she left to refuel from Kals' *U130*, leaving the ship burning and sinking. Kals too was out of torpedoes after an excellent maiden patrol to America, but still carried enough fuel for the voyage home, while *U109*, a Type IXB, lacked the diesel bunkerage. Thus Kals patiently waited for Bleichrodt as he made his final two sinkings, able to not only spare fuel for his flotilla-mate but make the return journey with a safety margin available.

Paukenschlag's success was welcome news to the U-boat service that had seen steadily dwindling accomplishment during the latter half of 1941. The five Type IXs of the 2nd U-Flotilla had destroyed twenty-five ships totalling 156,939 merchant tons, the majority between New York and Cape Hatteras. Combined with the destruction wrought off Canada by the supporting Type VIIs, forty-one ships had been sunk. Interestingly, though history often records *Paukenschlag* as the first enemy submarine attacks on mainland America, this is actually incorrect. Immediately following the raid on Pearl Harbor, submarines of the Imperial Japanese Navy attacked American installations both within the Pacific and on the United States' West Coast, though not with the same devastating results as *Paukenschlag*.

In Germany the first military contact with the United States received massive media

---

[95] After months of painful healing Tölle recovered and was invalided out of the services.
[96] Hirschfeld, pp. 125–126.

attention, newsreels being shown in cinemas across the country and within the occupied areas. Perhaps the most intriguing was footage of New York skyscrapers' bright lights against a peaceful night sky. Spectacular indeed, but unfortunately not shot by Tölle, or any other reporter for that matter, but faked in Berlin's Ufa studios.

7 February: In Kiel new boats *U154* and *U162* sailed for the North Atlantic, both transferred from the 4th U-training Flotilla at the beginning of the month. *U154* was planned to join those nearly ready to begin their attack in the Caribbean, but Kaptlt. Walther Kölle, reacting to sighting reports of a strongly escorted convoy, chased and found HX175. Over the next two days Kölle, a former company chief at Mürwik's naval school, attacked repeatedly, pressing home his approaches with great determination and resolve. Unfortunately for him, after firing all fourteen torpedoes he had not scored a single hit, four reported as dud hits on a tanker, the rest misses. Demoralized and perplexed, Kölle radioed his results and shooting reports to BdU and was ordered immediately to Lorient. On arrival on the first day of March Kölle reported to Dönitz while flotilla engineers checked his boat. It was found that the torpedo-aiming computer was out of calibration, an error that may have been picked up by a more practised commander.

U162 too was experiencing problems. Her commander, Kaptlt. Jürgen Wattenberg, was bound for the United States for his inaugural patrol, becoming embroiled in the hunt for convoy ON67 being shadowed by 10th U-Flotilla boat *U155*. After sighting the convoy on 24 February Wattenberg opened his attack alongside another 10th U-Flotilla boat *U158*, both firing at the same ship, British tanker SS *Empire Celt*, streaming Admiralty Net Defence from her flanks. The nets fouled Wattenberg's shots but the ship was hit and broken in two.

But after his first attack tubes one and two bow caps broke from their hinges and moved, blocking the field of fire for the remaining bow tubes. Despite surfacing and managing to clear the broken caps away and still possessing functioning stern tubes, Wattenberg was ordered away from his combat area to rendezvous with the blockade-runner *Osorno*, expected in the mid-Atlantic CD66 grid, west of the Azores by 7 March. The boat would have been jeopardized by any nearby depth charge without the outer caps on its torpedo tubes. But *Osorno* never materialized and Wattenberg waited until 11 March before breaking off and returning to Lorient, both the mission to America and escort duty aborted.

Reinforcements for North America and the Caribbean pounded west during February. *U126*, bound for waters north of the Greater Antilles, sailed on 2 February, while the veteran boat *U124* put to sea nineteen days later for Newfoundland. Mohr had lost his talented LI, Brinker transferring to the staff of the 2nd U-Flotilla as Chief Engineer, but his replacement Oblt. (Ing.) Egon Subklew soon proved as able as Brinker. Gone too was Zschech, due for commander training. By the month's end both *U105*, resupplied after its curtailed mission to rescue *Spreewald* survivors, and the brand new *U503* were also headed west.

The beginning of the month brought another benefit to the Kriegsmarine, albeit one of which they were unaware. Dönitz introduced the new four-rotor Enigma machine, leading shortly to a complete 'blackout' of the U-boat 'Triton' cipher; their opponents were now blind.

The second wave soon reported further success in action along the American coast, but only after *U108* began with news of a frustrating clutch of torpedo malfunctions. This maddening run of bad luck for Scholtz ended two days later when the Liberty ship SS *Ocean Venture* was successfully attacked east of Chesapeake Bay. It was the first of five sinkings made by *U108* before it headed back to Lorient bereft of torpedoes, arriving in France on 4 March.

Kaptlt. Werner Winter in *U103* was also experiencing a lucky streak. Having attacked and sunk his first ship of the operation on 2 February near Delaware he succeeded in savaging four vessels in total, plus an unconfirmed 'destroyer', with combined torpedo and gunfire before breaking off and heading home on 8 February, arriving in St Nazaire at the beginning of March. Forebodingly, however, he too had stories of torpedo failure to tell. Harald Gelhaus's *U107* added to both tallies – two ships sunk and three torpedo failures. The largest ship destroyed by this second wave of U-boats to America was the fast passenger/cargo liner SS *Amerikaland*, hit by torpedoes from *U106* north-east of Cape Hatteras on 3 February. It was the crowning glory of Hermann Rasch's patrol spent hunting off the Delaware, New York and Maryland coasts. Beginning on 24 January, Rasch sank five ships, his final victim, British MV *Opawa*, going down on 6 February in CB5582 while he was on his return journey.

Further south the longer-range Type IXCs *U128* and *U504* began to operate off Florida, sinking two tankers each against the backdrop of Daytona Beach's dazzling lights. Both U-boats had been given freedom of operation along the American seaboard, but weather had frustrated attempts at more northerly operations. Between Newfoundland and Nova Scotia ice shrouded every metal surface exposed to the elements as the temperature plummeted. Further south, between New York and Cape Hatteras, storms lashed the seas, nullifying attempted merchant interception and making life miserable for the U-boat crews. Near Florida the weather improved considerably, but was offset by an alternative handicap. With clear skies and in a sub-tropical climate, bright moonlit nights hindered inshore operations, even the low profile of a trimmed down U-boat dangerously exposed against the shimmering glow of moon on sea. Both boats moved yet further south, sinking another tanker each near the Bahamas. Heyse's *U128* destroyed the Norwegian SS *O.A. Knudsen* east of Great Abaco Island, taking the last of his eels and gunfire before the battered tanker would go down. Gröner's ship-recognition book provided the answer to Heyse's curiosity regarding the ship's resilience: she was German-built. Near Bermuda Heyse received the brunt of a brief air-attack, two shallow-set depth charges falling wide, shaking the boat as it crash-dived to safety. Heyse had been fortunate; the first of two VP-74 PBM seaplanes had released two depth charges just as U-boat's stern disappeared, but both were duds. The same plane made a second run minutes later, this time the depth charges exploding. But they had missed their chance and *U128* escaped.

U504 was the target of an intense search by aircraft based in Key West after sinking MV *Mamura* towards the end of February. Aircraft sighted a 'long grey object' north-north-west of the Bahamas and proceeded to depth-charge it while vectoring surface craft to join the hunt. After several bombing attacks American forces recovered the mutilated body of a whale. Poske's *U504* was by then en route for the waters east of Antigua where he sank British steamer *Manaqui*. The armed freighter exploded after Poske's torpedo strike, ammunition, stacked in holds between trucks and aircraft parts, detonating and tearing her apart. It was Poske's final success and he set course for Lorient, arriving on the first day of April, preceded by *U128* seven days earlier.

11 February: The newly operational *U505* sailed from Lorient alongside Merten's *U68*, both bound for the central Atlantic and a timely renewal of operations against West Africa. Now that the United States was at war with Germany all convoy traffic between Freetown, Bathurst, Monrovia, Lagos and Takoradi was fair game and vulnerable, Dönitz correctly surmising that, by reopening the combat theatre, any escort vessels available locally would be kept pinned to Africa instead of crossing the Atlantic and entering American service.

15 February: The Caribbean offensive was about to begin. Three *Neuland* boats were stationed in their designated areas, undetected amid the tranquility of a Caribbean Sunday. *U156* lay submerged off Aruba's San Nicholas harbour, *U67* similarly positioned outside Willemstad harbour in Curaçao. *U502* lay off the uninhabited islands of Los Morjie, preparing to move into the Gulf of Venezuela and attack the shallow-draught tankers that were the weakest link in the oil supply chain, few in number and difficult to replace. The last two boats were still cruising economically towards their assigned areas, *U129* heading for the sea lanes between Trinidad and Guiana, while *U161* was approaching the north coast of Trinidad, waters that her commander Kaptlt. Achilles had sailed often during his time in the merchant marine. His insider knowledge would soon pay big dividends.

The two U-boats outside the southern Dutch islands had been ordered to begin operations a little after midnight local time, opening with torpedo attacks against shipping rather than the proposed shelling that Raeder had pressed for. As the clock within the boat's *Zentrale* showed midnight Hartenstein ordered *U156* surfaced and began his run in towards the harbour. Hartenstein and his bridge watch peered through binoculars, the boat trimmed down so only the conning tower was above the waves. Slowly *U156* crept into firing position, Oblt.z.S. Paul Just ready at his UZO to unleash torpedoes. Two British and one American tanker lay moored in the harbour, swinging gently around their anchor chains as Just fired his first two torpedoes, followed immediately by two more, both British tankers his targets. The night sky was ripped apart by the shattering detonation against SS *Pedernales*, followed seconds later by another explosion in SS *Oranjested*, this second tanker shattered from keel to upper deck, heeling over before settling into the harbour mud. Oil poured from the fractured tankers, igniting and engulfing the harbour in a raging inferno. Hartenstein paused while his torpedo men laboured to reload the bow tubes for a fresh attack. Rather than retreat from the scene he allowed crewmen to come up and witness the panorama while repositioning for a second attack. Frantic men could be plainly seen rushing along the shoreline amid billowing black smoke as they sought to contain the fire.

One hour and forty-three minutes after his first attack Just loosed two more torpedoes, this time striking American SS *Arkansas* and slashing her hull open to allow thousands of tons more oil to feed the flames. Now Hartenstein chose to withdraw from the harbour, not to seaward of the island's fringing reef system, but eastwards towards the huge refinery. Phase two of his attack was about to begin. Having caused chaos and confusion in the harbour, he would shell the refinery before daylight arrived and *U156* approached with all weapons ready to fire. L.z.S. Dietrich von dem Bourne, the popular IIWO, climbed down onto the forward deck to oversee the artillery attack. As the main deck weapon was prepared the distant silhouette of several women and children crossing the line of fire, presumably bound for the nearby church, caused the opening shot to be checked while they moved away from the scene. This, perhaps, was the fatal moment when distraction caused forgetfulness that would soon end in tragedy. Hartenstein, clearly able to see the refinery's furnaces' dull red glow, ordered shelling to start and the gunner at the 10.5cm cannon opened fire. In a split second chaos exploded aboard *U156* as the shell impacted against the watertight tampion still screwed in place at the muzzle. The barrel burst, flinging fragments of steel in all directions. Smoke cleared to show *Matrosengefreiter* Heinrich Büssinger, the gun-layer whose job it had been to remove the tampion, lying in a vast pool of blood that trickled through the wooden decking onto the pressure hull below. The eighteen-year-old mechanic had transferred to *U156* only days before its February departure; now he lay mortally injured, stomach ripped open and both legs shattered. Gently he was carried below where minutes later he died. A second man had also been cut down, von dem Bourne, his leg slit open by the red-hot metal. Screaming in pain, he was taken below as Hartenstein realized *U156* was coming under attack from the large 155mm guns that formed the core of the refinery's defences. Boldly he ordered course steered for the smoke billowing from the harbour while engineers armed with a large hacksaw sprung on to the deck to slice the ruptured end of the barrel off. Hartenstein had come this far – he wasn't going to stop now.

Minutes later the useless metal was thrown overboard and an improvised clamp placed around the battered muzzle. *U156* emerged from the smoke and raced back toward the refinery to restart the bombardment. But by now the shore was alive with garrison troops and a searchlight probed the darkness. With blind shellfire crashing in the sea around him Hartenstein ordered his boat seaward of the reef system and to safety, two shells arcing from the repaired gun before the crew retreated inside their protective hull.

Meanwhile, as Hartenstein had been launching his second torpedo attack, von Rosenstiel's *U502* was beginning its assault on the Maracaibo/Aruba tanker route. His first target, west of Pen de Paraguaná, was the tanker SS *Tia Juana* sunk in flames with two torpedoes, followed three-quarters of an hour later by a second tanker, SS *Monagas*. As these first two shallow-draught ships sank, *U502* scoured the area for more traffic before sunrise and possible air attack, finding a third within an hour and sending SS *San Nicolas* to the bottom of the Gulf of Venezuela before retreating to deeper sea and shelter for the daylight hours.

The third *Neuland* U-boat to launch its attack that morning was Müller-Stöckheim's *U67* off Curaçao. The boat now bore a new symbol painted on its tower next to the *Sigrune* of the 2nd U-Flotilla, a chamois perched atop a star, the device conceived and hand-painted by the commander himself. A little over two hours after Hartenstein had opened the offensive, *U67* fired four torpedoes at tankers lying anchored outside the constricted space of Willemstadt Harbour. Seconds ticked away until four distant thuds drifted across the water. All torpedoes had hit, but none exploded. Incensed at the pointless failure of his attack, Müller-Stöckheim swung his boat through 180 degrees and fired both stern tubes at a third target. This time there was no failure and Dutch tanker SS *Rafaela* burst into flames, oil gushing from her burst hull. With all tubes empty Müller-Stöckheim ordered full ahead and raced for the sea outside Curaçao's reef system.

The islands of Curaçao and Aruba awoke the following morning in shock at the un-expected and sudden appearance of the war on their doorstep. On the wide sandy sweep of Aruba's Eagle Beach (San Nicholas) the sinister tube of an unexploded contact fused torpedo fired from *U156* had run part way up the beach. The dormant weapon became the subject of much attention before unexpectedly exploding during an attempt to defuse it, killing four Dutch Marines.

All three *Neuland* boats suffered weak air attack during the following day as they surfaced to report to Kernével, each easily evading the feeble harassment. Hartenstein knew there was no way that his onboard facilities or medical orderly could properly treat the injured von dem Bourne. His leg was in tatters and all attempts to clean the wounds resulted in agony for the injured man. Hartenstein radioed for permission from Dönitz to proceed north-east to Vichy Martinique and offload the wounded man. Consent was given and *U156* made way for the French island, aware that it was under heavy surveillance by American ships and aircraft, concerned that the small number of French warships in the main harbour could launch some kind of raid against the Panama Canal. The body of *Matrosengefreiter* Heinrich Büssinger was meanwhile wrapped in canvas and slipped over the side after a burial ceremony had been conducted in the control room.

Martinique's Vichy authorities were only too aware of their perilous position so close to the United States and were extremely reluctant allies to Hartenstein's plan. Nevertheless, on 18 February *U156* slipped into Fort de France Harbour on the island's western coast and was met by a French naval launch to transfer the wounded officer before leaving the exposed harbour.[97]

Meanwhile in Berlin Raeder was vexed that his directive to shell the Aruba refinery had not been pursued with greater vigour. His complaints became orders and both *U67* and *U502* were diverted to the island to undertake artillery attack. However, by the time they arrived the island was blacked out, shore batteries manned and a single stalwart Dutch launch doggedly patrolling the harbour entrance. Both boats retired and the refinery remained undamaged.

The day after Hartenstein's entry into Martinique the two remaining *Neuland* boats made their presence known. In one of the most daring operations of the Caribbean war Achilles took *U161* skilfully through the treacherous reef system that protected Trinidad's main city, Port of Spain. Incredibly, his presence had already been detected but no action taken. During the day as *U161* had slipped through the 'Dragon's Mouth' it crossed over one of seven magnetic detection loops laid in the approach channels to the Gulf of Paria, relaying the distinctive signature of a large metal object. Routine investigation by aircraft and patrol vessels turned up nothing and British and American military authorities decided that it was probably one of the patrol vessels 'out of station' that had triggered the reading. While propellers circled above, Achilles and his crew waited on the seabed. A little after 1900hrs *U161* surfaced and Achilles began his final run. Slipping past local fishing boats, the U-boat used the moonless night to creep into Port of Spain where Achilles launched his first attack with only twelve metres of water beneath his keel. The boat gave a slight lurch as two torpedoes sped away, *U161* already beginning its exit journey before a pair of explosions showed direct hits. Two tankers, SS *Mokihana* and SS *British Consul*, caught fire and heeled over as they settled on to the harbour floor. Achilles attempted a submerged escape but as the bow of *U161* cleaved into thick mud he was forced back to the surface. Trimmed down, Achilles switched on his navigation lights, running alongside numerous small American and British patrol boats criss-crossing the area in frantic search of what they presumed would be a submerged enemy. By sheer nerve Achilles passed before the silent shore batteries of Trinidad and Gaspar Grande Island, presumably taken for an Allied ship by watchers ashore. After a run of several miles *U161* was free, diving and passing again over the anti-submarine loop during its successful escape.

That same night Nicolai Clausen's *U129* was in position south-east of Trinidad, waiting for bauxite-carrying traffic from British and Dutch Guiana to pass his way. Clausen was directed by BdU to penetrate the shallow waters off Georgetown and Paramaibo but declined, radioing Dönitz that the "peculiarities of the inshore water [were] unfavourable for operations". By dawn the next morning he had sunk his first victim, the Norwegian tanker SS *Nordvangen* hit by two torpedoes and blown to pieces. Days later flotsam was found but no sign of her crew in an area soon to be known as 'Torpedo Junction'.

---

[97] Von dem Bourne's leg was later amputated and he was eventually repatriated to Germany.

25 February: KK Ernst Kals brought *U130* to rest against the *Isére* at the end of his *Paukenschlag* expedition. His was the last of the *Paukenschlag* boats to return, *U66* arriving on 10 February, followed by *U109* and a disappointed Folkers aboard *U125* on 23 February. Aboard *U130* Kals also had five Luftwaffe men rescued from their crashed Condor aircraft by outgoing *U587* before being passed to Kals' inbound boat off the coast of France. Kals arrived on Wednesday; by Sunday the first boat of the second wave returned. Kaptlt. Werner Winter's *U103* docked on 1 March, claiming five ships, including three tankers and an American 'destroyer'. While his warship claim turned out to be mistaken, he was correct with his other success reports, 26,539 tons of shipping left burning and sinking off the shores of Delaware and Maryland. Winter had also suffered four torpedo failures during his patrol, adding to the troubling statistics held in Kernével.

Kaptlt. Harald Gelhaus returned six days later from the American coast, *U107* entering harbour with two confirmed sinkings and a third ship damaged. Gelhaus had sailed the same waters as Winter, stretching from Chesapeake Bay to Bermuda. During his return to France Gelhaus had received orders to ship any spare fuel aboard the 1st U-Flotilla's *U564*, the smaller Type VIIC having run low on fuel after patrolling the United States coastline. Suhren had first been directed to link up with Winter in *U103*, but due to bad weather and faulty navigation the two boats had been unable to connect. Gelhaus, however, approached Suhren's boat on 13 February, hailing the irrepressible Suhren from his own conning tower. As they converged, Suhren, who had only recently woken from an afternoon sleep, misjudged his distance and rammed *U107* in its starboard fuel tank. The incident left Gelhaus with less fuel than Suhren, while *U564*'s bow torpedo tube caps were destroyed. Both boats started home, Gelhaus swearing long and loud in eloquent naval terms. En route for France *U107* was able to use its last torpedo, hitting and damaging the Norwegian tanker SS *Egda*, although the ship managed to slip away.

2 March: *Paukenschlag*'s star performer, Reinhard Hardegen, put to sea once more, bound again for the American hunting ground and again carrying a propaganda photographer, Rudolf Meissinger (soon dubbed '*Schön Rudi*', Handsome Rudi, by the crew). *U123*'s mid-afternoon departure was blighted by steadily growing fog until she unexpectedly juddered to a halt after losing sight of the *Räumboot* escort and running aground on a sandbank near Ile St-Michel. An embarrassed Hardegen broke out the boat's dinghy to inspect the situation himself, deciding that there was no damage and waiting for the fog to clear before pulling free. That night *U123* cleared harbour and made for the United States and round two of Hardegen's war against America.

The beginning of March witnessed unrelenting havoc in the Caribbean wrought by the *Neuland* boats. Their fuel and torpedoes were beginning to run low as they cut swathes through tanker traffic around Caribbean shipping choke points. While they found defences quicker to adapt and react than the *Paukenschlag* boats had experienced further north, they still outwitted their adversaries at every turn. Dönitz allowed his wolves to run wild, slipping the leash and giving the commanders freedom to decide where, when and how to strike. It was a strategy that returned greater success for *Neuland* as Dönitz's maverick commanders abandoned areas in which their own success had raised alarm and defences, moving to untouched hunting grounds. Allied merchant ships were warned to avoid certain well-travelled lanes and island-hop, hugging the coasts where it was felt the shallow waters afforded some protection. Unfortunately, most of these instructions were radioed uncoded, instantly picked up and understood by the U-boat hunters. Those few messages transmitted in code were swiftly broken by B-Dienst and retransmitted to the *Neuland* boats. The death toll mounted, particularly among tankers and, more crucially, the shallow-draught shipping vital for the transportation of oil from Lake Maracaibo. Finally the predominantly Chinese crews of those remaining vessels mutinied, refusing to go to sea without Allied escort. Their rebellion was short-lived as they swiftly found themselves in Dutch prisons. Nevertheless, tanker traffic ground to a halt and Aruba's vital refinery lay idle for days which the Allied war effort could ill afford.

Achilles struck the last truly spectacular blow as he cruised with *U161* west of the Windward Islands. His boat still carried two torpedoes and Achilles and his IWO L.z.S. Werner Bender were searching for targets in the suddenly depopulated seas. It was Bender who came up with a fitting finale to the operation that had started in great style in Port of Spain. Bender too had served within the merchant marine and knew the harbour of Port Castries on Saint Lucia from previous sailings. Saint Lucia, a British protectorate but occupied by a growing American garrison, had a small sheltered harbour where tankers called before attempting their Atlantic crossings. Determined to repeat his previous success Achilles arrived five miles from the harbour mouth a little before sunset on 7 March.

The harbour entrance was narrow and treacherously twisted, with sharp ragged reefs to either side, as well as sandbars that could spell grounding and certain death for *U161*. They would enter Port Castries surfaced, deck awash and gun crews ready for action. Again Achilles found navigation beacons burning as *U161* crept onwards on electric motors only. American defensive installations lay to left and right as Achilles conned his ship further into the anchorage until two large steamships tied to the harbour jetty in only ten metres of water became visible. One torpedo was fired at the furthermost target, a second arcing towards the other as Achilles ordered rudder thrown hard left and both diesels fired full ahead. Blue exhaust smoke coughed from the U-boat's stern and she began to gather speed for the exit as a column of water and debris was hurled skywards from the side of the Canadian steamer SS *Lady Nelson*, followed by the second detonation blowing a hole in the hull of British SS *Untata*, both ships on fire and settling. Houses fringing the natural enclave had windows blown out by the enormous explosions and bedlam exploded ashore while *U161* raced seaward, desperate to make clear water and submerge before retaliation. Achilles watched both ships explode, leading him to believe that they were probable write-offs, before ordering his gun crew below. As the U-boat charged through the channel entrance to safety a desultory burst of tracer flashed from the shore. But it did no damage and as it fell silent Achilles was already closing the hatch behind him, *U161* disappearing into the depths, its second harbour penetration a success. Although both merchant ships would later be repaired and returned to service, the mayhem of U-boat attack crept further into the Caribbean paralysing trade routes and generally instilling fear.

On 15 March Achilles made his last *Westindien* sinking, attacking the lighthouse tender USS *Acacia* on 15 March with artillery, all torpedoes already spent, sending her under with an hour-long barrage. It was the final *Neuland* victory. While Italian submarines operating on the eastern periphery continued to take their toll the five original German attackers retreated northwards to France, their sole reinforcement, Bauer's *U126*, alongside them, having sunk eight ships himself and damaged two others. It had been an astounding success for the Caribbean boats which in Winston Churchill's words had operated "with a freedom

---

[98] *The Second World War*, Winston Churchill, Vol IV, p. 108.

and insolence which were hard to bear": forty-one ships sunk, eighteen of them tankers.[98] Eleven other merchant ships had been badly damaged, including another seven tankers. Between the five boats they had sunk 222,651 tons of Allied shipping, over 70,000 more tons than Operation *Paukenschlag*.

While officers and men of the 2nd U-Flotilla celebrated their well-fought victories, Allied leaders contemplated what lessons were to be learned. The crisis off America's East Coast continued, while a temporary lull settled over the Caribbean theatre. The US Navy finally acknowledged their need for Royal Navy help, twenty-four ASW trawlers being ferried across the Atlantic to bolster a flagging defence. The frequency of North Atlantic convoy departures was cut from five days to seven, releasing ten US destroyers and two British and Canadian escort groups to patrol American coastal waters in what were the first steps towards the introduction of US convoying. To the south, demoralized Caribbean defences were bolstered by the arrival of several older American four-stacker destroyers, sixteen Coast Guard cutters, seventeen patrol craft, two minesweepers and the British 19th MTB Flotilla for Trinidad.

Furthermore there were political moves afoot to release the apparent German strangle-hold on the Western Atlantic. In response to a cable from Winston Churchill lamenting the "immense sinkings of tankers west of the 40th meridian" President Roosevelt appealed for bombing of submarine bases and repair yards. Churchill's reply drove another nail into the U-boat's coffin:

> "In order to cope with future U-boat hatchings, we are emphasizing bombing attacks on U-boat nests. . . . Admiralty and Coastal Command, RAF, have evolved a plan for a day and night patrol over the débouchés from the Bay of Biscay. . . . We hope that night attacks and menace by aircraft will hamper their night passage and force increasing exposure by day."[99]

11 March: The clash between Raeder and Dönitz over the need for a continual presence of U-boats within the fruitful Caribbean abated somewhat with the sailing of a second clutch of boats for the region. *U154*, transferred from Kiel to Lorient during February under the command of Kaptlt. Walther Kölle, left Lorient that day for its first proper war patrol. Kölle was joined by the end of the month by three other 2nd U-Flotilla boats, *U66*, *U130* and *U108*, the latter directed to the Florida/Bahamas area. Another valuable addition to this strike force was the 10th U-Flotilla refuelling submarine, *U459* – the first operational *Milch kuh* U-boat – leaving Kiel bound for the mid-Atlantic grid quadrant CC to resupply western Atlantic boats. The huge Type XIV U-tanker, commanded by First World War veteran KK Georg von Wilamowitz-Moellendorf (nick-named 'Wild Moritz'), sailed from Kiel on 21 March, heading to the North Atlantic after a layover in Heligoland. Ordered to remain in open ocean north-east of Bermuda, *U459* was scheduled to refuel fifteen combat boats, the first resupply undertaken on 20 April (two days later than scheduled) as Kaptlt. Klaus Scholtz brought *U108* to top up tanks before continuing towards the 'Golden West'. The refuelling was not without its problems, KK Wilamowitz-Moellendorf recording that the slip-hooks used to take the large Type IXB in tow repeatedly gave way under the U-boat's weight.[100]

---

[99] Churchill, Vol IV, p. 109.

[100] *U103* also experienced problems during its fuel transfer from *U459*, the pipeline severing at the *Milch Kuh* end, again due to the weight of the Type IXB.

16 March: The first *Neuland* boats arrived in Lorient. Escorted by minesweepers, Kaptlt. Jürgen von Rosenstiel docked *U502*, five confirmed sinkings and one American tanker damaged, all torpedoes fired. The following day Hartenstein's *U156* also arrived, their boat also empty of torpedoes. Hartenstein reported immediately to Dönitz who strode aboard with flotilla commander Schütze and various BdU officers to present him with the German Cross in Gold. With 'Hitler's Fried Egg' pinned to the lapel of his coat Hartenstein and Dönitz examined the deck gun's shattered barrel, still bearing its makeshift clamp.

Bauer's *U126* arrived on 29 March, while the final *Neuland* boat returning during March was Müller-Stöckheim's *U67* the following day, both boats out of torpedoes. Müller-Stöckheim's was the smallest tally from *Neuland*, two tankers sunk and one damaged in Willemstadt. His run of bad luck, which had begun with four successive torpedo failures, included an unexplained hole through his boat's pressure hull, presumably caused by corrosion, leaking seawater into the bilge near the second battery pack. The last ten days of the journey to port left *U67* with a limited diving capability, managing only thirty metres depth after the hole was temporarily sealed, a small margin of safety if under determined attack.

By 5 April all of *Neuland* had returned, Achilles' *U161* arriving on 2 April, Clausen's *U129* three days later. Clausen's boat had been damaged short of France when, just before midnight on 1 April, *U129* was sighted and attacked by a Whitley (VII 'F') of 502 Squadron. The pilot, Flight Sergeant V.D. Pope, approached from the boat's starboard quarter, roaring in unseen to drop six depth charges from a height of only fifty feet. As *U129* tardily crash-dived, a burst of air bubbles marked her position underwater, the U-boat suffering minor flooding. Pope was forced to break off his search and Clausen crept into Lorient for a month of repairs.

While all commanders and crews from the spectacular onslaught received lavish praise and attention, Achilles, the '*Frettchen des Port of Spain*' (Ferret of Port of Spain), in particular became the subject of an intense media campaign, his exploits reported frequently by Dr Goebbels' propaganda services. Clausen in turn received the Knight's Cross upon his return to port, the decoration already awarded while at sea by radio on 13 March, his tallied score by BdU reckoning over the 100,000-ton mark.[101] As usual the crew had already manufactured an on-board cross for Clausen, which he had worn since the radio announcement and again, as usual, he continued to cherish it, regularly wearing it instead of the official model presented by Dönitz. *Neuland* marked the end of Clausen's tenure within the 2nd U-Flotilla, he being transferred to Bremen to oversee the final stages of construction of long-range Type IXD2 *U182*, scheduled for launching in April. His replacement was Kaptlt. Hans-Ludwig Witt, ex-commander of *U161* during that boat's work-up period before breaking his leg and relinquishing command to Albrecht Achilles.

But already the newly opened battlegrounds were hardening against the Germans. Dönitz detected the barely perceptible shift of defences ranged along the United States.

> "On the whole, operations in American waters have become more difficult. . . . The formation of convoys as a defensive measure is to be expected soon."

Compounding the looming trouble, only four U-boats were in action off America on 16 March, Mohr's *U124* and the smaller Type VIIs *U71*, *U332* and *U404*. But they were

---

[101] In fact it was twenty-two ships for 67,572 tons, including the Vichy vessels sunk in error while in command of *U37*.

scheduled for reinforcement with fresh boats, including *U105*, *U123* and *U503*, as well as the 10th U-Flotilla's *Milch kuh U459*.

However, Kaptlt. Otto Gericke's *U503* was not going to add any weight to the American attack. On 10 March Gericke reported storm damage to his deck from inhospitable conditions near Newfoundland, then vanished, nothing but static answering repeated requests for updates. Five days after its final contact with home, *U503* was sighted approaching convoy ON72 east of Nova Scotia by a USN 82nd Patrol Squadron Hudson, which attacked the surfaced boat, sinking her with all hands. By 21 March Dönitz accepted the inevitable and *U503*'s short career ended as she was classified as *Vermißt ein Stern*.

Elsewhere in the Atlantic progress was sporadic. The two boats near Freetown found shipping patterns patchy, heavy traffic interspersed with extended periods of empty seas lasting up to a week. Both U-boats had reached their operational area by the first few days of March, after nearly a month spent in transit. Harassed by aircraft all the way, tempers became frayed aboard as they sweltered in the tropical heat. For the crew of Kaptlt. Axel Loewe's new *U505* the drudgery of the first month wore at their nerves. Crewman Hans Goebeler remembered:

> "A few times we ran the diesels at dangerously high speeds in order to catch a convoy. . . . You cannot imagine the excitement we crewmen felt during these chases. 'Finally,' we thought, 'we will get our first hit!'
>
> "But eventually we would hear the roaring diesels reduce to normal speed again and the Skipper would apologize to us over the intercom for guessing the convoy's course wrong. At those moments the crew's mood barometer would drop to zero and all the built-up frustrations and petty feuds of the past few weeks would come flooding back. Suddenly, once again you became conscious of the heat and the noise and the stench of whatever shit our cook was preparing for dinner."

Their patience was finally rewarded when *U505* attacked British steamer SS *Benmohr* on the evening of 5 March, missing with an initial two-torpedo spread but running the steamer down and hitting with a third shot. Once the merchant crew had abandoned ship, a fourth torpedo snapped its spine and sent it to the seabed. To the east, Merten's *U68* had also opened its scoring, sinking British SS *Helenus* two days previously. Both boats sank another ship apiece during the next week, *U505* receiving minor damage to her clutch by the blast wave of their second victim's cargo of 11,400 tons of oil exploding on torpedo impact.

However, the two U-boats became victims of their own success, British West African authorities thrown into shock by the attacks and holding solo ships in port while organizing convoys. An increase in Freetown's defences had begun during March 1942 when the Allies had started to fear the possibility of both Vichy-held Dakar and Casablanca being handed over to German control, leaving Freetown as the most strategic Allied base in the eastern-central Atlantic.

Air patrols were stepped up and the two U-boats continually forced underwater by circling 'bumble bees'. Loewe's crew were further harassed when they brushed with a Q-ship that briefly depth-charged *U505* before departing the scene. During days of niggling inactivity both boats requested permission to cross the narrow waist of the Atlantic and lie off Brazil, but relations with that country were already at boiling point, the pro-American government having broken off diplomatic relations with Germany on 27 January, and the requests were denied. Instead *U68* went south to Lagos where Merten's luck changed. Stumbling on massed shipping off Liberia he attacked with a combination of torpedoes and artillery, sinking four ships between 16 and 17 March.

It was the impetus that Dönitz needed and *U505* was directed to follow in *U68*'s wake, although Loewe encountered stiff opposition from escort ships and aircraft that foiled attacks on massed shipping off Cape Palmas. With crew at boiling point, frustrated by their inability to hit the enemy, Loewe pulled away from the coast, crossing the equator (with customary celebration) and sailed south. By chance two ships crossed *U505*'s path, both sunk with torpedo attacks. Loewe himself was nearly destroyed on 6 April when an approaching Sunderland prompted an immediate crash dive. In the course of submerging valves jammed and the resultant imbalance of weight within semi-flooded diving tanks caused the bow to dip under and stern to rise into the air. Oblt. (Ing.) Fritz Förster freed the valve while crewmen charged aft to bring their screws back into the water. In breathless anticipation they awaited the killing depth charges, but miraculously there were none, Loewe unwaveringly calm throughout the entire incident.

> "All sorts of gallows humour enlivened our work as we repaired the relief valve. The best joke was that the English pilot failed to attack because he thought *U505* was an ostrich, with its head buried in the water and its tail in the air."[102]

Meanwhile, *U68* had already begun its return voyage low on fuel, docking in Lorient on 13 April. *U505* achieved no more success despite being given freedom of action off Lagos. The seas were bare and they too arrived home on 7 May, having sailed a round trip of 12,937 miles. Dönitz was pleased with both commanders, eleven confirmed ships sunk and considerable disarray caused off West Africa, their performance helping make the 2nd U-Flotilla the highest scoring U-boat unit in action.

28 March: At 0250hrs telephone reports flooded into the Saltzwedel Caserne that St Nazaire was under attack by "twenty enemy cruisers and destroyers". 'Operation Chariot', designed to destroy the only dry docks capable of holding the *Tirpitz* in Western Europe, was under way. During the commando attack, taken as potential invasion, orders flashed to all flotilla bases and U-boats offshore.

Both *U109* and *U130* were still in Biscay, Bleichrodt having left Lorient during 25 March, the day after Kals. Unlike *U130* which was bound for the Caribbean, Bleichrodt's *U109* was again destined for America, this time the Florida Strait where conditions were thought to be the most favourable. Both boats received orders to proceed immediately to St Nazaire to help repulse the landings, both quietly ignoring them, experienced enough to conclude that the landings were a raid, not invasion, likely to be history by the time they had made any return journey. Sure enough the cancellation order arrived later that day and the two continued west.

In Lorient, however, there was considerable activity. An emergency directive drawn up by Dönitz and issued on 14 March was put into action and a condition of readiness, named 'Alarmstreife I' established. Under these instructions all available personnel were to proceed to the U-boat shelters. Secret documents and Enigma machines were to be removed from all boats and rushed to the flotilla offices for destruction. Any U-boat in wet dock, even if only carrying a partial crew, was to depart for coastal waters, prepared for battle. Once clear of dock, any boat putting out was ordered to report on 'Kustenschaltung' to receive orders from BdU. If for whatever reason they found themselves unable to contact head-

---

[102] *Steel Boats, Iron Hearts*, Hans Goebbeler, p. 42.

quarters they were to scuttle in shallow water, allowing the chance of salvage if invasion was successfully repelled. As for U-boats in Kéroman's dry dock, only the incline of the armoured slipway was to be blown up, the boats themselves made ready for destruction but awaiting orders.

Gradually it became apparent that the commando raid was over and KK Viktor Schütze, staff and men of the 2nd U-Flotilla stood down, U-boats rumbling slowly back to port. Dönitz, recently ordered to relocate to Paris away from his vulnerably exposed head-quarters, hastened his departure accordingly, albeit under protest. By 29 March BdU's new Paris headquarters was ready, control passing from Kernével the next morning at 1000hrs.

5 April: In a badly distorted W/T message BdU received a success report from Reinhard Hardegen aboard *U123*. It was mixed news. Hardegen had already destroyed two tankers after reaching Newfoundland and was turning south for more hospitable weather. Both tankers had been battered by combined artillery and torpedo attack east of Chesapeake Bay before going under in flames. However, the second tanker, MV *Empire Steel* had cost two torpedoes to no effect, the first a 'hot-runner' hung up inside its tube until manually ejected, the second launched by accident from tube five. Finally a third eel had brought her to a halt, whereupon she became the subject of a prolonged and fatal surface bombardment.

Three nights later, south-west of the previous sinking in fading daylight, lookouts sighted another solitary steamer, dense smoke issuing from her stack. Hardegen closed carefully, curious about so much smoke. The steamer then began zigzagging as heavy cloud obscured the bright moonlight. Seven hours after the initial sighting a single torpedo flew from tube two, streaking towards its target and exploding at the front edge of the steamer's bridge. Minutes later an SOS was picked up as the steamer sent its hurried distress call.

"SSS SS *Carolyn* torpedo attack burning forward not bad require assistance SSS . . ."[103]

The crippled ship rapidly lost way and Hardegen decided to finish her off with artillery. As the gun crews assembled in the control room waiting for permission to take their positions, Hardegen bellowed below for *Fähnrich* Holzer to come and witness the sinking. But Hardegen was nagged by an elusive doubt about the *Carolyn*. A single lifeboat had been lowered before the steamer had stopped moving, the damaged ship veering to starboard as *U123* crossed its wake to take up firing position.

To Hardegen's horror he realized that he should have listened to his misgivings as it became clear that the *Carolyn* was not stopping but had increased speed suddenly, intent on ramming *U123*. He shouted for full speed on both diesels as the Stars and Stripes unfurled on *Carolyn*'s jackstaff, machine-gun crews opening fire on *U123*. The American Q-ship USS *Atik* was going into action for the first time.

At the outbreak of war in December 1941 President Roosevelt, well known for his affinity for things novel and naval, initiated the US Navy's 'Q-ship' programme and SS *Carolyn*, a 1912 3,209-ton steel-hull steamer was requisitioned for that purpose. Now Hardegen watched in amazement as false bulwarks fell away to expose her 4" guns, depth charges and machine guns, which opened fire on Hardegen's frantically manoeuvring boat. Holzer, taken by surprise, fell to the deck with his entire right leg laid open by bullets that had passed through the conning tower plating. As gunfire drove the gun crew below and

---

[103] Communications Third Naval District, 27 March 1942.

caused the bridge watch to take cover, shells began falling dangerously close. Glancing hits on the deck from *Atik*'s main armament caused the U-boat to lurch, her engines momentarily cutting out before *U123* managed to pull ahead of its attacker, partially shielded by smoke from the diesels. Holzer was taken below as Hardegen judged it time to submerge, praying that the pressure hull would hold. Fortunately for him, damage was external and he turned *U123* to launch a second submerged attack. *Atik* then committed a fatal mistake, stopping to retrieve the 'panic party' that had made such a show of abandoning ship. Hardegen was too good a commander to let this stationary target pass and a second torpedo exploded against the ship's engine room, this time holing it fatally. As the hull sank lower in the water her boilers exploded, igniting stored depth charges. Although the crew had been seen to take to their lifeboats, no survivors were found, killed either by the blasts or the severe gale that lashed the area shortly afterwards. *U123* withdrew, chastened by the experience. By the time that the battle had been concluded Holzer was dead. Wrapped in canvas he was given a burial at sea later that night. It had been a costly mistake. On 9 April Goebbels' Propaganda Ministry reported on Radio Berlin that a U-boat had sunk an adversary after a "bitter battle", but gave no further details, *Atik*'s fate not revealed until after the war by captured German records.

Hardegen proceeded southwards past Cape Lookout, damaging an American tanker during the early morning darkness of 2 April but driven away by the unexpected appearance of Canadian *MTB 332*, panicked into diving in only thirty metres of water and expecting swift retribution from the new threat. However, there was none, the Canadian crew contenting themselves with having frightened their enemy. As *U123* retreated to deeper water the battered tanker escaped.

On 8 April Dönitz unharnessed the boats assembled along America's coast. He ordered them to operate without any consideration to fuel reserves to take advantage of the new moon period after weeks of bright nights, allocating *U459* to refuel them.

Scholtz's *U108* was one of those included in Dönitz's directive. Having been the last of four 2nd U-Flotilla boats to leave during March for the Caribbean, Scholz would sink five ships including two tankers with torpedoes and artillery before *U108* headed home to Lorient, arriving on the first day of June.

Dönitz had ordered his Type IXs to concentrate on four main areas of operation: the Windward Passage, a bottleneck for merchant traffic stretching between Jamaica, Cuba and Haiti, and Curaçao, Aruba and Trinidad. Again, a 2nd U-Flotilla boat was ordered to attempt bombardment of Curaçao's refinery, this time the duty falling to Ernst Kals.

The first of this second group to open its attack was *U154*, sinking two tankers north of Puerto Rico in early April. Aircraft of USAAF 45 Bombardment Squadron harassed Kölle's boat constantly as he attempted to slip through the Canal de le Mona during daylight. Forced to remain submerged, Kölle eventually slipped through the narrow passage and continued west past Isla Mona, looping through the Windward Passage and on to the Bahamas. During his sixty-day patrol Kölle sank a further three ships, including another tanker.

Outbound to Curaçao, *U130* opened with two successful attacks against tankers northeast of Puerto Rico. However, Kals' bombardment mission ended in relative failure. Arriving off Curaçao on the night of 18 April, *U130* found threading its way through the fringing reef system difficult, due in no small part to alert patrol craft reinforcements. Curaçao had learned from the *Neuland* attack and its defenders were sharpened and ready, additional elements of the 252nd Garrison Artillery battalion concentrated around the main harbour and Bullen Point refinery. Kals made a stealthy approach during the early morning of 19 April and, despite a successful blackout of the refinery, duly opened fire on its presumed location. As artillery rounds exploded within the main compound, retaliatory 155mm shells landed uncomfortably close to *U130*. After twelve rounds had been fired Kals wisely chose to retreat into the darkness, dashing past patrol craft to the open sea and safety. *U130* cruised for unproductive weeks before returning to France with no further successes, a victim of prior triumph, tanker traffic to Curaçao having been temporarily shut down after *Neuland*.

Zapp, cruising in the Windward Islands, had the most successful of these six patrols with six confirmed sinkings, including four tankers, and a British tanker damaged. Twenty of his twenty-five torpedoes had been fired and his official score by BdU reckoning rested at 142,000 tons. On 23 April Zapp received the award of the Knight's Cross by radio.[104] On return in Lorient on 27 May Zapp was relieved of command and moved ashore taking charge of La Rochelle's 3rd U-Flotilla, Kaptlt. Friedrich Markworth taking his place. With Markworth's arrival the ship's patronage changed as well, passing from the Bavarian Rifle Corps favoured by Zapp to Lorient's 806. *Marineflakabteilung*, its *Wappen* – a white Ace of spades – freshly painted on the tower front.

10 April: Mohr brought *U124* into Lorient, his 'lone wolf' patrol of the American East Coast adding seven ships, including five tankers, to his score. Notwithstanding exaggerating his total by three, this was the most productive of the American patrols to date and had sown disorder along the United States' seaboard.[105] Like Hardegen, Mohr, wisely or not, composed a verse for his success report to BdU:

> "The new-moon night is black as ink
> Off Hatteras the tankers sink
> While sadly Roosevelt counts the score
> Some 60,000 tons – by Mohr."[106]

By BdU reckoning Mohr had also passed 100,000-tons and on 27 March he was awarded the Knight's Cross by radio. The crew hid the message from their commander, making their own version of the medal to be accompanied by a cake during a presentation ceremony. The cake was decorated with the Cross and the words "Mohr has done his duty – Mohr can go".

By the end of April the bulk of the 2nd U-Flotilla was at sea, the majority either en route or on station in the southern American and Caribbean areas. After *U125* and *U507* had sailed on 4 April, the other new addition, *U162*, put to sea, followed by veterans *U103*, *U106*, *U107*, *U156* and *U502*. Three boats destined for Brazil were also putting out from France, *U126*, *U128* and *U161* travelling in company under secret instructions to attack shipping in the Fernando de Noronha Island region.

2 May: *U123* entered Lorient after its second patrol off the United States. Following his radio report to BdU on 5 April Hardegen had continued south into the Florida coastal traffic, the coast still radiant with lights, the tourist trade considered too lucrative to suffer

---

[104] By the patrol's end it actually aggregated 103,495 tons.

[105] The three-ship discrepancy between Mohr's claimed sinkings and those confirmed were those damaged but later returned to service.

[106] *Hitler's U-boat War*, Clay Blair, Volume One, p. 518.

a blackout. Much merchant traffic hugged the lee of the land in water dangerously shallow for U-boat safety, but the lure proved too much and the Georgia coast next witnessed *U123*'s destructive power as Hardegen attacked during the night of 8 April. Both SS *Oklahoma* and SS *Baton Rouge* were left burning fiercely, although the water was so shallow (barely fifteen metres deep) that they were later salvaged and returned to service. A third ship was destroyed off Georgia and Hardegen continued south to Florida, noting to his consternation intense phosphorescence in the water. The calm of the tropical climate led Rudi Meisinger to ask if he could row ashore to take photographs, a request denied by Hardegen.

In the early morning darkness of 11 April *U123* again cruised inshore to attack SS *Gulfamerica*, a new tanker belonging to the Gulf Oil Company and laden with 90,000 barrels of fuel oil bound for New York. Hit by one of Hardegen's remaining two torpedoes, the tanker instantly burst into flames. Unconvinced that she would go under Hardegen ordered deck gun manned and prepared to open fire on the blazing wreck. Suddenly he noticed a large crowd of stupefied Americans gathered on shore opposite the blazing inferno. Concerned that overshooting rounds might land among them or even among beach houses that dotted the coastline, Hardegen moved his boat shoreward of the tanker and opened fire. Forced close to their target by the shallow water *U123* was abruptly surrounded in flames as the muzzle flash ignited fuel spilling from the tanker's holed sides only 250 metres away. With tourists watching in horrified fascination, the gun crew peppered the hulk with shells, an offshore breeze keeping the firestorm at bay from Hardegen's men. Slowly *Gulfamerica* drifted offshore, eventually sinking four days later. *U123* prepared to slip away and run for deeper water, but it was not to be so easy for Hardegen this time.

American ASW forces rushed to the scene, an aircraft from nearby Jacksonville sighting the U-boat and dropping marker flares as Hardegen crash-dived in only twenty-two metres of water. As the aircraft roared away, destroyer USS *Dahlgren* charged immediately overhead and dropped six depth charges. The boat's interior was devastated, the crew flung about and machinery smashed in every compartment. Slowly Hardegen began to inch towards deeper water while propellers swept continuously overhead. Realising the futility of their plight, scuttling charges were set and the boat prepared for abandoning.

Hardegen climbed into the conning tower and began to open the hatch, water gushing into his face and freezing him with fear. He redogged the hatch in confusion. For the first time Hardegen was genuinely afraid and, as he admitted later, it was this dread that drove him back into the U-boat, cancelling scuttling orders and determined to save his boat. Amazingly, luck was with him. Above him the commander of USS *Dahlgren* mistakenly concluded that his blind attack on the location of the aircraft flares had not been against a U-boat contact and after searching the area he headed away leaving *U123* to recover. Barely able to blow tanks, Hardegen brought *U123* slowly to the surface in an empty sea, limping to deeper water on the starboard diesel, guns manned and crew alive with excitement. Despite the odds, *U123* had survived. As Hardegen later recorded:

> "I'm surprised that the enemy was not tougher, using depth charges in these shoal waters when he had us. . . . It shows how inexperienced the defence is."

U123 spent the following day heading south while repairs were carried out and the crew given some well-earned rest. Late on the evening of 12 April he fired his last torpedo, hitting and sinking SS *Leslie* east of Cape Canaveral, bound from Havana with a cargo of sugar. The following night a final kill was added to his tally, Swedish SS *Korsholm* laden with phosphate wildly estimated to be an '8,000-ton tanker' (5,500 tons over the mark) and obliterated with *U123*'s last ninety shells. Course set for home, Hardegen radioed his success to Dönitz, again using verse:

"For seven tankers the hour has passed
The Q-ship hull went down by the metre
Two freighters too, were sunk at last
And all of them by the same Drumbeater!"[107]

By his and BdU reckoning Hardegen had sunk ten ships, including seven tankers, for 75,837 tons. In fact the truth was a little less astonishing, seven ships sunk (excluding the tankers that were salvaged and repaired) for around 30,000 tons, still a formidable tally. Hardegen received congratulations of a special kind on 23 April, his KTB entry recording:

"1700. For the first time *U123* received a wireless signal from the Führer. The Commander has been honoured with an Oak Leaf Cluster. Everybody was delighted because everybody had earned it. A homemade Knight's Cross with Cluster was presented to me in a festive ceremony in the control room."

Five days later, on 28 April, *U123* rendezvoused with Kaptlt. Harald Gelhaus's westbound *U107* four days from Lorient, in order to pass over *U123*'s *Adressbuch* that provided keys for disguising grid references as per BdU instructions on tightened security. During mid-morning on 2 May *U123* arrived in Lorient under *R-boot* escort and tied up against the *Isère*. The boat suffered the brief indignity of running out of fuel at the harbour entrance to the Rade de Lorient, making the final stretch on her silent electric motors. Among the reception committee were both Dönitz and the OKM *Grossadmiral* Erich Raeder, on inspection tour of both local flotillas. Several days later Hardegen flew to East Prussia to receive his Oak Leaves from Hitler himself.

It was the end of Hardegen's command of *U123*. The battered boat required new drive shafts for its diesels and Hardegen was obliged to sail from Lorient to Kiel, then on to the dry docks at Stettin. At Kiel the U-boat, bedecked with forty-five pennants representing the boat's total claimed score, tied to the *Blücher Brücke* to be received by a welcome party including BdU (Org) Admiral von Friedburg. Commander and crew of *U123* then travelled to Hardegen's home town of Bremen to massed celebration from the city's inhabitants. Hardegen took his leave of the boat to begin his new post as commander of Gotenhafen's 27th U-training Flotilla, giving tactical instruction to prospective commanders. *U123* would remain in Germany until December under its new commander, ex-IWO Horst von Schroeter.

4 May: *U124* slipped from Lorient once more after a brief rest and refit for boat and crew. This time their destination was the North Atlantic and a spring resumption of Dönitz's convoy war. Conditions experienced in the foul weather of November had led Dönitz to suspend North Atlantic operations, satisfied that the occasional opportunistic sinking by boats en route to the Western Atlantic would suffice to keep escort vessels pinned to their convoy role.

The three Brazilian-bound boats, *U126*, *U128* and *U161*, had provided one such chance attack when they brushed with convoy SL109 north-west of the Cape Verde Islands, Kaptlt. Ulrich Heyse's *U128* sinking SS *Denpark* before Dönitz urged them on to

[107] *Operation Drumbeat*, Michael Gannon, p. 377

Brazil. Arriving on 1 June north of Fortaleza there was little to be found but a single Norwegian tanker, sunk by *U126* two days later. Sailing gradually northward they joined the Caribbean fray in June, ten U-boats already at work in the Caribbean and Gulf of Mexico, half of them from the 2nd U-Flotilla.

But cracks had formed in the German campaign. Allied radio-direction-finding units had at last moved into the region and on 22 May Mexico's President, Manuel Avila Camacho, deploring the loss of several freighters, declared war on Germany. While Mexico's military machine was not itself of major concern to Germany, the relocation of several American aircraft to the country was. There was also increasing tension with Brazil. Between February and April seven Brazilian ships had been torpedoed in the Western Atlantic, leading the pro-Allied country to arm its merchants. At the end of May Brazil announced that its air force would attack any U-boat sighted near its coastline. Dönitz, convinced that hostilities were imminent, planned a surprise attack on Brazil at the end of June, but, aware that such attacks could jeopardize relationships with pro-German countries such as Chile, Uruguay and Argentina, Hitler vetoed the suggestion. A mooted operation to use 2nd U-Flotilla boats to assault refrigerator ships leaving the River Plate was also refused. However, on 4 July, as Brazil became increasingly belligerent, Hitler authorized the attacking of all Brazilian merchant ships and warships engaged on convoy escort work. It was *U507* on its next patrol which would trigger the predictable result.

3 June: Beneath clear blue skies Kaptlt. Heinrich Bleichrodt brought *U109* to rest against the *Isére*. The boat motored steadily past the hulks of French cruisers *Strasbourg* and *Crapaud* (ex-SMS *Regensburg*) moored in Port Louis Bay before the Kéroman bunkers, barrage balloons tethered to their masts as protection against low-flying aircraft attack. KK Viktor Schütze walked down the gangplank to welcome commander and crew home.

U109 entered port flying only three pennants, not a great deal to show for nearly six weeks at sea. Bleichrodt had been ordered to the area east of Cape Hatteras, crossing the Atlantic in the face of hurricane force winds as the barometer tumbled ever lower. Finally, approaching Bermuda, the weather broke, *U109* stopping the Swiss-registered SS *Calanda* to examine its manifests before letting the small steamer go. Finally on 20 April, north-east of Bermuda, Bleichrodt's bridge watch sighted a smoke trail in the darkness of early morning ahead and to port and *U109*'s diesels were thrown full ahead. Bleichrodt finally sighted his quarry and brought *U109* as close as possible to launch a surfaced attack. Three torpedoes raced from the bow tubes, seconds ticking anxiously by until the realization that they had missed. Thundering ahead of the target and trailing a bright phosphorescent wash, *U109* drew in front and fired two eels from her stern tubes. In a blinding flash the steamer disintegrated as both impacted against the steel hull plates. SS *Harpagon* had been loaded with nitro-glycerine bound from Baltimore to Barry. All forty-one men aboard were killed, very little of their ship remaining. The blast had flung shrapnel in all directions, several splinters holing the boat's piping running from fuel bunker III, leaving a shimmering wake of oil behind *U109*.

For many bright moonlit nights *U109* cruised fruitlessly in what had once been rich hunting grounds, now devoid of merchant shipping as America tardily implemented its convoy system. So Bleichrodt decided to head south in search of the enemy. On 26 April, while running submerged off Florida's east coast, he sighted an American destroyer apparently following the faint oil slick. Unable to resist the sitting duck a mere 800 metres ahead of the U-boat's bow tubes, two torpedoes were made ready and fired at the exact moment that Oblt.z.S. (Ing.) Martin Weber lost trim control. As the bow cut under briefly the second torpedo raced from its tube pointing first downward and then hurtling back to its assigned depth of three metres, passing that level and 'porpoising' as it broke surface before going under again. It was all that the destroyer needed and its bow swung toward *U109*, engines racing as she prepared to attack. Bleichrodt bellowed for a crash–dive, but Weber botched that as well, placing the boat in dire jeopardy as he bungled compensatory flooding, *U109* seesawing to the surface. In haste Weber screamed for all off-duty men to run forward, flooding every available tank and sending *U109* shooting downwards to crash into the sea floor at a depth of only sixty metres. Bleichrodt calmly took control of the situation as his men braced for the impending attack.

The hammer blows of multiple depth charges shook the boat, knocking men to the deck as the main lighting flickered off. The Americans could not miss. A second and then a third attack threw the crew about inside their iron coffin, until the destroyer's propellers gradually receded. Incredibly there was little real damage. As even the weak emergency lighting failed, the shaky beams of numerous torches showed minor flooding through the vents – but no more. Weber's chaotic dive had saved the boat, *U109* plunging out of control and boring up to its *Wintergarten* in sticky mud that effectively cushioned the boat from damage.

With motors straining the U-boat finally managed to free itself from the thick sludge bank and surfaced off Jacksonville to the peace of a tropical summer night. Once more they had survived against the odds.

4 June: The day following *U109*'s arrival, Kaptlt. Harro Schacht returned from a more successful patrol aboard *U507*, nine pennants totalling 44,782 tons strung from the boat's extended periscope. Schacht, and the 10th U-Flotilla's *U506*, had been ordered by BdU to penetrate into the Gulf of Mexico, *U507* the first U-boat to enter this new territory, sailing on single diesels to conserve fuel during the Atlantic crossing. While passing through the Straits of Florida, Miami's halo of light visible to starboard, Schacht sank his first ship with artillery on 30 April, four nights later announcing his arrival in the Gulf by sinking SS *Norlindo*. Schacht fired one torpedo at the American steamer, hitting her at the water line, whereupon the American went down by the stern, standing vertically before sliding out of sight. Schacht later returned to the scene and yelled in perfect English to men huddled in lifeboats, asking the name of the vessel and their cargo. The merchantmen refused to tell him, but were nevertheless supplied with forty packs of cigarettes, tobacco, crackers, drinking water and a cake with French writing on its iced top.

Creeping paranoia in the United States that Germany operated a 'Fifth Column' of infiltrated saboteurs and spies was reflected in a curious newspaper report claiming that the new attacks were masterminded by Baron Edgar von Spiegel, a First World War U-boat veteran (commander of *U93*) and former German consul in New Orleans. Von Spiegel's fanatical and outspoken support of Nazi Germany had embroiled him in controversy, leading to his eventual expulsion from America as part of President Roosevelt's closing of German and Italian consulates during June 1941. Interviews with rescued merchantmen who reported being hailed by a tanned officer wearing shorts who spoke 'perfect American' convinced the gullible at least that the enemy lurked in their midst, lent some credence by the arrest during June of eight Abwehr agents landed in the United States by U-boat.[108] Needless to say there remains no evidence that Edgar von Spiegel or any other 'Nazi fanatic' was behind U-boat attacks in the Gulf.

[108] See Lawrence Paterson, *First U-boat Flotilla*, pp. 138–140.

Over the next two weeks Schacht cruised as far west as Louisiana devastating merchant traffic, soon joined by 10th U-Flotilla's *U506*. With no sign of American attempts at convoying, both U-boats began a shooting spree that culminated in the muddy delta waters of the Mississippi River. The turbid river outflow provided good cover at periscope depth and reduced the risk of detection by sound. However, Schacht experienced nine misses, failures or malfunctions from his stock of torpedoes, two of the latter suffering gyro-breakdowns, sending them in a circular trajectory back towards *U507* which crash-dived in alarm. On 5 May Schacht hauled out from the coastline to transfer torpedoes from deck canisters into the torpedo rooms at night. During this laborious task wire restraining gear broke and a torpedo slid out of control into the bow room, striking a radio operator and slicing his arm open to the bone. With no morphine aboard, Schacht radioed BdU and was instructed to rendezvous with *U506* to obtain medical supplies. Three times the meeting was planned, each time failing to materialize, while the radioman's wound festered in the hot, unhygienic U-boat.

Both boats suffered damage at the hands of inexperienced Coast Guard aircraft, but they pressed on, expending all their torpedoes before breaking away and heading for home. *U507*'s final victim was the Honduran SS *Amapala*, brought to a halt by concentrated machine-gun fire, no other ammunition remaining. As men rushed to abandon ship, Schacht closed the lifeboats and demanded that the freighter's Second Officer take a small German scuttling party aboard his abandoned ship. The U-boat men duly opened her seacocks, returning to *U507* just as a US Navy aircraft arrived on the scene. Hustling his men below, Schacht dived, scurrying away as salvagers attempted unsuccessfully to take *Amapala* in tow, the last of *U507*'s nine victories.

By 21 May *U106* had also reached the Gulf of Mexico to continue the offensive, bolstered by 3rd U-Flotilla's *U753* and a brief appearance from Werner Winter's *U103*, then enjoying phenomenal success on a patrol that would sink nine ships. Kaptlt. Hermann Rasch's *U106* would sink five ships by the end of its sojourn, returning to Lorient at the tail end of June carrying the dazed British occupant of a small liferaft spotted amid the Atlantic wasteland, a survivor from SS *Etrib*, torpedoed by Erich Topp's 'Red Devil boat' *U552* nine days earlier. By the end of the month nineteen more wrecks littered the Gulf. Combined with successes in the Caribbean, seventy-two ships, many of them tankers, were destroyed, totalling 364,000 tons, 78% of all sinkings for May.

7 June: As a victorious *U162* returned from the Caribbean during the afternoon flying ten sinking pennants, three of them the dark flag signifying tankers, Kaptlt. Axel-Olaf Loewe took *U505* out of harbour bound for the 'Golden West' alongside Kaptlt. Heinrich Schuch's *U105*. By 2000hrs the boats had cleared the French coast and headed for the southerly route that skirted around the bottom of the Bay of Biscay.

Four days from port as *U105* cruised slowly surfaced during the morning, lookouts were surprised by the sudden appearance of a 10 RAAF Squadron Sunderland dropping from the sky immediately astern. The aircraft was carrying new radar equipment into action, contact with *U105* initially established on the ghostly green screen. Her pilot, F/L E.B. Martin, had then seen the surfaced boat at a range of nearly five miles to the port bow, glimpsed through a brief break in heavy cloud. Using the thick cover, Martin crept unobserved toward his target before attacking. Lunging downwards the ungainly aircraft had built up considerable speed and roared overhead at a height of only 40 feet, six Torpex-filled depth charges dropping from her belly to straddle the boat, which emerged from the curtain of spray slewing to a halt. There was considerable damage to *U105*, the diesels knocked offline as Schuch raced from his bunk and the IWO ordered a crash-dive. The U-boat could be seen gaining speed as it started electric motors and frantically twisted to port, machine-gun fire peppering the water while *U105* submerged.

Aboard the shattered boat water poured through several large fractures in the pressure hull, too much for the bilge pumps to deal with, leaving Schuch with little choice but to surface. He recognized that the boat should have attempted evasive manoeuvres rather than diving and so, with water pouring into the control room, the U-boat rose toward the surface. Depth gauges were smashed, so Schuch climbed into the conning tower and simply heaved on the hatch until it opened. Above them Martin and his ten crewmen were surprised to see *U105* appear again after less than a minute and immediately opened fire while preparing a second attack. German gunners could be seen racing onto the conning tower to man AA guns and the Australian crew braced themselves for the defensive barrage that would follow. To Schuch's horror he found that the barrel on one 2cm AA gun had been bent by the blast, while the second was disabled, with its ammunition feeder ripped off. The diesels obstinately refused to fire and *U105* sat, a lame duck, at the Australian's mercy.

Radio messages flashed to both BdU and surrounding boats, *U505*'s Loewe hearing the appeal for help and immediately changing course to render whatever assistance he could. Aboard *U105* Schuch frantically ordered another dive, but flooding soon threatened to overwhelm the boat and with no functioning depth gauge they would simply slip into oblivion. Once again the boat blew all tanks and rose to the surface to face their enemy. The Sunderland made two more attacks from astern, dropping a single anti-submarine bomb on each attack and smothering the U-boat in machine-gun fire. German gunners tried desperately to make whatever repairs they could to the boat's AA weapons while other men on the bridge fired with machine pistols broken out of the boat's weapons locker. Amazingly they hit their attacker, a line of small bullets stitching across the port wing tip. Smoke was now drifting from the boat's conning tower from brief but fierce fires inside, but all that the Sunderland could do was to circle beyond effective range of machine-gun fire, its bombload expended.

Schuch again radioed BdU for help, pleading for fighter cover, but there was none available. Then, abruptly, messages from the damaged boat ceased and Lorient ordered *U505* and other nearby boats to hunt for survivors. Less than an hour later this order was cancelled and aboard the 'rescuers' there was unspoken understanding of depressing significance. However, this time they were mistaken. Radio problems aboard *U105* had interfered with transmission, but contact was finally regained and Schuch was ordered to make for El Ferrol for emergency repairs. The boat lay low in the water, only one diesel now functioning as it crawled to the port some 200km distant. By that time the Sunderland had been forced to leave, low on fuel, and *U105* made good its slow escape.

Eventually Spain hove into view and *U105* crept into El Ferrol, her Enigma machine and secret documents already thrown overboard in weighted sacks. Following morsed instructions, Schuch tied his shattered boat alongside the Spanish destroyer *Almirante Antequere* where an Abwehr agent, Herr Bendel, and the Spanish commander of the El Ferrol Naval Arsenal, *Capitán de Fregata* José Ragel, came aboard to help assess the boat's damage.

U105's commander and crew were made welcome by their Spanish equivalents and placed in the depot ship *Canaris* while their boat was taken to a Spanish dry dock for nearly two weeks of repairs. Their presence seemed, amazingly, to go unnoticed, although several unusual British reconnaissance flights passed low over the U-boat, beaten off by Spanish

AA weapons. There were no diplomatic complaints and *U105* was ready for the short journey to France by 28 June, putting to sea with the Spanish destroyer *Melilla* as escort as far as the Spanish three-mile limit. From there KG40 Junkers Ju88 aircraft shepherded the boat back to Lorient, where she arrived battered but intact on 30 June.

By then Dönitz had already issued orders regarding U-boat passage across Biscay. As of 24 June they were to proceed submerged by day and night, surfacing only long enough to recharge batteries. *U105*'s experience, combined with other attacks in Biscay, spurred Dönitz to visit *Reichsmarschall* Herman Göring to ask for greater air protection over Biscay. Although relations between the two had remained frosty since early 1941, Göring relented and twenty-four more Ju88 aircraft were earmarked for the Atlantic squadrons. It was to prove an inadequate defence.

22 June: Kaptlt. Werner Winter brought his veteran *U103* into Lorient to the customary welcome from flotilla and BdU staff and the 'Grey Mice' nurses of Lorient's Wehrmacht medical facilities, all clustered aboard the *Isére*. Schütze in particular always made the crew feel welcome, the U-boat that he had helped to make famous a welcome memory of his own significant combat record. By that stage of the war *U103* had destroyed a confirmed forty-three ships totalling nearly 228,000 tons, nine on its latest mission. This would place the boat that carried the single 'S' rune on its tower as the third most successful after *U48* and *U99*.

Winter had amassed a considerable score, survivors of his third victim, SS *Orgontz*, remembering him approaching their lifeboats with the immortal words, "Sorry for sinking your ship, but this is war". Bringing a wounded man aboard, Winter had personally supervised medical treatment before stocking the lifeboats and departing into the darkness.

The aged Type IXB *U103* required an extensive refit in Kéroman before it would sail again, this time with a new commander. Winter had passed the required tonnage by BdU reckoning and as he strode ashore he received his official Knights' Cross, awarded by radio and crew on 5 June. Winter stayed in Lorient as *U103*'s commander until July when Kaptlt. Gustav-Adolf Janssen, ex-commander of the training Type IXA *U37*, relieved him. For Winter there was promotion and transfer to command Brest's 1st U-Flotilla.

26 June: 'Jochen' Mohr brought *U124* in once more from the Atlantic. His boat had been part of the six-strong *Hecht* group formed by Dönitz to relaunch the Atlantic convoy battle in order to prevent experienced escort vessels transferring from 'safe' convoy routes into either the Caribbean or the American Atlantic coast and also to take advantage of any lapse in preparedness that the absence of U-boats may have caused. Radio intercepts had shown that the British were using the Great Circle from the North Channel to Newfoundland for their trans-Atlantic merchant trains. By positioning *Hecht* approximately 300 nautical miles north of this supposed route Dönitz allowed the boats to hunt in a south-westerly direction. Supported by the temporary U-tanker *U116*, *Hecht* could search, but, if failing to make contact, could continue in that direction to the coast of the United States.

Hecht, comprising *U124* and five Type VIIs, was heading for its assigned area when the 3rd U-Flotilla's *U569* sighted the forty-one merchant ships of ON92 and its accompanying warships on 11 July. Ocean Escort Group A3, headed by US Navy destroyer USS *Gleaves* and comprising a US Coast Guard cutter and four Canadian corvettes, had never worked together and none of them carried HF/DF. Ironically it was the merchant ship SS *Bury* which did carry HF/DF as an aid to searching for damaged or lost ships. Only corvette HMCS *Bittersweet* had the powerful new Type 271 centimetric radar, but its operators were inexperienced. It was *Bury* that pinpointed the radio burst from *U569* during the morning. After passing the information on to USS *Gleaves* the convoy skippers were stunned that the American commander, Captain John B. Heffernan, made no move to investigate.Later that day, as the remaining *Hecht* boats closed the convoy, *Gleaves* and the Coast Guard cutter USCGC *Spencer* sighted what they took to be a surfaced submarine seventeen miles ahead. The two ships gave chase and became involved in a prolonged hunt for the mystery U-boat, taking them far away from the vulnerable convoy as night fell.

By then two other *Hecht* boats were in contact, one of them *U124*. By 0115hrs on 12 May Mohr was ready and had penetrated undetected between the first and second convoy columns. Remaining surfaced, he fired two bow torpedoes, followed by a single stern shot, before attempting to dart out of the convoy perimeter. The first torpedo struck lead starboard ship, CAM SS *Empire Dell*, sending her to the bottom. The third torpedo hit another British steamer, SS *Llanover*, travelling in ballast and going under by the stern, her empty holds torn open. With pandemonium erupting everywhere, the U-boats closed in. Canadian corvettes dashed about attempting to sight the enemy, the loss of the two American warships away on futile searching sorely felt. In *U124* Mohr twisted desperately, seeking the shelter of darkness to reload. Hemmed in by corvettes, *U124* re-entered the convoy's columns where sirens shrieked madly. Shooting between two other corvettes, with only 800 metres to spare on either side, Mohr was in his element as *U124* charged ahead, firing its last stern torpedo at another freighter. During the chaotic battle, with U-boats and corvettes racing around each other, several times narrowly missing collision, Mohr sank two further ships, his confirmed score four freighters destroyed, totalling 21,784 tons.

Reinforced by the remaining *Hecht* group, contact was kept until late the following day when heavy rain and poor visibility allowed ON92 to escape. Seven ships had been sunk, the two Americans nowhere near the action.

Dönitz moved his group ahead of the convoy, but it eluded them, so *Hecht* trailed southwest, briefly brushing ON94 before fog allowed it too to slip away. On 25 May *U124* eased up to *U116* to refuel, *U96* also appearing, her commander, Oblt.z.S. Hellriegel, rowing over to *U124* for a brief visit. Torpedoes were shipped aboard as 132m³ of fuel oil flooded into *U124*'s bunkers. Extra provisions, capable of sustaining the boat for seven weeks, were also taken aboard. Finally the resupply was complete and Mohr headed away for the next *Hecht* patrol area, Dönitz deciding that the group again deploy in the Great Circle.

In intermittently bad weather brief unsuccessful contact was made with convoy ON96 before Mohr's bridge watch sighted convoy ON100 during the night of 8 June, shadowing and sending beacon signals. Escort Group C1, comprising one Canadian destroyer, two British corvettes and two French corvettes, escorted thirty-nine merchant ships. All escorts bar the French *Mimosa* carried Type 271 centimetric radar, *Mimosa* relegated to the convoy's stern, zigzagging to prevent U-boat penetration from that quarter. Mohr, frustrated by the offending corvette in his attempts to do exactly that, fired a pair of torpedoes at *Mimosa*, blowing a hole in the small ship's hull, exploding boilers and stored depth charges finishing what Mohr had begun. Only four of her crew survived. It was later discovered that the other French corvette, *Aconit*, had established a 'small radar contact' but thought nothing of it. *U124*, the blip they had observed, raced away and dived to reload. During the following four days ON100 was repeatedly attacked in deteriorating weather, Mohr sinking one more freighter in the face of fierce retaliation before losing contact.

Still *Hecht* searched for fresh targets, soon locating ON102. But this time the escort was formidable, beating off repeated attacks with accurate location of the surfaced U-boats. *U124* made a single sinking before *Hecht* disengaged and headed home. The precision of the Allied counter-attack prompted Dönitz to inquire of Mohr by radio whether he felt that the enemy were equipped with a "new locating device", but Mohr demurred, stating that he could avoid pursuit with rapid evasive manoeuvres. He was wrong.

8

THE TRANS-ATLANTIC WAR:
1 JULY TO 31 DECEMBER 1942

4 July: The 2nd U-Flotilla's oldest boat, *U43*, sailed from Germany to begin transit to the North Sea. New commander Oblt.z.S. Hans-Joachim Schwantke was headed for the North Atlantic to join *Wolf*, sweeping towards Newfoundland.

Elsewhere boats left Lorient for West Africa. Kals' *U130* and Schacht's *U507* travelled in loose company through Biscay until sighting northbound convoy SL115 on 14 July. Kals immediately began to shadow, given freedom of attack by Dönitz while continuing to transmit updated position reports for the benefit of nearby *U507* and the Italian boat *Pietro Calvi*. At 2243hrs *U130* and the Italian had linked up and were conferring atop their conning towers using megaphones when escort sloop HMS *Lulworth*, running down HF/DF contact on Kals' transmissions, surprised the two boats, driving them both under. Kals lost contact in the darkness until sighting distant flames a little after midnight. Racing past, he realized that it was *Pietro Calvi* on fire and unable to dive after being hit by *Lulworth*'s depth charges and pulverized by artillery. *Lulworth* finally rammed the Italian before slewing to a halt, Royal Navy boarders preparing their assault. Kals attempted a surface attack on *Lulworth*, but missed, submerging where *Lulworth* made sonar contact, firing several wild depth charges in his direction. It was enough to dissuade *U130* and Kals left the scene. Meanwhile, SL115 had slipped away, Kals and his men listening to the sound of receding propellers as both *U130* and *U507* were called off from attempts at pursuit.[109]

The two boats continued southward, reaching Freetown by the end of July. Kals sank a Norwegian tanker travelling in ballast en route and now he began a small run of success during August that would total six further ships sunk, including two more large Norwegian tankers. The Captain and First Engineer, Jan M Jacobsen and Peder Johan Olsen of SS *Malmanger*, were taken as prisoner aboard *U103*, Kals complying with new BdU directive to capture the master and chief engineer of any torpedoed ship, thus depriving the enemy of skilled personnel and also to elicit whatever useful intelligence could be gleaned.

By the time Kals began his return voyage at the end of August his sinkings in *U130* had reached eighteen ships for 116,500 tons and he was awarded the Knight's Cross by radio on 1 September.

Both *U130* and U*507* were refuelled by *U116* at the end of July, but Schacht's fortunes aboard *U507* had not mirrored Kals' success. The boat encountered nothing but aircraft and Schacht asked for permission to cross the Atlantic to Brazil. His request was cleared by BdU providing he was "extremely careful" in regard to Argentinian and Chilean shipping. For 'political reasons' *U507* was also expressly forbidden to enter Brazilian harbours or bombard them.

---

[109] The British boarders found no more than a logbook and chart aboard *Calvi*, which abruptly upended and sank, taking the commander of the British boarding party with it to the bottom.

On 16 August Schacht reached the Brazilian coastline, sailing so close to the shore that the crew were able to watch locals enjoying a game of tennis. *U507* immediately began an extravaganza of sinkings in international waters barely beyond the three-mile limit, three ships torpedoes by midnight south of Aracaju. Two more were sunk the next day, a third escaping after the single torpedo fired at it prematured. In less than two days 14,822 tons of Brazilian shipping were destroyed. The 90-ton yacht *Jacyra*, shelled to oblivion on 19 August, proved the final straw for President Getulio Vargas who declared war on Germany three days later.

Brazil's declaration of war had little real effect on the immediate prosecution of the U-boat campaign. American aircraft had already begun operating from Natal, Brazilian aircraft and merchant shipping under orders to attack on sight. However, the Brazilian Navy was:

"not expected to embarrass our operations."[101]

On the other hand, Germany's Foreign Ministry became nervous of adverse reaction in neighbouring South American countries and OKM ordered *U507* withdrawn 500 miles from Natal.

7 July: Kaptlt. Hartenstein brought *U156* in from its second successful Caribbean patrol, eleven ships sunk and two damaged during ten weeks at sea, a line of inflated inner tubes suspended from the U-boat's forward jumper wire and piles of tyres stacked before the conning tower in mute testimony to SS *City of Melbourne*'s cargo, despatched by torpedo east of the Guadeloupe Passage.

Three days later *U68* returned from the same theatre equally successful, Merten having sunk seven ships. *U68*, suffering problems from a defective diesel exhaust valve letting water enter the boat when submerged, had been compelled outbound to sneak quietly into El Ferrol, mooring alongside the *Max Albrecht* for repair and topping up of fuel bunkers.

After leaving Spain Merten headed for his target area off the Panama Canal, sinking ships en route. By the end of the first week of June *U68*, accompanied by 10th U-Flotilla boats *U159* and *U172*, lay astride shipping lanes to and from Panama, where they remained for several days savaging the vulnerable merchant traffic. *U68* suffered moderate damage from one of its three victims sunk on 10 June. After hitting SS *Surrey* with a single torpedo, its British crew made haste to escape their sinking ship. Curiosity aroused, Merten closed upon a single survivor swimming frantically away. Hauled from the sea, the British seaman explained that *Surrey* was loaded with nitro-glycerine, the volatile cargo exploding as if on cue. The blast wave lifted *U68* bodily from the water in what Merten recorded as "the strongest blow *U68* has yet experienced" and sent it crashing back down, both diesels temporarily out of action, gauges destroyed and belongings strewn everywhere.

At that moment lookouts reported another cargo vessel in sight, valuable time being lost getting the diesels back on line before Merten took up pursuit. Realizing that his lagging boat could not overhaul the target, Merten fired a single long-range shot, miraculously hitting MV *Port Montreal* and sending her under. Radioing success to BdU, his confirmed score of sixteen ships (102,234 tons) qualified him for the Knight's Cross, awarded by radio three days later. The onslaught continued with other long-range U-boats also turning the Caribbean into an inferno of torpedoes and artillery. Merten retreated

[110] Hessler, Chapter V, p. 41.

from Panama towards Aruba, his sixth sinking, Vichy tanker SS *Frimaire*, torpedoed on 15 June, the Frenchman's identity remaining unknown to him with no survivors or wreckage found. Merten's was to remain the most successful patrol of the Caribbean in terms of tonnage sunk, 50,898 tons of shipping cluttering the seabed.

Commanders were now compelled to travel by train to Paris to make their reports, Dönitz still insisting on line-by-line examination and explanation of their War Diaries. Following Hartenstein's statement made after his return, Dönitz extended an invitation to use his own car to tour the French capital. Hartenstein accepted and, in the company of Kptlt. Karl Thurmann of 7th U-Flotilla's *U553*, he left in BdU's limousine. By 8pm that night the car and its two occupants had still not returned, a fuming Dönitz forced into alternative transport for his evening appointments. Hours later Dönitz returned to still find no car waiting for him.

Early the following morning Hartenstein and Thurmann appeared, both barely able to stand after thoroughly acquainting themselves with Paris's nightlife. Dönitz's aide-de-camp ordered them to report to Dönitz, but thought better of it when he realized their condition, ordering them to bed instead.

> "Hartenstein, however, felt himself called by his commander's voice. He straightened himself out, put on his uniform and made his way to Dönitz's quarters. Dönitz, who was in the habit of working late into the night, complained bitterly that the two had taken advantage of his generous gesture. Hartenstein listened to the tirade unmoved, then saluted his commander and replied, slightly altering the famous lines attributed to Baron Munchhausen, 'On many a flag have I laid my hand swearing loyalty in this wicked war, many an Admiral have I served . . .' before he simply turned around and left. The next morning at breakfast Dönitz retold the whole story to the amusement of his staff."[111]

The crew of *U156* later accompanied their commander to his Saxony city of birth, Plauen, which had 'adopted' *U156* while still under construction in Bremen. Under the morale-boosting *Patenschaft* scheme Plauen became sponsoring city of boat and crew, the city crest adorning the U-boat's conning tower. During *U156*'s commissioning ceremony Plauen's Burgomeister, Eugen Wörner, and several other civic officials had been present, handing over an accordion, fifty mouthorgans, gramophone records and, for each crew member, a book on Plauen's history. In July 1942 Hartenstein was presented with the Freedom of the City.

13 July: Kaptlt. Klaus Scholtz sailed to reinforce the Caribbean fight. *U108* left to a familiar fanfare from flotilla officers and men, but the character of war in the western Atlantic had begun to change. *U153* was declared *Vermißt ein Stern* on 15 July. KK Wilfried Reichmann of the class of 1924, but inexperienced in combat, had brought the Type IXC to France during May after Baltic training that had not been without incident, *U153* colliding during night exercises with the brand new Type VIIC *U583* on 15 November, the latter sinking with all forty-five men aboard. After reaching France Reichmann's boat was prepared for the Caribbean, putting to sea on 6 June, the third flotilla boat that month destined for that region.

Reichmann began his patrol inauspiciously, attempting to attack a darkened steamer but foiled by engine trouble during the chase. Things brightened when Reichmann sank the

---

[111] Topp, p. 85.

MV *Anglo Canadian* on 25 June and another two American ships shortly afterwards south-east of Bermuda before entering the Caribbean through the Windward Passage. The boat's last message was received on 30 June from an area north-east of Puerto Rico.

On 5 and 6 July two separate B18 bombers of 59th Bombardment Squadron reported damaging a U-boat, *U153* being the only one within that immediate area. Reichmann next made his presence felt by firing at the American net layer USS *Mimosa*, sixty miles off Almirante, Panama, one streaking past the small ship's bow, another passing below her, either failing to explode or contact fused. That night a Catalina made radar contact with a surfaced U-boat, dropping parachute flares that illuminated *U153* and straddling the boat with four depth charges. With no debris found, the Catalina was soon joined by patrol craft USS *Evelyn R* which found a 'moving oil slick' at 1000hrs on 11 July and depth-charged the area. Still no debris was seen.

The destroyer USS *Lansdowne* then arrived and immediately established sonar contact and dropped four 600lb depth charges. The sonar trace disappeared, no wreckage betraying what in all probability was the last resting place of *U153* and its fifty-two crewmen, the first boat <u>officially</u> declared as lost in the Caribbean. However, it was not the first to be sunk, the 2nd U-Flotilla having already suffered its first Caribbean casualty on 13 June, although BdU continued to plot the boat's presumed position for weeks, supposing *U157* to have a problem with its W/T gear. KK Wolf Henne, also from the class of 1924 and also lacking combat skills, had taken the new *U157* from Lorient on 18 May. Henne had transferred to Lorient during the beginning of the month, spending eight days in France before being sent to the western Atlantic. Ordered to the Mississippi Delta, followed by *U67* and *U129*, *U157* briefly patrolled the Greater Antilles until 11 June when it sank American tanker SS *Hagan*, laden with molasses, off Cuba's Cayo Guajaba. The American Gulf Sea Frontier commander immediately ordered all the forces at his disposal to "hunt this submarine to exhaustion" and the torment of *U157* began.

On 11 June the surfaced boat was picked up on radar by a B18 bomber and attacked, although the outcome was unknown as *U157* escaped. But, less than two hours later, a commercial Pan-American flight spotted the surfaced *U157* headed west. American sea and air forces continued their relentless hunt until 13 June when Coast Guard cutter *Thetis*, attached to Key West's East Coast Sound School, picked up a strong sonar trace and carried out a single devastating depth-charge attack. A huge shimmering oil patch and bubbles of escaping air rose to the surface as reinforcements converged on the scene, plastering it with twenty-two more depth charges. In all likelihood *U157* was already destroyed. When the chaos subsided *Thetis* recovered two pairs of leather submariner's trousers, a tube of grease marked '*Gemacht in Düsseldorf*' and splintered teak decking. There were no survivors.

It was only two months later that Dönitz officially listed *U157* as presumed lost. The grudging admission in the BdU War Diary on 13 August read:

> "*U157* last reported its position as DN73 on 10 June. Boat was operating off New Orleans. As several submarines and submarine attacks have been reported in this area and *U67* suspected the presence of another boat it is quite possible that his radio has broken down. *U157* was therefore considered to be operating until fuel and provisions were calculated to be exhausted. Boat had not reported again. It must be presumed lost."

The loss of this 2nd U-Flotilla boat in the Western Atlantic followed on the heels of another disaster for a Caribbean veteran, but this time in Biscay. On 5 July *U502* was on its final leg into Lorient after successfully sinking ten ships, expending all ammunition in the process. Von Rosenstiel had linked up with *U156* for the majority of the voyage, Hartenstein passing over surplus fuel to *U502*.

They separated to begin overseeing Biscay where at 0445hrs on the night of 6 July Wellington 'H' of 172 Squadron detected the surfaced *U502* on radar at a range of seven miles. American Pilot Officer W.B. Howell prepared to use a new weapon, untried in combat. Hanging beneath the belly of the Wellington, in place of the obsolete retractable 'dustbin' turret, was a 22,000,0000 candlepower, 24" searchlight. Named the Leigh Light, after its inventor Squadron Leader H. de V. Leigh, it had first been tested in March 1941, deemed a complete success and issued to active RAF Coastal Command squadrons in April 1942 in conjunction with ASV radar.

As the aircraft roared towards its target Howell prepared to ignite the massive searchlight as the radar echo became distorted by 'clutter' from the sea. Less than one mile from target and only fifty feet from the wave-tops, the light crackled into life and *U502*'s startled watch found themselves blinded and taken completely unawares. Howell raced over the boat from starboard dropping four depth charges across its bow as the boat began to crash dive. Rising away, the Wellington's tail gunner sprayed the submerging conning tower with machine-gun fire before the depth charges exploded. As the spray subsided Howell returned to drop flame floats, revealing a massive spreading oil slick. Of the fifty-two men aboard the U-boat none survived.[112]

The loss of this experienced crew so close to home again prompted Dönitz to issue fresh instructions regarding the Biscay transit on 16 July.

> "The danger of unexpected attack from radar-equipped aircraft is greater by night than by day, so in future boats shall proceed surfaced by day and submerge only in the extreme sections when daylight is not sufficient for the whole journey."

By then both *U128* and *U126* had returned again from the Caribbean, the former sinking five ships, the latter seven. Bauer's *U126* played host to several 'temporary prisoners' during the cruise. The first group were from the Dominican schooner *Nueva Alta Garcia*, sunk by artillery south-east of Saint Lucia. Bauer had taken the eight-man crew aboard his boat after discovering that their liferaft was unseaworthy, handing them over to a passing sailing vessel the next day.

The other had more bizarre consequences. In the early hours of 16 June *U126* attacked and sank two American steamers west of Grenada. The second, SS *Kahuku*, had already taken aboard survivors from *U161*'s victim SS *Scottsburg* some days previously. After the sinking Bauer fished out of the water a lone survivor, a tall young Texan from the *Scottsburg* named Archie Gibbs. Gibbs was placed under confinement for four days as the U-boat continued its patrol until Bauer stoped the Venezuelan motor skiff *Minotaura* and handed over the dazed Gibbs, who returned to the United States to tell of his tale in a dramatized book called *U-boat Prisoner* published in 1943. This in turn made the silver screen as a heavily fanciful 1944 Columbia Studio cinematic version of events in which Gibbs disguises himself in the uniform of a dead Gestapo agent, is picked up by the U-boat and manages to trick the crew into believing his new identity, overpowering them and rescuing a group of captured Allied scientists. What Gibbs, or indeed Bauer, thought of the film remains unknown to this author!

---

[112] Wiley Howell, who won a DFC and later transferred to the US Navy, made a second successful Leigh Light attack on 12 July against *U159*. Although not sunk, the 10th U-Flotilla boat was badly damaged.

But the tide of war was beginning to flow inexorably against the 2nd U-Flotilla. The large boats which had wielded such power in the first half of 1942 began to lose effectiveness as groups mostly comprising smaller Type VIIs reopened the Atlantic convoy war. Too unwieldy for the dangerous Western Approaches, Type IXs were constrained to free-roaming lone wolf patrols, rapidly losing their bite against improved defences. During the latter half of July only a single merchant ship was sunk in the Caribbean. During the two- to four-week transit periods from France situations could radically alter, making BdU staff's operational planning reliant on accurate trend prediction.

Two 2nd U-Flotilla boats put to sea during the last week of the month, *U106* leaving on 25 July and *U125* sailing two days later, bound for Freetown. as Rasch's *U106* crossed Biscay a small fleet of Breton sardine fishing boats was spotted, one of them altering course towards *U106*. Suddenly the unmistakeable shape of a Wellington bomber roared towards the U-boat from the same direction and Rasch, with no time to dive, ordered AA weapons to open fire. Wellington 'A' of 311 (Czech) Squadron charged into the attack, nose gunner blazing away as the twin flak weapons on *U106* sent tracer rounds hurtling towards him. The Wellington roared overhead, dropping four Torpex depth charges from a height of only fifty feet in a clean straddle before climbing away for a second attack. The first blasts sent the lookouts gasping to the steel floor as *U106* slewed to a halt, listing slightly to star-board. IWO Günther Wißmann lay dead and Rasch wounded, as men struggled to get him through the narrow hatch and the boat dived. Oblt. (Ing.) Albert Helmer blew tanks and *U106* slipped underwater with the main hatch still open, only the inner control room hatch stopping the boat from flooding as a second pair of depth charges exploded along-side. Badly damaged, *U106* limped submerged towards Lorient where she was hauled from the water into dry dock the following day. Wißmann was buried with full honours and Rasch was hospitalized. It would be two months before *U106* would sail again, but when she did Rasch was back at the helm.

With declining fortunes, BdU again pinned hopes of success for the larger boats on concentrating around West Africa and another attempt at attacking Cape Town. The daunting prospect of a 6,000-nautical-mile journey from France to South Africa meant that Type IXCs would require the full support of *Milch kuh* tankers.

> "From our point of view the most important thing was that we should retain the initiative and that the various blows we struck should come as a complete surprise to the enemy . . . exploit his weaknesses before he has had time to eradicate them by re-routing his shipping or strengthening its escort."[113]

It was decided to send four experienced U-boats. Named Group *Eisbär* (Polar Bear), in an attempt to disguise the group's destination, Hartenstein's *U156*, Merten's *U68*, Poske's *U504* and Emmermann's 10th U-Flotilla *U172* were to be supported by tanker *U459*. Following behind would come four Type IXD2 U-cruisers, now entering service and destined ultimately to cross into the Indian Ocean.

With complete surprise a pre-condition of the operation's success, a paranoid SKL issued orders to BdU on 1 August to:

> "forbid [the *Eisbär*] submarines to attack while en route beyond the equator. They must also maintain complete radio silence. Only attacks on battleships and aircraft carriers are permitted – providing firing data is certain."

[113] Dönitz, p. 240.

Although recognizing the imperative of surprise, Dönitz ensured that his commanders were aware of their freedom to attack enemy shipping before the equator was reached. This 'free-fire' area was later enlarged to 5° south latitude, an extension soon of great significance to Hartenstein.

The first two *Eisbär* boats, *U156* and *U172*, sailed on 19 August, *U459* leaving Bordeaux that same day for quadrant GG where it would hold a refuelling station. The following day the remainder followed and the small task force began its trek.

Abwehr agents had reported massed shipping passing Cape Town in either direction, while only six aged destroyers and several guardboats were on guard. The operation was to begin after *U156* and *U172* had made a thorough reconnaissance of the Cape Town roadsteads. Success against an estimated fifty anchored ships was to be radioed to BdU, acting as a cue for the other boats to open fire.

5 August: Lorient received an unusual visitor, the huge 2,584-ton Japanese *Kaigun/B1* class long-range submarine *I30* arriving in France after over four months journeying from Japan. Commanded by *Chu-sa* (Commander) Shinobu Endo, the huge submarine (thirty-four metres longer than a Type IXC) eased into Lorient carrying vital cargo for the Wehrmacht. The entire 2nd and 10th U-Flotilla staffs, headed by both Dönitz and Raeder, turned out to greet the Japanese crew as *I30* slowly edged into its moorings against the *Isére* before transferring to the relative safety of the Scorff bunker. It was the first of three successful transport journeys undertaken by Japanese submarines from the Far East to France.[114]

7 August: The extraordinary Kaptlt. Albrecht Achilles entered Lorient with a heavily damaged *U161* after his second war patrol, again spent in the Caribbean. Heading initially for prospective operations against Brazil, Achilles and two accompanying boats, *U126* and *U128*, arrived off the South American coast toward the end of May. After their Brazilian attack was cancelled the three boats headed north to the Caribbean. Dispersing near the Lesser Antilles, Achilles sailed for his favoured hunting ground of Trinidad, while his two companions positioned themselves east of the Windward Isles.

Although Achilles was once again in his element, the odds had changed. The Allies had gained the protection of the convoying, a sign of steadily increasing escort and aircraft presence in the region. Coupled with this was the periodic torrential downpour of tropical rain obliterating visibility and making life wretched for sailors exposed to the elements. An hour before midnight (local time) on 14 June Achilles sank his first ship of the new patrol, SS *Scottsburg*. The giant American steamer had been travelling in a small coastal convoy. Approached by Achilles at periscope depth, two torpedoes soon shot from the U-boat's bow tubes. Achilles was rewarded with twin direct hits, *Scottsburg* immediately sinking low in the water, until minutes later she was gone, five crew entombed within her. Unfortunately for Achilles, he had failed to notice that in the few seconds before impact the entire convoy had begun an emergency turn, the G7a torpedoes' wakes seen by alert

---

[114] When she sailed for her return journey on 22 August, codenamed *Kirschblüte* (Cherry blossom) she carried a cargo that included a torpedo data computer, *Bold*, 'Seetakt' radar, Metox, Enigma machines and G7a and G7e torpedoes. *I30* would reach Singapore on 13 October, stopping for only six and a half hours before sailing for Japan. Outbound from Singapore harbour she strayed into a Japanese defensive minefield and was sunk for the loss of fourteen of her 110 crewmen.

lookouts. When they exploded chaos erupted, as turning ships twisted to avoid collision with *Scottsburg*. SS *Kahuku* slowed to search for survivors while Achilles ordered his boat deep in anticipation of escort retaliation. Hydrophones revealed only low rumbling merchant propellers heading in several directions, leading Achilles to presume that the convoy was scattering, an ideal moment for a second attack. Rising to periscope depth surrounded by the cacophony of whirling screws, Achilles climbed into the conning tower in preparation for raising the boat's *spargel*. Abruptly *U161* reeled to port as a freighter's keel smashed against the conning tower, the shriek of rending metal reverberating through *U161*. Amazingly there seemed no damage to the pressure hull and as soon as the boat had broken free of its unwitting assailant Achilles ordered her dived away to sanctuary.

Hours later *U161* surfaced in an empty sea to inspect the damage. Climbing gingerly through the conning tower hatch Achilles found the starboard shielding of the conning tower buckled inwards and the spray deflector completely missing on that side, but no damage to vital systems. Both periscopes were untouched and the ship remained water-tight. While the forward jumper wire had been ripped from its mountings it didn't take long for the radio crew to rig their antennae to the battered tower and raise Kernével again. The patrol would continue; behind them the *Scottsburg* was gone.

U161 sailed west toward Panama where it sank the small yacht *Cheerio* with artillery before leaving the barren area for Costa Rica. Because of the sparse pickings, Achilles met with *U159* of the 10th U-Flotilla to exchange torpedoes for food, before deciding on yet another of his trademark attacks. Creeping into Costa Rica's only Caribbean harbour, Porto Limón, during the night of 1 July, Achilles fired two torpedoes at the sole freighter in sight. Both struck the Panamanian steamer *San Pablo*, tied up at the pier, and the crippled ship settled upright while Achilles successfully retraced his course and escaped.[115]

Slipping through the Windward Passage bound for France, *U161* had one last stroke of fortune. During mid-afternoon on 16 July distant smoke was sighted south of Bermuda issuing from fast convoy AS4 – nine cargo ships heading from America to Suez and escorted by a formidable pair of cruisers and seven destroyers. Diving for a submerged attack, Achilles fired four torpedoes, two water columns erupting alongside the 6,165-ton American SS *Fairport*, taken to be a "9,000 ton tanker", just over two and a half minutes later. A third detonation was heard as Achilles took his boat deep, although Allied records show no trace of this. Now Achilles would pay as USS *Kearny* and *Wilkes* charged over-head to begin nine hours of depth-charging, resulting in severe damage to *U161* and an (incorrectly) claimed kill. Harrowing though the attack was, Achilles survived and continued his return journey, entering Lorient a hero once more.

Ironically *U161* had unwittingly proved Dönitz's contention that convoy interdiction was the surest way of swinging the war in Germany's favour. SS *Fairport*'s holds were crammed with 300 Sherman tank engines being ferried to the North African desert where the Afrika Korps appeared on the verge of crushing the British Eighth Army. Tobruk had fallen to the Germans, 33,000 men surrendering to a smaller attacking force. In despera-tion, Churchill had appealed to Roosevelt for "as many Shermans as you can spare" and six ships were soon loaded with cargo for the embattled British, five carrying 317 Shermans and 100 Priest SP guns, while *Fairport* carried the engines for the stored Shermans.[116] In one single blow Achilles nearly altered the course of the North Africa war. However, with

[115] The *San Pablo* was later salvaged and returned to service.
[116] Churchill, Vol IV, p. 316.

American industry hitting high gear, a second ship laden with engines was despatched immediately, actually arriving in Egypt before AS4.

The day following Achilles' homecoming Kaptlt. Günther Müller-Stöckheim also returned, U67, empty of torpedoes, trailing a minesweeper escort into Lorient after a number of sinkings off Florida and within the Gulf of Mexico. Flying eight success pennants, Müller-Stöckheim was celebrating the best patrol of his career. Brief interference from a Sunderland bomber in Biscay had caused light damage, the diesel's power-operated clutch rendered inoperative, emergency hand-operated equipment allowing U67 to continue home.

15 August: U107 sailed from Lorient bound initially for the South Atlantic, while the oldest Type IX in active service returned from an unsuccessful and frustrating patrol. U43 had sailed on 4 July to join the aptly named Wolf pack, proving unsuccessful despite sighting a westbound convoy on 13 July which escaped as Wolf struggled against heavy seas, losing contact. Dönitz ordered Wolf south and the patrol line straggled towards its allocated area, preparing to refuel from Milch kuh U461. On the verge of refuelling, convoy ON113 was spotted, but the U-boats had little success in the face of a strong escort. One, U90, was sunk and the attack was called off on 26 July after three days of frustration.

As Dönitz considered there to be a glut of U-boats heading for the Caribbean during July, seven of the remaining Wolf boats refuelled as planned from U461 before heading north to intercept convoy ON115 sighted by the 10th U-Flotilla's U164 on 29 July south-east of Cape Farewell. Forty-one fast ships under escort by the experienced Canadian C3 escort group were heading west. While Wolf moved towards the convoy they were joined by U164 and four others to bolster the attack, the whole dozen renamed group Pirat. On the evening of 2 August the convoy blundered into the Pirat line just as thick fog descended on the battlefield. In the confused action that followed torpedoes began to explode on target. As Kaptlt. Hans-Joachim Schwantke prepared U43 for its first assault a blinding starshell exploded directly astern, surprising him and revealing HMCS Sackville turning to attack. Schwantke bellowed for a crash dive, which began an ordeal later described in his War Diary:

> "Unable to close the conning tower hatch. The catch has jammed in the socket. Could find nothing which might be impending it. . . . LI blew tanks briefly, but I had to get down and I ordered him to flood. Two men were hanging on to me as the water started to pour in. I managed to thrust the catch home (later examinations showed that the catch had been turned a little too far, with the result that the straight edges of the catch had come up against the claw lugs on the rim of the conning tower, instead of the bevelled edges)."

The time spent trying to dog the hatch, coupled with the LI's understandable hesitation at diving, added a crucial half-minute to the boat's already slow submergence, there being barely twenty metres of seawater above it when the first Canadian depth charges exploded. The boat was hammered sideways by the blast and all main lighting flickered and died, while one man was hurled to the deck by the severe concussion, suffering internal injuries. Every depth gauge in the boat ceased to function and all that Schwantke and his men could do was guess their position in the water column. With both electric motors knocked off-line, Schwantke climbed to the troublesome conning tower hatch and opened the 'piddle-cock', a small valve inset for test purposes. The thin stream of high-pressure water that jetted forth confirmed his suspicion that U43 was plummeting out of control. With the corvette's screws still audible above them, Schwantke ordered trim adjusted so that *U43* lay down by the stern, starboard electric motor coaxed back on line and pushing the boat forward, the port motor still seized. Abruptly the U-boat began rocking in a gentle swell and to his horror Schwantke realized that they had broken the surface, probably in the path of the oncoming Canadian. He bellowed for a second crash dive and *U43* plunged under again, this time the Papenberg 25-metre depth gauge springing back into life and showing an alarming descent rate. The boat had reached an estimated 120 metres before the second pattern of depth charges exploded overhead causing more damage. But *U43*'s luck held and the corvette's screws gradually faded away.

Schwantke waited until hydrophones declared the sea above empty before bringing his boat to the surface, flinging open the hatch as water streamed from the conning tower. *U43* was badly damaged; both on-board compressors had broken down and two bow caps were jammed half-open. Although the hull was sound, Schwantke radioed Lorient that he was returning and was ordered to rendezvous with *U461* two days later in order to receive a Junkers compressor to facilitate diving and surfacing while crossing the Bay of Biscay. It was fortunate that they did so as lookouts had sighted a periscope in grid square BF4964 and they crash-dived away from what was presumed to be a lurking British submarine before entering Lorient.

On **19 August**, as the last *Eisbär* member, *U504*, sailed from Lorient, an emergency alert was radioed to three U-boats outbound near the Western Approaches, including 2nd U-Flotilla's *U107*, ordering them to make all speed for the Allied landings at Dieppe, feared to presage invasion. Gelhaus had no choice but to comply and *U107* raced north-east towards the hazardous entrance to the English Channel and the prospect of tackling an invasion fleet.

It was in fact the Allied débâcle of 'Operation Jubilee', where, in front of the Norman town of Dieppe, a massed landing by predominantly Canadian troops had started a little before 0500hrs. Aboard *U107*, apprehension regarding their forthcoming anti-invasion role was assuaged at 1600hrs as the diversion was cancelled, the beach at Dieppe silent but for the crackling of flames and the groans of wounded men after a bloody victory by the fierce German defence which killed or captured nearly half the attacking force.

After successfully escaping the clutches of Biscay, Gelhaus radioed Lorient that his newly installed Metox set had helped evade six separate aircraft attacks, proving the apparent worth of the new addition to the U-boats' arsenal. Distribution of the radar detector had begun during August and Gelhaus' report provided the first indication that it worked in operational use. An extra *Obermaat* was added to the boat's crew to monitor the new equipment, reporting any enemy radar impulse detected immediately to the commander. Boats returning from combat and thus unequipped with Metox were ordered, where possible, to form small convoys with at least one Metox-equipped U-boat leading during the dangerous Biscay crossing. Although temporarily effective, blind faith in Metox would soon provide the Allies with several new successful aerial sinkings.[117]

However, the perils of Biscay continued to plague Dönitz and his men. The previous March Churchill had expressed his determination that U-boats transiting Biscay would be hounded day and night. Now the effect began to erode operational U-boat performance:

---

[117] Metox was the first radar detection device issued to U-boats as counter to increasingly effective aerial detection. Named after the Paris firm that built it, the small unit was installed with a rigid wooden-frame aerial that earned the unit the nickname 'Biscay Cross'.

"Numbers of enemy aircraft [in Eastern Atlantic] have increased . . . equipped with an excellent radar set against U-boats. All these factors have made the conduct of the U-boat war in the East Atlantic very difficult.

"Outward and inward-bound boats in the North Sea and Biscay are exposed to grave danger by daily, even hourly, hunts by aircraft. . . . If development continues at the present rate those problems will lead to irreparable losses, to a decline in successes and consequently to a decline in the chances of success of the U-boat war as a whole."[118]

23 August: Luckless *U154* arrived in Lorient after the most unsuccessful Caribbean and Gulf of Mexico mission to date. KK Walther Kölle had sailed from Lorient on 4 June without serious incident before pounding across the Atlantic and penetrating the Windward Passage during early July. As *U154* slipped through the Canal de Yucatán into the Gulf of Mexico, Kölle sank his first ship, the 65-ton Panamanian motor trawler *Lalita*, with gunfire on 6 July. It was his sole success.

During the next two weeks *U154* patrolled the Alabama and Florida coasts in search of targets, reporting two misses against a fast enemy freighter near the Dry Tortugas on 9 July, the fan shot disappearing without trace. Apart from neutrals there was no traffic and Kölle requested permission to proceed to Galveston in search of the elusive tankers. Hounded by constant aircraft presence, he awaited orders. On 13 July the sudden appearance of aircraft prompted a crash-dive to safety, *U154* plunging to eighty metres. It was while congratulating themselves on their successful escape from detection that the crew noticed *Maschinenobergefreiter* Rudolf Bahner missing from his post. Bahner had been on deck at the time, using the detachable wooden 'outdoor toilet', clipped to the guidewires. As the bridge crew scrambled below and the boat dived Bahner was completely forgotten, left swimming in the swirl of the submerged U-boat. Realizing the potentially tragic oversight, Köller ordered his boat surfaced. Circling the area, lookouts sighted Bahner, as well as the ominous and unmistakeable dorsal fin of a large shark nearby. With several men breaking out pistols and shooting toward the shark the terrified Bahner was pulled back onboard, shaken but otherwise none the worse for the experience.

Morale slumped lower as the boat headed for Galveston in sweltering heat. Skin rashes and boils plagued the men cramped together in the humid hull. With the constant aircraft threat there was little chance to go on deck where seawater, sun and fresh air would clean their filthy bodies. Their miserable voyage was curtailed on 19 July when a leaking fuel tank left a shimmering oil track, an irreparable problem. After initially refusing permission to shorten the patrol, Dönitz relented when Kölle began to complain of feeling unwell, *U154* aborting to Lorient and rendezvousing with a sceptical Reinhard Suhren aboard the 1st U-Flotilla's *U564* to transfer torpedoes.

After also transferring spare water the two boats parted company and Kölle resumed his homeward trek, welcomed with a subdued reception. Reporting to Dönitz, he was relieved of command and returned to Mürwick, the remainder of *U154*'s crew being transferred to *U105*, still in dry dock undergoing repair. *U105*'s experienced crew, still led by Kaptlt. Heinrich Schuch, was given *U154* in return, the boat being overhauled in Lorient in preparation for an October sailing.

[118] BdU KTB.

25 August: The last of the flotilla's boats which had sailed during the first half of June, *U505*, entered port after a luckless and fraught patrol. The Atlantic passage was spent mainly surfaced, *U505* making good speed towards the Caribbean. Hans Goebeler remembered:

> "My favourite moments were passed on bridge watch, especially during the relatively cool nights. . . . Around midnight Anton 'Toni' Kern, our boat's cook, would come to the bridge with his steaming pot of *Mittelwächter*, a much welcome mixture of very strong coffee laced with rum. I remember the first time he tried to make a big pot of hot tea for the crew. Most Germans are coffee drinkers, so Toni had not been trained to make tea during his four-week cook's course in U-boat school. In his ignorance, he used the same measure of tea leaves as one would use for coffee. He then boiled the leaves until the tea was as black as old motor oil. The stuff tasted bitter as poison when we tried to drink it.
>
> "Well, Kaptlt. Loewe's mother was Dutch, so the Skipper was a big tea drinker. Naturally he demanded that it be properly brewed. It was very amusing to watch the Skipper hovering over the stove like a patient old man, instructing a very embarrassed Toni on the intricacies of tea making."[119]

Loewe's first action of this, the boat's second war patrol, was on 28 June north of the Leeward Islands, when, after a seven-hour surface chase, Loewe dived and torpedoed SS *Sea Thrush* crowded with aircraft parts.

The following day a second American steamer was also run down and hit by submerged torpedo attack. But it was at that point that the U-boat's luck changed. Sailing into the Caribbean on 4 July, *U505* began two weeks of humid patrolling towards Colombia in the face of thunderous tropical storms. Newly deployed Liberator bombers carrying centimetric radar hounded the boat by day and night; constant aircraft alerts grating on the men's nerves until the entire crew were depressed and fractious.

Finally on 21 July a three-masted schooner was sighted near Isla de San Andreas. With the sailing ship suspiciously zigzagging, Loewe ordered battle stations and deck guns manned. Firing a warning shot, IIWO Stolzenburg's first shell unfortunately took down the schooner's main mast and in panic the sailing ship attempted to flee as the Colombian flag was run up the neutral's yard. Feeling he had little alternative than to finish the work the single shell had begun, Loewe, after some hesitation, ordered his guns to open fire and minutes later the *Roamar* from Cartagena was nothing but splintered debris as *U505* hastily left the area.

The experienced and respected Loewe appeared seized by sudden depression and nervousness, IWO Herbert Nollau assuming more and more the mantle of command. In deteriorating weather *U505* sailed back and forth off the South American coast with no result until finally it became clear that Loewe was physically ill and on 1 August he requested and was granted permission to return to Lorient. Refuelling from *U463* en-route, *U505* entered port to an enthusiastic reception. Once safely ashore Löwe was diagnosed as suffering from appendicitis, immediately relieved by an emergency operation.

However, the commander continued to show depression over the schooner sinking, a judgement that he was to regret. The *Roamar* was the property of a Colombian diplomat, prompting yet another South American country to declare war on Germany. Loewe, respected by Dönitz, was relieved of his command and put on the staff of Hans Rösing's

[119] Goebeler, p. 56.

FdU West as *Referent W.*[120] It was the third poor return for the expensive and time-consuming commitment of Type IXs to distant waters. More catastrophically for Loewe's crew, *U505* received a new commanding officer. Kaptlt. Peter Zschech, former IWO aboard Mohr's now-famous *U124*, arrived to occupy the vacant post. The crew of *U505* were well aware of the reputation that Mohr's crack crew had built for themselves and hoped their new skipper would bring renewed success. As time would show, they were tragically mistaken.

10 September: KK Klaus Scholtz's *U108* also arrived in port from the Caribbean, followed two days later by Ernst Kals' *U130* from success off Freetown. Scholz had begun his patrol inauspiciously, five days after departing Lorient attacking convoy OS34 with a full salvo of six torpedoes missing each target. Disappointed and harried by escorting aircraft, *U108* withdrew in the face of aerial depth-charging.

Sailing south-west, *U108* skirted the Caribbean, patrolling east of Trinidad and sinking the solo-sailing British tanker MV *Tricula* on the night of 3 August and the Norwegian freighter MV *Brenas* the following night. Captain Oscar Kløcker was taken prisoner, identified as Scholz nosed *U108* through the scattered debris.[121]

Redirected to concentrate off French Guiana, Scholz sank his third victim on 17 August, although subsequent retaliation from locally based American bombers inflicted serious damage on the submerged U-boat, which returned to France. On the day of his return Scholtz was awarded the Oak Leaves to his Knight's Cross.

Meanwhile, Kals had sunk seven ships off Africa, claiming 51,718 tons in total, also reporting a missed long shot against the fast liner *Empress of Canada* south-west of Sierra Leone on 24 July. Additionally, *U130*'s final victory of the patrol, SS *Beechwood*, provided a set of confidential Admiralty sailing instructions for West Africa traffic, carried by the master A.M. Tilsey when he was taken prisoner aboard *U130*. Bereft of torpedoes, Kals, sporting the Knight's Cross made by his crew, returned to Lorient, suffering slight damage after being caught surfaced by a Boeing B18 bomber west of Cape Finisterre.

Despite decorations and flowers, the pendulum of fortune had swung against Germany's *Unterseebootwaffe*. The benefits of air power, centimetre radar, increasing escort strength and hard-won experience irrevocably turned the tide of battle in the Allies' favour. The Caribbean had finally become too dangerous for high-level U-boat concentration and by early September boats were moved to Trinidad and further east into New York convoy routes. The narrow choke points where U-boats had initially hunted now worked against them, Allied strength in the Caribbean able to swarm over the slender passages from the Atlantic, making them unreasonably risky for U-boat penetration. Off Freetown results had declined after Kals' July successes, solo shipping now intercepted as it sailed some 500 miles west in the central Atlantic. Only new theatres promised an immediate boost to success for distant operations.

By early September the *Eisbär* group were well on their way towards Cape Town when, on the morning of 12 September, Kaptlt. Werner Hartenstein's bridge watch sighted the smudge of distant smoke. *U156* had already sunk one ship when, on 25 August, the four

---

[120] Loewe later became a member of the *Reichsministerium für Rüstung und Kriegsproduktion* from August 1944 to April 1945, then commanding the *I. Marine Panzerjagregiment*.

[121] He would later be put ashore in Lorient and incarcerated, freed after nine months and sent home to Norway in July 1943.

Eisbär boats were temporarily diverted to attack convoy SL119 east of the Azores and, although approaching the new cease-fire latitude, the chance of one more sinking was too hard to resist and Hartenstein gave chase. At 2207hrs he ordered tubes one and three fired. Three minutes later both torpedoes hit their target.

As the ship began to founder, the sudden splutter of a Morse message came from the radio operator's headset.

"SSS, 04.34 south, 11.25 west, *Laconia* torpedoed, SSS."

The *Laconia* was soon found in Gröner's merchant fleet index: Cunard, White Star Line, 19,965 tons, requisitioned troop ship, a lucky hit for any U-boat. Hartenstein, realizing the danger the radio message posed to his U-boat, decided to try and find the *Laconia*'s captain while his radio crew jammed the outgoing distress message and the steamer heeled to starboard and began to go down by the bow. *U156* eased into the floating debris to interrogate survivors. It was at that moment that the distant sound of voices shouting for help drifted across the sea – Italian voices.

The *Laconia* had left the Bay of Suez on 12 August bound for the United Kingdom. It was the return half of a voyage transporting troops to North Africa and at the time of sinking was carrying 268 British military personnel returning to England, many of them badly wounded in the fight against Rommel's Afrika Korps. About eighty women and children were also aboard and 1,800 Italian POWs, guarded by a contingent of 103 Polish troops. Captain Rudolf Sharp, an experienced merchant master had, by coincidence, captained two other Cunard ships enshrined in military history before *Laconia*. Prior to the First World War he had been master of the *Lusitania*, later sunk in 1915 by *U20*. In 1940 he captained the troopship *Lancastria*, sunk by German bombers in the Charpentier Roads before St Nazaire during 1940's 'Operation Aerial'. The tragic loss of that ship, crammed far past its capacity with Allied troops, remains to this day the most costly British maritime tragedy in history. Now, once more, his ship was embroiled in war but this time Sharp did not survive. In the finest tradition of sea captains, Sharp and his First Officer George Steel remained on their bridge as it sank below the waves.

As *U156* circled the scene of devastation, the distinct cry of "*Aiuto! Aiuto!*" (Help! Help!) drifted towards her. Fishing several survivors from the sea, the Germans were shocked to discover the *Laconia*'s huge number of Italian passengers and Hartenstein ordered his crew to begin rescuing survivors. As numbers of bedraggled half-naked Italians grew aboard the boat he also ordered an emergency message flashed to BdU:

"Sunk British *Laconia*, unfortunately with 1,500 [sic] Italian prisoners. 90 rescued so far."

Without waiting for further orders, Hartenstein continued his mission of mercy, pulling friend and foe alike from the water. Many Italians became aggressive towards rescued Poles, several of the recent POWs showing visible bayonet wounds after being kept away from lifeboats by their Polish guards. Coupled with the bayonet wounds was another worrying injury – shark bites. The scene of the tragedy was beginning to attract the predators and many survivors disappeared in a flurry of spray.

In Paris Dönitz faced a dilemma. To endorse the rescue and direct other boats to assist would place their crews in jeopardy. However, the alternative was to order *U156* to throw survivors back in the sea and continue its mission. This was unthinkable and Dönitz, a professional seaman since before the First World War, was unable to sanction such an action. In all probability Hartenstein would not have complied anyway. Within a few hours BdU made his decision and messages were sent out to the remaining three *Eisbär* boats, *U459*, nearly *U506* (10th U-Flotilla) and *U507*, the latter homebound from Brazil. Even the BETASOM boat *Capellini* was ordered to make all speed for the sinking as one of the unlikeliest rescue operations of the war got under way. Dönitz ensured that the Italian government was apprised of the situation, as well as Vichy authorities through the Armistice Commission in permanent session in Wiesbaden. By involving the French Dönitz hoped to be able to hand survivors over to nearby Morocco at the earliest possible opportunity.

However, Berlin would not endorse the rescue. Hitler was furious with Hartenstein, declaring that he should have left the scene immediately, allowing nothing to interfere with the *Eisbär* mission. Through Raeder he demanded that the Cape Town U-boats resume their journey, the rescue to be left to Vichy ships *Gloire*, *Annamite* and *Dumont d'Urville*, all having sailed after Raeder added his weight to a formal request for assistance.[122] The Führer's temper was not improved when Dönitz passed on Hartenstein's request that the area of the sinking be the subject of a "diplomatic neutralization" (cease-fire) in order to complete the rescue. This too Hitler refused. Dönitz complied with his superiors' instructions – but only in part. He ordered the remaining *Eisbär* boats and *U459* to continue with their original orders. Merten's *U68* was to take over the role of Hartenstein's boat during the attack on Cape Town. However, *U506* and *U507* remained under instructions to converge on Hartenstein whose boat was now full of survivors with several lifeboats in tow. *U156*'s decks were covered in shipwrecked men, while the injured and women and children were quartered below. Doris Hawkins later told French author Léonce Peiliard:

> "The Germans treated us with great kindness and respect the whole time. . . . One brought us eau-de-Cologne, another cold cream for our sunburn which was really bad; others gave us lemons from their lockers, articles of clothing and tins of fruit. The commander was particularly charming and helpful; he could scarcely have done more if he was entertaining us in peacetime. I did not hear 'Heil Hitler' once; I saw no swastikas, and only one photograph of Hitler, in a small recess."[123]

On the morning of 13 September Hartenstein tried to instigate his own truce. Radioing in plain English he sent the message:

> "If any ship will assist the shipwrecked *Laconia* crew I will not attack her, providing I am not attacked by ship or air force. I have picked up 193 men. 4° 52 south 11° 26 west. German submarine."

On 15 September British authorities in Freetown notified the merchant ship *Empire Haven* of the rescue operation revealed by Hartenstein's radio message and directed her to rendezvous with the U-boat and assist. They also contacted the newly established American airbase on Ascension Island to provide 'air cover' to the *Empire Haven*. It proved to be a poor choice of words.

The following morning *U506* and *U507* reached the scene and began rescuing survivors. But, almost inevitably, the apparent progress could not last. An American B24 Liberator

---

[122] Vichy ships that sailed from Dakar were specifically released by the British blockade for this purpose.
[123] Léonce Peiliard, *U-boats to the Rescue*, p. 145.

bomber in transit from Brazil to Africa refuelling at Ascension had scrambled with a full weapon load to provide the necessary 'air cover' for *Empire Haven*. The pilot, James D. Harden, was two and a half hours into his flight when he sighted *U156*. At that moment Hartenstein had 115 shipwrecked survivors on board and was towing four lifeboats. He deployed a two-metre square improvised Red Cross flag, the banner held on the forward deck above the 10.5cm deck gun. To reinforce his intentions, Hartenstein ordered a signalman to flash messages to the aircraft, a British officer offering to send the message instead, signalling:

> "RAF officer speaking from German submarine. *Laconia* survivors on board, soldiers, civilians, women, children."

The aircraft made no reply. Flying away to the south-west, Harden radioed Ascension for instructions. Commander of American 1st Composite Squadron, Richard C. Richardson III, replied with little hesitation after conferring with his superior Colonel Ronin: "Sink sub".

Minutes later Harden began the first of five attack runs, dropping three depth charges. In his report he recounted that the lifeboats had moved away from *U156*, something hotly disputed by other eyewitnesses. Two of the first charges fell wide, the third exploding close to the U-boat's stern, capsizing a lifeboat and killing several people in the water. Hartenstein ordered tethers to the other boats cut and all British survivors overboard – he must submerge. The next three bomb runs were unsuccessful, but the final attack dropped two bombs immediately below the control room. Inside *U156* the crew reported chlorine gas and flooding as panicked *Laconia* survivors, Italians now included, were hurried out of the cramped interior. Ordering *U156* dived, Hartenstein retreated from the site, his guns having remained silent throughout the attack. Above him Harden reported the U-boat as "rolled over" and "last seen bottom up", crew abandoning ship and claimed *U156* as sunk.

Damage aboard *U156* was indeed heavy – but not crippling. It was soon discovered that there was no danger from chlorine and that, although leaking, the pressure hull had not been ruptured and flooding could be controlled. Oblt. (Ing.) Polchau reported to Hartenstein that seven battery cells had been destroyed, the sky periscope jammed in its well, diesel-cooling flange broken off, wireless incapacitated and both sounding gear and hydrophones inoperable. With gusto the German crew set to work as Hartenstein lowered his boat into the depths for repairs to begin. Hours later his technical crew had done what he recorded in his War Diary as a "first class repair job", all the damage that could be patched up at sea repaired. That evening, several miles from the *Laconia* survivors, *U156* surfaced and used its mended radio to contact Dönitz in Paris:

> "Hartenstein. While towing four lifeboats, in clear weather and displaying large Red Cross flag from bridge was bombed by American Liberator. Aircraft dropped five bombs. Have transferred survivors to lifeboats and am abandoning rescue work. Proceeding westwards. Repairs in hand."

Dönitz immediately ordered all remaining rescue attempts cancelled if boats were in danger of further attack. The large-scale attempt at humanity had backfired, compounded the following day by *U506* also being bombed by Harden. The boat suffered no real damage and Würdemann surfaced to transfer his cargo to the newly arrived Vichy sloop *Annamite*. Schacht also put his load aboard the French ship. Altogether *U507* had carried 129 Italians, sixteen children, fifteen women and a British officer, while towing seven lifeboats with 330 more survivors. As *U507* retreated from the scene it still carried two prisoners: *Laconia*'s Third Officer Thomas Buckingham and an RAF Flying Officer named Smith, Schacht judging that they had seen a great deal of the U-boat's Metox apparatus and could possibly pass on their knowledge to the Allies. The two Britons fared well on their journey, Smith in particular playing chess against IIWO Eckehard Scherraus, while German crewmen remembered Buckingham as "a great consumer of salt water soap" during the voyage.[124]

Aboard *U156*, although the crew were deeply troubled by what they had just experienced, there was at least the reward of a radioed message from Dönitz on 17 September, awarding the Knight's Cross to Werner Hartenstein for his accumulated claims. The *Laconia* rescue was over and 1,041 people had survived. Seething at the bombing of the humanitarian gesture, Dönitz radioed a final message on 17 September to all U-boats, also distributing it to flotilla headquarters everywhere. It has since become known as the 'Laconia Order' and was used by Prosecutors at the Nuremberg trials to indicate Dönitz guilty of war crimes:

> "1. No attempt of any kind must be made at rescuing members of ships sunk; and this includes picking up persons in the water and putting them in lifeboats, righting capsized lifeboats and handing over food and water. Rescue runs counter to the rudimentary demands of warfare for the destruction of enemy ships and crews.
>
> 2. Orders for bringing in captains and chief engineers still apply.
>
> 3. Rescue the shipwrecked only if their statements will be of importance to your boat.
>
> 4. Be harsh, having in mind that the enemy take no regard of women and children in his bombing attacks on German cities."

In total war there are seldom issues that can be taken as purely black or white, particularly complicated command level decisions. On the Allied side USAAF Captain Robert C. Richardson III had faced a thorny dilemma: let the U-boats go, whereupon they could later sink more Allied shipping, or attack. He had chosen the latter. In 1963 the *Sunday Express* ran a series of articles about the *Laconia* incident, in which it interviewed Richardson:

> "I gave the order to bomb the *Laconia* survivors. We did not know there were British among them. But even if we had, it would have made no difference. I would have given the order anyway."[125]

The Allies had suffered a communication breakdown, Americans asserting not to hear of the *Laconia* rescue in progress, the British steamer *Empire Haven* never arriving and at best a feeble British rescue attempt. Indeed, when Ascension Island was alerted by British authorities that Vichy warships were 'on the way' they prepared ground defences for what they assumed was to be a full-scale French invasion!

---

[124] Smith later died in a POW camp near Stuttgart. Buckingham was liberated by British troops from Milag Nord on 29 April 1945.

[125] *The Enemy Killed My Friend*, p. 116.

16 September:

"*U162*, commanded by Commander Wattenberg, an experienced boat, has not reported since 1/9/42. She was lost operating in the area of Trinidad and was probably destroyed by aircraft. Nothing further is known. Boat must be presumed lost."

Kaptlt. Jürgen Wattenberg had sailed from Lorient on 7 July, destined for the Caribbean, arriving west of the Windward Islands during mid-August and heading for Trinidad and recent heavy convoy activity. On 19 August, in pre-dawn darkness, Wattenberg sighted a convoy west of the Grenadian capital St George and homed 1st U-Flotilla's *U564* on to the fourteen merchant ships of 'feeder convoy' TAW(S), escorted by two destroyers, two patrol craft and circling aircraft.[126] Wattenberg circled wide before launching a surface attack, hitting American freighter SS *West Celina* and sending it slewing out of control in flames, before being pounced on by a Hudson bomber dropping flares and depth charges and forced to dive and escape.

The use of flares to illuminate the U-boat led many to conclude that aircraft did not have radar but relied on visual sightings. They were half-right. Although radar sets aboard the attacking aircraft could pick up the surfaced U-boat hull, many German commanders confused the attackers by turning to the convoy's course and speed when Metox betrayed enemy radar contact. Pilots then were forced to confirm the contact with flares as the impulses returned by a small patrol vessel and U-boat were indistinguishable.

Wattenberg then sailed east, sinking three more ships before intending to begin the return journey to France. On 31 August Wattenberg radioed BdU to arrange a fuel transfer and once again it was Suhren's *U564* that met *U162* to transfer oil east of Saint Lucia, the smaller boat already refuelled from a *Milch kuh*.

Two days later, as *U162* lingered in the shipping lanes between Barbados and Trinidad, Wattenburg spotted what he took to be a single destroyer heading roughly his way. Determined to add the prestigious crown to his patrol, he submerged and closed to attack. Inexplicably *U162*'s hydrophone operator failed to report that there were three high-pitched destroyer screws approaching. HMS *Pathfinder*, *Quentin* and *Vimy* were travelling in line abreast bound for Trinidad and escort duty. Closing to torpedo range, Wattenberg fired a single bow torpedo. It is hard to know precisely which impression struck the forty-one-year-old veteran commander first – that his torpedo had malfunctioned, broached and run off course or that there were three destroyers approaching instead of one. Only minutes before, *Pathfinder* had obtained ASDIC contact to port and begun to change course to intercept. The wildly running torpedo was plainly visible and heading towards *Quentin*, which immediately took evasive action, the eel skipping harmlessly wide to starboard. *U162* dived to escape as *Pathfinder* roared overhead to attack. Guessing his enemy would go deep, ten depth charges set between medium and maximum depth were fired from either beam and rolled off the destroyer's stern. The ensuing blasts shook Wattenberg's boat but commander and crew held tight and weathered the storm, *U162* creeping away on silent routine to the south. Their boat, however, began to suffer. As the other destroyers joined in the attack, the U-boat's hydrophones were put out of commission, coupled with damage to one of the diving tanks. The hunters above could detect the audible noise of

---

[126] This 'feeder convoy' had left Trinidad on the first leg of a journey to Key West and, ultimately, the United Kingdom after growing in size and receiving an HX number once the final conglomeration of ships joined out of Halifax, Nova Scotia.

escaping high-pressure air and they continued to drop accurate patterns of depth charges, losing ASDIC contact in the swirling aftermath but quickly regaining it. Damage continued to mount aboard *U162* with many systems affected and minor flooding in the engine room, but still the tenacious Wattenberg held his crew together and as the brief tropical sunset graced the horizon the destroyers lost contact.

In what he knew was darkness above, Wattenberg decided that the only way to escape was to surface and run for it on diesels, now that he had put some distance between himself and the hunters. However, his opposite number was himself a seasoned veteran and came to the same conclusion. HMS *Vimy*, the only one of the three with the new Type 271 centimetric radar, was detailed to stay put while the remaining two, with inferior Type 286 metre-wavelength radar, searched to eastward. Minutes later *Vimy* obtained the firm contact at 2,800 yards of *U162*'s conning tower breaking surface and the chase began.

Wattenberg tossed open the hatch and ordered diesels fired as *Vimy* called her comrades to converge on the target ahead. *Vimy*'s forward gun began to fire and in the light of exploding shells *U162* attempted to run. It was an uneven contest and Wattenberg must have known it unwinnable. British veterans are adamant that they hit the conning tower of the boat with one of their shells, although German survivors disagree vehemently. Wattenberg tried a last desperate ruse, firing two red flares into the sky, temporarily blinding their assailant's bridge crew. *U162* swung to port as *Vimy* attempted to ram and the two ships began a last battle of tight circles. Wattenberg ordered his boat scuttled and rushed the crew on deck. In the ensuing confusion *Vimy* impacted *U162* with its port screw, chewing through the U-boat's engine room, the shriek of tearing metal accompanying a brilliant shower of sparks as the hardened pressure hull proved too strong and *Vimy*'s propeller sheered off. While the German crew leapt from their boat *Vimy* limped away, her commander determined to make sure the sinking U-boat could not get under way again and escape. A single depth charge was dropped below the sinking U-boat, exploding in the water and injuring many of the struggling survivors, throwing others off the splintered decking into the sea. Below decks the last man aboard, LI Oblt. (Ing.) Edgar Stierwald, was engaged in ensuring the boat's scuttling as the depth charge exploded. He never came out and *U162* upended and went under. Wattenberg and forty-eight of his men were pulled from the sea, Stierwald and one other remaining unaccounted for.[127]

During the second half of September five 2nd U-Flotilla boats put to sea to continue their distant lone-wolf patrols, but the focus had swung permanently away from the Caribbean, back once more to West Africa. During September BdU Staff had begun to withdraw boats from the Caribbean and position them to the Atlantic side of Trinidad where there was still some tanker traffic to be attacked. The halcyon days of Caribbean operations were over and returning U-boats generally recounted the same stories of aircraft and depth charges. Only *U67* and *U129* sailed for the Indies, while *U128*, *U161* and *U126*

---

[127] Wattenberg and his men were later handed over to American Intelligence officers who found them disciplined and security conscious. The relentless Wattenberg was later housed in an Arizona POW camp in Papago Park from which, in a plan of his devising, he escaped along with twenty-four others in a 250-foot tunnel. They picked their way through granite with screwdrivers and coal shovels. Three of them squeezed wood, canvas and tar through the tunnel, hoping to build a boat with which to navigate along the Gila River, to the Colorado and into the Gulf of California to Mexico, from there they hoped to find their way home to Germany. Wattenberg was at liberty the longest – thirty-six days – before he was recaptured in Phoenix.

were all destined for the central Atlantic. While *U128* was aimed at merchant traffic centring on Freetown, the latter two were tasked with an offensive reconnaissance of the Gulf of Guinea and Congo Delta where Abwehr intelligence told of heavy shipping activity, troops and stores unloading bound for North Africa.

The sole glimmer of success from the dwindling Caribbean campaign was *U66* on 29 September, Kaptlt. Friedrich Markworth flying nine pennants as it entered Lorient. During three months at sea he had also laid six mines in St Lucia's Port Castries, severely damaging a small American Coast Guard cutter and two MTBs, forcing the harbour's closure. While returning to France, the celebratory atmosphere was muted somewhat by the death of *Matrose* Horst Keller on 13 September from illness, the young seaman buried at sea that day. Shortly afterward an error during replenishing from *U462* left insufficient diesel for a return to France and *U66* was instructed to head for El Ferrol for emergency refuelling from *Max Albrecht*, completed on 25 September, during which Markworth also transferred dangerously ill *Maschinengefreiter* Helmut Ehrlichmann aboard for surgery.[128] *U66* slipped quietly from harbour before dawn and eventually reached Lorient. It had been a remarkable combat command debut for Markworth.

3 October: In Kiel *U520* and *U521* left for the front, accompanied by *UD3* transferring to 10th U-Flotilla. The pair of Hamburg's *Deutsche Werft* boats were beginning their first war patrol after months of shakedown in the Baltic where they had encountered brief and unproductive attacks from Russian submarines. Both were bound for the frozen Canadian coast. A third brand new boat, *U522*, followed five days later, leaving Kiel on 8 October. The three new boats were to reinforce recent success by two 10th U-Flotilla Type IXCs operating in the Gulf of St Lawrence. They were also on hand to reinforce any gains made by the thirteen-strong *Veilchen* group planned to occupy a patrol line sweeping south-west, 400 miles east of Newfoundland.

4 October: *U505* left Lorient under new command. The crew already had misgivings about their new skipper, one of Zschech's first orders upon taking command in Lorient being for his men to undergo infantry combat training while the boat was refitted (including installation of a new Metox set).

Zschech, appearing eager to get to grips with the enemy, arrived alongside several fresh faces, including a new IWO, Oblt.z.S. Thilo Bode, and as *U505* sailed from port the relationship between commander and crew dipped yet lower. In Hans Goebeler's compelling autobiography he mentions his strong suspicion of a homosexual relationship developing between Zschech and his IWO, something that could spell disaster within the Third Reich and great unease for the seamen under their joint command. *U505* received the traditional send off from well-wishers ashore and headed under minesweeper escort for the Bay of Biscay. Her conning tower and deck festooned with flowers, several sailors began to throw the garlands overboard, maritime suspicion maintaining that flowers should be removed from the boat before losing sight of land lest they bring the ship bad luck. Zschech exploded in a rage, screaming at his men to stop. Bewildered, the boat's IIWO Stolzenburg attempted to explain what was happening whereupon Zschech turned his rage on him. The flowers remained as *U505* sailed west.

---

[128] After returning to Lorient and recovering from his stomach operation, he was ready to put to sea before the next patrol.

6 October: *U109* sailed into Lorient. Bleichrodt uncharacteristically sporting a white commander's cap and an immaculate uniform, his thick black beard trimmed into a tidy goatee reminiscent of privateers of a bygone age. It had been a successful voyage, five ships sunk in the waters 500 miles west of Freetown before Bleichrodt had been forced to retreat with only 8m³ of diesel remaining to rendezvous with *U460* in more secure waters south-west of the Canary Islands. His success had also earned Bleichrodt the Oak Leaves, awarded by radio on 23 September and celebrated on board *U109* that evening. By that stage of the cruise Bleichrodt had taken three British prisoners aboard, two ship's captains and a chief radio operator, the three men sharing their captors' lives for sweltering weeks of Africa before *U109* headed towards France. From one of the three incarcerated Englishmen, master of SS *Peterton* sunk by torpedo west of Sierra Leone, confidential material detailing the Freetown–Lagos–Takoradi trade route was recovered from a sealed pouch.

As *U109*'s crew disembarked, flotilla mates thousands of miles to the south-west were making a stunning and devastating discovery. The *Eisbär* group were finally within striking distance of Cape Town, anticipating an assault reminiscent of *Neuland*'s Caribbean attack. Refuelling south of St Helena the U-boats took up their positions, *U68* and *U172* rendezvousing north-west of their objective where Merten visited *U172* to confer with Kaptlt. Carl Emmermann on their best approach. However, instead of scores of anchored merchant ships Emmermann found the roadstead empty, while Merten radioed the presence of a heavy searchlight barrage before Table Bay and thick small-craft transit traffic. It was an unpromising start to their mission. Dönitz responded that night, giving *Eisbär* freedom of action as of 8 October, guessing that the presence of Japanese submarines off Madagascar might have alerted the Allies to Cape Town's potential vulnerability.

Although the operation had begun on a dour note, the *Eisbär* boats managed to sink fifteen ships in three days. Bolstering the attack were four 10th U-Flotilla Type IXD2 U-cruisers, the first to arrive, *U179*, opening fire simultaneously with the *Eisbär* boats and sunk that same day after a single victory.

By mid-October the weather began to deteriorate and the rash of sinkings died away, the *Eisbär* boats being forced away from Cape Town in search of milder weather. However, by 1 November they had sunk twenty-two ships, many laden with valuable war material, and including three troop transports, the furthest east sunk by Poske's *U504* off Durban. On 1 November the remaining Type IXD2s arrived to continue applying pressure as the *Eisbär* boats began their return. Merten and Emmermann went first, both sinking one further ship each as they headed north. For Merten it was to be a chilling reminder of Hartenstein's *Laconia* experience and the horrors of unrestricted submarine war.

On 6 November Merten sighted what he took to be an 8,000-ton cargo freighter which he subsequently hit with two torpedoes. As his radio operator monitored distress calls during the time it took the ship to sink he was able to identify it as the SS *City of Cairo*, carrying 125 passengers, mainly women and children. Although unable to rescue survivors, due to both practical reasons and Dönitz's 'Laconia order', Merten took *U68* among the lifeboats, directing by megaphone the recovery of people in the water. After providing a course for St Helena, some 500 miles south, Merten left, his final words, "Goodnight, sorry for sinking you". The event left a cloud of depression over *U68*'s crew, aware of the ordeal in store for the survivors.

Eleven days later Merten, whose claims amounted to over 200,000 tons, was awarded the Oak Leaves to his Knight's Cross for the sinking of a confirmed total of 27 ships (170,248 tons). The boat continued to sail towards its French base, the crew relying heavily on their Metox to warn them of any impending aircraft threat. Realization that Metox was not proof against centimetric radar had not yet dawned on the U-boat service and, of course, there were other drawbacks to such mechanical reliance. Oblt.z.S. Walter Meyer later wrote of *U68*'s return through Biscay:

"During the whole night we sailed unmolested by the enemy. Nor did we expect to see any aircraft, as our Metox would have told us in good time, now we were convinced that Metox was the sailors' trusty friend. Later, when safely home, the dockyard experts found that the cable had broken in sixteen places and Metox could not have 'spoken' even if the entire RAF had shown up!"

12 October: Following the *Laconia* tragedy Schacht's *U507* returned to Lorient after over three months at sea. During his voyage Schacht had opened attacks against Brazil, the seven ships sunk during this assault the only successes of the patrol. Carrying his two prisoners into harbour, the U-boat received a jubilant reception, although the nurses who arrived to welcome the boat home had first to contend with several men stricken with dysentery. During a rendezvous with U-tanker *U460* on 28 September Schacht had received a new Metox set, while one of his most seriously ill men was transferred aboard the *Milch kuh*, a tanker crewman replacing him. However, only days later as Schacht headed home he was forced to summon urgent aid for another seriously ill man. This time it was too late, *Obersteuermann* Kurt Warkentin dying of dysentery. Even when *U507* was safely in port the disease took its toll on the weakened crew, two more later dying in Lorient's naval hospital.

13 October: Radio reports of depth-charge damage on the previous night were received in Kernével as *U126* reported the effectiveness of an Allied convoy escort at work. En route to the sweltering heat of the Congo Delta *U126* sighted a small coastal convoy south of Liberia. Earlier that year Liberia's head of state, President Edwin Barclay, had signed a defensive treaty with the United States allowing USAAF aircraft to base at Roberts Field, securing the narrow 'waist' of the Atlantic for Allied aircraft.

With diesels at flank speed Kaptlt. Ernst Bauer attempted to haul ahead of the merchant ships, skirting around them in order to submerge and make a broadside attack. As the U-boat pounded forward the sudden and unexpected appearance of an American aircraft from Liberia forced him under in a hurried crash-dive. Worse still, it alerted destroyer escorts to his proximity. That night, as Bauer finally prepared to launch his submerged attack, *U126* was located in extremely clear underwater acoustic conditions by British ASDIC while still at a distance of seven kilometres. Depth-charged accurately, Bauer was forced deeper as the glass shattered and men were thrown to their knees by concussion. Outside the circular pressure hull, deck plates were wrenched free and external torpedo canisters received heavy damage. With the fractured containers flooding, *U126* plummeted out of control, the crew watching in terror as the depth gauges dropped steadily past the factory-rated maximum depth, continuing downward before settling at 240 metres, LI Oblt. (Ing.) Johannes Graf von Ballestrem blowing emergency ballast and running the electric motors at full ahead to bring *U126* to heel. There was silence as the crew anxiously listened to the creaking hull, squeezed by nearly 336 pounds per square inch of pressure. Any moment they expected the collapse of their life-preserving capsule, having reached the greatest depth of any surviving Type IXC

U-boat. Then the needle began to rise; *U126* was headed upwards towards the waiting British.

Bauer was left with no alternative but to surface, his batteries nearly dead, no more compressed air available and the ship still dangerously unstable. If they attempted to submerge again it would be their final dive. Ironically, as *U126* broke surface a little before 2100hrs the boat was able to creep away from the searching destroyers as near as 600 metres astern. One diesel stubbornly refused to start and *U126* limped slowly away heading seaward as engineers laboured over repairs. Despite their record-breaking plunge, the U-boat was relatively undamaged and soon ready for action once more.

Ultimately the Congo was to prove a wasted journey for both Bauer and Achilles, none of the anticipated heavy shipping being sighted. It appeared to the German observers that the harbour of Cabinda was preparing to receive major traffic. However, with fresh dockside construction still going on, it did not seem imminent. Enemy patrol craft and warships regularly sailed the waters and *U126* opted to retreat. Achilles was about to do the same when he decided on one swift attack, torpedoing and damaging the 'Dido' class anti-aircraft cruiser HMS *Phoebe*, fresh from the Mediterranean and the supply convoy 'Operation Pedestal'. Achilles hit her twice before leaving the apparently floundering ship. The damage was severe and, after temporary repairs at Pointe Noire, *Phoebe* was forced to undergo extensive renovation and was inoperative until July 1943. Meanwhile the two U-boats sailed into the Gulf of Guinea, although conditions were still not ideal, glittering phosphorescence betraying their passage and prompting aerial depth charges.

The Gulf proved unrewarding. Achilles managed to sink one American steamer and damage a second off Takoradi, but subsequently reported heavy seas and strong currents, making shallow-water operations useless. Bauer in *U126* had managed to find and sink three merchant ships, but in late November both boats were given permission to head west for Brazil. Despite crossing the Atlantic successfully and patrolling previously busy shipping lanes, neither U-boat experiences success. Harried by air and surface activity, including a severe and accurate depth-charging for Achilles on 14 December, the boats eventually broke off their frustrating sortie and began their return to Lorient five days before Christmas, arriving in the New Year.

19 October: KK Heinrich Schuch's *U154* was seven days from port and headed for the central Atlantic as escort for *Kapitän zur See* Haase's inbound blockade runner *Tannenfels* from Yokohama, Japan. Making contact at 1400hrs on 22 October, *U154* cruised in company with the 7,840-ton ship, which had weathered intense British air searches, fire on board and a hurricane during its two-month journey, until handing over escort to Bordeaux's *Torpedoboot* and resuming her war patrol.

Schuch's previous command, *U105*, was nearing the end of its extensive refurbishment following the bombing off Spain. Under the new command of 26-year-old Oblt.z.S. Jürgen Nissen, the boat's readiness for action was barely impeded by the increased tempo of Allied air attack on the Kéroman bunkers. The same was not true, however, for one of the 2nd U-Flotilla's most prestigious veterans: *U124* was in the process of a comprehensive overhaul when she incurred further damage. On 21 October the dry-docked 'Edelweiss' boat was moving from one bunker to another within Kéroman II, the hull resting on the slowly moving cradle, under the watchful eyes of crew members and flotilla engineers. Suddenly air raid sirens heralded another of the USAAF's daylight attacks. High above were sixty-six Eighth Air Force B17 bombers and twenty-four B24s, despatched to hit Kéroman. However, low-lying cloud prevented all but fifteen B–17s from bombing. Their bombs rained down around the dock area, also striking the virtually impregnable roof of the U-boat pens. But amidst the explosions several near misses damaged *U124* lying vulnerably in the open, the cradle moving at a snail's pace, two crewmen badly injured by flying splinters and another month added to *U124*'s repair time.

29 October: KK Ernst Kals took *U130* out of Lorient for the boat's fifth war patrol, the last of three flotilla boats leaving port in late October destined for the central Atlantic merchant lanes from Cape Town. Kals had been preceded by eight days by veteran *U103* under its new commander, Kaptlt. Gustav-Adolf Janssen, sailing from France after a four-month shipyard refit. On 25 October KK Ralf-Reimar Wolfram had also left Lorient in *U108* for his first patrol in command. Kals crossed Biscay successfully, although plagued with diesel problems, and began heading south, oblivious to an impending maelstrom centered on North-West Africa.

Janssen in *U103* was interrupted during his southbound passage by orders to join the seven boats of the *Streitaxt* group already involved in attacking convoy SL125 south-west of Madeira. In the course of the seven-day battle that followed, German commanders claimed the sinking of eighteen ships (actually twelve, totalling 80,000 tons). Janssen despatched the already damaged MV *Tasmania*, loaded with food and iron, on 31 October, claiming a second ship hit and sunk in the same attack that remains unconfirmed. *Streitaxt* then broke away, attempting to intercept a 'carrier group' reported by Luftwaffe sighting and sailing south, unaware of the pending tempest.

Far to the west the three new 2nd U-Flotilla boats designated for Canadian waters – *U520*, *U521* and *U522* – neared the Gulf of St Lawrence. But weather conditions had deteriorated noticeably and as barometers plunged BdU redirected them to Halifax in search of eastbound convoys. On 30 October Kaptlt. Herbert Schneider, ex-IWO on *U123* and new commander of *U522*, reported sighting SC107 near Cape Race and the hunt began. Schneider was no newcomer to action. He had joined the navy in April 1934, transferring to the Luftwaffe two years later and spending two months as part of the Condor Legion. Returning to Germany and the fledgling naval air arm, in October 1940 Schneider rejoined the navy and began U-boat training.

Thick fog descended and the three 2nd U-Flotilla bloats jockeyed for firing positions as thirteen *Veilchen* reinforcements raced towards the scene. The first assault did not bode well for the Germans, the convoy escort being reinforced with local ASW craft after U-boat radio chatter alerted them to the incoming threat. Schneider's *U522* made an unsuccessful attack against the four-stack destroyer HMCS *Columbia* which in turn located *U522* and turned to attack. Schneider loosed two torpedoes in a highly unlikely bow-shot, terrifying his own crew if nothing else, before diving deep to escape. Bargsten's *U521* did not even achieve firing position, located on the surface by a 145 Squadron Hudson and bombed, forcing Bargsten under and away. The last of the trio was less fortunate. Kaptlt. Volkmar Schwartzkopf, former IWO of *U109*, was surprised on the surface by a 10 Squadron Digby bomber that fell from the foggy sky to drop four 450lb Mark VII depth charges on the boat and its startled bridge watch. There were no survivors.

However, the tenacious Schneider had not finished and, as *Veilchen* boats began to engage SC107, *U522* continued shadowing and attacked again on 2 November. That morning Schneider torpedoed three ships, sinking two and heavily damaging the third in conjunction with *Veilchen* boat *U438*, later that evening returning to sink another.

Bargsten's *U521* had also clung to the convoy, narrowly missing torpedoing escort corvette HMCS *Moosejaw* when the torpedo exploded just short of the target. After a run of eight minutes and two seconds, the submerged *U521* reverberated with the detonation, incorrectly leading Bargsten to claim the corvette sunk. An hour later Bargsten finished off SS *Hartington*, already damaged by *U522*, and sank another the next morning. By the time that the convoy battle had ended on 6 November due to lack of fuel or torpedoes and incoming Allied air cover, the Germans claimed a total of twenty-three merchant ships sunk, plus a destroyer and Bargsten's corvette. In fact they had substantially overclaimed their success: fifteen ships confirmed sunk aggregating 88,000 tons (as opposed to 136,000). Nevertheless it was still a notable achievement against the strongly defended convoy, the fourth most successful attack of the war.

Far to the south-east Hartenstein's *U156* had resumed operations, diverted to patrol north-north-west of Ascension Island. It was here that Hartenstein sank the third and last ship of this voyage, his crew still dejected after their *Laconia* experience. On 19 September he sighted in the early morning darkness the British steamer SS *Quebec City* carrying 6,600 tons of general cargo and cotton from Alexandria to England. A chase of nearly nine hours ensued before Hartenstein submerged and fired tube 6, hitting the steamer amidships and bringing her to a halt. The battered ship refused to sink and, wary of her defensive weaponry, Hartenstein surfaced and prepared to finish the ship off with gunfire. He also mounted an armed watch atop the conning tower as the first of fifty-eight 3.7cm cannon shells smashed into the ship's hull. The boat's IIWO, Max Fischer, ordered the 10.5cm gun to open fire as the *Quebec City* refused to sink. Finally, after eight rounds, stored ammunition exploded at the stern and she finally sank. Hartenstein approached the lifeboats cautiously, remembered by a Welsh Cadet Officer from the steamer, David Cledwyn Jones:

> "I saw the gold Knight's Grand Cross at his throat and it was obvious he was a disciplinarian who had perfect control of his crew. But when he spoke, in perfect English, it was in a very gentle manner. He was sorry he had to blow up our ship, sorry we had to meet in such circumstances. I liked the man. I liked his approach."

U156 continued its lonely vigil throughout October, the horizon bare of any shipping, but under constant air patrols. Finally on 30 October Hartenstein radioed from the central Atlantic that his boat had suffered damage, a small inaccessible leak in the region of the battery compartment defying attempts at repair. The boat was only capable of shallow depths and Hartenstein announced his return. Arrival in Lorient on 16 November prompted celebrations, Dönitz awarding the *Ritterkreuz* to the enigmatic commander. Despite criticism during debriefing of Hartenstein's handling of the *Laconia* affair, Dönitz wrote of a 'well executed' mission in *U156*'s war diary.

6 November: Kaptlt. Ulrich Folkers brought *U125* into Lorient alongside two other returning Type VII boats *U203* and *U602*, six success pennants to show for fourteen weeks at sea. Despite being among the higher average of sinking figures for 2nd U-Flotilla boats in the tail end of 1942, it was a relatively poor return for an operation that required two *Milch kuh* refuelling rendezvous. Like many of his flotilla mates, Folkers arrived bearing prisoners, the captain and chief engineer of SS *Empire Avocet*, picked up from their lifeboats and held aboard *U125* since 24 September. The two Britons were led away by Kriegsmarine guards, eventually to incarceration in MILAG Nord – the *Marine Internierten Lager Nord* – for captured merchant seamen (technically civilians and thus 'internees' not prisoners of war) in Westertimke, ten miles north of Bremen.[129] Folkers' crew paraded outside the Saltzwedel barracks before going on leave in Germany, their boat pulled from the water into Kéroman I for weeks of overhaul.

8 November: In the early morning Allied forces landed in Casablanca, Algiers and Oran, the beginning of 'Operation Torch' – the Allied invasion of Vichy North Africa. Under pressure from Stalin, President Franklin Roosevelt and Winston Churchill instigated the opening of a second front against German forces to take the pressure off embattled Russia. While Roosevelt had pushed for an invasion of France, Churchill correctly surmised that such a project was too ambitious to undertake at that time. The compromise 'Operation Torch' aimed to divert German military strength from the North African front and ultimately Russia. As Allied soldiers came ashore facing 100,000 Vichy troops, there was only sporadic Vichy resistance, Admiral Jean-François Darlan, C-in-C of Vichy North African forces, surrendering on 11 November, sparking German occupation of Pétain's Vichy state in France.

Remarkably, the huge invasion force had remained undetected by both German intelligence agents and maritime forces. Condor aircraft sighted naval forces sailing south from Gibraltar, but this was interpreted as fresh moves to convoy to Malta and Egypt. Indeed on 20 October OKM had issued a situation report that characterized the formation of an Allied second front as "militarily impossible".

Meanwhile, on the morning of the invasion, the telephone rang in Karl Dönitz's Paris headquarters to inform him that 'Torch' had begun. The only weapon with which to strike against the Allied armada was the U-boat and Dönitz immediately ordered all battleworthy boats between Biscay and the Cape Verde Islands towards Morocco to attack the landings and its supply convoys. Eight U-boats, including *U103*, *U108*, *U130* and *U173*, sped toward the landings as part of the hastily formed *Schlagetot* group. Later that day Dönitz broke off all Atlantic operations, boats being ordered to the Gibraltar region. Their crews were exhorted to new heights, receiving a characteristically uncompromising personal message from Hitler:

"I expect a completely victorious operation."

Dönitz added his own words to Hitler's:

"I expect the same of the boats off Morocco and Gibraltar. We must relentlessly carry out the Führer's will with our tested brutal methods of attack."

The first U-boat arrived on station on 9 November, 3rd U-Flotilla's *U572* failing to penetrate the anti-submarine destroyer screen.[130] It was not until 11 November that a single transport ship was sunk by *U173*, a tanker and USS *Hambleton* damaged in the same attack. That day retribution fell on *U108* as it neared Casablanca. A single destroyer picked up

---

[129] The *Marine Intermierten Lager* was first created as one of two compounds inside Sandbostel Concentration Camp, south of Bremervorde, Germany, for the purpose of housing captured merchant seamen. An adjoining compound, MARLAG – the *Marine Lager*, was created for captured Royal Navy personnel.

[130] The cautious Heinz Hirsacker was later tried for cowardice, the only U-boat commander to be so judged in the Second World War. Found guilty, he was sentenced to death, but friends slipped a pistol into his cell where he committed suicide.

KK Ralf-Reimar Wolfram's boat on ASDIC and battered it severely with accurate and sustained depth-charging. The boat's hydroplanes were damaged and *U108* limped out to open sea to effect repairs. By 16 November Wolfram radioed that repairs could only be partially completed and he was ordered to abort to Lorient.

Oblt.z.S Hans-Adolf Schweichel's *U173* outran its lucky streak while attempting to mount a second attack off Casablanca. Flushed with earlier success, *U173* had torpedoed another transport on 15 November, but was detected the following day by three prowling American destroyers, depth charges shattering the submerged U-boat and ending its second war patrol with all fifty-seven men entombed in the deep water.

It was left to Ernst Kals to deliver the most effective blow to 'Torch' shipping at Fedala. After arriving at night on 11 November, he was detected by radar while surfaced and repeatedly driven off. Frustrated by the lack of success, he devised an alternative, and extremely hazardous, line of advance.

"12 November. 1321hrs . . . My intention is to go inshore until I reach the 15 fathom line and then proceed along the coast to Fedala roadstead and attack. The patrols will hardly expect a U-boat to approach so close inshore."[131]

He was correct and as the U-boat grazed the bottom at a depth of only twenty metres Kals crept south, reaching the roadstead and finding "some twenty vessels", including an aircraft carrier, a cruiser and two tankers. With the sea absolutely flat calm he could only afford the barest glance through the periscope and fired a full bow salvo before turning to fire stern tube six (five out of action with mechanical problems). Kals was rewarded with hits on three troop transports, sinking them all. He then sailed north away from the scene, entirely undetected, barely enough water concealing the conning tower from circling destroyers hunting to seaward. It was the greatest individual success against 'Operation Torch', but prompted Allied planners to move their unloading operation to the more easily defended Casablanca. In total the twenty-five U-boats rushed to counter 'Torch' sank eleven ships and damaged five more for the loss of three U-boats sunk and eight others damaged and forced to abort. The invasion was barely impeded at all.

Dönitz and his staff despaired over the ruinous exchange rate suffered off North Africa. His boats were under constant aircraft and escort and hunting destroyer attack. Dönitz railed against his boats' dispositions, particularly the use of large heavy Type IXs so close inshore, and finally achieved permission from OKM to move them further west, a dozen boats left behind in a north-to-south patrol line designated *Westwall*. Even this futile deployment, contested unsuccessfully by Dönitz, was finally cancelled on 23 December.

While most of the Atlantic boats had been transferred to North Africa, there remained nine still active in the North Atlantic, bolstered by seven more either fresh from Germany or too low on ammunition and fuel to be usefully diverted. Designated *Kreuzotter*, they included *U521* and *U522* and were directed west of Ireland in search of convoy traffic.

On 15 November Kaptlt. Klaus Bargsten's *U521* contacted thirty-three merchant ships of convoy ON144 protected by one British and four Norwegian corvettes of escort group B6. He tried to send homing signals but was prevented by defective transmission equipment. Charging towards the convoy, Bargsten fired all six torpedoes at great range,

[131] Dönitz, p. 280.

claiming success, but actually missing; four of the explosions heard were caused by end of run detonations, another pair from random Norwegian depth charges.[132]

Still Bargsten continued to dog the convoy, drifting in and out of thick fog banks. His technical crew succeeded in repairing the transmitter and he vectored the remaining boats toward the convoy. Among them was *U184*, a Type IXC recently transferred to Schütze's flotilla from training and eight days out from Bergen. Her commander, Kaptlt. Günther Dangschat, ex-IWO of *U38*, also launched a surfaced long-distance attack, claiming three ships sunk where in fact he had fatally hit only SS *Widestone*, killing forty-two of her crew. During the next few hours the U-boats grappled with aggressively handled escort corvettes, all equipped with Type 271 radar sets. At some time during the confused mêlée *U184* was lost, credited by the British to the Norwegian *Potentilla*, although it remains relatively conjectural, the corvette depth-charging a contact and reporting oil and debris afterwards. Whoever actually sank the boat, there were no survivors in what had been a tragically short addition to the 2nd U-Flotilla.

By 19 November, with American reinforcements arriving, the U-boats broke off. Their collective claims amounted to eighteen ships, including a destroyer and corvette. In fact they had sunk five merchantmen and a single corvette. However, the misery of the *Kreuzotter* boats endured as the worst North Atlantic winter for fifty-one years battered them as they prepared to refuel by U-tanker. Those with sufficient supplies of food, fuel and ammunition, including *U522*, formed the new *Dragon* patrol line, while others were forced to drift through extremely high seas, so low on fuel that they were unable to run diesels even for battery recharging. For days miserable crewmen were reduced to eating cold meals as all electric current was hoarded in case of a need to dive. Eventually Bargsten's *U521* managed to replenish his boat from the *Milch kuh*, also transferring a sick crewman aboard the tanker for treatment, before setting course for Lorient. *U521* arrived at its new base on 8 December, six days after *U522* which had put in flying five victory pennants.

9 November: Kaptlt. Markworth took *U66* out from port once more, the boat fresh from Kéroman rust treatment, its conning tower now sporting Metox's flimsy wooden cross. However, it was a material failure in the boat itself that posed greater jeopardy than aircraft. When *U66* submerged, two days from port, water suddenly gushed into the pressure hull, both electric motors and batteries rapidly flooded and clouds of chlorine gas crept from the bilges. Markworth was forced to surface, ventilating his boat while engineers tried to solve the problem, breathing apparatus gripped between their teeth.

There was no chance of repair and, as the Metox chirped multiple threat warnings, Markworth ordered course set for home. Flak crews, all wearing deflated life jackets, manned every available anti-aircraft weapon, ammunition piled on deck to facilitate rapid reloading as they awaited the anticipated onslaught. Sure enough, that night, as the Metox readings reached a crescendo, the blinding Leigh Light of a 172 Squadron Wellington bomber pierced the darkness, followed by machine-gun fire as it roared into the attack. Markworth's crew returned fire, *U66* thrown into emergency evasion as eight grey cylinders tumbled from the Wellington's belly.

U66 disappeared amid the plumes of water, her gun crews and bridge watch soaked by the deluge and thrown off balance. Miraculously, there was little real damage and

---

[132] Dönitz later admonished the experienced commander for taking such long-distance shots when Bargsten underwent minute examination of the boat's War Diary with his commander-in-chief.

Markworth shook off the Wellington as he set sail for Lorient. *U66* headed due east using the so-called '*Kernleder*' route before reaching rendezvous point 'Kern' the following day. There he was met by three *Vorpostenboote*, flak guns aboard converted trawlers armed and ready arrived to escort Markworth home, while overhead a pair of KG40 Ju 88s provided more cover from air attack.

By 2100hrs on 11 November *U66* had docked, tying up to the *Isére* before disarming and transferring into the Kéroman dry docks for repair. It was during the thorough over-haul that followed that the boat received modification to its *Wintergarten*, a second platform carrying the heavy 3.7cm AA gun added to the conning tower to augment the twin 2cm weapons on platform one. Unusually, *U66* retained its deck 10.5cm cannon, usually removed to counterbalance the increased load. By this stage of the war deck weapons were all but obsolete, new weaponry all pointing skyward toward the gravest danger they now faced. Correspondingly, while the boat underwent its refit most of the crew were sent on anti-aircraft training near Bordeaux.

Elsewhere the aircraft plague caused further havoc to the 2nd U-Flotilla. On 10 November *U505* was 150 miles east of Trinidad, sailing surfaced beneath a dangerously low cloud canopy. The patrol, begun with ill-temper and bad feeling, had not improved. Zschech had sunk a single steamer, but was unable, or unwilling, to improve relations with his crew. The IIWO L.z.S. Stolzenburg's request for a double bridge watch, or at least to have the boat trimmed down ready to dive while in weather that clearly favoured an aircraft attacker, further inflamed Zschech's ill temper.

Inevitably, at 1514hrs a Hudson bomber of Trinidad's RAF 53 Squadron dropped from the cloud and straddled *U505* with depth charges. The attack took the Germans completely by surprise, Flight Sergeant Sillcock having perfected an attack technique that turned the Germans' reliance on Metox against them. When searching the area of a suspected U-boat sighting, Sillcock would acquire the target at extreme range by radar before switching off his set and approaching until he established visual contact. Then, cutting his engines, he would glide out of the sun until at bombing altitude, then restarting his engines and swooping over the startled U-boat.

The depth charges were a perfect drop and exploded all around *U505*. Unfortunately, however, the attack was too precise. One canister landed on the stern deck and exploded prematurely, directing the full force of the blast upwards against Sillcock's aircraft which plunged into the sea and her entire crew were killed.[133] Inside *U505* there was pan-demonium. The explosions had hammered the submarine, her crew temporarily stunned. Zschech raced to the conning tower and screamed for the crew to abandon ship, an order belayed by Obermaschinist Otto Fricke. Fricke stormed into the control room angrily declaring, "Well, you can do what you want, but the technical crew is staying aboard to keep her afloat!"

Miraculously *U505* was still buoyant and looked able to stay that way. A large hole in the pressure hull was plugged by Fricke and his engineers, as were numerous small leaks in the port diesel. Bilge pumps brought flooding under control and smoke was sucked from the inside by switching the starboard diesel air supply to the choking interior. Order was restored as Zschech stood bewildered in his control room. Although the conning tower was covered in blood none of the bridge watch were killed by the blast, Stolzenburg

---

[133] Yellow aluminium from the downed Hudson was found all over *U505*'s decking, collected and later fashioned into small axes, the emblem of the boat, for crewmen's caps.

being the most badly wounded with burns and numerous metal fragments and splinters embedded in his head and body. The injured men were carried below and the crew began to take in the narrowness of their escape.

> "The wooden planks of the upper deck aft of the conning tower looked as if a bull-dozer had ploughed across them. In the centre of the damage, an enormous hole gaped half way across the entire topside hull of the boat, exposing a jumble of smashed and broken equipment below. . . . Fully half of the steel side plates of the conning tower were either gone or hanging limply, clanging against each other in time with the gentle rocking of the waves. One depth charge had exploded on the pressurized tubes where the spare torpedoes were stored, completely destroying one of the torpedoes except for the warhead section. If that torpedo warhead had gone off, none of us would have survived."[134]

The crew salvaged steel plating which they welded over the hole in the pressure hull and *U505* was then able to dive to forty metres. Although trailing a thick oil slick, she was otherwise sound. However, whatever relief the crew may have felt at their narrow escape vanished when Zschech made known his desire to take the crippled boat into Port of Spain in the style of Albrecht Achilles. The madness of the plan was apparent to all the crew, who simmered in rage. *U505* staggered towards Trinidad before Zschech attempted an attack against a distant freighter, missing and bringing swift and accurate retribution from RAF bombers. Stormy weather followed and, while the crew cursed at the conditions, it at least kept enemy aircraft at bay. Even Zschech was forced to abandon his bizarre scheme, reinforced by radio messages from Lorient directing *U505* to rendezvous with *U154* in grid square EE60 to obtain whatever assistance Schuch could provide, transpiring to be only twenty ampoules of morphia for the wounded men below decks.

Zschech was ordered to rendezvous with *Milch kuh U462* on 22 November, meeting while the tanker was in the act of refuelling *U68*. Merten's boat handed over a small quantity of spares for Zschech, while *U462*'s doctor came aboard to check on the wounded. As *U505* resupplied, a substitute IIWO, L.z.S. Helmuth Knocke, came aboard to replace Stolzenburg, removed to *U462* for immediate and life-saving surgery.

U505 then continued its homeward trek, Zschech still making every attempt to attack distant shipping, his single functioning diesel engine unequal to the chase. The temporary repairs began to leak as Zschech made his final long-distance shot only days short of Lorient, the torpedo malfunctioning and circling, striking *U505* at an oblique angle, insufficient to trigger detonation. Finally on 12 December the crew's torment was over and the tattered boat came up the Kéroman slipway for extensive and time-consuming repair.

16 November: Kaptlt. Hartenstein brought the battered *U156* home, three pennants, including one for the *Laconia*, flown from its periscope. That same day the first disquieting report of Metox failure was received at BdU in Paris as *U43* was forced to veer away during a surfaced approach on a steamer east of Newfoundland by unexpected, and unheralded, aircraft attack. Oblt. Hans-Joachim Schwantke had left Lorient on 23 September bound for Canada alongside Rasch's *U106*, making the deepest penetration of the St Lawrence by U-boat, reaching Point St Peter at the tip of the Gaspé Peninsula. Harassed by aircraft and closely coordinated surface destroyer groups, Schwantke noted that regional commer-

---

[134] Goebeler, p. 91.

cial traffic had ceased and his Metox worked only occasionally. Diagnostic inspection showed the Metox to be in order, indicating that either the equipment was unreliable or the Allies had perfected radar on a different wavelength. But, although Metox's short-comings were becoming obvious, the Kriegsmarine continued to rush the equipment to front-line boats, Dönitz bristling as problems with parts delivery led to severe "irrespon-sible and insufferable" delays within flotilla engineering yards.

Two days after Hartenstein's arrival Kaptlt. Gelhaus brought *U107* safely home after three months at sea operating from the Azores to Freetown. Three ships had been sunk and on 7 November Gelhaus had met the heavily damaged *U333* to transfer his passenger, *Kommandant Konfirmand* Kaptlt. Lorenz Kasch, to replace her commander Kaptlt. Erich Cremer, badly wounded in action against HMS *Crocus*.

As *U107*'s crew disembarked in Lorient, the wail of air-raid sirens heralded thirteen USAAF B24 bombers arriving to plaster the docks with high explosive, identical raids aimed at St Nazaire and La Pallice as American bombers based in England began to get into their stride. It was apparent that the days of the Saltzwedel barracks were numbered and work had already begun on an alternative site for the flotilla's men.

The remainder of November and most of December saw a monotonous chain of depar-tures for the western Atlantic and returning boats boasting little real success in that theatre. The South African attack had proved more rewarding, although, at four months, it was an expensive use of operation U-boats. On 11 December *U504*, last of the 2nd U-Flotilla's *Eisbär* boats, arrived home in Lorient five days after Merten's landfall in *U68*. KK Fritz Poske had sunk six ships for 36,156 tons and used his full load of torpedoes, earning the Knight's Cross during early November.

For both Poske and Merten it marked the end of their front-line careers. During January 1943, as *U68* underwent extensive overhaul, Kaptlt. Karl-Friedrich Merten left to take command of the 26th U-training Flotilla in Pillau where he oversaw instruction of the art of torpedo shooting. Poske in turn was rotated out of combat in January to take command of Neustadt's *I. Unterseebootlehrdivision* (U-boat school).

15 December: *U518*, a new flotilla addition, entered Lorient at the conclusion of its inaugural war patrol. Oblt.z.S. Friedrich-Wilhelm Wissmann, former minesweeper commander and IWO on *U109*, had left Kiel on 26 September bound for the Strait of Belle Isle. Wissmann, known among his fellow officers as *Wissmännchen* (Wise Guy), was a recent arrival aboard *U518*, her first commander, FK Hans-Günther Brachmann having been removed after a crew delegation protested at his leadership methods. Wissmann assumed command, tasked on his first patrol with an additional *Sonderaufgabe*, alongside expected interception of Belle Isle traffic. As *U518* slipped from Kiel for refuelling in Kristiansand she carried an extra passenger, Abwehr agent Lt Werner von Janowski, bound for Canada. Janowski had lived in the small Ontario village of Ailsa Craig before the war, accepted by the local population despite his often vociferous pro-German attitude. In 1938 he left Alisa Craig, resurfacing in wartime Germany.

Although committed to landing the agent, Wissmann had been granted much latitude as to how and when, deciding first to emulate a successful attack carried out by 10th U-Flotilla's *U513* during September. Creeping surfaced into Newfoundland's Conception Bay during the night of 2 November Wissmann torpedoed and sank two anchored ships, scheduled for loading with iron ore, and damaging a third when a torpedo struck a loading wharf. Within four hours of entering the bay *U518* was out and racing surfaced for deeper water. With no Metox warning, a B18 Digby dropped from low clouds and narrowly missed the rapidly diving U-boat before fog rolled over and in rising seas the aircraft lost *U518*'s scent.[135]

Wissmann then turned *U518* into the Gulf of St Lawrence in order to drop von Janowski. Choosing the secluded Baie des Chaleurs as the landing site, *U518* nosed quietly into position near New Carlisle on electric motors beneath a moonless and calm night sky in the early hours of 9 November. Unable to see the darkened coastline Wissmann continued gently moving forward with his bow diving tanks flooded to dip the U-boat's nose until the keel grounded softly, an inflatable dinghy being immediately launched with two crewmen, von Janowski and his three suitcases of equipment. As the dinghy disappeared in the dark a moment of near panic gripped Wissmann's lookouts as car headlights on shore swung closer and closer. Ducking so as not to show pale faces above the conning tower rim, the crew prepared to abandon their mission and retreat when the light vanished. The car had passed and seen nothing.

The dinghy returned and *U518* was able to reverse seaward on the rising tide in what had been a text-book operation. But within twenty-four hours von Janowski was behind bars. Leaving a trail of clues behind him, he was soon cornered on a train, stating matter-of-factly "I am caught, I am a German officer" at the time of his apprehension.[136]

Unaware of the agent's failure, Wissmann returned to the hunt in the Gulf of St Lawrence, entering Lorient on 15 December with a score of two tankers damaged, two sunk and a pair of captured officers from his last victim, SS *Caddo*, destroyed south-east of Cape Race. It was an impressive debut for Wissmann and the new *U518*.

21 December: *U67* returned from three months at sea east of Trinidad and the Windward Islands. Kaptlt. Günther Müller-Stöckheim's patrol had begun badly after reaching the battleground. In company with three other boats, *U67* tried to attack an eastbound convoy from Port of Spain but was fended off by heavy RAF air cover from Trinidad, aided by a glistening full moon. Later, on 25 October at 0640hrs local time, *U67* was surprised by the sudden appearance of the small steamer SS *Peter Minuet*, which also sighted the surfaced U-boat and turned tail to flee. With Müller-Stöckheim in hot pursuit, the freighter raced away, passing Norwegian MV *Primero* and frantically urging her to take flight as well. Aboard *Primero* Captain Hjalmar Johansen ordered engines to full power and vainly tried to keep pace with *Peter Minuet*, the Norwegian's holds filled with salt as ballast from Aden. *U67* drew closer until a single G7e torpedo shot from the bow toward *Primero*. Johansen ordered the wheel thrown hard over as the torpedo prematurely detonated midway between the two.

Stöckheim fired a second eel, this time the G7a leaving an arrow-straight trail of bubbles as it sped away on target. Johansen saw the threat and ordered hard to port, bracing himself against the inevitable impact. As *Primero* heeled over, Stöckheim saw that the torpedo would strike and awaited the telltale roar and column of water and debris. To their mutual amazement the G7a struck the Norwegian's hull with a resounding clang; the angle too oblique to detonate the contact pistol. Worse still for *U67*, Johansen had not ordered the

---

[135] This second attack on the Wabana anchorage forced its abandonment altogether until anti-submarine defences were strengthened.

[136] Von Janowski was later used by the RCMP as a double agent, radioing reports to his controllers in Hamburg. His success has never been properly established although it is thought that von Janowski was considered a reliable agent by BdU for his news of fictitious departing convoys. See Michael Hadley's *U-Boats Against Canada*.

wheel taken off hard-a-port and now the 4,414-ton ship was pointed almost directly at the U-boat's beam, the merchant master already with his wits about him and preparing to ram. Stockheim frantically manoeuvred to starboard on full diesel power, before skilfully ordering engines cut, *U67* swinging quietly as *Primero* struck her a glancing blow along the port side. The merchant's stem impacted forward of the conning tower and rode part-way along her deck before the two were free of their embrace, Johansen realizing that his one chance had failed. Firing diesels again, Stockheim took careful aim and fired both stern tubes at the Norwegian; they exploded in the motor vessel's engine room.

The *Primero* was doomed and Stockheim watched as lifeboats were lowered and he withdrew to weigh up his own damage, torn decking and torpedo storage canisters showing signs of being partially crushed. A damage control party was assessing the exact extent of their injury when a cry of pain rent the air, *Matrosenobergefreiter* Heinz Hartmann lying mortally injured. He had opened one of the crushed torpedo canisters to check the state of the stored torpedo, the damaged cover flying suddenly open, striking him on the chest and smashing his rib-cage, broken bones puncturing both lungs. He died in seconds, his body later buried at sea. *U67* drew away for repairs, ironically firing a single long-distance torpedo at SS *Peter Minuet* which again blundered into the U-boat's path. It missed. Stöckheim had used five torpedoes to sink one ship in ballast, losing a crewman into the bargain.

The remainder of *U67*'s patrol harvested four more victims from the waters east of Trinidad and Barbados, his last the Norwegian MV *Tortugas*, yielding two prisoners. The ship went down in eight minutes, finished off by the last of Stockheim's torpedoes. *U67* then nosed among the lifeboats, assuring they were provisioned, and taking her master Captain Rolf Endresen and Chief Engineer Trygve Jensen as prisoners bound for MILAG-Nord. Stöckheim refused a request by Endresen's wife to be taken with her husband, but by November 1943 the two Norwegians were repatriated reuniting the couple. A final ship was damaged by shellfire on 28 November as *U67* sailed to refuel from *U460* for the homeward trek.

The boredom of long journeys home without torpedoes aboard to strike at enemy shipping was a constant problem for U-boat commanders whose crews chafed against the enforced inactivity. Aboard *U67* the crew were entertained every Tuesday and Friday evening by the *Kameradschaftdienst* radio broadcasts. As well as the radio there was, as on other boats, a gramophone and record collection enabling a 'concert' to be held on Sundays, music played from the small radio room broadcast through the U-boat's loudspeaker system. A rotating system of relief allowed the entire crew to listen, and occasionally Müller-Stöckheim raised the level of normality by allowing a strictly controlled but very welcome ration of beer to the crew.[137]

During this voyage Müller-Stöckheim had also passed the required mark for the award of the Knight's Cross and as his boat entered dry dock he flew to Paris in company with Kptlt. Carl Emmermann and Kaptlt. Büchting (CO 1st S-Flotilla) for the for the presentation of the medal in BdU's new headquarters.

By the time *U67* returned, her first commander was on the verge of mental collapse at sea east of Trinidad. Kaptlt. Heinrich Bleichrodt had sailed *U109* on 28 November for the Western Atlantic experiencing accurate depth-charging after failed attempts to engage an

---

[137] Boats often had favourites tunes, *U67*'s unknown to the author. For the irrepressible Jochen Mohr's *U124* it remained Irving Berlin's 'Alexander's Ragtime Band'.

enemy destroyer. Arriving off French Guiana on Boxing Day, *U109* attacked a merchant ship which, according to Bleichrodt, subsequently depth-charged his boat. In its attack *U109* recorded a double miss, single miss and triple miss, each attack followed by one to three depth charges. Later interrogation of crew members and scrutiny of the boat's log led Dönitz to conclude that the merchant vessel had not been a Q-ship, but detonations caused by end of run torpedoes sinking to a depth where water pressure forced an explosion. Nonetheless this appears to have widened the crack in Bleichrodt's condition. He radioed BdU requesting permission to return "due to nervous state after Q-ship engagement". Denied his request, Bleichrodt radioed again the following day:

> "For ten days the commander has been suffering from nervous debility with loss of energy, together with a serious depression. Request return."

Again the appeal was denied, BdU conceding on New Year's Eve that Bleichrodt could hand over command to his IWO Oblt.z.S. Joachim Schramm, but that the mission "must be carried out". On the first day of 1943 Bleichrodt gave up, radioing that he was returning due to "lack of fuel". Bowing to the inevitable, Dönitz ordered all spare torpedoes handed over to other boats south of the Azores, Bleichrodt transferring four G7a torpedoes to *U575* before breaking off for home. Finally on 23 January *U109* docked in St Nazaire and Bleichrodt was quietly lifted off the boat and taken to hospital where he was certified as suffering from what amounted to 'shell shock'. It was the end of his operational career, but, in a remarkable display of man management by his commander-in-chief, not his naval career. In March 1943 he was transferred to Gotenhafen's *2.U-bootlehrdivision*, promoted to *Korvettenkapitän*. Here he again flourished. Bleichrodt would survive the war; *U109* was not to be so lucky.

23 December: *U183* docked in Lorient three months after leaving Kiel for its maiden marathon voyage. KK Heinrich Schäfer's first patrol as commander had been initially barren as part of the *Luchs* group west of Ireland in late September. After *Luchs* dispersed, *U183* travelled west to Nova Scotia in company with Wissmann's *U518*, sweeping north to Newfoundland. After mechanical difficulty a single straggler from ON146 was sunk off Sable Island before *U183* shaped course for Lorient.

Three days after his arrival Kaptlt. Rasch's *U106* also entered Lorient with a meagre single confirmed sinking from its foray alongside *U43* into the Gulf of St Lawrence. Rasch complained of feeling "like a dolphin" under constant aerial harassment. However, despite the disappointment Rasch had achieved a proud combat record and on 29 December he received his Knight's Cross. The boat's tower emblem of two duelling sawfish received the decorations as well – one sawfish for Oesten's *Ritterkreuz*, the other Raschs'. Days later *U103* also returned to Lorient. Kaptlt. Janssen had sunk two confirmed ships, damaging a third and claiming another as part of *Streitaxt* and *Westwall* before heading for Lorient once more.

The most successful of the North African boats, *U130*, arrived on 30 December. Ernst Kals' audacious shallow-water assault near Fedora was followed by relegation to aircraft target as part of *Westwall*, constantly under aerial harassment. Tying the battered but intact *U130* alongside the *Isére* Kals left the boat for the last time as its commander. He too was to rotate ashore, due to occupy a staff position in the New Year. KK Viktor Schütze was about to be promoted to *Führer der Unterseeboot Ausbildung*, Kals being his replacement as chief of the 2nd U-Flotilla.

The *U-bootwaffe* reached a high water mark in 1942. In November they had sunk

802,160 tons of Allied shipping, the highest monthly total of the war. The latter half of 1942 saw 2,600,000 tons of shipping destroyed, as opposed to 600,000 tons during the same period in 1941, helped enormously by the 'Shark' blackout in England. Crucially, on 13 December Bletchley Park's ULTRA staff broke back into Triton (Shark) following the capture of material from *U559* in the Mediterranean. These priceless documents, earned at the cost of two Royal Navy men's lives, provided clues to a flaw in the four-rotor Enigma which in turned opened a back door into the four-rotor net, quickly opened by Allied cryptanalysts.

Before their success, the Enigma 'blackout' matched by B-Dienst success in Berlin had allowed U-boats to intercept more convoy traffic than ever. During April B-Dienst had been at the height of its powers – solving 5–10% of intercepts in time for Dönitz to use the information tactically. They had broken the Royal Navy's Cipher Three (convoy code) in February and managed to read it for the rest of the year until the British deduced through Enigma intercepts that their cipher was compromised. The Admiralty changed their system, but, after two months of concentrated work, briefly broken again until June 1943 when the Admiralty changed ciphers again, closing the window to German intelligence for the remainder of the war.

9

DEATH FROM ABOVE: 1 JANUARY TO 31 MAY 1943

As KK Ernst Kals took command of the 2nd U-Flotilla his unit numbered twenty-eight boats, the most his flotilla would carry. Eight had been lost in battle during the previous year, three others transferring without seeing action (the two Type XBs and *UD3*), seventeen new boats entering the flotilla base at Lorient to offset these depredations.

The opening half of January saw five 2nd U-Flotilla boats return to their French base at Lorient: *U129* on 6 January; *U126* and *U154* the following day; *U161* on 9 January and *U128* on the 15th. KK Hans-Ludwig Witt's *U129* had had success east of the Caribbean, five ships sunk, including two tankers, but at a cost of over three months at sea. Nevertheless, the young commander received his prize – the Knight's Cross award radioed to him on 17 December for claims totally well over the 100,000-ton mark (a confirmed total of sixteen ships sunk for 74,184 tons). Both *U126* and *U161*, engaged in hunting first off the Congo and later unproductively north of Natal, Brazil, returned with meagre success. For Bauer aboard *U126* it was the end of his combat career, leaving Lorient during February and transferring to the staff of the 27th U-training Flotilla. His award of the Knight's Cross for combat achievement followed him on 16 March. Achilles on the other hand received his overdue decoration on 16 January a week after the return of *U161*. The young commander refused to go ashore and returned to his beloved boat as she lay in dry dock for two months' overhaul.

Kaptlt. Heinrich Schuch's *U154* continued the meagre accomplishment of the 2nd U-Flotilla. After crossing the Atlantic to the sea east of the Caribbean he succeeded in sinking three ships, eight-nine days at sea yielding 17,936 tons sunk. It was Schuch's final patrol as skipper, transferred ashore to the U-boat's Weapons Service, his replacement, Oblt.z.S. Oskar-Heine Kusch, ready to take command for the first time.

When the latter boat had left France the previous September Germany's military star appeared to still be in the ascendant, but by January 1943 the end of the Third Reich had begun on all land fronts. At sea things were no better. U-boats were hard-pressed and a hair's breadth from losing the initiative once and for all, while in harbour the destruction of the U-boat threat had been again named top priority for RAF Bomber Command. The British War Cabinet issued a directive sanctioning area bombing of cities that were French Atlantic U-boat bases.

6 January: *U66* slipped from harbour during the afternoon, sailing surfaced across much of Biscay. Aboard Kaptlt. Markworth's boat was an extra body, Frenchman Jean-Marie Lallart, arrested for espionage ,in France during November 1941 and supposedly 'turned' by the Abwehr. Now he played the role of Axis agent, bound for Free French-held Mauritania. Although the country had been loyal to Vichy since June 1940, with the success of 'Torch' it had unhesitatingly swapped allegiance during November. The area chosen for Lallart's covert disembarkation, code-named '*Sturm*', was on the edge of the

Sahara, a forbidding expanse of wind-blown shifting sand dunes, covering nearly half of the country, fringed with what were reputed to be beaches pounded by Atlantic surf.

During daylight on 20 January *U66* was offshore, observations through the periscope showing no sign of surf along what seemed an empty coastline. Allowing the boat to float southwards with the current, Markworth paused until a secluded bay drifted into view before bottoming *U66* and awaiting nightfall. Lallart prepared for disembarkation while two of the U-boat crew's strongest swimmers, *Botsmaat* Wagner and *Matrosenobergefreiter* Daschkey, were detailed to row him ashore. By 2000hrs that evening the sun had long set and Markworth surfaced beneath an idyllic night sky, beginning the run towards the distant beach.

The first unforeseen problem was not long in coming. By the time that *U66* was in shallow water with only twenty metres beneath the keel the beach was still two kilometres distant. However, the men readying their dinghy were undeterred and, launching their small craft, all three climbed aboard to begin their long row to shore.

Markworth was still concerned that the surf line, although much smaller than feared, may yet prevent the dinghy returning once Lallart had been landed. In this event the two Germans were instructed to signal *U66* by torch before walking north to Cape Blanc where they could swim out to the waiting *U66*. As the dinghy approached land lookouts could plainly follow its progress, bright moonlight illuminating the tableau before them. The dinghy was seen reaching the shore where it was finally lost in the shadow of several large rocks. Confusingly, some accounts state that the dinghy was not lost from view but seen being dragged ashore, crucial in the light of things to come. Lallart was plainly silhouetted emerging from the shadows and running inland over sand dunes until he too disappeared. Markworth waited.

As minutes dragged by with no sign of the dinghy Markworth became concerned. Indeed within ten minutes Lallart was seen to re-emerge from the dunes, racing back to the beach. But there was still no sign of the two crewmen. At that point surf began to pound on to the coastline with renewed vigour and Markworth feared the dinghy's return would be thwarted by the heavy waves. He ordered a signal flashed for the two men to head north, awaiting confirmation. There was nothing but darkness from the rocks. By now it was eight hours since the U-boat had begun its approach to the bay and Markworth was perplexed as to what could have happened. Still he waited, until at 0700hrs the tinges of dawn to the east forced him to withdraw from the shallows and submerge.

Loath to abandon his men, he decided the area was barren enough to risk surfacing and approached the coast once more looking for them, but there was no sign and with a heavy heart Markworth resigned himself to the fact that there was no choice but to depart, thirteen hours after the operation began.

Within ten days he received a signal from BdU concerning the missing men. Naval Intelligence reports stated that all three had been captured by Free French troops, taken to Port Etienne in Morocco and handed over to the British as prisoners of war. It transpired that the swell had indeed capsized the dinghy, its occupants swimming ashore. Though Lallart still had all his equipment, the two U-boat men had only unmarked shirt and trousers. Knowing the area well, the Frenchmen led his comrades to a nearby former Foreign Legion fort at Port Etienne held by Free French forces where he had them arrested as spies. Unable to prove that they were sailors, Daschkey and Wagner were detained for several weeks before finally being taken to POW camp.

Meanwhile, near Brazil, disaster had struck for *U507*, KK Harro Schacht and his fifty-four crewmen bombed to oblivion by a Catalina of VP83 north-north-east of Camocim.

Schacht was eventually posted as missing towards the end of January. He had sunk three ships off Brazil's north-east coast, taking two masters prisoner and reporting their capture to BdU. It was these very reports that allowed Allied ground stations to DF *U507* and vector the Catalina towards it. Both British captains went to the bottom with their captors.

By this time the Royal Air Force had begun to reduce Lorient to rubble, despite Air Marshal Sir Arthur 'Bomber' Harris, Chief of Bomber Command, complaining at the diversion of air power from the assault on Germany. His lone voice was quickly overruled and, after missing their opportunity to damage the U-boat pens during their vulnerable construction, the RAF chose to attack the French ports that housed the U-boat units, Lorient being top of the list. Ironically, as this new area-bombing, onslaught began, personnel and services of the 2nd and 10th U-boat Flotillas were moved from Lorient to Lager Lemp, between Pont Scorff and Caudan, sixteen miles north of the town. The first new raid started at 2355hrs on 14 January.

On that night Kaptlt. Heyse's *U128*, just returned from his final lengthy war patrol near Freetown and Brazil, was tethered to a hulk before the Saltzwedel barracks, a skeleton watch of seven men still aboard. As the first flares and bombs began to rain down, fire endangered *U128*, which moved on electric motors to relative safety in the center of the Scorff River. Above them 122 aircraft guided by pathfinders dropped a deluge of bombs later described by British Intelligence as 'wild' and inaccurate.

Two small steamers anchored in the mouth of the Scorff River were sunk during the attack and the 2nd U-Flotilla's officers' quarters in the *Prefecture Maritime* devastated by the explosion of fifty torpedoes stored nearby. The crew quarters in the Saltzwedel Caserne were reduced to a roofless ruin. The *U-bootheim* was partially destroyed, while local cafes and brothels were obliterated, at least 120 buildings and two churches being destroyed and at least twelve people killed.

The day brought chaos to Lorient. Civilians emerged from the blasted ruins to begin their exodus to the countryside, the night's attack, the heaviest so far, a clear harbinger of things to come and repeated the following night, while, masked by the bomber stream, nine Wellingtons dropped mines in the harbour approaches.

The administrative structure of the 2nd U-Flotilla was slightly impeded, not least by the destruction of recent promotion orders. However, problems were minor and, while administration was now taken care of in offices in Kéroman II U-bunkers, flotilla crews were accommodated out of town or bunkers prepared for the inevitable and expected destruction of Lorient. Kéroman III, the 'wet bunker', was now virtually completed and bays in the building made available to U-boats, although the entire bunker would not be declared fully operational until May.

Personnel now spent the greater part of their time at Lager Lemp. Started before the intensive air raids had begun, the camp was in the process of much extension during January, soon providing complete living and recreational facilities for officers and men of both the 2nd and 10th U-Flotilla, as well as the Personnel Reserve of the base. Situated off the main road from Pont Scorff to Caudan, the camp stood in the extensively wooded grounds of the requisitioned Moulin Kersalo, a lakeside mill. Hundreds of paid French workers had constructed comfortable buildings of solid concrete foundation and wooden superstructure, the huts heated and camouflaged, painted a uniform green to blend with the surroundings. Kersalo Lake, fringed by a walkway that incorporated a solid jetty from which the Kreigsmarine men enjoyed boating on the placid water, was soon covered with metal scaffolding supporting a dense curtain of camouflage netting, all designed to deny RAF pilots the distinctive landmark. Due to the successful disguise there were few anti-aircraft gun emplacements and even fewer air raid shelters, slit trenches being thought to provide enough in case of discovery, and bombardment and air raids indeed remained minimal. The perimeter was patrolled, but not closely enough to prevent U-boat men slipping under the wire to rendezvous with a local farmer selling home-brewed Calvados to the thirsty Germans.

The U-boat commanders and crews would now stay in Lorient for only two or three days before sailing, housed in both the Kéroman bunkers and buildings near the Porte du Morbihan. Men of the 2nd U-Flotilla stayed either in the single large bunker near the Place Alsace-Lorraine, or two air-raid shelters alongside the ruins of *Haus Kleinschmidt* within the courtyard of the Saltzwedel barracks, while technical personnel benefited from the construction of new air-raid shelters added to the side of Kéroman I. Coupled with this development, the pen's roofs themselves received further reinforcement. To detonate bombs and direct the blast to an open six-and-a-half-foot-high explosion chamber below, German engineers designed the *fangrost* or 'bomb trap' superstructure of inverted concrete U-shaped beams set on parallel slabs. An enclosed concrete layer under the explosion chamber continued down to a further solid platform and on to a triangular void. Serving as a second bomb trap, this void formed by tilted concrete beams also redistributed the enormous weight load to exterior walls. This combination of solidity and void redirected bomb impacts and contained their explosive power, seven irregular and dense overlays up to eight metres thick protected the U-boats.

Thus, while Lorient burned, the U-boat shelters sustained little damage. Kéroman remained in full and uninterrupted operation, as did the older two-berth Scorff bunker near the Caudan Bridge. Undamaged also were the pyramid-shaped *Dombunkers* and the torpedo and ammunition storage bunkers near the abandoned *U-bootheim* in Kéroman. However, the population finally took their opportunity to escape the burning town, clogging road and rail in all directions by their exodus.

6 February: *U123* returned from its first patrol with Oblt.z.S. Horst von Schroeter in command. After slipping from Kiel in early December *U123* participated in two U-boat groups, *Spitz* west of Ireland and *Jaguar*. In late December von Schroeter shared in the destruction of two ships from ON154 in a battle during which the Germans sank fourteen ships at no loss to themselves. Later, during January, *U123* joined *Jaguar* north-east of Newfoundland in some of the worst North Atlantic gales for decades. Hampered by meteorological interference with radio communications and appalling visibility, saturated lookouts rotated watches wearily as *U123* blundered along its allotted patrol lines. The expected convoys did not materialize and eventually *U123* sailed for home.

The turbulence at sea was matched by political turmoil in Berlin. On the penultimate day of January *Grossadmiral* Eric Raeder resigned as Kriegsmarine C-in-C, pushed beyond his limit by an enraged Hitler demanding that Germany's surface fleet be scrapped following a poor showing in the Arctic. Karl Dönitz was one of two candidates for succession; he accepted and was promoted to *Grossadmiral* and *Oberbefelshaber der Kriegsmarine*.

In February what remained of Lorient was virtually destroyed by high explosives and incendiary. During the month-long offensive 4,000 tons of bombs had obliterated Lorient at a total cost of twenty-four RAF aircraft. While the flotilla's home port was devastated, returns for the hard-pressed crews at sea shrank yet again, several Type IXs sailing for operations stretching between the Caribbean and the Canary Islands for little tangible result. The Germans were beginning to suffer from ULTRA's recovery of the 'Triton' net, routing convoys around waiting U-boats. During February also Hitler's supposed intuition led him to determine that the Allies intended a full-scale invasion of Portugal. Correspondingly Dönitz was compelled to move U-boats west of Lisbon to counter any seaborne threat, despite himself strongly doubting the likelihood. On 7 February *U103* sailed from Lorient to the area, *U107* also sent from the disbanded *Hartherz* group to join her. Other reinforcements flooded to the region, including the successful group *Delphin*, arriving after sinking seven of the nine-tanker convoy TM1 west of the Canaries, the 2nd U-Flotilla's *U125* and *U522* accompanying them.

Kaptlt. Ulrich Folker's *U125* had been at sea since early December and, like the other *Delphin* boats, was low of fuel when ordered to lie in wait for the imaginary invasion force. One of the few recently successful flotilla boats, *U522* commanded by the aggressive Kaptlt. Herbert Schneider, had damaged two tankers from TM1 on the morning of 9 January, later returning to sink both ships. A week later he received his reward, the Knight's Cross granted for what was a confirmed total of seven ships sunk (45,826-tons) and two damaged.

By 12 February Dönitz had waited long enough and those boats with sufficient fuel were ordered to intercept KMS9, sailing into fierce aerial resistance and strong escort forces. The Germans were driven off, two Type VIIs sunk and the attack abandoned, *U125* freed to return to Lorient.

Meanwhile two further groups had formed in the hunt for middle Atlantic convoy traffic. *Rochen* gathered first, comprising ten boats in total, *U43*, *U66*, *U504* and *U521* among them, *Robbe* then assembling with *U103* and *U107*, the only two Type IXBs among its eight boats. These new hunting groups, soon joined by remnants of *Delphin*, were alerted to a large inbound 'Torch' convoy, due to pass the Azores during the middle of February. Dönitz ordered all boats to lay doggo, submerged in tightly controlled lines to avoid air detection and enhance hydrophonic tracking of the low thump of oncoming merchant propellers. But ULTRA intelligence had betrayed the trap and the convoy rerouted around both groups.

In the interim, having failed in the hunt against KMS9, Kaptlt. Schneider's *U522* sailed south of the Azores to refuel from *U461* before heading for Morocco. Schneider, flushed by the award of his recent *Ritterkreuz*, seemed to be on a roll of luck when on 22 February his lookouts were electrified by the sight of southbound UC1, thirty-two merchant ships en route to Curaçao. Guarding the convoy, which included seventeen tankers in ballast, was a strong and determined escort force, six warships of British Escort Group 42, augmented by an American 'Hunter-Killer' group of four new destroyers.

U522 began to shadow, homing eleven *Robbe* and *Rochen* boats to the attack. As soon as the first reinforcement arrived BdU cleared Schneider for action and he charged into the attack. Torpedoes sped on their way, hitting and sinking British tanker SS *Athelprincess*, and escorts began beating suspected U-boat sectors as *U522* raced ahead of UC1, submerging again for an ambush. It was here that Scheider's remorseless thirst for attack came to its end. Detected by escorts, *U522* was fiercely depth-charged by the sloop HMS *Totland*, oil and debris welling up from the depths, all that remained of Schneider and his fifty crewmen.

By the time of Schneider's death nine other U-boats were in contact and combat began in earnest. Over the ensuing night seven U-boats attempted to break through the escort cordon, exhorted by radio messages from Dönitz to strike without pause. Torpedoes criss-crossed the wakes of charging destroyers and white distress rockets cast their ethereal glow over the chaos. All three 2nd U-Flotilla boats involved, Schwantke's aged *U43*, *U504* under its new commander Kaptlt. Wilhelm Luis and Klaus Bargsten's *U521*, launched unsuccessful attacks and by morning the struggle was over, both sides separating to regroup and count their losses. BdU rejoiced in his commanders' reports of one destroyer and eight tankers sunk. The truth was that three tankers had been sent to the seabed, two others damaged but successfully reaching port in the Caribbean. Schneider and his crew were the only German casualties.

But Schneider's loss was not the only grim news for flotilla commander KK Ernst Kals in Lorient. *U519*, engaged on its second war patrol under Kaptlt. Günter Eppen, had sailed from Lorient on 30 January. Brief involvement in the unsuccessful *Hartherz* group had ended on 8 February whereupon Eppen sailed west. On 10 February a final position report was radioed from *U519* followed by silence. Thirty-year-old Günther Eppen and his forty-nine crewmen disappeared, their combat career spanning eighty-six days at sea with no recorded success.

13 February: The leading 'ace' of the 2nd U-Flotilla, Kaptlt. Jochen Mohr, brought *U124* into port, moderately successful again after patrolling east of the Caribbean. Having sailed in late November *U124* suffered repeated engine problems, particularly from the starboard diesel, outbound from Biscay. As the mechanical crew sweated over their faulty diesels Dönitz radioed to Mohr that large quantities of fuel oil had been sabotaged in Lorient. According to his commander-in-chief, Mohr's boat had taken fuel aboard that contained a chemical added that would cause "the fuel pumps to corrode, jamming the fuel injector valves".[138] Mohr was given the choice of continuing or aborting after instructions to clean the engines thoroughly and run them for twenty-four hours at full revolutions. Mohr complied and waited a day for results before electing to continue, although requesting a new fuel pump from his next *Milch kuh* refuelling.

Although it is undeniably possible that workers in Lorient had sabotaged the U-boats' fuel, it may have been a maintenance error that caused the sudden periodic diesel failures. The 10th U-Flotilla's *U513* had suffered a similar problem near Canada. On reaching base it was discovered that the interior of the fuel bunkers had been painted with red aluminium paint. This paint, a standard procedure, had not been given enough time to harden before the bunkers were filled with fuel. Gradually the paint softened and flaked off into the fuel supply, clogging injectors and pumps, periodically choking off the fuel supply.

Mohr's problems were entirely reminiscent of those suffered by *U513*. As the boat was sailing surfaced diesel revolutions would rapidly falter, particularly if running high, before shutting off entirely. Often after several minutes enough fuel would have leaked through to enable engines to restart, again failing when run at moderate revolutions. It was a daunting prospect for men who relied on speed and manoeuvrability for survival.

Nevertheless *U124* sailed onwards. Mohr refuelled from the Type X1B temporary tanker *U118*, picking up 300m³ of lubricating oil, 20m³ fresh 'clean' fuel, new valves and the pump for his starboard engine. As they continued westward Mohr used the supposedly 'contaminated' fuel first, saving his clean diesel for action in the combat zone.

The boat lurched towards the Caribbean, engineers driven to distraction by daily breakdowns, until on 15 December *U124* sighted convoy mastheads 600 miles off Trinidad. Shadowing in company with Type VIID *U217*, Mohr attacked that evening claiming two tankers hit, although no Allied records of these hits can be found.

Drawing away to reload, Mohr sighted aircraft and dived to avoid detection, losing sight of his quarry and unable to regain contact. Although unconfirmed, it was a good start. A

[138] Gasaway, p. 225.

second convoy was sighted days later to the west, but now Mohr paid the price for his diesel problems. Calling all hands to battle stations, engines thrown to full ahead, Mohr was dismayed at the sudden faltering of engines refusing to engage higher revolutions. Oblt. (Ing.) Subklew was forced to lower engine speed or face a total cut out and Mohr could only watch in frustration as his target drew away. It was a pattern that continued for the next weeks on patrol.

Despite this handicap *U124* gradually harvested a toll from its enemies, Mohr's skill as a commander was stretched to the very limit as he operated his defective boat with his customary daring and vigour. The experienced crew excelled, rewarding their commander with a total of five more confirmed sinkings, four of them from attacks on southbound convoy TB1 off Guiana during the pre-dawn darkness of 9 January.

Shark meat plucked from the tropical seas by Oblt.z.S. Willi Gerlach's fishing prowess augmented their diet of mouldering or tinned provisions as *U124* skirted the eastern edge of the Caribbean. On 13 January a welcome radio message arrived in the cramped communications room – Mohr had been awarded the Oak Leaves to his Knight's Cross, the 177th Wehrmacht soldier to be so decorated. Finally it was time to return and *U124* again lurched laboriously across the Atlantic, resupplying once more from *U118*. In the face of extreme difficulty Mohr had destroyed three tankers and five merchant ships aggregating 46,000 tons of enemy shipping, the most successful of the Western Atlantic boats in the first months of 1943, even when unconfirmed sinkings are subtracted. As *U124* eased into Lorient's Scorff River the crew were given an enthusiastic welcome by flotilla mates, the 'Edelweiss' crew grimly noting Lorient's dilapidation. Mohr had a further appointment to keep and was flown to Hitler's Ukrainian headquarters to receive his Oak Leaves from the Führer in person. His four hours spent with Germany's leader Mohr later described, in a fairly noncommittal way, as "very interesting". Mohr, still the youngest U-boat commander at that stage of the war, was now the proud father of a baby boy, his wife Eva nursing hope that her husband would be relegated to a staff position as Dönitz routinely did with such highly decorated men. Mohr, on the other hand, would not be separated from his beloved boat and pleaded successfully for one last cruise before transfer, *U124* went into the Kéroman bunkers for refit before her eleventh war patrol against a strengthening enemy.

14 February: The day following Mohr's return, Kaptlt. Jürgen Nissen sailed *U105* into Lorient at the end of his patrol as commander. Nissen too had been to the western Atlantic, indeed entering the confined Caribbean Sea during early January, one merchant ship already sunk north-east of Guiana. Nissen made a single artillery sinking before retreating through the Windward Islands, sailing through the island chain and sinking the abandoned wreck of British tanker MV *British Vigilance* the following day. Another ship fell to Nissen's torpedoes as *U105* sailed homebound, not the glory once achieved by U-boats within the 'Golden West' but saved the indignity of a barren patrol like that of the damaged *U108* returning on 24 February.

During the remainder of February two more rejuvenated veteran 2nd U-Flotilla boats, *U106* and *U130*, sailed from Lorient, while in Kiel the first of four reinforcements during February and March began its transfer voyage. The Type IXC-40 *U190* slipped from the *Tirpitz Hafen* to begin transit through the Kiel Canal to the North Sea. This new generation of U-boat, of virtually identical outward appearance to the IXC, had a slightly larger outer hull, housing enlarged fuel bunkerage. *U190*'s commander Kaptlt. Max Wintermeyer had long since cut his teeth in U-boats as Watch Officer aboard *U105* during late 1940 and early 1941 when the U-boat's star was truly rising. Now after months of training he took to the sea as commander. The paper transfer of *U190* from the 4th U-training Flotilla to Kals' front-line unit was accomplished by the beginning of March, Wintermeyer already en route west of Ireland as part of the new ten-strong pack called *Neuland*.

March saw the remaining three Type IXC-40 reinforcements sail from Kiel, *U168*, *U191* and *U532*, the latter commanded by veteran KK Ottoheinrich Junker who had sailed *U33* against the Spanish Republicans six years before. Junker had spent the intervening years as a member of the TEK and BdU staff before requesting front-line action once more.

Meanwhile the veterans who had put to sea from Lorient were west of the Azores in wait for Gibraltar shipping. Kaptlt. Hermann Rasch's *U106* had originally been ordered to the United States before being redeployed. *U130* was also ordered to join the group, named *Unverzagt* (undaunted), the boat's new commander Oblt.z.S. Siegfried Keller, ex-Watch Officer aboard Bleichrodt's *U109*, finding northbound convoy XK2 during the evening of 5 March while en route to the group area. In a blistering single attack Keller fired all torpedoes and sank four British ships, totalling 16,350 tons. Although prevented from launching a second strike by strong escorts, it was a staggering debut and seemed to bode well for the young native of Gotha.

A week later the six *Unverzagt* Type IXs had congregated where B-Dienst predicted the American ships' path to lie. *U130* and *U106* were the group's only 2nd U-Flotilla boat's and on the evening of 12 March *U130*'s watch sighted the distinctive shadow of oncoming merchants. Keller immediately began sending beacons to home on UGS6 – forty-three laden merchant ships escorted by seven brand new US Navy fleet destroyers. All the American escorts were equipped with centimetric-wavelength radar and privy to the latest intelligence from shore-based HF/DF stations as to likely enemy dispositions, Dönitz's demand for radioed reports betraying his boats' presence.

Shortly afterward, radar aboard USS *Champlin* detected a surface contact two nautical miles dead ahead. Her commander, Lt.Cdr. C.L. Melson, ordered flank speed and all hands to battle stations and *Champlin* quivered under full power. It was a little before midnight, but the sanctuary of darkness now held no security for *U130* under the unflinching gaze of radar.

U130 surfaced and was lying directly in front of the destroyer as Melson ordered his 5" guns to start firing. No doubt startled, Keller crash-dived to escape the onrushing American, although the dive appeared slow and hesitant. The conning tower had submerged barely minutes before *Champlin* raced overhead and delivered the first of five depth-charge attacks. Keller and his fifty-two young crewmen, aboard one of the five boats that had launched Germany's attack on the United States thirteen months before, never resurfaced.

As UGS6 wallowed east the remaining *Unverzagt* boats attacked stubbornly, driven off by equally determined American escorts. BdU organized fresh reinforcements and a second group was formed, *Wohlgemut* including the recently sailed *U67*, *U103* and *U109*. Combined with *Tümmler* boats still possessing sufficient fuel, Dönitz saw a real opportunity to deal the Allies in North Africa a crippling blow. At the scene of the clash order was quickly lost as German and American wrestled over access to the vital merchant ships. Torpedoes and depth charges ripped the Atlantic and it soon became apparent that the defenders were gaining the upper hand. Among the boats joining the struggle was Klaus Bargsten's *U521*, claiming three ships sunk. Bargsten was lucky to avoid collision after his last salvo, floundering to a halt as another U-boat crossed his bow only fifty metres distant.

During this evasive manoeuvering *U521* was detected by escorts and driven under for a severe depth-charging, shaken by seventy depth charges. Bargsten used the newly developed 'Bold' launcher to throw his assailants off the scent, later scornful of his enemies for their 'lack of tenacity'. However, he had not escaped unscathed, a slightly bent propeller shaft being the most serious damage inflicted. Of his three claimed sinkings none were ever confirmed.

Later Bargsten did succeed in sinking a single verified ship. On the night of 17 March as UGS6 neared Gibraltar and began to receive an aircraft umbrella *U521* chanced upon a drifting and damaged Liberty Ship, the SS *Molly Pitcher*, holed by 1st U-Flotilla's *U558* and hove to, guarded by a corvette. Five torpedoes were fired and one hit, ending the freighter's torment, the final ship sunk from UGS6 which, despite the presence of seventeen U-boats, had lost only four merchants, the remaining thirty-nine safely reaching North Africa.

While Allied bombing razed Lorient, aircraft also made their mark on the flotilla at sea. KK Werner Hartenstein's *U156* had crossed the Atlantic from Lorient during January, arriving in position east of Trinidad by the middle of February. His was the last of three new boats based east of the Lesser Antilles, *U68* and the 10th U-Flotilla's *U510* rounding out the trio. None found targets, enemy aircraft blighting their tenure. While racing fully surfaced after small convoy TB4 *U156* narrowly avoided serious damage from an attacking B18, forced under repeatedly and receiving ferocious bombardment. The Americans began a concerted hunt for *U156*, which now trailed a thin but fatal oil slick from a slight tear in its fuel bunker. Airships and bombers tracked the damaged U-boat as it crept submerged from the danger area.

During the night of 5 March Hartenstein radioed BdU with critical information. Coupled with reports of the impossibility of operations between Trinidad and Grenada due to aerial saturation, Hartenstein also recounted a lack of Metox warnings. Allied centimetric radar had become standard on ASW aircraft, immune to Metox's meter-length detection waveband. Unhappily for Hartenstein, American shore receivers had triangulated his transmission and streams of bombers flew in search of the elusive boat, *U156* sailing east to effect repairs.

During the early afternoon of 7 March a US Navy Catalina of Trinidad's VP-53 detected a radar contact at twenty miles. Skilfully manoeuvering his aircraft using available cloud cover, pilot Lt. John. D Dryden approached *U156*, sighting it visually seven miles distant. Hartenstein must have felt that he had placed enough distance between himself and the hunters, allowing many crewmen on deck to survey their damage and enjoy a glimpse of equatorial sunshine. At point blank range Dryden broke cover and dived from the clouds in a shallow attack, forward machine guns blazing. His surprise was total. Dryden and his crew could see several Germans 'sunbathing' on deck as the machine-gun splashes 'walked' towards the U-boat. Roaring overhead at only thirty metres, Dryden dropped four depth charges, blasting the steel hull and blowing it cleanly into three segments which sank rapidly. As Dryden circled he noted eleven survivors, including what appeared to be 'an officer in a white shirt'. He dropped a life raft into the struggling men and five of them managed to pull themselves aboard, while the remaining six slipped below the waves, possibly too badly injured to keep themselves afloat. Signalling the survivors' presence to his home airfield at Chaguaramas, Dryden stayed for thirty minutes before leaving the scene. Later that afternoon American destroyer USS *Barney* was sent to haul the survivors from the sea. They were never found. Hartenstein and his crew were gone.

13 March: Another old hand from the heady days of 'Operation *Westindien*' sailed from Lorient, Kaptlt. Albrecht Achilles taking *U161* out alongside Oblt.z.S. Horst von Schroeter's *U123*. Both boats were bound for the United States, although von Schroeter was first attached to the *Seeräuber* group south of the Canary Islands.

After making a rendezvous west of the Azores with returning Axis blockade-runners *Regensburg* and *Pietro Orseolo* to pass over radar equipment and sailing instructions, he proceeded west, arriving off New York in early April alongside 10th U-Flotilla's *U174*. Both boats were directed to Nova Scotia where they were battered by foul weather. The weather and the strong aircraft menace eventually proved too much and on 27 April a USN Ventura from Newfoundland destroyed *U174* with all hands.

Discouraged, Achilles broke off the hopeless operation and trudged southwards to calmer waters off the United States. Still hindered by constant air patrols he made a single sinking, stopping the small Canadian brig *Angelus* and allowing her crew to abandon ship before shelling it out of existence. It was a bitter pill for Achilles to swallow, heading to Lorient with a single sailing vessel sunk, entering port again on 7 June. His depression reflected in the words of his report to Dönitz where he described U-boat activity off Canada and the United States as "hopeless" in the face of such air superiority.

During March four veteran 2nd U-Flotilla boats – *U105, U154, U124* and *U126* – sailed for Freetown, joined by Mohr's ex-crewmate Werner Kenke aboard 10th U-Flotilla's *U151*. On 2 April, while sailing south for the central Atlantic, Mohr caught site of convoy OS45 heading from Britain to Sierra Leone, immediately beginning to shadow and radioing sighting reports to BdU.

Dönitz radioed Mohr, authorizing a single attack as he was the sole U-boat in that vicinity and the convoy was fast approaching formidable aircraft cover from North Africa. Mohr, never one to let an opportunity pass, slipped towards the convoy that evening and fired a full torpedo salvo, hitting and sinking two British ships, transporting between them 13,000 tons of stores, 1,000 tons of ammunition and sixteen aircraft.

As a conflagration of burning oil illuminated the scene, escort sloop HMS *Black Swan* detected a surface contact on its centimetric radar and with all guns manned raced at speed toward the radar blip. Suddenly the conning tower with its huge Edelweiss emerged from the darkness off the sloop's starboard bow, sliding under in what must have been a hurried crash-dive. Too close for the main guns to depress and take aim, *Black Swan* careered over-head and dropped a group of depth charges. A second corvette, HMS *Stonecrop*, detected *U124* on ASDIC and another salvo floated down toward the submerged boat, exploding at their primed depth and causing both escorts to lose contact in the turbulence. They never regained any trace, as *U124* was no more. The 'Edelweiss' boat, fourth most successful U-boat of the Second World War, was never heard from again, no sign of its passing found by the British ships save for a shimmering rainbow of diesel lying on the water. Eventually Dönitz was forced to admit the loss of Jochen Mohr and his men, declaring them officially *Vermißt ein Stern*. Months later, on 3 January 1944, Wolfgang Frank, head of the Kriegsmarine Propaganda Arm, wrote a final tribute to "a born convoy fighter" in the *Brüsseler Zeitung*. Dönitz, as shocked at the loss of the exuberant young commander as the rest of Germany, ordered on 6 April that the large Type IX U-boats would only be used to reinforce convoy battles already underway, the unwieldy boats too slow and clumsy to operate alone against heavy escort presence. But the large boats were soon to prove too ungainly for the rough and tumble of any fast-moving convoy action, as events in April and May were to show.

Freetown's allocated U-boats continued their extended patrol off Sierra Leone, losing

Oblt.z.S. Oskar Kusch's *U154*, redirected to Brazil during early May. Results were mixed. Both *U105* and *U126*, under its new commander Obtl.z.S. Siegfried Kietz, ex-Minesweeping officer and IWO of *U130*, managed to destroy a single ship each while Kaptlt. Horst von Schroeter found great success, *U123* sinking five merchant ships and the British submarine *P615*. But for the veteran *U105* it was a swansong, surviving its final victim by eighteen days. Kaptlt. Jürgen Nissen's Type IXB was detected by the French Potez flying boat *Antarés* of 141 Squadron near Dakar sailing homebound. The French-man was engaged in coastal escort duty and swooped down on the surprised German, straddling her cleanly with depth charges. *U105* crash-dived but lost the race for survival, Nissen and his fifty-two men never resurfacing.

24 March: Kaptlt. Markworth's *U66* arrived in Lorient at the end of its seventh war patrol, sailing into harbour alongside KK Wilhelm Luis's *U504*. Luis had had no success in two group operations and Markworth also had achieved little. After the débâcle of the Western Saharan agent landing *U66* had continued on her ordained patrol pattern, joining the *Rochen* group where she sank her first ship of the voyage, the French trawler *Joseph Elise*, by gunfire east of Las Palmas. A second victim on 27 February, when Markworth torpedoed the independently sailing British SS *St. Margaret*, yielded the ship's captain as prisoner, turned over to the *Milch kuh U461* two days later as *U66* received fresh provisions and oil.

Within the last six days of March *U107*, *U103*, *U521*, *U190* and *U43* all reached home, aggregating a mere nine confirmed sinkings, although claims exceeded this number considerably. Of those definite kills, five were sunk by *U107* alone, Kaptlt. Harald Gelhaus torpedoing four of them with a full torpedo salvo during 12/13 March in a bold single night attack on convoy OS44 west of Vigo, Spain.

More tragically, the single victory logged by Kaptlt. Schwantke's aged Type IXA *U43* as a 'Dunedin Star' or 'Dunnottar Castle' type ship sunk on 3 March later turned out to be the overdue blockade runner *Doggerbank* sailing to Bordeaux from Japan with a cargo of 7,000 tons of rubber, animals fats, vegetable and fish oils. *Doggerbank* had begun the war as British steamer *Speybank*, captured by the raider *Atlantis* during January 1941 and later commissioned into the Kriegsmarine at Bordeaux as auxiliary minelayer *Schiff 53* '*Doggerbank*'. It was she who laid successful minefields around Cape Town before heading to Yokohama, Japan, to collect cargo for the cruise back to occupied France.

Doggerbank's experienced master, Paul Schneidewind, was unfortunately and inexplic-ably sailing well outside the charted area marked as safe passage to France during the final leg of his thirteen-month round trip. Steaming 1,000 miles west of the Canaries, three torpedoes from *U43* crashed against the steel hull, blowing gaping wounds in the ship and sending her and her precious cargo to the bottom in less than three minutes. As *U43* retreated from the scene only a dog named Leo and fifteen of the crew, including Schneidewind, survived to board a raft, stranded without food or water. Twenty-six days later, on 29 March, the Spanish tanker SS *Campoamor* found the last remaining survivor, Fritz Kürt. As an afternote to the disaster, which only became apparent to OKM after Kürt's rescue, the entire incident was erased from *U43*'s War Diary, the third occurrence of BdU removing pages from a U-boat's KTB.

The beginning of April saw continued failure to intercept Allied convoys. *U109* returned to 1 April after barely a month at sea under new commander Oblt.z.S. Joachim Schramm, no successes to boast against Gibraltar traffic and damaged hydroplanes to boot. Likewise for Kaptlt. Hermann Rasch returning from the Biscay battle aboard *U106* with no pennants flying from the periscope three days later, *U67* following bruised and empty-handed on 13 April.

In the port itself further USAAF bombing churned the devastated wreckage. The smell of smoke that clung to everything in Lorient added its all-pervading stench to an already wretched atmosphere. German troops could take some measure of comfort in the strong concrete fortifications that afforded them protection, but haunts they had enjoyed between patrols were now just rubble and dust. Even nearby Nantes, where repairs to delicate U-boat optics were undertaken, soon received several tons of high explosive and incendiaries.

It was left to Kaptlt. Friedrich-Wilhelm Wissmann to revive spirits on 27 April when *U518* returned from three and a half months off Brazil. Four ships had sunk, *U518* taking officer prisoners from its final victim, the Swedish MV *Industria*. Initially BdU was concerned when Wissmann reported failure of eight out of fourteen torpedoes fired in a two-day attack on convoy BT6, but from his War Diary and torpedo charts it was concluded that he had launched his weapons at excessive range.

1 April: In late March Dönitz formed the *Meise* group lying off Newfoundland in wait for Halifax convoys. On April Fool's Day *U108* slipped from Lorient to join the group, followed shortly by new boats *U189*, *U531*, *U191* and *U532* on their inaugural missions. Intelligence from Italian and B-Dienst sources showed Slow Convoy SL126 due to pass near the *Meise* line and Dönitz positioned them accordingly. But the quarry slipped the net as SL126 veered south and eluded them. Despite this disappointment, BdU soon fastened his sights on a second cluster of three convoys, HX234, ON178 and ONS4. Ordering all available boats to the scene, even the Type IXs, previously considered too clumsy, he prepared for another clash. It was the beginning of a German disaster that dragged on until the end of the month.

Meise boat *U306* sighted HX234 on 21 April and began shadowing, homing others on to the forty-three merchant ships. Among the six boats within range to open the attack were *U108* and *U189*, the latter commanded by Kaptlt. Hellmut Kurrer, ex-IWO aboard *U128*. Immediately Allied direction-finders picked up the incoming threat and VLR Liberators were despatched to provide cover, weather conditions permitting. In the ensuing clash two merchant ships were sunk and another damaged, but one U-boat was destroyed and a second heavily damaged – both by aircraft. The U-boat lost was Kurrer's *U189* sighted sailing alongside *U413* and attacked on the night of 23 April by RAF 120 Squadron B24 VLR Liberator. The pilot, Flying Officer John K. Moffat, attacked the nearest boat, surprising the Germans with accurate depth charges. When the spray subsided Moffatt and his crew could see nearly the entire German crew abandoning their boat, radioing the convoy's Escort Group of the submarine's destruction only to be told there were no ships available for rescue work. Kurrer and his crew were never found. *U413* reported their loss. *U189*'s operational career lasted three weeks.

The attack on HX234 was abandoned in the face of thick fog, fierce storms and intermittent air cover as other *Meise* boats picked up the trail of ON178 on 21 April. Dönitz redirected his boats briefly towards the new target before cancelling in favour of a concentrated attack on the third convoy, ONS4. Shadowed by *U732*, four other U-boats rapidly gained contact and were cleared to attack, among them *U108* and *U191*. Veteran KK Ralf-Reimar Wolfram's *U108* had already claimed an unsubstantiated Liberty ship sinking and again attempted to gain firing position but was constantly frustrated and depth-charged. Kaptlt. Helmut Fiehn's *U191* had also sunk one ship from ON178 before latching onto ONS4. Firing a full bow salvo in a submerged daylight attack, Fiehn was frustrated by four misses. Pulling away to reload, *U191* issued a brief progress report to BdU, immediately DF'ed by Commander Donald Macintyre in his escort destroyer HMS *Hesperus*. Meanwhile, commander of British Escort Group B2, raced toward the contact with corvette HMS *Clematis* accompanying, surprising the surfaced *U191* which promptly tried to submerge. In crystal clear water affording perfect hydrophone reception, *Hesperus* located Fiehn's boat and began its attack. Using the new Hedgehog weapon, inexperienced crewmen bungled their shot. Macintyre's order to fire on his first attack run was greeted with nothing, the safety pins not having been removed. As this oversight was rectified, other weapons were readied aboard the destroyer while *Clematis* roared over the ASDIC contact with its first depth charge attack. The two British ships then proceeded to hound *U191* for thirty minutes, *Hesperus* deploying an experimental two-thousand-pound depth charge from its torpedo tubes before finally firing the Hedgehog. The clear sound of two explosions from the sinking Hedgehog contact-fused projectiles indicated a direct hit on what must have already been a severely battered boat. Helmut Fiehn and his fifty-four men went to the bottom.

ONS4 slipped away to safety and Dönitz was left to count the cost of his operations: five ships from three convoys attacked by nearly forty U-boats. Three U-boats had been lost, two of the 2nd U-Flotilla's fresh reinforcements from Germany and the 1st U-Flotilla's 'ace' boat *U203*. *Meise* was disbanded on 25 April.

There were still a great many U-boats astride the North Atlantic convoy routes and Dönitz reshuffled his remaining battleworthy forces into three packs: *Amsel*, *Specht* and *Star*. The first two totalled thirty-two U-boats strung out opposite Newfoundland in a patrol line nearly 500 miles long. The last group, totalling a further sixteen boats, lay eastward of the others, in wait for traffic using the northern route.

Two westbound convoys, SC127 and HX235, under strong American escort, including the 'Jeep' carrier USS *Bogue*, were able to weave through the combined *Amsel-Specht* line without being sighted thanks to precise decoding of the U-boats' dispositions. A brief nine-day ULTRA blackout starting on 10 March had ended and the convoys' ninety-three merchant ships escaped unscathed. At that moment diaster struck the Allies. Dönitz shifted his two packs further south, aware of the Allies' successful evasion and ordered *Star* to remain athwart the convoy lanes between Iceland and Newfoundland. On 26 April ULTRA again lost the key to the four-wheeled Enigma and suddenly there was no current intelligence on the three drifting wolf packs. On 28 April *U650* of the *Star* group sighted slow outbound ONS5 south-west of Iceland. The unwieldy forty-ship formation had already suffered enormously from savage weather conditions, but, strongly escorted by British Escort Group B7, led by the experienced Commander Peter Gretton, the clumsy convoy stagged on towards New York.

In steadily worsening weather, U-boats shuddering and creaking their way through mountainous seas, the battle unfolded. Denied cohesive air cover by the elements, ONS5 came under unsuccessful attack by *U650*, other boats then joining the fray. KK Ottoheinrich Junker aboard *U532* fired a full salvo and claimed two ships hit, although Allied records hold no trace of these strikes. *U532* was rocked by severe depth-charging from HMS *Snowflake* and *Tay* shortly after and, damaged and vulnerable to further attack, Junker broke off and headed for France. By the time of his arrival on 15 May the attack had been called off, one ship sunk for the loss of a single U-boat (*U528*) and two severely damaged, limping home.

The depleted *Star* group was dissolved and the North Atlantic boats were reorganized again into two large groups, *Amsel* and *Fink*. The latter totalled twenty-nine boats in all, veteran *U125* joining *U168* and *U531*, while *Amsel* was subdivided into four smaller groups of six boats each in an experiment by BdU to confuse the Allies. Another pair of veteran 2nd U-Flotilla boats that had recently sailed, *U107* and *U504*, formed part of *Amsel I*. The stage seemed set for a battle royal as the largest conglomeration of U-boats in the North Atlantic prepared to meet skilfully defended convoy traffic in waters that raged with great rolling seas.

Combat began on the night of 4 May as slow convoy ONS5, by now straggling badly, stumbled into contact with fifty-three U-boats. Unexpectedly, as the Germans gathered the weather cleared and balanced shifted in favour of ONS5 with the arrival of Canadian aircraft. Two British support groups of destroyers, frigates and corvettes had also begun to appear in dribs and drabs and before the U-boats had even managed to close to attacking distance two were sunk by aircraft. Fog began to settle over the North Atlantic and during dusk the fifteen U-boats that had gained contact began their onslaught, the first to fire being Kaptlt. Ulrich Folkers' *U125*. He made a series of surfaced attacks, torpedoes striking a straggling ex-French steamer now running under the Union Jack, ironically named SS *Lorient*. None of the remaining convoy members saw her sink, her entire crew perishing in the Atlantic.

Other boats attacked, but by morning of 5 May the Germans lost contact, driven under by aircraft as the fog and darkness cleared, leaving the bedraggled convoy with seven ships less than they had started the night with. That evening as fog descended again the Germans recovered contact, attacking once more. In *U125* Folkers had good reason for optimism and jockeyed for position as midnight passed and the early morning darkness of 6 May offered the illusion of shelter. Preparing a surface attack, *U125* was stunned by escort destroyer HMS *Oribi* bursting from drifting fog banks after having fixed them on radar, leaving Folkers no time to escape. *U125*'s helm was flung hard over as *Oribi*'s bow crashed headlong into the U-boat's flank. *U125* reeled and began to submerge, breaking free of its attacker while aboard the departing destroyer there was jubilation at what must have been a certain kill, *Oribi* having struck *U125* at nearly twenty knots.

However, the veteran German crew were still very much alive. Desperately fighting to stop flooding, it soon became apparent that their boat was doomed. At 0331hrs Folkers nursed his crippled boat to the surface and transmitted an urgent distress message, Dönitz wasting no time in directing *U552*, *U381*, *U413* and *U260* to assist.

As *U125* lay damaged and barely mobile escort corvette HMS *Snowflake* received firm radar impulses at 0345hrs, closing rapidly in thick fog. When the contact lay a scant 100 metres distant, starshell was fired and the unmistakable sight of a heavily damaged U-boat, apparently already sinking, was revealed. *Snowflake* instantly attempted to ram but Folkers was unwilling to concede defeat and dragged *U125* about, inside the corvette's turning circle. Knowing the end was near, Folkers ordered the boat scuttled, leaping into the sea as five explosive charges detonated aboard *U125* while almost alongside *Snowflake*. The Germans now lay at the mercy of their enemy and as a second corvette, HMS *Sunflower*, reached the scene its commander radioed the temporary escort commander Lt Comm. R.E. Sherwood aboard frigate HMS *Tay* – Gretton and HMS *Duncan* having been forced to detach for refuelling in St John's – for permission to rescue survivors. The reply was unequivocal:

"Not approved to pick up survivors."

Both corvettes reluctantly turned away from the bobbing heads of fifty-four German survivors. Folkers and his crew were never seen again.

This was the second U-boat sinking that HMS *Sunflower* had been involved in. Earlier that night the new 2nd U-Flotilla boat *U531* had been detected by ASDIC aboard destroyer HMS *Vidette* and subjected to a sharp violent depth-charging. Forced to the surface by the bombardment Herbert Neckel's boat was then rammed by *Sunflower* before crash-diving again in a desperate bid to escape. A brief shower of Hedgehog bombs and the diesel life-blood of *U531* drifted up from the depths, again taking all fifty-four men with her.

By the battle's end on 6 May six U-boats had been lost for the destruction of twelve merchant ships. The ruinous exchange rate worsened with the addition of boats from other packs that had tangled with ONS5, raising the total lost to nine – four Type IXs and five Type VIIs.

Nor was that all. Elsewhere the heavy Type IXs had suffered further loss. On 17 May *U128* had been at sea one day short of six weeks, her new commander Oblt.z.S. Hermann Steinert taking his first patrol as commander after taking over from Kaptlt. Ulrich Heyse on 17 February while the boat had new batteries fitted in Kéroman II. He had added a symbol to the U-boat's conning tower – the Olympic rings of the officer class of 1936, Steinert's stamp on the veteran boat.

U128's new command hierarchy featured the unusual position of IWO, Kaptlt. Siegfried Sterzing, outranking the commander. However, this appeared to cause no problem, they and their crew conceding that Steinart possessed more submarine experience. *U128* had been ordered to escort a blockade-runner from Japan, cruising vainly in the Bay of Biscay until advised that the *Silvaplana* had been intercepted and sunk. Course was set of northern Brazil and *U128* cruised at economical surface speed until arriving off Bahia, within sight of the city's lights. There her luck ended. At 1450hrs on 16 May *U128* was sighted running surfaced by a patrolling aircraft, which immediately depth-charged the crash-diving boat. The nearby explosions shook *U128* as it crept away submerged. That night a Catalina was sent out to keep the U-boat harassed and under, but as the airplane carried no radar she was unable to locate *U128*, which spent the night ventilating and charging batteries before submerging at dawn, the low rhythmic thumping of propellers from convoy TB13 clearly audible on hydrophones. After establishing the convoy's mean direction, *U128* took up pursuit, travelling at flank speed on diesels, hoping to close the distance between her and the convoy.

A patrolling US Navy PBM sighted *U128* during mid-morning at a distance of eighteen miles, the Catalina in turn spotted by Steinert's bridge watch. Ordering a crash-dive, the boat experienced a sudden failure in its high-pressure manifold and valuable minutes were lost before vents were opened manually. *U128* tardily submerged, followed within seconds by six Mark 44 depth charges dropped ahead of its path. All were set at the shallowest setting of 25 feet and exploded around *U128*'s bow. The effect was catastrophic. The pressure hull was ruptured near the forward starboard torpedo tubes and water poured in, as well as gushing through the galley hatch. Both electric motors and the gyrocompass were out of commission and men rushed along the slanting deck into the boat's stern compartments to attempt to regain trim. Gradually their descent was arrested and Steinert ordered all emergency tanks blown to save his crew. Three minutes after the Catalina's attack *U128* broke surface, both diesels bursting immediately into life as *U128* made off at full speed in the direction of the South American coast. Steinert's *Obersteuermann* laid course by roughly estimating the stand of the sun and men raced atop the *Wintergarten* to man the anti-U-boat guns. But in the meantime a second aircraft had arrived and made a low-altitude attack with six more depth charges, increasing the damage aboard *U128* and continually strafing any attempts at returning fire. The IIWO and a rating were badly wounded, Steinert himself crawling on to the bridge to administer morphine. Although hoping for deliverance, Steinert prepared for the inevitable and sent men outside, sheltering behind the conning tower in readiness to abandon ship.

At about 0930hrs those men clustered behind the tower sighted USS *Moffett* and *Jouett* on the horizon. With no hope left, Steinert gave the order to abandon ship and scuttle, all vents and hatches opened and hydrophones on dive. Within twenty minutes most of the crew had left the U-boat, but, since no white flag was showing, both destroyers opened fire. Amid spumes of shellfire *U128* slipped under the surface a little after 1000hrs. Steinert was among the last to leave his first and final operational command.

Later, under American interrogation, it became apparent that most of the prisoners believed that *U128* could have survived the damage done by the first depth-charge attack and might even had got away after the second one, had not the destroyers come upon the scene. They also felt that the disaster would not have befallen them had Heyse still been in command, although there appeared no resentment against Steinert. USS *Moffett* rescued fifty-one Germans, four of whom later died, Oblt. (Ing.) Gustav Stutz succumbing to the effects of chlorine gas seeping from the batteries during the boat's last moments. Superficial wounds from machine-gun fire and a single shark bite were treated aboard USS *Moffett*, whose officers and crew received unanimous German praise for their humanity.

U128 was the fourth 2nd U-Flotilla boat sunk during May and the only one to have left survivors. *U109*, another veteran boat, had been lost in the North Atlantic on 4 May, six days after leaving Lorient. She too was surprised by aircraft north-north-east of the Azores, her mainly inexperienced crew unable to learn the realities of U-boat war quickly enough. The pilot of the RAF 86 Squadron Liberator that bombed the boat to oblivion recalled seeing the faces of the bridge watch transfixed in horror by his approach, only beginning to crash-dive when it was far too late. Six shallow depth charges exploded around the boat's central section, four more jamming *U109*'s rudder and sending her in circles to port trailing a thick wake of oil. It took half an hour for *U109* to sink taking her crew to the bottom. No men were seen to exit the conning tower, leading to the belief that the hatches had been buckled, trapping the crew. It was not until June that *U109* was officially listed missing. Wolfgang Hirschfeld had missed his boat's sailing, put ashore on sick leave with a skin infection.

> "I remember Ferdinand Hagen. When we had shared a last drink together . . . he had said to me with a resigned smile, 'Wolfgang, believe me when I tell you that we won't be coming back from this trip. . . . Do me a last favour and tell my fiancée when you hear for sure.'
>
> "It was a glorious June morning when, on entering the [Prefecture] bunker, I glanced automatically at the pigeon hole for *U109* and saw to my grief that it was empty. The cards lay face down on the table. *U109* was gone. I turned on my heel and walked out into the sunshine."[139]

When combined with eleven other Type IXs sunk during March and April, Dönitz concluded that he must withdraw the large boats from the North Atlantic. They were not agile enough in quick-fire combat and would revert to long-distance solo hunting that had seen their greatest successes. Both *U66* and *U190* had left Lorient at the end of April for just such missions, the former sailing on 27 April bound for the Caribbean and the thin U-boat presence maintained there, the latter on 1 May to the United States. *U66*'s attempt

---

[139] Hirschfeld, p. 186.

at leaving France was, however, cut short, the boat forced back into harbour after diesels began belching fumes, filling the boat's interior and curtailing the voyage. She sailed again on 29 April.

Other U-boats putting to sea from France during May sailed into the teeth of a brand new Coastal Command aerial offensive over Biscay – 'Operation Derange'. But the losses suffered by 2nd U-Flotilla were not the only matter for concern in Lorient. Nine of the flotilla's U-boats arrived in port having sunk between them only six enemy freighters. *U168*, *U103*, *U107* and *U504* – the last putting into the Gironde, docking in Bordeaux on 29 May – returned from the North Atlantic pack attacks with nothing but damage to show for their labours. Kaptlt. Janssen's *U103* unloaded two officers as prisoners, the British sailors plucked from the liferafts of SS *Fort Concord* torpedoed previously by *U456* of the 1st U-Flotilla.[140]

The slim pickings that had been taken were spread between *U183* (one Honduran freighter) and *U68* (two freighters) operating in the Caribbean and *U129* near Bermuda. Kaptlt. Witt's *U129* had suffered severe depth charging by USS *Swanson* during a foiled convoy attack on the night of 21 April, but later redeemed her failure by sinking two independently sailing ships west-south-west of Bermuda.

Three further boats sailed from the 2nd U-Flotilla during May. Kaptlt. Klaus Bargsten put to sea from Lorient aboard *U521* on 5 May, ordered to the United States, Kaptlt. Müller-Stöckheim's veteran *U67* following five days later, bound for the Caribbean. Meanwhile in Kiel the latest addition to the flotilla strength slipped from the Tirpitz Harbour bound for two months off West Africa. KK Hans Pauckstadt, prewar commander of *U34* and briefly *U30*, conned his first wartime patrol as the new Type IXC/40 *U193* sailed west. Pauckstadt, despite a lack of combat experience, was a veteran naval officer with years of peacetime seagoing experience. He had spent the war thus far in staff positions, serving primarily within BdU (Org) before a brief period as temporary commander of the 5th U-Flotilla. As Pauckstadt put to sea once more, his Commander-in-Chief began to count the cost of his Atlantic battles.

May's results were appalling and it rapidly became apparent to Dönitz that his forces faced a complete rout in the North Atlantic. Ignoring scant success achieved elsewhere, while engaged against six separate North Atlantic convoys, located with superb B-Dienst assistance, the U-boat service had managed to sink only six ships in total. In return during the month of May Dönitz lost a total of forty U-boats to enemy action, fifteen in the North Atlantic. Tellingly, not only were radar and radar-equipped aircraft held to be decisive factors in the collapse of the U-boat campaign, but the carrier HMS *Biter* had helped swing the balance firmly in the Allied favour when it appeared among the escort groups.

During what was later known as 'Black May', Dönitz was actually in Rome, having flown there to confer with Italy's Naval Command regarding strategy against an expected Allied attack on Sicily. Everywhere Germany was in retreat. Tunisia had fallen, opening the 'soft underbelly' of southern Europe to possible invasion, the Italians already viewed as wavering allies, Mussolini's grip on the country slipping with each day that passed. In Russia the Soviet juggernaut gained momentum and the Wehrmacht slowly retreated in a withdrawal to the west that would never be convincingly halted. The guns on the Russian front could now be heard in conquered Warsaw, then in the midst of uprising and fierce SS counter-action. The last frontier, the Atlantic, was now disintegrating entirely, after months of vainly papering over hundreds of cracks in the U-boat frontier.

---

[140] *U456* was sunk soon afterwards. See *First U-Boat Flotilla*, Lawrence Paterson, p. 192.

The Allies had won the 'Battle of the Atlantic' and would never again face starvation in Europe. American, British and Canadian convoy escorts were multiplying rapidly and the VLR Liberator had closed the central Atlantic air gap. By April 1943 a virtual 'shuttle' operation provided continuous air cover for convoy traffic, while the glut of escort ships allowed formation of hunting groups devoted to chasing U-boat contacts, no longer pinned strictly to defence. It was the end of the U-boat war within the Atlantic and on 24 May, even before the losses were fully appreciated, Dönitz directed all U-boats at sea to withdraw south-west of the Azores.

10

THE END IN THE ATLANTIC:
1 JUNE TO 31 DECEMBER 1943

Another U-boat slipped from Kiel bound for Lorient at the beginning of June. Kaptlt. Rolf Schauenburg, who had celebrated his thirtieth birthday the previous day, ordered lines cast off his new Type IXC-40 *U536* and the boat eased from its berth towards the Holtenau locks for the canal transit to Brunsbüttel. Schauenburg had already had a long and varied naval career, begun as flak artillery officer aboard the *Admiral Graf Spee* during its first and last raiding voyage. Interned in Uruguay in 1939, he had managed to return to Germany the following year, crossing South America disguised as a cloth merchant, twice recaptured and finally freed by the German consul in Argentina. Once home he enlisted in Dönitz's submarine service in 1941, spending two months as *U432*'s Executive Officer before commander training and assignment to *U536*, heading for the front line and combat.

However, the boat's inaugural patrol was not to be the fighting role that Schauenburg and his men had hoped for. With U-boats pushed out of the North Atlantic to less perilous waters south-west of the Azores, many needed refuelling and *U536* was one of three new U-boats tasked to act as auxiliary tankers (the others 10th U-Flotilla's *U170* and *U535*) in support of the only available Type XIV at sea, *U488*.[141] Schauenburg sailed the northern coasts of Britain and eventually rendezvoused with Type VIIC *U84*, refuelling her before following BdU orders and passing all remaining surplus fuel to *U488* to give the tanker an extended period on station. The two 10th U-Flotilla auxiliary tankers followed suit and all three sailed for France in company.

The most treacherous part of their return journey to Lorient lay within the killing ground of Biscay. Yet another Coastal Command offensive, 'Operation Musketry', was in full stride and in a desperate bid to reduce losses Dönitz had issued new orders for crossing Biscay. U-boats were now instructed to remain surfaced by day where they could visually detect any aerial threat, grouped together with anti-aircraft weapons fully manned. Recent Allied successes had left a bitter legacy for Rolf Schauenburg's *U536* and its consorts.

On 12 June *U68* had left Lorient for the western Atlantic in company with *U155*, *U257* and *U600*, hoping for the safety in numbers. Two days from port they had been sighted and attacked by Mosquitoes of 307 (Polish) Squadron. The agile fighter-bombers streaked into attack, the U-boats throwing a hail of defending fire at them. It was only partially successful. Machine-gun and cannon fire bracketed both *U155* and *U68*, slashing through the flimsy metal of conning tower and gun shields. Both boats received so much damage that they abandoned their passage and returned to Lorient. Aboard *U68*, machine-gun fire had wounded her commander, Kaptlt. Albert Lauzemis, the IIWO and *Obersteuermann*.

---

[141] A fourth boat, *U530*, was also assigned the role of tanker, but nearer to the Canary Islands.

Lauzemis' jaw was broken and he was in extreme pain as the boat entered the Scorff River on 16 June, scheduled for dry-dock repairs. Unwilling to let his command go, Lauzemis petitioned Dönitz in writing from the naval hospital to hold *U68* for him in the event that the U-boat was repaired before his own recovery.

A similar fate befell *U518*, putting out from Lorient on 24 June. Three days outbound along the Piening route that fringed northern Spain Kaptlt. Friedrich-Wilhelm Wissmann's boat was damaged by two depth-charge attacks by a 201 Squadron Sunderland flying boat, despite a thick flak barrage. Diving to safety and narrowly missing more serious damage, Wissmann was compelled to return to base. He had fallen victim to 'Operation Seaslung II', running concurrently with and west of 'Musketry', the considerable power of Coastal Command's 15 and 19 Groups dedicated to U-boat hunting. They were unwilling to let go of Wissman and *U518* was attacked again by a Sunderland on 30 June, this time the 10 (RAAF) Squadron bomber suffering injury itself, the rear gunner killed by the fierce defending fire. But *U518* had been damaged again and Wissman faced the very real possibility of losing his crippled boat. It was directed immediately to the nearest Kriegsmarine base, Bordeaux, docking on 3 July.

The Biscay offensives claimed another 2nd U-Flotilla boat during early July. Kaptlt. Siegfried Kietz's *U126* had damaged two ships during its West African patrol, suffering severe aerial depth-charging himself before heading home. On the night of 2 July as *U126* sailed surfaced through Biscay in company with *U154* returning from Brazil, a blinding shaft of light from a 172 Squadron Wellington framed the U-boat squarely, machine-gun fire racing out of the darkness towards her. *U126* twisted wildly, but depth charges were already tumbling her way. Buckled and torn, *U126* stood no chance and immediately began to sink. There were no survivors, *U154* carrying the news to Lorient.

Oblt.z.S. Oskar-Heinz Kusch's aggressive Brazilian patrol had bagged a single confirmed sinking and two ships damaged, although claiming three freighters sunk during a surfaced night attack, FK Ernst Kals (recently promoted) remarking in *U154*'s War Diary that Kusch had proved himself

"Well qualified to be a U-boat commander".

Days later Kaptlt. Rolf Schauenburg's *U536* and two companion U-boats thundered through a mild swell towards Lorient during daylight on 5 July, flak weapons armed and ready in obedience of Dönitz's 'fight back' edict. When the inevitable attack came it was from an RAF 53 Squadron B24 Liberator. Its pilot, New Zealand Flight Sergeant W. Anderson, sighted the three surfaced boats and dived to attack. Flaming tracer drifted slowly towards him, gaining speed as the anti-aircraft shells flashed past the bomber's fuselage. Jinking wildly, his gunners returning fire, Anderson avoided serious damage on his first pass and wheeled about to attempt a second. This time the B24 went straight for Schauenburg's boats, bullets ripping through *U536*'s teak decking and showering German gunners and lookouts with thousands of needle-sharp splinters. Thundering low overhead Anderson cursed as his depth charges failed to release on what could have been a perfect attack. Gunfire smashed through the bomber's steel skin, causing heavy damage as Anderson nursed his bomber back into the air. It was the signal that the three U-boats had been waiting for and, as gunners ran for the conning tower, one by one they began to submerge. But Anderson and his crew were not finished. Swinging around again, the Flight Engineer had rectified their weapon problem and the B24 zeroed in on the last disappearing boat, 10th U-Flotilla's *U535*. Watching it disappear, Anderson dropped eight shallow-set depth charges ahead of the swirling water, the Torpex exploding seconds later and destroying *U535* with all of her crew. The remaining U-boats escaped underwater while Anderson nursed his damaged bomber home. For Schauenburg's crew it had been a singular lesson in the dangers of British air power.

Early July brought more tribulation for *U505*, putting to sea and suffering diesel failures, breakdowns of both Metox and the GHG hydrophone array and a leaking propeller shaft. A leaking external fuel bunker also left a shimmering trail of diesel for enemy aircraft and destroyers to harass them every step of their return. Showing considerable skill, Zschech slipped free of pursuit by combining high-speed night-time surface runs near the Spanish and French coasts with submerged travel by day, limping into port on 13 July for further dockyard repair. In the Kéroman pens it was discovered that myriad watertight seals were corroded to the point of failure – battery acid having been poured over them.

The boat's silhouette had undergone considerable change, reflecting the effects of losing control of the skies. The entire conning tower had been reinforced with new shielding. An extended lower-platform *Wintergarten* carried the improved firepower of a four-barrelled *Vierling* anti-aircraft weapon and two twin-barrelled 2cm cannons mounted on the platform above. The deck gun, superfluous to requirements at that stage of the war and in danger of overweighting the boat with the increased conning tower weaponry, had been removed. It was not just the boat's appearance that had changed, but also the manner in which the crew were assembled for departure. Now all but those essential inside were ordered on deck wearing life jackets and kneeling, felt to afford the majority of the crew their greatest chance of survival if mined.

3 July: Three boats put to sea from Lorient for a new and untried battleground. Kaptlt. Helmuth Pich's *U168*, KK Heinrich Schäfer's *U183* and FK Ottoheinrich Junker's *U532* all left as part of the *Monsun* group, their destination the Indian Ocean and ultimately Penang.[142] None of the three had experienced much success recently, smarting from severe treatment handed out by Allied escort and ASW forces during May and June.

In total eleven U-boats sailed from France as part of *Monsun*, the majority Type IXDs of the 12th U-Flotilla. Their committment to the Far East was a continuation of OKM proposals from 1941, although at that time Dönitz expressed little enthusiasm for a relocation of U-boat strength. Flushed with the apparent ease in which the Imperial Japanese forces swept all before it, Tokyo also had no desire for German 'trespassing' on their sphere of influence.

But by 1943 all had changed for both powers. Japan had suffered the humiliation of Midway and stagnation on all fronts, as well as the first setbacks in China and the Solomon Islands. German defeat in the Atlantic forced an opening of the new combat zones before ASW capabilities in the Far East improved. Furthermore, U-boats shuttling between France and the Far East could continue the valuable work of blockade-running, now virtually impossible by surface ship.

The 12th U-Flotilla's *U178* left Bordeaux for Penang as *Monsun*'s spearhead. Once in Malaysia the boat's commander, FK Wilhelm Dommes, would become *Chef im Südraum*, leader of the Far Eastern U-boat presence, coordinating the establishment of German bases, work already begun by Admiral Wenneker, Naval Attaché in Tokyo. Wenneker's relationship with *Sho-sho* (Rear Admiral) Ichioka Hisashi, commander of the local Eighth

---

[142] The group was so named because they were timed to arrive in the Far East at the end of the monsoon season.

Submarine Group of the Imperial Japanese Navy, was excellent and during spring 1943 Batavia (Jakarta) and Singapore were made ready for loading and clearing German blockade-running U-boats, while the small island of Penang off Malaya's west coast would be used by combat boats between patrols. There was a base established at Georgetown's former Imperial Airways seaplane installation and soon the *Monsun* boats began to tie up to Swettenham Pier, a safe sheltered harbour on the north-eastern promontory of the island of Penang (*Pulau Pinang*). As Jürgen Oesten later wrote of his experiences there:

"Relations with the Japanese were reasonably good. We were the only white people running around free, this was a bit of a problem as the Japanese had established a kind of 'racial war' in order to improve their position with the native population."[143]

The Type IXC-40 U-boats of the 2nd U-Flotilla did not have the extreme range that their larger IXD cousins did, so a system of refuelling was organized for their voyage from France, their first refuelling stop being with a *Milch kuh* before reaching Cape Horn. Later two German tankers were available for resupply within the Indian Ocean, the 7,474-ton *Charlotte Schliemann*, finally free of its cage in the Canary Islands, and the larger 9,925-ton *Brake*. It was a complicated schedule and one vulnerable to attack.

As the three 2nd U-Flotilla boats headed southwards toward their first refuelling, aircraft from USS *Core* attacked and sank *U467*, the Type XIV earmarked for their resupply. Furthermore, the emergency replacement, a Type IXC sent from Bordeaux, was also sunk by *Core*'s aircraft. An extremely complex reshuffling of U-boats both to and from the Americas was made by Dönitz which resulted in the *Monsun* boats receiving their diesel after days of uncomfortable milling about in the refuelling zone. By the time that the replenishing was complete the eleven-strong *Monsun* group had been whittled down to five by marauding enemy aircraft, all three 2nd U-Flotilla boats among the survivors.

But *Monsun* was not the only group to suffer. On 13 July *U43*, the oldest Type IX in service, sailed from Lorient bound for minelaying off Lagos. Oblt.z.S. Hans-Joachim Schwantke sailed his aged boat from France with twelve TMB mines, south-west of the Azores by the month's end and on track for Nigeria. Meeting with the smaller Type VIIC *U403*, also bound for West Africa, in order to transfer fuel from the larger U-boat, the two sailed in tandem on the surface as they prepared to begin fuel transfer. An Avenger-Wildcat team from the carrier USS *Santee*, acting as distant escort for convoy UGS10, sighted the pair and immediately attacked, the U-boats blundering by immediately diving. *U43* was peppered with machine-gun fire before a single Fido homing torpedo was launched into the surface eddies left behind the submerging boat. Within seconds an enormous explosion, probably the sympathetic detonation of stored mines, rent the Atlantic swell and *U43* with its fifty-six crewmen vanished forever.

Kaptlt. Müller-Stöckheim's *U67* also received short shrift from American carrier-borne aircraft. Abandoning attempts to enter the Caribbean due to a faulty Metox set, Müller-Stockheim instead cruised between Puerto Rico and Bermuda while awaiting replacement equipment. Finally, after ten weeks at sea, *U572* supplied a substitute Metox, although by then fuel and supplies aboard *U67* were dangerously low and Müller-Stockheim faced an empty-handed return to France. However, *U67*'s uneventful return was interrupted on 16 July by aircraft from USS *Core*, the carrier given freedom of action while distant escort for Gibraltar convoys. Streaking into the attack a single Avenger surprised the inattentive

---

[143] Correspondence with Jürgen Oesten, 15 June 2002.

bridge watch, headed by the IWO Oblt.z.S. Walter Otto, and dropped four well-placed depth charges. The resultant explosions pitched one of the four lookouts into the sea, the remainder suddenly flailing in the water as *U67* disappeared below them at a 45° angle, air streaming from the open hatch as the remaining forty-eight crewmen remained trapped inside the doomed U-boat. Later that day USS *McCormick*, part of the carrier's escort screen, fished Otto and two others from the sea, *U67*'s only survivors.

27 July: *U129* sailed from Lorient, desperately pushed into service as a U-tanker, a role it would fulfil with the resupply of seven boats south-west of the Azores. The Allied assault on the *Milch kühe* was beginning to hit home and as *U504* also sailed from Lorient, KK Wilhelm Luis' boat rendezvoused with two U-tankers from Bordeaux shortly after clearing the coastline and heading south. *U461* and *U462* were sailing under destroyer escort augmented by a *Sperrbrecher*, six minesweepers and (increasingly rare) air cover from six KG40 Junkers Ju88s. The German procession sailed through Biscay, the formidable escort finally departing on 29 July at 2300hrs. Staying surfaced, the three U-boats continued with flak weapons manned, Metox searching for any sign of incoming enemy aircraft. They had not long to wait.

The next morning a Coastal Commander Liberator of 53 Squadron, engaged on a 'Musketry' patrol, sighted the three surfaced boats and began to shadow, keeping well out of range of the swivelling AA guns. Next a 228 Squadron Sunderland arrived, briefly fired on before also dodging out of range. However, the appearance of a single Ju88 caused the Sunderland to jettison depth charges and evade, reducing the enemy again to the single Liberator. Soon a 210 Squadron Catalina, acting as distant escort for Captain Walker's veteran 2nd Escort Group, joined the Liberator. Walker's group had been attached to the Coastal Command offensive, working in tandem with the aircraft and they immediately altered course towards the reported sighting. The group comprised HMS *Woodpecker*, *Wild Goose*, *Wren*, *Starling* and *Kite*, with heavy cruiser HMS *Scylla* in support should they brush with German destroyers. Aboard *U461* Kaptlt. Wolf Stiebler was only too aware of the threat and frantically radioed for air cover. Nine Junker Ju88 fighter-bombers were ordered to help, but they had insufficient fuel for the task. The three boats were on their own.

By 1115hrs a second Liberator, from USAAF 19 Squadron, had arrived, joined by the Sunderland that had successfully shaken its Junkers pursuit. A fourth aircraft, a 502 Squadron Halifax, also made contact with the Germans and watched in dismay as they circled menacingly anti-clockwise. Unbeknown to the Germans there was considerable confusion above them as the aircraft tried to coordinate attacks, all using separate radio frequencies. It would take minutes before they began to communicate coherently. Two more aircraft were arriving, another 502 Squadron Halifax and a 461 Squadron Sunderland, when the initial Halifax opened the assault.

Flying Officer W.S. Biggar raced in to attack, flak exploding all around as he released three 600lb bombs wide of the mark, cannon shells ripping through his fuselage while the bomber's machine gunners flayed the U-boat's decks. By then the second Halifax had arrived and Flying Officer van Rossum made his attack run. At 3,000 feet he overflew *U462*, sailing on the port quarter. Dropping single 600lb AS bombs, the Halifax made two passes in the teeth of heavy and concentrated flak, severely damaging the U-tanker with his second pass, *U462* slewing to a halt belching smoke and sinking. The spell now broke and the remaining aircraft launched their own assaults. *U461* was next, by now Stiebler having received orders to separate and attempt individual escape. But *U461* was squarely bracketed by Flight Lieutenant D. Marrows' 461 Squadron Sunderland, machine-gun fire cutting down several of the U-boat's flak gunners, enabling the flying boat to depth-charge *U461*, disappearing in a haze of spray and smoke and sinking with all but fifteen of her crew.

By this stage the bombers were suffering from severe flak damage, one Liberator forced to sheer away and make for Portugal where its crew was later interned. KK Luis' *U504* continued to put up a fierce wall of flak when the unexpected splashes of heavy artillery fell nearby. Walker's 2nd Escort Group was now less than five miles distant and had opened fire. The aircraft, having sunk the two valuable tankers, took the opportunity to break off their action and leave it to Walker, *U504* using the pause to submerge and attempt underwater escape. At 1234hrs Walker's HMS *Kite* made ASDIC contact and soon began hours of creeping depth charge-attacks. By mid-afternoon oil, debris and pieces of torn flesh were found on the surface and Luis and his fifty-two men were confirmed dead. For the first time British Biscay forces had eliminated an entire U-boat group.

The ensuing days saw one more 2nd U-Flotilla boat sent to the bottom of Biscay. On 28 July Oblt.z.S. Wolf-Dietrich Damerow, former IWO on *U521*, sailed for his first cruise as commander of the veteran *U106*. After beginning the voyage in company with *U107*, the two separated once free of Lorient's coast and Damerow traced the now standard outbound course above northern Spain in an attempt to avoid unwelcome attention. It was a forlorn hope and on 2 August, after successfully fending off one aircraft attack, a Canadian Wellington of 407 Squadron badly damaged *U106*, forcing Damerow to effect temporary repairs before aborting to France. Radioing his position to BdU, three torpedo boats (*T22*, *T24* and *T25*) from Bordeaux were despatched to provide escort, four Junker Ju88s also being assigned to the rescue mission. Three light destroyers had been engaged in exercises off Concarneau when sent on an abortive rescue mission for Kaptlt. Horst Kremser's damaged *U383* of Brest's 9th U-Flotilla. On arrival at the scene, the circling torpedo boats found no trace of her save for a large patch of floating oil south-west of Fastnet. However, they were well placed for their second errand of mercy and immediately fired boilers for full speed to the next disaster scene.

Aboard the crippled *U106*, sailing at periscope depth, hydrophones picked up the three torpedo boats' propellers searching for them. But, to Damerow's dismay they appeared to swerve away to the north and he was forced to surface, running in pursuit. This proved his undoing and *U106* was soon sighted by a 228 Squadron Sunderland, which had been shadowing the torpedo boats three miles to the north-west. Approaching this more profitable target, Flying Officer R.D. Hanbury tried to close *U106*, but received a wall of flak forcing him to break away and circle out of range. Shortly a second 461 (RAAF) Squadron Sunderland arrived and the two began an alternating series of depth-charge and strafing attacks.

"On reaching favourable positions they attack from each bow, with blazing guns. . . . The port engine-room switchboard is torn from its mountings and catches fire. The starboard diesel stops. Thick smoke fills the boat which lists to port with a bad leak. Fire minutes later the aircraft return to the attack . . . bombs fall very close and cause further damage. The port diesel also stops. Both electric motors are out of action. The boat is out of control and settles appreciably by the stern because of the inrush of water. Chlorine gas is coming from the batteries. At 2008hrs [sixteen minutes after the attacks began] a third attack is made and since casualties among the gun crews have been replaced with non-gunnery ratings, our fire is less accurate.

The aircraft, engaging with all her guns, drops four bombs which detonate about ten metres away."[144]

It was the end for *U106* and, after confirmation that she was going down from *Leutnant* (Ing.) Johann Gruber, Damerow ordered her abandoned. As men raced to the deck to jump overboard, several also attempted to man the guns again, but were cut down by machine-gun fire. In short order, after Damerow and his remaining crew were adrift clutching debris and four small dinghies, *U106* exploded inside and slid under stern first, cheered by her surviving crew. Their work done, the two aircraft flew for home, broadcasting the position of the approaching torpedo boats for other aircraft. Although later attacked unsuccessfully by a Coastal Command Halifax, the three warships rescued thirty-six survivors of *U106*, including Damerow still clutching the boat's KTB. Slipping through a gathering net of Royal Navy destroyers, they set course for France. After landing, *U106*'s crew were transported back to Lorient where Damerow, severely wounded during the battle, was immediately hospitalized. There he died on 21 May 1944.

Its sister ship destroyed, *U107* ploughed onwards to the United States, briefly brushing with a 502 Squadron Halifax that emerged from cloud to find *U107* straight ahead. This time luck was with the U-boat as the Halifax dived in for an immediate depth-charge attack that inflicted no real damage. By the time the Halifax had swung around for a second pass its quarry had crash-dived.

Losses to aircraft in July and early August during the 'Seaslug' and 'Musketry' offensives shocked Dönitz who immediately recalled all boats that had sailed at the beginning of August. Coastal Command's impressive results had seen twenty-five anti-submarine squadrons launch attacks against fifty-five of the eighty-six U-boats transiting Biscay between 1 July and 2 August. Of those attacked, sixteen were sunk by aircraft, *U504*, the seventeenth, destroyed by 2nd Escort Group. Dönitz cancelled all further group sailings across Biscay, ordering U-boats to proceed submerged except when recharging batteries. Incoming boats were ordered to hug the Spanish coast (ignoring the issue of territorial waters) before reaching France and heading northward to their home ports. Dönitz had been defeated again. Flexible British tactics had overwhelmed his policy of fighting the aircraft with massed flak weaponry. Aircraft would accumulate before attacking, dividing the flak between them and lessening its impact. If unable to breach the U-boats' defences they could circle and call on naval support. Any attempt to submerge in the face of Royal Navy warships would render submarines defenceless to air attack for the vital seconds it took to clear the bridge and dive. It was a virtually unwinnable situation for the Germans.

Furthermore Dönitz believed (erroneously) that he had found the reason for successful night-time location of U-boats by enemy aircraft. Following a casual (and possibly calculated) remark from a captured Allied airman that Metox radiation could be tracked, Dönitz instigated tests with Luftwaffe aircraft flying experimental sorties around several Metox receivers on the French coast. They found that Metox did indeed radiate, the impulses detectable at a range of up to fifty kilometres. Metox use was thus severely curtailed as of 13 August, only to be used in poor visibility and immediately switched off if impulses were detected. Dönitz and his staff suffered from a rigidity of thinking and their final conclusions were wrong, the secret of airborne centimetric radar, against which Metox was useless, continuing to elude them. Meanwhile new radar search receivers emerged from the

[144] Extract from *U106* KTB, *Conflict over the Bay*, p. 215.

Hagenuk Company's factory, the W.Anz G.I (*Wellenanzeiger*) ordered immediately fitted to all U-boats preparing to sail. *Wanze* (this nickname, 'Bedbug', replacing the official designation of FuMB-9) was a more sophisticated set than Metox, automatically scanning the 120cm to 180cm radar frequencies using a 'round dipole' antenna comprising two small dipoles mounted on a pressure-resistant mesh-enclosed cylinder. *U161* was the first U-boat to put to sea carrying the new apparatus.

Dönitz again stressed to his superiors the urgent need for fighter support, pushing for reinforcement of the Luftwaffe's Atlantic forces. This time his requests were treated sympathetically and on 5 August twin-engine Messerschmitt Me110 fighters flew in to Kerlin-Bastard's pitted and scarred runway, soon joined by the far superior Focke Wulf FW190 fighters. The Luftwaffe finally caused some hindrance to Coastal Command's monopoly over Biscay, sixteen ASW bombers and six RAF fighters being shot down during the rest of August. But it was too little too late – the damage had been done to the western U-boats.

8 August: Kaptlt. Albrecht Achilles' *U161* sailed from Lorient, passing safely from Biscay along the Spanish coast, reaching the Atlantic and heading south-west. The safe passage of his and other boats was taken as vindication of both the *Wanze* search receiver and Dönitz's new instructions, no U-boats lost in Biscay during August as they surfaced only at night amid the radar clutter of the Spanish coastline. Before beginning his mission proper Achilles was ordered to rendezvous with incoming Japanese blockade-running submarine *I8* south of the Azores, approaching France under the code name '*Flieder*' (Lilac). After successfully meeting with *I8* and transferring two Kriegsmarine officers with a *Wanze* receiver to her by dinghy, Achilles set course for Brazil.[145]

1 September: A battered *U66* crept into Lorient, the crew relieved to have landfall once more. The patrol had begun promisingly, slipping from port in company with two Type VIIC boats. After clearing Biscay and passing the Azores *U66* thundered onward toward the Americas, surfaced with experienced watch keepers aware of the threat posed by VLR aircraft.

Until 10 June *U66* had experienced no success in attack until the crump of an exploding torpedo marked the end of tanker MV *Esso Gettysburg*, on course for Charleston. A frantic aerial search ensued for the assailant, an airship seen by periscope hovering overhead as *U66* crept away at dusk. Sailing eastward, Kaptlt. Markworth sank a second tanker with artillery and torpedo attack on 2 July, not hitting his third target until three weeks later when he damaged the turbine tanker *Cherry Valley* with a spread of three torpedoes. Although badly hit, the tanker's guns fired on *U66* as it surfaced to administer an artillery *coup-de-grâce*. Markworth glided away submerged, anxious not to spend too long in one place for the benefit of American air and sea searchers. By then he had received news to lighten spirits aboard *U66*, awarded the Knight's Cross on 8 July.

---

[145] *I8* arrived in Lorient at month's end carrying quinine and an extra crew of forty-eight sailors destined to man the brand new *U1224* and pilot her back to Japan, a gift from the Führer. It had been a sixty-one-day voyage for the overloaded submarine. *I8* moved from Lorient to Brest in September 1943. For their return home they embarked torpedoes, aircraft engines, AA guns and 10 German advisors. *Tai-sa* Uchino sailed his submarine into Japanese waters in December 1943.

By mid-July fuel and supplies were running low and with little U-tanker support *U66* began her return to France, remaining submerged for the most part due to heavy air cover south of Bermuda. Markworth had a planned refuelling rendezvous with *U117*, betrayed to the Americans by ULTRA decryption of radio messages flashed from BdU to *U117*. With the meeting position compromised, it was only a matter of time before *U66* was found and on 3 August at 2018hrs an Avenger-Wildcat team from USS *Card* sighted *U66*, the Wildcat immediately strafing the surfaced boat. As heavy-calibre bullets smashed through decking and conning tower three men were killed almost instantly, IIWO Oblt.z.S. Kurt Schütze and *Matrosengefreiter* Erich Lorentz dead before they hit the ground, *Mechanikergefreiter* Heinz Nitsch wounded, dying soon after. Markworth ordered guns manned as the Avenger swept towards his boat preparing to drop depth charges and a Fido. In heavy flak the attack miscarried, the Avenger hurtling overhead and strafing *U66*, claiming more victims. Markworth was hit in the stomach and IWO Oblt.z.S. Klaus Herbig received agonising bullets in his knees. A *Fähnrich* had suffered a chest wound while another man had his entire heel blown away by the attacking aircraft. With four others lightly wounded, *U66* seized the brief opportunity to dive and escape. Too late the Avenger managed to drop its weapon load, causing heavy damage but not the killing blow.

The boat was in bad shape when it resurfaced later that day beneath an empty sky. Reporting their situation to BdU, they doubted their ability to reach France and requested urgent assistance. On 6 August *U66* met *U117* in early morning darkness on 7 August, starting the refuelling process by which it would receive ten cubic metres of diesel and provisions. *U117*'s IWO Oblt.z.S. Paul Frerks went aboard *U66* to assume temporary command, accompanied by the Type XB's medical officer, MStA Dr Schrenk, who treated the badly wounded men. As dawn stained the eastern horizon another *Card* Wildcat-Avenger team found the two boats, the oil transfer was interrupted and hoses hurriedly cast off as Frerks ordered *U66* dived. A hasty Fido attack missed *U66* as it submerged safely, but for *U117* there was no escape. Despite fierce flak two further American double teams arrived and the large minelayer was obliterated after repeated attacks. Frerks and Schrenk aboard Markworth's boat were the only survivors from *U117*. The remainder of *U66*'s return journey was mercifully uneventful, ending in the Scorff bunker on 1 September opposite the burnt-out shell of the Saltzwedel Caserne. By now Lorient was deserted and off limits to all but German and Vichy military personnel and *Organisation Todt* workers. Markworth had sailed his last voyage aboard *U66*, relieved by Oblt.z.S. Gerhard Seehausen, posted to command the 23rd U-training Flotilla after his stay in hospital.[146]

During the rest of September the 2nd U-Flotilla's boats that had been recalled to Lorient began to put to sea again. *U68* sailed on 8 September, followed ten days later by *U103* and *U505*. Unfortunately for Kaptlt. Peter Zschech and *U505*'s crew it was once more a short-lived cruise, more mechanical difficulties rendering *U505* unserviceable and arriving in Lorient on the last day of September. The dispirited crew recalled a change in their unpopular commander, his fragile emotional state sagging in a slough of despondency. Zschech became the subject of rumours regarding his courage and competence and what confidence he had once possessed evaporated completely.

---

[146] Paul Frerks later commander *U975*, surviving the war as a UAA instructor. The fate of *U117*'s Medical Officer is currently unknown to the author.

3 October: Oblt.z.S. Volker Simmermacher brought *U107* into Lorient. Following the end of its last below-par voyage, Kaptlt. Harald Gelhaus had taken a well-earned transfer to a staff position in OKM, Simmermacher promoted from IWO to captain, his first patrol a moderate success. After brushing with a Halifax bomber in Biscay, *U107* continued an uneventful passage to the United States, his cargo of twelve TMB mines destined for the bottom of Charleston harbour, South Carolina. While following the coastline south Simmermacher sighted the Liberty ship SS *Albert Gallatin* and made a textbook attack, striking the merchant's side with one of three torpedoes fired. Expecting the dull roar of an exploding warhead, Simmermacher and his crew were aggravated to hear the unmistakable clank of an unexploded torpedo. Dispirited, *U107* slunk away to continue its primary mission, the enemy alerted to his presence, hounding the unwelcome intruder.[147]

U107 successfully penetrated Charleston harbour during the night of 4 September, laying its minefield before retreating to safety while the cylindrical killers activated. It was, however, a wasted effort. British minesweeper *J967* triggered one of the weapons sixteen days later betraying the field's presence, the remainder safely swept. *U107* launched a final attack before slogging home, but US Navy tanker *Rapidan* escaped unscathed. It was a modest end to the tour of duty, but they had at last reached Lorient despite fears for their safety after little communication from Simmermacher.

Elsewhere, on the same day that Simmermacher put her into Lorient *U183*, the first of the 2nd U-Flotilla *Monsun* boats, arrived in Penang. Despite high expectations of fresh merchant slaughter in the Indian Ocean, Kaptlt. Heinrich Schäfer had sunk nothing during the seventeen-week voyage. After successfully refueling from *Brake* on 11 September near Mauritius, *U183* had cruised between the Seychelles and Kenya, sighting little. The few attacks mounted by Schäfer had resulted in eight electric torpedoes either missing their targets or malfunctioning. Conditions had been demanding for both men and machinery. German battery-powered torpedoes suffered enormously from the effects of tropical humidity, resulting in extremely unreliable performance. Likewise the boats' batteries, built to withstand relatively temperate climates, had also deteriorated, while diesels suffered from excessive exhaust temperatures, using large amounts of lubricating oil and requiring constant nursing. For the men there was insufficient on-board refrigeration with the corresponding spoilage of fresh food during the long crossing. U-boats possessed no air-cooling system aboard and the interiors became like a hot sticky oven, crews suffering from not having acclimatized to the new environment. Skin infections were rampant as *U183* finally eased into harbour on Penang, the bearded Germans reeling on sea-legs as they took their first steps on terra firma for several months. The frustrating voyage had strained Schäfer and he was transferred from the boat's command into a local personnel reserve pool.[148]

Schäfer's was the only complete failure of the three 2nd Flotilla boats. *U532* arrived in Penang on the last day of October, followed by *U168* on 11 November. Kaptlt. Ottoheinrich Junker had dispatched four freighters during his voyage by combined torpedo and artillery attacks, while Kaptlt. Helmuth Pich's *U168* had sunk a single

---

[147] SS *Albert Gallatin* was later sunk by *I26* in the Indian Ocean.
[148] Schäfer was later placed in command of the commandeered Italian boat *Reginaldo Guiliani*, renamed *UIT23* by the Kriegsmarine, but died on 8 January 1944. His last command succeeded him by little over a month, sunk by HMS *Tally Ho* on 15 February.

confirmed freighter and six cargo sailboats. Pich had also been on the receiving end of a brief but uncomfortably close depth-charging from an unidentified Catalina as he attempted to close the only convoy spotted, driven under and losing contact.[149]

However, there was little that FK Ernst Kals in distant Lorient could do for his boats in the Far East. Somewhat illogically the three *Monsun* boats from his unit would remain on strength of the 2nd U-Flotilla until September 1944 when they were transferred to the newly established 33rd U-Flotilla.

The idea that the *Monsun* boats would open a full-scale offensive in the Arabian Sea never fully materialized. Allied intelligence had monitored their progress as they passed South Africa, Enigma decrypts providing a virtual step-by-step track chart of the German submarines. Convoys had largely been diverted away from the cruising threat, minimizing what little impact they could have had. Cooperation with Japanese forces was patchy at best and in total the Far Eastern boats achieved little in the face of nominal Allied ASW measures. Their various missions undertaken from Malay a failed significantly to hamper merchant traffic, although large Type IXD U-cruisers of the 12th U-Flotilla continued to be sent to the area in vain pursuit of promising rewards. Likewise, the transport of raw materials back to Europe by U-boat also proved unsuccessful, few reaching Europe again. In total the 2nd U-Flotilla despatched four U-boats to the region. None would return to France, passing from the flotilla ranks during September 1944, only one surviving to the war's end.

4 October: The first of three reinforcement Type IXC-40 boats for the 2nd U-Flotilla put out from Trondheim after nearly a month in Norway. AG Weser's *U841* sailed under command of twenty-six-year-old Kaptlt. Werner Bender, former IWO for Albrecht Achilles on board *U161*. Bender left Norway under a cloud. The boat's popular IIWO, L.z.S. Ernst Huffmann (son of Knight's Cross holder *Generalleutnant* Helmuth Huffmann), had committed suicide before departure after Gestapo agents found 'secret documents', including keys to the Enigma, in his hotel room. The next day KK Wolfgang Heller's *U842* sailed from Bergen, *U843* following from Kiel on 7 October. The latter boat was also commanded by an ex-IWO, Kaptlt. Oskar Herwartz having served four months aboard *U67* in the second half of 1942 after transferring from the Luftwaffe.

For two of the departing newcomers their careers were brief and brutal. Ordered from Norway to the North Atlantic, both *U841* and *U842* joined the *Schlieffen* patrol line east-south-east of Cape Farewell. Contrary to the policy of not using Type IX boats in the North Atlantic, the three new 2nd U-Flotilla boats were cast into the maelstrom, their heavy and impressive anti-aircraft firepower making them valuable assets. By the time that

---

[149] Among the more bizarre additions to the *Monsun* boats' on-board armoury was the Focke-Achgelis Fa 330A-1, *Bachstelze* (Wagtail). This one-man three-bladed powerless rotor kite was designed to be towed aloft by a moving U-boat in order to extend the visible horizon to search for targets. While not in service the Fa 330 was stored in two metal tubes built into the conning tower, one tube containing the blades and tail, the other holding the fuselage. The Fa 330 took to the skies from a small platform attached to the *Wintergarten* railing, trailing a tow cable. The pilot, often the U-boat's medical officer, communicated with the submarine via a basic interphone system. When the pilot was ready to land, the Fa 330 was simply winched back aboard. However, should the U-boat come under attack the pilot was obliged to jettison the tow-cable and deploy a parachute, awaiting the later return of the U-boat to rescue him. Results from use of the *Bachstelze* were uninspiring.

U841 received orders to fight its way through to ONS20, located on 16 October, destroyer and aircraft attacks were already pounding the attackers. On 17 October *U841* was found by Lend-Lease destroyer escort HMS *Byard* which blasted it to the surface with ten depth charges. As cannons mauled the crippled German, killing many men as they emerged from the conning tower, Bender was seen on the battered superstructure brandishing a pistol and firing it at the British destroyer. Austrian Hermann Ptacovsky began waving a small white flag in surrender and, giving way to the inevitable, Bender ordered *U841* abandoned and scuttled.

> "One officer, five petty officers and twenty-one other ratings were picked up. . . . The officer, a young German of 23, whose wife was expecting her first baby that day, had swum over supporting a wounded man and was the only prisoner not distressed.
>
> "One dead Hun was a nuisance, for he had tied himself on the end of a rope and then proceeded to drown and get himself into the main circulating pump inlet where he was a source of annoyance until washed clear.
>
> "[Another] seemed to think he was about to be tortured and it was not until the Chief Stoker made motions threatening to put the Hun's head in the vice in the Engineer's workshop that he refrained from struggling."[150]

Bender was not among those rescued, going to his grave with the boat and twenty-four other crewmen. *U841* had lasted thirteen days in action. The sole British casualty of the skirmish was a sentry who managed to shoot himself through the foot while guarding the prisoners.

U842 outlasted its sister ship by nearly three weeks. *Korvettenkapitän* Wolfgang Heller also took part in the disastrous *Schlieffen* attack before they were cancelled after six U-boats were lost for a single merchant. Heller was then assigned to *Siegfried*, 500 miles east of Newfoundland. Successfully avoided by convoy traffic, the group was dissolved, its boats reformed into two separate packs, *Jahn* and *Körner*, the former including *U842*, while newly arrived *U843* was in the latter.

On 3 November Heller's *U842* was assigned to one of five smaller sub-groups, numbered *Tirpitz 1* to 5. Among their opposition was Captain Walker's legendary 2nd Escort Group, alerted by an aircraft sighting of *U842* and racing toward Heller. Making swift ASDIC contact, a brief depth-charge attack from Walker's HMS *Starling* followed, but with no result, HMS *Wild Goose* then being ordered to prepare a creeping attack. But *Wild Goose* mishandled the attack, only dropping some of the planned depth charges and Walker berated the hapless sloop's commander for his poor performance. As the tirade continued by radio a large underwater explosion was detected, followed moments later by upwelling oil, splintered wooden wreckage and human remains. *U842* and her fifty-six crewmen had perished.

The last of the trio, *U843*, emerged intact. Pressed into four more unsuccessful wolf packs, Kaptlt. Oskar Herwatz finally staggered into Lorient on 15 December. By then the flotilla was inundated with reports of other casualties, among them Werner Bender's mentor, the celebrated Albrecht Achilles. *U161* was missing presumed lost as of 8 October after failing to report for nearly two weeks. Achilles had sailed to Brazil after his August rendezvous with *I8*, sinking three ships and reporting successes on 26 September. The

---

150 *Afloat and Ashore with the Fourth Escort Group*, document in the U-boat Archiv.

following day *U161* was sighted and attacked by a Mariner aircraft of VP74 250 miles west of Bahia. Damaged by accurate flak from the U-boat, the Mariner nonetheless made two strafing runs, dropping depth charges on both passes. As the pilot, Lt H.B. Patterson, nursed his crippled aircraft away from the scene he radioed for further support, a USN Ventura arriving at the reported position soon afterwards. There was no trace of *U161* and Achilles and his men were never heard from again.

7 November: Six 2nd U-Flotilla boats had put to sea during the first week of November, veterans *U129*, *U505*, *U193* and *U190* from France and new transfers *U538* and *U801* from Germany. Like many before and after it, Kaptlt. Johann-Egbert Gossler's *U538* survived only briefly in action. Gossler, former IWO on *U125*, was detected while sailing to join the *Schill* group west of Spain. Escort sloop HMS *Crane*, from combined convoy MKS30/LS139, charged into the attack with depth-charge salvoes. Joined by frigate HMS *Foley*, the two warships pounded the intermittent target until finally producing wreckage from *U538* and pieces of her crew.

The grim state of the 2nd U-Flotilla was not lightened by the return of two boats on Sunday 7 November, both entering port under Luftwaffe protection. *U123* eased into Kéroman III claiming unconfirmed torpedo hits on a Liberty ship and tanker east of the Windward Isles in late September. Those fleeting 'successes' were followed by the award of the German Cross in Gold to *Obersteuermann* Walter Kaeding on 6 September for his service with the boat since its commissioning in 1940. *U123*, the boat that had opened the war against America, milled aimlessly around the Western Atlantic fringe before Oblt.z.S. von Schroeter took her home to France. While crossing Biscay on 7 November a 248 Squadron Mosquito armed with the heavy-calibre 57mm gun attacked the surfaced boat and killed one man, wounding two others before von Schroeter submerged to shelter from the heavy weapon, the damaged boat shepherded into port by two torpedo boats and a fighter-bomber umbrella. Worse still, *U505* arrived after less than a month at sea that had resulted in depth charges, damage and suicide.

Kaptlt. Peter Zschech left Lorient on 9 October *U505*, edging through and refusing to surface any more than absolutely necessary even once in the Atlantic proper. At 100 metres the boat skulked silently onwards, ambient water pressure disallowing use of the WC, the stinking contents of a bucket adding to the miserable conditions.

On 24 October a distant tattoo of exploding charges moved surreptitiously nearer until at 1948hrs the hydrophone operator reported engine noise. Zschech, brooding behind the green curtain that sealed off his commander's bunk and virtually absent during the voyage, finally emerged into the control room. He appeared ashen, eyes glassy as he walked silently to the ladder and ascended into the conning tower that housed the periscopes. His men were puzzled. At that depth there was no chance of using the scope and no orders had been forthcoming from Zschech. His IWO, Oblt.z.S. Paul Meyer, hovered below the open hatch, virtually begging for instructions as propellers swished overhead, audible to the naked ear as the probing fingers of ASDIC played over the boat. They had been located and soon the sound of large canisters were reported hitting the surface far above, drifting silently downward before exploding. On *U505* all hell broke loose. Lights blew and shards of glass flew through the air, loose objects joining the mess on the steel floor plates.

> "Finally, Zschech came down the ladder. . . . His expressionless face, illuminated by the fluorescent paint on the air ducts, was ghostly white. We all stared at him, anticipating some orders for manoeuvres, but still he said nothing. Instead, he walked

zombie-like through the forward hatch into the radio room. As he passed me, I could see his wide-open unblinking eyes shine in the half light."*

The Allied warships circled above, unleashing their might onto the barely moving target. Amid the flying debris and cacophony inside *U505*, Zschech stood in the control room hatchway, slowly leaning over onto the decking. In the thunder of explosions and general confusion nobody realized the significance of a small bang until a gradually spreading pool of blood seeped from Zschech's head and the full horror of the moment gripped his crew. He had shot himself with his Walther service pistol.

The chief radio operator lifted the commander on to his cot. But Zschech clung to life. He had bungled the attempt and lay making grotesque noises from deep in his throat, the rattle of a slowly dying man. The boat still hammered by explosions, four strong hands pushed a pillow over their commander's face to hasten his demise. Peter Zschech, a man tormented by his own inner demons, was dead.

Oblt.z.S. Meyer immediately took command and finally gave the orders needed to survive. *Bold* capsules were fired from the *Pillenwerfer* and the boat sent into a series of evasive manoeuvres, the chemical cloud left behind successfully decoying the enemy as *U505* stole away to safety. Later, at 2129hrs when the sound of explosions was only a distant rumble, the War Diary received a brief entry, tragic epitaph for a troubled man:

"*Kommandant tot.* (Commander dead)."

U505 endured another accurate depth-charge attack that night before finally slipping away for good, surfacing to bury their commander at sea without ceremony or remorse. The majority of the crew, whom Zschech had ridden mercilessly, felt that he had abandoned them when they had been in most need of firm command. There was no mourning aboard *U505* as it radioed its situation to Lorient and trekked home once more.

The German U-boat effort was sliding further downhill since the withdrawal of forces from the Atlantic. New weaponry continued to be the hook on which Dönitz hung all hopes. *Wanze's* lifespan was brief. Although immediately after its introduction Biscay sinkings had declined, this was as much due to a scarcity of U-boat presence and reduced Coastal Command activity as to any protection from radar. On 20 September aircraft surprised *U386* without any *Wanze* warning, further unheralded attacks soon following. The new receiver still failed to cover centimetric wavelengths and was as useless as Metox. On 5 November Dönitz banned its use, issuing the primitive stopgap FuMB-10 'Borkum' set that emitted shrill beeps when scanned by radar, although it gave no directional information. Germany had long since lost the electronics war.

After the introduction of *Wanze* had come the much-lauded *Zaunkönig* acoustic torpedo. The Kriegsmarine had developed the FAT and LUT looping torpedoes in answer to the problem of unguided and long-distance attacks against merchant columns, but now they possessed an anti-warship torpedo. In early 1943 the relatively unsuccessful and short-lived *Falke* acoustic torpedo had entered service, but it was not until the *Zaunkönig* that the U-boat service truly believed they had found the answer to enemy destroyers, its guidance system tuned to the pitch of escort propellers. Designated T5, the *Zaunkönig* was first available in August 1943. With a maximum range of 5,750 metres the torpedo had a limited speed of 24.5 knots (slower than 1939's torpedoes). Its velocity had been reduced due to noise produced by faster passage through water interfering with the acoustical guidance

* Goebeler, p. 175

system, the jewel of the T5. Enthusiasm for the torpedo was rampant as U-boat officers witnessed night-time demonstrations in the Baltic, the warheads replaced by luminous nose cones that homed unerringly on the stern of a twisting target ship.

However, there were two serious flaws that would only later become apparent. The *Zaunkönig* had a short arming range, only 250 metres, meaning that in order not to become a target itself the firing U-boat had to dive deep immediately after release. Correspondingly, in the months to come frequent successes were reported by submerged captains as their torpedo exploded after a reasonable run, without any further corroboration of a hit. The second problem, related to the first, was that the Allies knew all about the torpedo's development and had already engineered the 'Foxer' decoy towed behind warships to attract the *Zaunkönig*'s attention away from its intended target. Described variously by puzzled submariners as approximately the noise of a "circular saw, a continuous gnawing or the rattle of a DKW engine" the 'Foxer' if properly deployed would negate the effectiveness of an already dubiously efficient weapon.

But in late 1943 these problems still lay in the future and on 9 November *Obermechaniker* Reinecke gave a short lecture course on maintenance of the T5 in Lorient, enthusiastically attended by all available technical personnel of the 2nd U-Flotilla.

16 November: Kaptlt. Volker Simmermacher eased *U107* out of St Nazaire where it had been undergoing four days' installation of heavy flak weaponry. After leaving the Loire *U107* nosed out towards the Atlantic. Simmermacher was headed for the *Weddigen* group west of Portugal, hunting American convoys supplying the Allied armies now advancing up the boot of Italy.

As Simmermacher's boat battered through Biscay towards its patrol area the 2nd U-Flotilla lost yet another U-boat in a convoy battle. Kaptlt. Rolf Schauenburg's *U536* had been returning from a bizarre and unsuccessful rescue mission in Canada after sailing in late August. Code-named 'Operation Kiebitz' (Magpie), the plan was the brainchild of KK Otto Kretschmer, incarcerated in Bowmanville's Camp 30 on Canada's Lake Ontario. There Kretschmer and several other key U-boat officers grouped together in the self-titled 'Lorient Espionage Unit', preparing an ambitious escape attempt in which they intended to tunnel out of the camp and rendezvous with a U-boat.

> "I had an atlas that I got in England; it was a nice school atlas that we could only use to study the Canadian Atlantic shoreline.
>
> "At the point where the St. Lawrence empties into the sea, along the shores of its wide mouth, we located a large number of bays. One of them, called the Chaleur Bay, attracted our attention because of a cape that protruded into it and which would favour an escape. The cape was called Pointe Maisonnette.
>
> "We could easily reach Pointe Maisonnette in three or four days if walking conditions were the least bit favourable. . . . The critical part was convincing . . . Admiral Dönitz, to send us a submarine."[151]

The plan had been communicated to Dönitz using a simple code hidden in mail to Germany and BdU authorized the attempt to be made. In Bowmanville preparations began in earnest and as their tunnel inched beneath the wire messages continued to be sent to

---

[151] *Trop loin de Berlin. Des prisonniers Allemands au Canada (1939–1946)*, Yves Bernard and Caroline Bergeron, p. 216.

Germany providing Dönitz with progress reports. In August 1943 Dönitz received a prospective date for the breakout of four key prisoners, replying by code that a U-boat would be waiting for them, surfacing near Pointe Maisonnette for two hours every night over a two-week period beginning on 23 September. Kretschmer would have fourteen days to make his rendezvous.

Dönitz himself was conscious of the propaganda coup of a successful escape, the U-boat service still mourning Kretschmer's capture. At first BdU assigned the rendezvous to Brest's 1st U-Flotilla, but the assigned Type VIIC *U669* was sighted by an RCAF Wellington bomber and sent to the bottom with no survivors on 7 September. Dönitz radioed *U536*, his backup, on 12 September:

"Execute Operation Kiebitz, no amplification."

Schauenburg headed west, while the 'Lorient Espionage Unit' continued digging, their progress followed by RCMP personnel with microphones. Unbeknown to the Germans, Allied camp authorities had intercepted their coded mail and were fully aware of the scheme, seeing not only the chance to foil an attempted escape but perhaps net an operational U-boat into the bargain. Instructions, maps and forged material had been intercepted by the Canadian authorities, secreted within the covers of books sent to the German prisoners ostensibly from the Red Cross. Dissecting, photographing and then replacing the documents before passing them on, the assignation had been given away and *U536* sailed blithely unaware towards the waiting trap.

At first the Canadians made elaborate plans to let the prisoners escape and signal the waiting U-boat, before arresting them and sending a select team of commandos in order to capture it. Ideas for a German-speaking Canadian to impersonate a Wehrmacht general and assume command of the unwitting U-boat were mooted before sanity prevailed and British pleas to sink the U-boat were accepted. Code-named 'Operation Pointe Maisonnette', the Canadians planned their strategy.

But one week before the scheduled breakout disaster struck the German tunnellers. With nowhere to put excavated earth except into barrack roofs, wooden ceilings strained under the extra weight. One night heavy rainfall seeped through the tar-paper exterior into the compacted soil, a ceiling finally gave way, burying several prisoners beneath a landslide of glutinous mud. Guards, alerted by the noise, immediately saw the earth bulging from the windows. Faced with hard evidence, they set about searching for its source, no longer able to pretend ignorance. Scouring the camp, they deliberately failed to find the main tunnel, 'discovering' two decoys dug for that purpose. But the charade was short-lived. Only days later a German prisoner not privy to the escape plan unwittingly dug close to the boundary fence to fill his flower boxes with earth. Unexpectedly, the earth beneath his shovel gave way and he fell headlong into the third tunnel. The Canadians had no choice but to place the tunnellers under arrest.

However, faced with the failure of Kretschmer's plan, Kaptlt. Wolfgang Heyda, commander of *U434*, put forward his own simple scheme for a separate escape attempt. Basing his arguments on the expected presence of the German submarine off Canadian shores, Heyda convinced Kretschmer, the senior camp officer, to accept his proposal. His idea was basic, almost reckless. Provided with well-forged papers, including an Admiralty Pass, and dressed in civilian clothing, Heyda would scale a perimeter fence using home-made crampons. There he would climb into a jury-rigged bosun's chair and slide along nearby cables over the fence to freedom.

His daring plan went without hitch. A dummy took his place for the evening prisoner count on 24 September and after nightfall, taking advantage of a diversion orchestrated by other prisoners, Heyda left his hiding place, climbed the fence and launched himself to freedom. With no sign of pursuit, Heyda began his journey to the coast. He made his way by rail to Bathurst, New Brunswick, on 26 September before continuing on foot to Pointe Maisonnette. En route he was intercepted by a military patrol, but his false papers, civilian clothing and Admiralty pass, allowing him into the area to take geological samples, saved him. Finally he arrived at the rendezvous site and camped in an unobstrusive corner to await rescue.

In the meantime the Royal Canadian Navy formed a flotilla of ships to patrol the southern area of Chaleur Bay. On 25 September a destroyer, four corvettes, five minesweepers and Fairmile MTBs were assigned to blockade the bay. Combined with their daunting strength the RCN used a new camouflage technique to attempt some measure of stealth. Corvette HMCS *Rimouski* was fitted with a system of projectors, using the 'diffuse lighting' technique designed to render the ship virtually undetectable at night from afar.

Professor Edmund Godfrey Burr, of Canada's McGill University, had accidentally discovered the principle in 1940 while evaluating optical instruments for the National Research Council of Canada. While monitoring aircraft flying at night without navigation lights, he noted their shapes were easily distinguishable, attributing this to the contrast that exists between a completely blacked-out plane and the slight luminosity of the sky, never completely black even when the darkness appears total. He logically wondered if it would be possible to diminish the visibility of aircraft by reducing this contrast.

On the night of 4 December 1940, a sudden and unexpected demonstration of the principle occurred by chance. A plane that Burr was monitoring in flight disappeared suddenly as it approached landing. Burr deduced that the area surrounding the aircraft was covered in freshly fallen snow and moonlight reflecting off this white surface had illuminated the underside fuselage when the aircraft was at low altitude. This 'diffused lighting' had eliminated the contrast in luminosity between the plane and the sky, rendering the aircraft invisible.

Lieutenant Pickford commanded HMCS *Rimouski* during the operation against *U536*:

> "They had installed a radar station and observation posts on the beach, and when they received an indication of the presence of the U-boat, HMCS *Rimouski*, with her diffuse lighting, was to abandon the patrol and enter the bay on her own. Sailing slowly with her navigation lights and her diffuse lighting, she would create the illusion of being a small ship until she was able to capture the submarine."[152]

On shore Heyda had encountered problems. He was finally stopped by sentries who knew of the operation unfolding at sea and taken to the Pointe Maisonnette lighthouse to be questioned by Lieutenant Commander Desmond Piers, coordinating the Canadian trap. Heyda did his utmost to convince Piers that he was a former member of the Royal Canadian Engineers released to join the Northern Electric Company helping build anti-submarine equipment. But he erred by revealing a handmade compass and chocolates stamped by the German Red Cross. These conspired with other small details of his forged documents to betray him until he admitted his identity and surrendered. He was returned to Bowmanville three days later.

---

[152] Excerpt from the collection of interviews, *Salty Dips*, Vol. 1, pp. 4–5.

As the drama ended on land *U536* eased into the bay. But the ring of enemy warships gathered near the rendezvous point had already raised Schauenburg's suspicions. Passing only 200 metres from the shoreline, it soon became apparent that the operation was blown. A brief message came into the U-boat's radio room but not on the agreed frequency. Finally a German-speaking Allied officer attempted to entice the U-boat in by flashing '*komm, komm*' by torchlight at the barely visible conning tower and Schauenburg, not fooled, hastily moved *U536* offshore and dived.[153] The boat plunged to the bottom in only 30 metres where crew were confined to bunks, all noise-generating machinery shut off, including the softly humming gyrocompass. In frustration the Canadians began hunting their elusive quarry, releasing random depth charges. Schauenburg correctly guessed that the Allied ships would expect him to make a break for deep water and stayed in the shallows where sonar echoes were confused by ground clutter and ships were unable to release depth charges for fear of damage to themselves. On the night of 26 September, nearly twenty-four hours after submerging, *U536* eased itself from the bay at a depth of between twenty and thirty metres. Explosions periodically echoed around the bay, the tension taking a tremendous toll aboard the U-boat, its interior thick with the stink of her confined crew. Men drifted in and out of the stupor of oxygen deprivation as Schauenburg adeptly extricated his boat from the trap. Near Ile de Miscou, as *U536* had nearly reached safety, she suddenly became entangled in a trawler's nets, fishermen wrestling with their impressive catch before *U536* burst free and raced for deep water.

It was only after nightfall that Schauenburg decided to surface. As the conning tower broke free, he climbed to his bridge, fetid air belching from the U-boat's interior, her crew gathered beneath to gulp the sea air. But Schauenburg was alarmed to see three destroyers and an unknown fishing vessel at a range of only 300 metres. In turn, the Canadian ships opened fire as they spotted the U-boat, her conning tower and jumper wires still festooned with fishing net. Schauenburg dived once more. Again creeping closer to the shallow shoreline, *U536* eventually shook loose her pursuers, surfacing once more and breaking away from the bay to safety. Schauenburg remembered:

> "I had only one objective: finding a quiet area 600 nautical miles south, that is to say far from the enemy's operational flying zone. We urgently need to surface to allow the men to recover and to make repairs. The experience in the Chaleur Bay had severely tested us."[154]

In due course Schauenburg communicated to Dönitz that 'Operation Kiebitz' had failed. *U536* then began weeks of unsuccessful hunting before beginning the return to France via the Portuguese coast. There Schauenburg was unexpectedly vectored to take part in operations against Gibraltar convoys as part of group *Schill 2* and luck finally deserted them.

Shadowing the sixty-six ships of convoy MKS30/SL139 and running at a depth of 190 metres, ASDIC impulses pinged loudly on the pressure hull, followed by a series of rapid and accurate depth charges. The sanctuary of depth that had saved many U-boats was no longer available, the capture of *U570* in 1941 having shown the Royal Navy that their adversaries were able to cruise at depths they had never before imagined, depth charges being modified accordingly.

The explosions threw *U536* into chaos; lights failed, water gushed into the stern torpedo

---

[153] Interestingly, he did not record sighting the approaching HMCS *Rimouski* approaching from seaward. This was the only time the diffused lighting was ever used in action.
[154] Bernard and Bergeron.

compartment and fire blazed from a shattered fuse box. The boat plunged to 240 metres before Kaptlt. (Ing.) Wilhelm Kuja arrested its descent. Chlorine gas seeped from the bilges and Schauenburg ordered his men to prepare to abandon ship as Kuja brought it to the surface. Bursting free of the water, the conning tower was soon battered by artillery from corvette HMCS *Snowberry* only metres away to port. Two other Canadian ships, corvette HMCS *Calgary* and frigate HMCS *Nene*, closed the crippled boat and hosed the decks with machine-gun fire, German sailors jumping overboard as they tried to escape. A final message to BdU informed them that they had been rammed as *Snowberry* passed close enough to brush the U-boat's flank. Gradually the smashed conning tower slid backwards into the depths, thirty-eight crewmen including the LI, going with her. Schauenburg and sixteen of his men were rescued, ironically soon incarcerated in Canada.

1 December: *U518* returned from Florida and the Gulf of Mexico, empty-handed and frustrated by torpedo failures and enemy harassment. Kaptlt. Friedrich Wilhelm-Wissmann further incurred the wrath of Dönitz by not replying to status requests for fear of being DF'ed and hunted. By then *U518* was suffering numerous problems. Their *Wanze* had malfunctioned, the boat's batteries were ailing and two barrels of the *Vierling* AA weapon were inoperative. The heavily patrolled Gulf of Mexico and Florida Straits were no longer to be taken lightly with such defects although avoiding contact with the enemy went against the grain for Wissman.

> "I am in the area of air traffic from Miami and under the eyes of the aircraft, which may be civilian or transport, but I cannot justify attacking the steamer by full moon. If I want to get out of here, I cannot risk being detected, because I need the nights to recharge my weak batteries. . . . These decisions run contrary to all our teachings about attack, attack, attack."[155]

It was to be Wissman's last patrol as commander. Already having upset his Commander-in-Chief and then returning empty-handed from patrol, he then argued with Dönitz, stating baldly that he refused to sail with "the ridiculous Biscay Cross device" aboard his U-boat, demanding "proper radar" of the Luftwaffe-developed *Hohentweil* type. He soon found himself attached to the 26th U-training Flotilla, commander of the depot ship *Waldemar Kophamel*, handing over command of *U518* in January to Oblt.z.S. Hans Offermann, ex-IWO from *U129*. After four months at sea *U518* was to undergo an extensive seven-week overhaul.

Wissman's was not the only boat to arrive in Lorient empty-handed. *U843* sailed into the Kéroman III pens on 15 December after unsuccessful pack operations in the North Atlantic, *U154* following five days later from South America. Only the veteran *U68* arrived with any further laurels for the U-boat's crown.

Oberleutnant zur See Albert Lauzemis, scarred by his bullet wound in the jaw, had taken his boat to the South Atlantic close to West Africa after leaving Lorient in September. Refuelled en route by *U488*, Lauzemis claimed his first unconfirmed ship of the patrol a month after leaving France. On 22 October he stalked a small coastal convoy in the Gulf of Guinea, firing a total of seven torpedoes but hitting nothing. Lauzemis surfaced and immediately opened fire with all available deck weapons. In the ensuing battle he sank the small ASW trawler HMT *Orfasay* and Norwegian tanker SS *Litopia*, afterwards releasing an Aphrodite radar decoy balloon to lure any prospective hunters away from *U68*.

155 *Torpedoes in the Gulf*, Melanie Wiggins, p. 214.

British freighter SS *Columbia* was torpedoed off the Ivory Coast on 31 October before the final kill for *U68* a month later at the beginning of its return voyage to Lorient. French freighter SS *Fort de Vaux* was attacked at night, two torpedoes fired, the first exploding against her port hull and sending the ship under in thirty-seven minutes, the second passing narrowly astern.

U68 returned to harbour still carrying five torpedoes on 23 December, air attack in the Bay of Biscay having inflicted last-minute damage on the elderly submarine, several outboard tanks holed by machine-gun fire as she dived. *U68* was difficult to control after submerging, leaking ballast tanks eventually coming under control after elaborate trim calculations by quick-thinking Oblt. (Ing.) Franz Volmari. For his actions, which saved the boat, Volmari was later awarded the German Cross in Gold, the same honour being bestowed on Lauzemis.

During its extended period of overhaul *U68* had three external torpedo containers removed and received a new 3.7cm AA gun. The removal of the storage canisters had been suggested by Dönitz as a possible solution to several losses among Type IX U-boats. He felt that nearby depth charges were possibly cracking the canisters, extra weight induced by their flooding causing the U-boat to tumble out of control until water pressure splintered the hull.

The year 1943 had been one of unmitigated disaster for the Kriegsmarine. The U-boat losses had rocketed beyond sustainable levels. But still they continued to put to sea. In December the brand-new Type IXC-40 *U545*, fresh from working up in the 4th U-training Flotilla, sailed from Kiel. From Lorient *U505* was the only boat to leave during the month. At the helm was a new commander, an experienced sailor who had served since the war's beginning in *Sperrbrecher* and *Corpostenboote* before transferring to U-boat service in 1941. Oblt.z.S. Harald Lange had moved on to become IWO and then commander of *U180* before transfer to *U505*. Once again departure was delayed by five days with mechanical problems before they finally slipped from harbour on Christmas Day, Lange having celebrated his forty-first birthday two days before. He was tall, calm and spoke to his crew with an air of quiet authority. Insisting on shooting the stars with a sextant himself, he was every inch a seaman, the antithesis of the tragic Peter Zschech and his crew loved him for it.

The Lorient that *U505* sailed from was quiet and desolate. A single flotilla mate played the boat on its way with his accordion, FK Ernst Kals and flotilla staff making a small farewell party. But the times had changed and the sense pervaded that this may be the last time that *U505* would see home and friendly faces. Around them there was nothing but ruin. During 1943 Lorient had been the most heavily bombed French Atlantic U-boat base, receiving 6,102 tons of Allied bombs, all of it aimed at the U-boat pens and docks, but flattening everything around them. It was a city of ghosts.

11

'IN THE NAME OF THE FÜHRER . . .':
1 JANUARY TO 30 JUNE 1944

The New Year dawned with 2nd U-Flotilla strength at nineteen operational U-boats, *U547* passing from the 4th U-training Flotilla to Kals' command that day. However, even the most stalwart of crews felt some trepidation entering the Atlantic. U-boats in service were outdated and virtually obsolete, as was their mode of operation. BdU could no longer accurately control groups of boats, commanders at last realizing that their radio communications had betrayed them to steadily improving Allied direction finding, while Enigma penetration by the ULTRA codebreakers in both the United Kingdom and United States contributed greatly, though not flawlessly, in redirecting convoy traffic around assembled wolf packs. Thus, in early 1944, the costly convoy assaults were gradually abandoned, U-boats resigned to tying valuable Allied air and sea forces to escort duties.

Preparing for an Allied assault on Europe, defences were improved around the French Atlantic U-boat bases, now designated 'Fortresses' (*Festungen*). At the beginning of 1944 *Festung Lorient* was under the command of infantry *Oberst* Karl Kaumann, a forty-eight-year-old officer who had served in the front line since November 1939. Most recently commanding the 422nd Regiment (126th Infantry Division) on the Eastern Front, he was promoted to *Oberst* and moved west to Lorient, appointed *Festungkommandant*. Turrets of obsolete French tanks began to sprout from concrete fortifications that straggled to north and south and during April the legendary 'Desert Fox', *Feldmarschall* Erwin Rommel, inspected Lorient's defences as part of his tour of French coastal emplacements, content with what he saw but ironically doubting that the Allied invasion would fall on the Atlantic coast.

The German Navy also continued its dogged occupation. Despite cancellation of a planned extension to the submarine bunker facilities, (designated Kéroman IV and designed to hold twenty-four Type XXI U-boats), there remained considerable naval activity in port. Alongside *Sperrbrecher*, *Vorpostenboote* and *U-bootjäger*, fourteen small armed trawlers arrived during December 1943 from Brest to form the Lorient Harbour Defence Flotilla (*Hafenschutzflottille*).

December 1943 had seen heavy losses for Brest's 4th Torpedo boat flotilla and destroyers of the 8th Destroyer flotilla during a bold foray to escort the German blockade-runner *Alsterufer* through Biscay. The German fleet encountered British cruisers HMS *Glasgow* and *Enterprise* and during the ensuing clash lost the destroyer *Z27* and Torpedo boats *T25* and *T26*.

While the battle raged *U505* was ploughing steadily through the Bay of Biscay's wind-whipped water, thick cumulus clouds threatening rain to add to the misery of the shivering crew. Through the steel walls the crash of distant battle echoed through the seawater. Tension rose at 1900hrs on 28 December when an urgent message from BdU directed *U505* towards the gunfire. In short order FK Ernst Kals radioed further information to

Lange – *Z27* was dead in the water, the remaining ships still attempting to fight their way to the French coast and coastal artillery support.

By the time *U505* reached the area in the early morning of 29 December the sea was rising, icy wind throwing spray over the bridge crew as they searched for survivors in poor visibility. Blankets were accumulated and coffee put on the stove in the cramped galley as binoculars scanned the sea. Of the ship there was no sign and as the first shipwrecked crew were found it became apparent that she had gone under, as had other warships – these men were from *T25*. Lange remained on the bridge as rafts of hypothermic sailors were found and *U505* eased alongside to provide some shelter, survivors lifted aboard, barely able to hold the ropes thrown to them. The last man to be saved was KK Wirich von Gartzen, *T25*'s commander, who had rescued the crew of *U106*. Von Gartzen was inconsolable at the loss of so many of his men, refusing treatment until the search was finally abandoned.

With no more survivors to be found and to ease the cramped conditions where frozen men unused to the violent yaw of a U-boat at sea vomited swallowed diesel and seawater into the bilges, Lange submerged. The initial tilt of the boat as it slid downwards brought some of the more delirious men to a frenzy of panic and many were tied to bunks lest they run amok. Gradually peace descended aboard *U505*, diverted to Brest, home base of the 5th T-Flotilla.

Lange ran submerged as much as possible, a crash dive in any emergency virtually impossible with the overloaded boat. The stink aboard rose to hideous proportions. Many of the rescued men were suffering from diarrhoea as well as seasickness and, with no means of emptying the filth from the boat when at depth, it accumulated in overflowing buckets.

After radioing the headquarters of the 1st U-boat Flotilla Lange brought *U505* to its rendezvous with escort ships, shepherded past Pointe St Mathieu and into Brest harbour on 2 January. There a barge loaded with war correspondents pulled alongside and, much to the submariners' chagrin, climbed aboard with heavy camera equipment to film the cramped interior. Suddenly a massive flash came from the electric motor room, while billowing white smoke and a huge blue bolt of electricity arced across the starboard motor, starting a small fire and stampeding the terrified newsmen and *T25* survivors into the control room.

> "We crewmen knew immediately what had happened because it had happened before; it was another short in the electrical control panel. The boys in the motor room used the CO^2 fire extinguishers to good effect and within ten minutes the fire was out. . . . Privately, we just had to shake our heads – it just wouldn't have been *U505* if something like this hadn't happened."[156]

As the terror subsided *U505* eased toward Brest's huge bunkers, the headquarters staff of the 1st U-Flotilla and the 5th T-Flotilla present alongside a brass band, an echo of a victorious past. One final indignity was inflicted on *U505* as it entered wet-pen C1. A group of torpedo boat sailors, overjoyed to be nearing their home base again, rushed to disembark. One of them slipped from the ladder and landed on the helmsman, *U505* swerving to starboard, brushing the concrete mooring bay and bending the forward dive plane's shaft. The boat would need dry-docking and at least two weeks of repair. But the nearest replacement shaft was in Bordeaux; it would be considerably longer than a fortnight before she sailed again.

---

[156] Goebeler, pp. 206–207.

7 January: *U103* arrived in Bergen from its final lengthy combat patrol. The aged Type IXB was heading for retirement, her last mission spent laying mines off Takoradi and patrolling near Freetown. On 19 November *U103* had parted with a single crewman when Kaptlt. Gustav-Adolf Janssen had been compelled to stop the Portuguese steamer SS *Angola* in order to offload a man suffering from tuberculosis. After months at sea neither the mines nor free-ranging hunting yielded any results and *U103* passed out of the 2nd U-Flotilla into Gotenhafen's 2 ULD where she remained until decommissioned in March. Eventually she would be transferred to Hamburg during February 1945 for use as a generator boat, ending the war scuttled at Kiel, an inglorious end for a boat that had survived eleven war patrols and sunk forty-five ships.[157]

The day after Janssen's appearance in Germany *U107* and *U801* arrived in Lorient. Battered by depth charges in the North Channel, neither boat had achieved anything. The trend continued throughout the month, *U190* returning on 15 January empty-handed after three months at sea off Brazil, *U129* docking in Lorient on the last day of January, a single pennant from an action north of San Salvador to show for sixteen weeks at sea.

While the war at sea ground remorselessly on, Dönitz recognized the near-folly that his campaign had become. It was a grim logic that kept the U-boat campaign running:

> "In the war at sea the U-boats, suffering heavy losses, fought on with deliberate self-sacrifice and no prospect of visible success. Their only objective could be the tying down of innumerable enemy forces which might otherwise be used against Germany itself, forces that included a large number of heavy four-engine bombers which could otherwise have been switched to air-raids on our civil population."[158]

He reveals in his own words how he reacted to the plot against Hitler's life later that year in July 1944. The nation's very existence was at stake and

> "any strife within the fortress itself could not but adversely affect and weaken its efforts against the besiegers outside."

In Lorient this point of view would tragically claim the life of *U154*'s skipper, Kaptlt. Oskar-Heinz Kusch. Twenty-four-year-old Kusch was arrested in Lorient on 12 January. He had been denounced by his IWO Oblt.z.S. Ulrich Abel, a doctor of law and a dedicated National Socialist. There are many descriptions of the tall, quiet Kusch. He was said to have been "blond, strongly built, a Germanic type, and a very good sportsman . . . somewhat quiet and serious, unlike most of us". Perhaps more tellingly, a devout Catholic who kept a small crucifix on the wall of his quarters, he was "pleasant, thoughtful, forthright in his views, and formidable in discussion".[159] It was the last trait that ultimately ended his life. Kusch either failed to grasp, or simply didn't care, that in a frenetic climate like Nazi Germany's freedom of speech was often a luxury. He believed, correctly, that U-boat strategy was fundamentally flawed and was not shy in stating this within the crowded confines of *U154*. He had already antagonized Abel by tearing the regulation portrait of Adolf Hitler from the officers' mess wall, exclaiming, "There will be no idol worship here!"

---

[157] Janssen also passed out of the flotilla ranks. He was transferred to the 25th U-training Flotilla until January 1945 when he took command of the Type XXI electro-boat *U3533*. The boat was never completed.

[158] Dönitz, p. 402.

[159] Vause, *Wolf*, p. 88.

The ideological divide that separated the two men had widened during their last patrol together. That he disliked Abel was no secret. Kusch goaded him by tuning the ship's radio on to the BBC, not an uncommon act but forbidden nonetheless. However, it was personal spite that finally prompted Abel to take action. Having completed two patrols as the boat's IWO, he faced the possibility of training for a command of his own. Kusch wrote his report on Abel's abilities for FK Ernst Kals. Although suitable for the command of a U-boat, Kusch also recorded that he felt Abel to be an "inflexible, rigid, and one-sided officer [possessing] average talent". Abel filed a formal charge of sedition against Kusch, and Kals, whose opinion on the matter has never come to light, was faced with little choice but to acknowledge the charge and arrest him. Many attempted to dissuade Abel from his course of action, but to no avail. Five days after his arrest Abel filed a separate charge of cowardice in the face of the enemy, backed by the IIWO and *Obersteuermann* from *U154* as well as a *Fähnrich* present during the last patrol. By then Kusch was imprisoned at Angers, base of operations for FdU West K.z.S. Hans Rudolf Rösing, in command of all judicial matters relating to the western U-boats. In Lorient there was outrage from officers and enlisted men alike. Kals took great pains to quieten the men of his flotilla as Kusch's fate hung in the balance. The day following the second charge, Kusch was brought before a court martial to answer charges of sedition and "listening to foreign broadcasts", the cowardice indictment being immediately dismissed by the court.

Among others, KK Werner Winter and Kaptlt. Gustav-Adolf Janssen, who had both served alongside Kusch in *U103*, sprang to their comrade's defence. But Kusch, who had been disillusioned with the National Socialist government since 1935 when he quit the Hitler Youth, refused to deny the charges, his principles allowing him to place the events in context but not to disavow his beliefs. He was found guilty of sedition on 29 January and sentenced to death. Perhaps more damning for the mythology that has built up around the U-boat service as an unassailable 'band of brothers' led by *Onkel Karl*, neither Dönitz nor any BdU representative visited Kusch during or after his trial. He was incarcerated in Kiel and shot on 12 May 1944. It is a bitter memory even today for many of the surviving U-boat veterans and continues to provoke heated argument.

Kusch's boat, *U154*, sailed again on 30 January, her new commander Obl.z.S. Gerth Gemeiner, putting to sea to maintain the token Caribbean U-boat presence.

10 February: Radio reports reached Kals that one of his new U-boats transferring, via the North Atlantic, to Lorient had ben sunk, two of its crew lost in the action. Kaptlt. Gert Mannesmann's Type IXC-40 *U545* had been surprised that evening on the surface in dim visibility amid patches of fog and banks of low cloud whipped by strong southerlies. Having already operated in the *Rügen 2* group and damaging SS *Empire Housman* straggling from ON217, it was sheer bad luck for Mannesmann; the 612 Squadron Wellington bomber that found him had been blown eight miles off course by strong winds as it flew convoy support.[160] At 2037hrs Sergeant David Smith made radar contact at a distance of eight miles, queried by Pilot Officer Max H. Paynter lest they mistakenly be

---

[160] *Empire Housman* was later sunk under tow by *U744*. During the attack in which Mannesmann made a one-hour submerged run through the convoy screen he reported three steamers sunk and a fourth damaged, saving two stern T5s for any expected counter-attack. The torpedoes remained unused. Apparently Mannesmann was incorrect, sinking noises that led to his exaggerated claim still unaccounted for.

homing on Rockall. With confirmation of the target, Paynter flew directly for the radar trace, sighting the surfaced boat at one mile and delivering a perfect depth-charge straddle.

The blast killed two men instantly and Mannesmann immediately realized that *U545* had no hope, water flooding the interior and engines wrecked. Ordering his men out, he ordered the boat scuttled after a hurried SOS. As the Wellington passed overhead minutes later its crew remember seeing the oval shapes of several liferafts, each winking a weak orange light. Their SOS had been received and three U-boats despatched to their rescue, the Type VIIC *U714* arriving first and picking up survivors the following day, Mannesmann having kept them together through a difficult night.

19 February: Kaptlt. Oskar Herwartz's *U843* left Lorient bound for the Far East. In mid-June he arrived, one British steamer sunk en route. Like all other boats stationed in the Japanese sphere of operations, *U843* transferred t the 33rd U-Flotilla and, like most, it would never return, Herwartz and his crew lost in action in April 1945.

A second boat from Kals' flotilla sailed also for the Orient a week after Herwartz's departure. Kaptlt. Hans-Joachim Brans began *U801*'s second mission with no victories to boast of yet, the distant hunting grounds of the Indian Ocean promising potential reward for the young skipper. However, on 17 March, he and all but ten of the U-boat's crew were pulled aboard American destroyers USS *Bronstein* and *Corry*, prisoners of the US Navy. For two days aircraft of the escort carrier USS *Block Island* had hunted the boat west of the Cape Verde Islands, inflicting casualties in a strafing attack. Brans was forced to broadcast urgent appeals for help, one man killed and nine wounded by the hail of gunfire. But the damaged boat leaked a revealing slick of oil from ruptured fuel tanks and was finally brought to the surface by depth charges from the two destroyers, survivors abandoning ship while Chief Engineer Kaptlt. (Ing.) Franz Schiemann scuttled the boat, going down with it.

On 24 February newly transferred *U856* sailed from Kiel on its inaugural mission. Oblt.z.S. Friedrich Wittenberg, ex IWO on *U506*, took his Type IXC-40 from Germany bound for the North Atlantic where he cruised south of Newfoundland. On 7 April the boat was located by destroyers USS *Champlin* and *Huse* and destroyed by depth charges with twenty-seven of its largely inexperienced crew, Wittenberg being among those rescued.

25 February: The battered *U193* inched its way into Lorient, scars from its brush with disaster still marking the U-boat. For the second time in as many war patrols FK Hans Pauckstadt's boat had been severely mangled by Allied aircraft. Pauckstadt had left La Pallice in October 1943 and spent weeks patrolling the Gulf of Mexico. On 3 December 1943 he had attacked and sunk the brand new turbine tanker *Touchet* en route from Houston to New York west of Cape Romano, torpedoing the American with three eels and sending it under with its cargo of 140,000 barrels of heating oil and the lives of ten of her eighty crew. Although the only success of his patrol and a paltry result for four months at sea, *Touchet*'s destruction marked a historical finalé – the last ship sunk in the once beleaguered Gulf of Mexico by U-boat attack.

In total German submarines had sunk fifty-six ships in the region, twenty-four of them tankers. Months later the Allies had their revenge on Pauckstadt. Twice attacked by American aircraft while in the Gulf, it was not until 9 February as *U193* approached Biscay that it received such severe punishment at the hands of aircraft that the crippled boat was compelled to limp into Spain's El Ferrol for emergency repair. Nine days of makeshift work on the heavily camouflaged boat were undertaken before it again put to sea for home. Once in Lorient the boat was hauled from the water for extensive repair, passing out of the 2nd U-Flotilla and into the 10th during April as she lay in the Kéroman dry dock.[161]

The end of February marked another watershed in the U-boat war. Dönitz formed his last real wolf pack – thirty-two Type VIICs named *Preussen* (Prussia). The huge group attacked and sank two small British warships for the loss of seven of their own. March continued the dismal regularity of 2nd U-Flotilla boats leaving and returning with no victories to speak of. Among the arrivals was the Japanese blockade-breaking submarine *I29* (code-named *U-Kiefer*). *Chu-sa* (Commander) Kinashi Takakazu and his crew had carried fourteen passengers from Japan, including scientists, engineers and the new Japanese Naval Attaché for Berlin, Vice Admiral Kojima. After meeting outbound *U518* to collect sailing instructions for the final leg of their journey, *I29* arrived in Lorient on 11 March, her cargo of rubber, wolfram and two tons of gold bullion unloaded as the huge boat was at Kéroman. Although the US Navy had managed to track them through ULTRA intelligence, they lagged one step behind and never launched an effective search for Takakazu. Their boat safely ensconced beneath concrete, the Japanese crew resided at Lager Lemp with their 2nd U-Flotilla hosts, enjoying the local U-boat recreation centres, touring subjugated Paris and indulging in the hitherto unknown game of football against the German flotilla's team. *I29*'s officers even hosted a reception dinner on 20 March in the mess hall at Lager Lemp, attended by the Admiral Commanding Western France VA Ernst Schirlitz. A brief menu translation (*Speisefolge*) was circulated for officers of the 2nd U-Flotilla, allowing suitable advance warning for the European palette to digest items such as seaweed (raw and cooked), sushi, fungi and sake. *I29* left Lorient again on 16 April for its three-month transit back to Penang.[162]

27 March: Kaptlt. Albert Lauzemis took *U68* from Lorient bound for the Caribbean. Although her crew were unaware of their exact destination, tropical kit had been issued, indicating a return to the equator. Escorted by a single *Sperrbrecher* and minesweeper, *U68* left Lorient, her electric motors purring until the narrow entrance channel had been cleared and diesels fired. Once into Biscay the two escorts turned away, replaced by a destroyer that stayed on station until *U68* had passed Cape Finisterre.

Lauzemis' boat had received new equipment installed within the conning tower casing. The latest radar set, FuMO-61 or *Hohentweil*, had been fitted in Lorient, *U68* among the first Type IX U-boats to take delivery of the new device. Designed as a replacement for the outmoded and ineffectual GEMA sets, the *Hohentweil* was based on the successful Luftwaffe design fitted to Condor maritime aircraft. The direct lineage of the radar set could be seen in the fact that early U-boat installations still sported a switch to be thrown

---

[161] *U193* also received a new commander in March. OlzS Dr Ulrich Abel, ex-IWO of *U154* and main accuser of his erstwhile commander Oskar Kusch, took command of *U193* before its transfer. His single voyage aboard the boat ended on 28 April 1944 when he and his 59-man crew were lost at sea, bombed by a 612 Squadron Wellington.

[162] *I29* reached Singapore on 14 July disembarking a majority of its passengers, several carrying plans for the German radar, communications gear and Me163 and Me262 fighter aircraft. *I29* and its entire crew were then sunk in the Luzon Strait after being intercepted by USS *Sawfish*, one of three submarines lying in wait for her, alerted again by ULTRA intelligence.

when operating at altitudes under 3,000 metres! *Hohentweil*'s receiver was located in the radio room rather than the control room where GEMA's had been situated, although this did lead to certain difficulties in operation. The mattress-antennae was 1.5 metres wide and 1 metre high and, whenever its operator wished to raise and rotate it, word has to be passed through the control room allowing lookouts to duck out of the way. Ten centimetres wide at its base, narrowing to four centimetres at the top, the antennae was a large obstruction atop the tower and prone to damage unless great care was exercised. With no automatic locking device to align the aerial correctly, it could be severely damaged while lowered hydraulically if not correctly aligned.

As *U68* pounded towards the South Atlantic near the Portuguese island of Madiera BdU passed on reports of an American escort carrier within her immediate vicinity. During the night of 9 April nineteen-year-old *Matrosengefreiter* Hans Kastrupp remembered being off watch and asleep in the forward torpedo compartment when he was awakened by the sound of distant depth-charge explosions. It was the noise of an American hunting group attacking suspected U-boats, at the group's core the carrier USS *Guadalcanal*.

Only hours later it was *U68*'s turn. Sailing fully surfaced in the moonlight of pre-dawn, sharp lookouts reported enemy aircraft approaching. Confident of his AA arsenal, Lauzemis ordered all guns manned and Kastrupp ran through the boat's interior, scaling the ladder to his post at the aft-most weapon, the 3.7cm gun. Mayhem ensued aboard *U68* as the attacking aircraft, an Avenger from *Guadalcanal*'s VT58, swooped above, a second Avenger and a Wildcat flying into view and awaiting their turn to fire. Eight rockets raced from the lead aircraft's wings as heavy flak buffeted the Americans. All three aircraft plastered *U68* with rockets, bullets and Mark 47 depth charges. In the mêlée Lauzemis must have known that he was outgunned and suddenly Kastrupp heard the blare of the siren signifying a crash dive. *U68* had been badly hit and was trailing a slick of leaking diesel as it slowed and began to submerge. Gunners ran for the open conning tower hatch, Kastrupp helping first to secure the 3.7cm gun and then beginning his charge to safety. As he turned to sprint for the hatchway he noticed a badly wounded man on the *Wintergarten* decking. Lifting him, he struggled forward with his heavy burden, reaching the conning tower hatch when, to his horror, it slammed shut and seawater flooded over his feet. In seconds the two men were in a solid wall of water, pulled under with *U68* by strong suction before struggling to the surface. Kastrupp's lifejacket had been holed by machine-gun fire, but he continued to support the wounded man in the water with him. His comrade had been hit in the stomach and leg and soon lapsed into unconsciousness. Meanwhile the attack on their boat continued. At 0634 the second Avenger aircraft roared over the U-boat's swirl and dropped several more depth charges, ending *U68*. Probably already fatally damaged by accurate rocket attacks, an enormous air bubble broke surface immediately after what the Americans described as a "large underwater disturbance". *U68* and the fifty-five men aboard were destroyed. Kastrupp was alone with his unconscious comrade when one of the two attacking Avengers passed overhead and dropped a small dinghy which he climbed into, losing consciousness soon after he had hauled his companion aboard.

Three hours later the sole survivor of *U68* and his crewmate's corpse were taken aboard an American escort vessel. Further debris, including fragments of cork, cloth, food, a leather jacket and human remains, were observed floating in the pool of oil that was *U68*'s sole memorial.

In Germany Dönitz grasped for solutions to the rate of attrition. Capture of British centimetric radar sets from aircraft shot down over Germany finally solved the riddle of location by aircraft and new *Naxos* radar warning equipment was rushed forward for installation in the combat boats. With heavier AA weapons, *Bold* sonar decoys, Aphrodite balloons, *Hohentweil* radar and new torpedoes U-boats continued to batter the teeth of a snarling enemy. The Biscay crossing alone weighed heavily on men's nerves. Where in 1940 it had taken four days, U-boats now crossed the bay in ten to twelve, creeping submerged for most of the time before forced to surface and recharge straining batteries. As they sailed above the waves AA weapons were constantly manned in a high state of nervous alert. Morale bent, but never broke.

The newly developed *Schnorchel* was also rushed into production. Based on a pre-war Dutch design that had fallen into the hands of German invaders in 1940, the *Schnorchel* concept had lain abandoned for years before Professor Helmuth Walter reinstigated development and production of the device under the auspices of an enthusiastic Dönitz. The *Schnorchel* mast would allow U-boats to travel submerged while their diesels were running, fresh air drawn in through its valved head and exhaust vented out to bubble its way to the surface. Dönitz reasoned that this would give his boats faster submerged passage and make radar detection by the enemy more difficult. It was a flawed system but one eagerly grasped and by April 1944 the 2nd U-Flotilla's *U107* was the first of Kals' boats to receive the new device.

7 April: Oblt.z.S. Hans-Werner Offermann's *U518* docked in Lorient after eleven weeks at sea, patrolling the Caribbean as part of the last gasp of U-boat operations in the once abundant hunting ground. A single Panamanian steamer, SS *Valera*, had been torpedoed and sunk during what was an otherwise unsuccessful patrol. Other flotilla boats had achieved as little, if not less. The veteran *U123* entered Lorient three weeks later, having sunk nothing and requiring extensive maintenance, her batteries worn beyond use by constant submergence. The boat's veteran *Obersteuermann* Walter Kaeding was awarded the Knight's Cross in a ceremony at Lager Lemp for his exemplary service after having sailed on every single patrol, accumulating nearly 700 days at sea.[163] *U154* followed into Lorient on 28 April from the Caribbean, no successes to boast of, only fear and fatigue engendered by hours of depth charging by American and Colombian warships.

2 May: Kaptlt. Helmut Schmoeckel's new addition to the 2nd U-Flotilla arrived in Lorient, *U802* having torpedoed and sunk a small British steamer from coastal convoy SH125 off Halifax, Nova Scotia, and claiming three other unsubstantiated sinkings in the same attack. A second convoy attack on HX286 in early April produced another unproven sinking, leading *U802* to return to port flying five pennants from its periscope as it motored into Kéroman III after a difficult voyage.

> "The good times for submarines to get successes were gone long ago and the main thing was to survive. . . . We had spent five months without supply . . . and [in the St Lawrence] could see the Canadian coast on both sides. It was not very good there!"[164]

---

[163] That was not the end of Knight's Cross awards to *U123* veterans. On 1 June Oblt.z.S. Horst von Schroeter received his prior to departing for command of *U2506*, followed by Chief Engineer Oblt. (Ing.) Reinhardt König on 8 July.
[164] Interviews of Stephen Ames, 1992 (courtesy of www.uboat.net).

Between April and the end of May three boats of the 2nd U-Flotilla sailed from European ports to their allocated combat zones. Oblt.z.S. Heinrich Niemeyer left Lorient as the new commander of *U547* on 30 April bound for the West African coast, the only flotilla boat to sail from Lorient during that month. New addition *U534* put to sea from Bergen on 8 May, entering the flotilla ranks in its first combat role. Kaptlt. Herbert Nollau's boat had been commissioned as long ago as December 1942 but consigned to the 4th U-training flotilla for all of the intervening period. Nollau had previously been Kaptlt. Axel Loewe's IWO on *U505*, transferred to command *U534* in December 1942.[165] The last of May's departures was from France, *Schnorchel*-equipped *U107* leaving on 10 May bound for Canada.

In Lorient Kals was concerned for one of his flotilla's longest serving boats. On 5 May BdU had received a flurry of brief messages from *U66* reporting supply state and progress. It had been a remarkable patrol to that point, Oblt.z.S. Gerhard Seehausen having sunk four ships off Freetown and in the Gulf of Guinea. On board the U-boat two prisoners from *U66*'s third victim shared the miserably cramped accommodation, British master of the freighter SS *John Holt* and an agent of the John Holt Shipping Company, taken aboard as their ship foundered in less than five minutes. On 23 April Chief Engineer, Oblt. (Ing.) Georg Olschewski, was notified by radio of his Knight's Cross of the Iron Cross, awarded for service on all nine of *U66*'s patrols.

But American direction finding located their approximate position, radio messages requesting resupply and directing *U66* to rendezvous with the *Milch kuh U488* providing the necessary transmission bursts to track and the Allied net was cast wide to find her.[166] Periodic and brief aerial sightings were made as Seehausen went from map reference to map reference in search of resupply. Both *U68* and *U515* had been instructed by Dönitz to meet with Seehausen, radio messages vanishing into the ether, both U-boats already long sunk. Finally *U188* received instructions to meet Seehausen who listlessly waited for the large 12th U-Flotilla boat to appear. By then, after nearly four months at sea, *U66* was in grim shape. Fuel and rations were extremely low and the boat's inexperienced medical officer, *Sanitätsmaat* Wolf Loch, had discovered to his horror that, due to an error in Lorient, the large supply of vitamin pills he had expected to carry had turned out to be one small inadequate bottle. By early May the crew were exhibiting the classic symptoms of scurvy, reduced mental capacity and lethargy. While they waited for replenishment they were gradually forced to spend more and more time surfaced as the aged batteries proved unable to hold a full charge.

In the early morning darkness of 6 May as *U66* surfaced beneath a clear moonlit night Seehausen was startled by the sight of aircraft carrier USS *Block Island* lying less than 5 kilometres distant. The hunter-killer group centred on the carrier had followed their direction finders towards Seehausen before obtaining radar contact on the surfacing U-boat. Aboard *Block Island* the American group commander ordered his carrier turned away from the threat and detached escort destroyer USS *Buckley* to investigate. Seehausen's final messages to BdU boded evil for his boat:

---

[165] *U534* has one of the most incomplete service records of Dönitz's U-boats. The author has followed the logical assumption that she remained a training boat for the majority of her early career. Personally, the author does not hold any credence to claims made post-war about *U534* smuggling high-ranking Nazi officials out of Germany. Herbert Nollau, one man who could perhaps have answered these allegations, committed suicide post-war.

[166] *U488* had by that stage already been sunk as part of the concerted drive to destroy the U-tankers.

"0518hrs: Lüdden [*U188*] not met. Supplying impossible since [we have been] D/Fed constantly since the 26th . . . Central Atlantic worse than Biscay . . .

"0615hrs: Plane keeping in touch.

"0622hrs: Being attacked by destroyer."

Seehausen was faced with a disastrous choice. His batteries were virtually drained and yet he stood little chance of staying alive surfaced. According to his own flashed messages to BdU he loosed a single torpedo towards the enemy carrier, but neither surviving Germans nor Americans remember this. Grasping the only alternative left to him, he ordered AA guns manned and diesels full ahead in an attempt at a running escape. It was at that stage that his sluggish lookouts spotted an Avenger TBM1-C shadowing *U66*. By Seehausen's reckoning the Avenger was most likely armed with depth charges and able to rush into the attack as soon as the gun crew began to go below if they attempted to dive, out of the question at any rate with *U66*'s empty batteries. Periodic bursts of flak seemed to dissuade the Avenger from coming any closer, although it continued to make short approach runs toward *U66*. Unbeknown to Seehausen it was a bluff, the aircraft possessing no weaponry, adapted for extended night patrols by the removal of all armament in exchange for extra fuel tanks. However, its pilot, Jimmie J. Sellars, continued to goad the U-boat into preparing to fight it out on the surface while homing USS *Buckley* on to *U66*. The carrier also responded to the confirmed contact by despatching a group of Avenger and Wildcat aircraft carrying their full weapon load, but by the time they arrived on the scene *Buckley* had made contact.

U66 came into full view, silhouetted against the moon at a range of 4,000 yards. The American commander, twenty-eight-year-old Captain Brent Abel, maintained flank speed, altering course to bring the U-boat dead ahead. Seehausen ordered emergency firing of a stern torpedo, which flew harmlessly wide, before opening fire at 0419hrs with flak weapons at the closing American juggernaut. Abel responded one minute later, *Buckley*'s forward armament belching flame.

The very first 3" cannon salvo impacted just forward of *U66*'s conning tower, tearing a hole in the forecasing. Seehausen, possibly wounded by the blast, realized that there was no prospect of escape and ordered his men to abandon ship. Tracer from flak weapons and smaller calibre MG34 machine guns continued to race towards *Buckley* and a second torpedo was fired as the German crewmen emerged, ready to leap overboard. Abel ordered all available arms to open fire and soon smaller calibre cannons showered *U66*, silencing her weapons. Flames licked from the battered conning tower as *Buckley* gained rapidly on its quarry, still running at maximum speed. Ironically the conflagration was extinguished by another direct hit from *Buckley*'s main armament.

At 0428hrs Abel rammed *U66*, his ship riding onto the U-boat's foredeck and staying there. Seehausen feared his boat was about to be boarded, but felt unable to scuttle her while men were still below decks. He bellowed for his IWO, twenty-two-year-old Oblt.z.S. Klaus Herbig, to take any men he could find and board *Buckley*, creating a diversion to allow time for evacuation and scuttling. Herbig climbed the steel ladder, gathering eight men with him and leaping onto the destroyer's rails, pulling themselves on deck intent on capitulation.

Abel was aghast at what he thought was a German boarding party reaching his ship and in minutes American sailors swarmed to do battle with the invaders. Small arms fire broke out and bullets and less orthodox weaponry greeted the German crew.

"Ammunition expended at this time included several general mess coffee cups, which were on hand at ready gun station. Two of the enemy were hit in the head with those. Empty shell cases were also used."[167]

Several U-boat men were killed by the combination of blunt instruments and handguns before it was realized that they were surrendering and the fusillade petered out. Meanwhile *Buckley* had reversed engines and disengaged from the twisted mess of *U66* to avoid further boarding, seconds later blue smoke belching from the U-boat's exhaust as *U66* roared away again, crewmen jumping overboard as *Buckley*, bows crumpled and bent, gave chase with guns blazing. Suddenly at 0435hrs *U66*, still making eighteen knots, veered sharply towards *Buckley* and struck a glancing blow, grinding its way under the forward engine room in a welter of twisting steel. Battered yet still defiant, *U66* rolled over to an angle of 60° and disengaged from the American, running at full speed as she disappeared beneath the surface, open hatches belching flame and thick oily smoke. As the recently decorated Olschewski leapt to safety, his scuttling successful, underwater explosions marked *U66*'s end. During the next three hours *Buckley* rescued a total of thirty-six survivors, Herbig, Olschewski and the two other Watch Officers among them. Kaptlt. Gerhard Seehausen and twenty-three of his men were killed.

29 May: Kals and the heads of all Atlantic U-boat flotillas met FdU West Hans-Rudolf Rösing at La Baule to discuss strategy and tactics in the event of Allied landings on mainland Europe. Only days later the expected blow fell. On 6 June 1944 'Operation Overlord' came ashore in Normandy with the massed landings of paratroops, seaborne infantry and armour. Type VIIC U-boat crews despatched to hamper the invasion fleet sailed into a tempest of flying steel and died in droves. Too clumsy even to contemplate entering the English Channel, the 2nd U-Flotilla boats remained focused on the Atlantic fringes to west and south. The flotilla would eventually face the enemy which swarmed ashore in Normandy, but not at sea. In Germany new boats *U858* and *U1225* left Kiel during June for operational cruises as twilight descended on Nazi Germany.

While *U190* returned from the Gulf of Guinea empty-handed on 20 June, *U548*, another new transfer, came to rest at Kéroman four days later, her only sinking felt dearly by her crew, the destruction of an enemy 'destroyer' with a T5 *Zaunkönig* acoustic torpedo. During the night of 6 May Kaptlt. Eberhard Zimmermann's *U548* chanced upon Canadian Escort Group C-1 returning to port after escorting ON234. Zimmermann immediately dived and ordered a single T5 fired before turning away and plunging deep. In minutes the resounding boom of impact against Canadian frigate HMCS *Valleyfield* signalled destruction of the enemy warship, *Valleyfield* breaking in two and sinking with all but thirty-eight of its crew.

---

[167] Official after-action report by Captain Abel.

12

DEFEAT AND EVACUATION:
1 JULY TO 31 AUGUST 1944

On the first day of July BdU calculated that 434 U-boats were in commission. Of the thirty-three operational Type IXCs the 2nd U-Flotilla accounted for sixteen, one of which had only two more days to live.

U154, engaged upon its second patrol after the arrest and execution of Oskar-Heinz Kusch, had left Lorient on 20 June 1944 destined for Cape Hatteras, an area where prolonged submersion was difficult due to high summer water temperatures. But the problem proved academic, *U154* and its crew of fifty-eight men depth-charged by USS *Inch* and *Frost* on 3 July while still north-west of Madeira. They had outlived Kusch by fifty-two days. However, it was not until 6 October that BdU admitted the boat *Vermißt ein Stern* in an assumed location.

> "*U154* has been lost off the North American coast. . . . She has not answered several orders to make a situation report, so that she was probably sunk by patrol vessels off the coast."

July also saw a fresh onslaught against Biscay. The Royal Navy's 'Operation Dredger' targeted U-boats and their vulnerable escort ships. Its first battle fought off Brest on 6 July ended with two escort trawlers sunk, although their U-boat charges escaped. As a result Dönitz ordered all U-boats to have a T5 torpedo ready to fire when leaving base. However, wildly excessive claims of *Zaunkönig* success overstated the weapon's effectiveness. By the end of July BdU rated the T5 as having a 58% success rate – 175 hits and twenty probables from a total of 341 operational shots. This outrageously optimistic figure was based on the claimed destruction of one cruiser, 128 escort vessels (destroyers or corvettes), three submarines, eighteen freighters and two tankers, with a further twenty-three probable destroyer kills, a colossal exaggeration. Postwar analysis shows seventy-seven ships sunk from 700 T5 shots – a return of 11%.

15 July: *U518* put out from Lorient, her commander Oblt.z.S. Hans Offermann taking his boat on its sixth war patrol, this time bound for the United States. The conning tower and forward decking now hosted the ungainly thick trunk of the *Schnorchel*, installed during three months in harbour. The extensive refit had been tested during a six-day trial, quickly aborted and *U518* forced to return to Lorient for repair of several mechanical faults. This time there were no serious defects as Offermann lowered his boat into calm water and began the long *Schnorchel* cruise to the Atlantic. It was the last time that *U518* would see France.

That same day Dönitz recorded the loss of one of Kals' new boats:

> "*U1225 Vermißt ein Stern*. It is assumed . . . due in the main to fast Mosquitoes."

While Mosquitoes of the Banff Strike Wing hammered German shipping that plied the Norwegian coast, *U1225* had in fact been the victim of an amphibious PBY-5A Canso. The 162 (RCAF) Squadron aircraft attacked Oblt.z.S. Ernst Sauerberg's boat as it sailed surfaced at high speed north-west of Bergen. Sauerberg elected to remain surfaced and opened fire as the Canadian dived to attack. *U1225* swung through evasive manoeuvres to throw the Canso off its aim and allow all flak guns to bear. At a range of 1,200 yards the PBY's front turret opened fire at the U-boat's guns, but a jammed machine gun reduced its firepower by half. Heavy and accurate flak pummelled the oncoming aircraft, two large holes ripped in its starboard wing and oil pouring from the engine. Soon the entire starboard wing was wreathed in flame as the oil ignited, endangering the aircraft's fuel tanks. Flight Lieutenant David Hornell held his course until the Canso came over *U1225* at a height of only fifty feet, straddling her perfectly with four depth charges. As the Torpex exploded all firing ceased from Sauerberg's stricken U-boat and, ripped almost in half, it slid stern first to the depths with most of the crew trapped inside. Many of those that had been on deck manning the AA weapons were pitched into the sea, facing a slow inexorable death.

But Hornell was also in trouble. The heavy flak had shattered his aircraft and it vibrated badly as the pilot wrestled with its controls. Suddenly the burning starboard engine fell off and knowing there was no way they could reach their home at Wick, Scotland, Hornell ditched into heavy swell.

As their aircraft sank the eight Canadians abandoned it in a single dinghy designed to hold four men. Taking turns in the water they waited for rescue. A Norwegian Catalina sighted them and began to circle, also spotting 'about forty' men from *U1225* three miles distant. One by one the Germans vanished from sight until all fifty-six crewmen lay with their boat on the seabed. Meanwhile a Wellington bomber passed over the exhausted Canadians, dropping a second raft that landed 500 yards downwind, the men too fatigued to reach it. Gradually life ebbed from their weary bodies. Two died from exposure before a high-speed RAF rescue launch arrived to pluck them from the water. Hornell, who had encouraged his beaten crew with "cheerfulness and inspiring leadership" was blinded and completed shattered as he was pulled aboard, dying twenty minutes later.[168]

For Dönitz the loss of *U1225* with all its crew was yet another bitter blow and he advised all boats outbound from Norway to:

> "Proceed submerged only, using *Schnorchel*, from the time they part from their escort until they reach large square AL."

16 July: The probable sinking of another 2nd U-Flotilla boat was recorded, attached in cold typewritten language to FK Kals' flotilla War Diary. The report was in error, but just how badly mistaken they would not discover until after the end of the war.

> "U505 must be presumed lost. This boat was operating off the coast of Liberia and made a situation report on 15/5 which was received very corrupt. . . . Nothing is known of date or cause of loss."

---

[168] Hornell was awarded a posthumous VC for gallantry, his crew one DSO, two DFCs and two DFMs between them, the two dead gunners mentioned in despatches.

By the time this conclusion was entered into the War Diary *U505* was already in Allied hands, hidden from sight in Bermuda where the United States Navy had taken their prize, the first enemy vessel captured by the American navy since 1815.

Oblt.z.S. Lange had headed quickly through Biscay, risking extended surface sprints rather than creeping submerged beneath the heavily patrolled waters. His chance paid off and *U505* cleared the 'Valley of Death' in good time, directed by sealed orders to hunt the waters off Freetown.

Approaching the equator the weather worsened considerably, forcing Lange to submerge regularly in order to rest his crew. Finally, towering waves were replaced by a long swell that, although less dramatic, slowed their progress considerably and ensured that any new sailors remained in the grip of sea sickness.

It was a frustrating journey, aggravated by a lack of merchant shipping. Lange scoured the seas, going as far as entering several ports, but still found nothing. A single surface chase offshore thwarted by an enemy destroyer until, towards the end of May, Lange threw in the towel and began the slog home.

Enemy aircraft regularly drove *U505* underwater, so much so that Lange was forced to again spend extended periods submerged, unequipped with *Schnorchel* and so unable to charge the boat's steadily depleting batteries. By then he was far from the coast and the constant aerial attention led him to conclude that he had become the focus of a Hunter-Killer group, the hub of which was an aircraft carrier. As events revealed, he was correct, but he chose an unfortunate path of action. Believing the enemy carrier group to be in the proximity he sailed east toward Africa, into the arms of American Task Force 233, led by USN Captain Daniel Gallery aboard the carrier USS *Guadalcanal*. Lange again showed a cunning ability to risk all, running surfaced when possible to recharge batteries, correctly believing that the Allies were well aware of the German need to surface but reckoning they would never think a U-boat foolhardy enough to do so in daylight, thus relaxing their vigilance. The ploy worked until 4 June when *U505* blundered into Gallery's Task Force.

A little after midday reports of a faint hydrophone trace were passed to Lange. Rising slowly to periscope depth, Lange mounted the ladder into the conning tower to take a look. An unusual sound outside, loud metallic 'clinking', reached the control room and most were puzzled as to its source. Abruptly it halted, replaced by Lange's bellow: "Destroyer!"

Slamming the scope back into its well, *U505* was already trying to lose buoyancy and dive away. The strange sound had been machine-gun bullets from many aircraft overhead, Lange spying the entire Task Force intent on their destruction.

A single T5 was fired in the carrier's direction, more in hope of creating confusion among the charging enemy than actually hitting anything. *Bold* capsules were ejected and the water around *U505* churned with the decoy's bubbles as Hedgehog missiles rained down. As explosives detonated alongside the U-boat, water gushed into the control room, filling the bilges, light bulbs burst and seconds passed before the emergency lighting flickered on. Men didn't need their eyes to know the U-boat was filling with water, increased air pressure squeezing eardrums painfully as the U-boat lay in its death throes. The stern torpedo compartment reported that it was unable to control flooding and Lange ordered the watertight bulkhead sealed after the compartment had been evacuated. The main rudders were jammed and now that the stern was flooded and sealed off there was no way to use the auxiliary helm. *U505* drifted to starboard in a slowly descending circle, the boat gradually losing buoyancy as the seawater engulfed it.

The pain on the crew's ears increased as *U505* sank lower into the gloom, depth gauge creeping past the maximum rated depth of the Type IXC. Lange knew that there was no hope and ordered her surfaced, his crew using all the skill they possessed to arrest their descent. Slowly *U505* began to rise.

Above them the Americans could tell that *U505* was mortally injured and circling out of control, destroyers staying outside of the turning radius still hurling depth charges. In a flurry of spray *U505* broke surface. Lange had readied his men to abandon ship and as the boat began to rock in the swell he cracked the seal on the conning tower hatch, almost pushed out of the boat by the intense level of air pressure. Following his duty to lead his crew from their ship, Lange heaved himself on to the conning tower, followed by the IWO Paul Meyer. Lange fell instantly, hit by shrapnel from an exploding AA shell. Meyer briefly attempted to man a flak gun before also falling wounded. The Americans pumped hundreds of smaller calibre shells into *U505*, their intention to keep men away from their weapons but not to sink her. Gallery had spied the potential for capture and the timeless cry of 'Away Boarders!' echoed aboard several ships as whaleboats hit the water and raced towards *U505*. On the crippled U-boat Lange crawled painfully to the open hatch and urged his men to scuttle the boat and abandon ship.

In the ensuing stampede of frightened crewmen many were hit by flying bullets as aircraft swooped into the attack. The barrage only slackened once it became obvious that the U-boat was being abandoned. The victors moved closer to *U505*, her stern dragging underwater. Among the men who leapt from the crippled submarine was the LI, Josef Hauser, his duty of ensuring that scuttling charges were set ignored in his haste to get outside. In the absence of officers, Engine Room *Obermaat* Holdenried organized several men to take over the task of destruction. One of them was Hans Goebeler.

> "We waited a minute or two for the last of the men to evacuate the compartment. It seemed like an eternity. The very second they were clear, we tried to open the valves to let water into the tanks. All went well except for forward main diving tanks number six and seven. We tried again and again to open those damn valves, but with no luck.
>
> "Desperate to find another method of letting water quickly into the boat I suddenly remembered the sea strainer located on the deck close to my duty station."

The sea strainer that Goebeler rushed over to undo was a filter mechanism for the main water-cooling pump. Its removal would allow seawater to flood quickly into the bilges and eventually send *U505* to the bottom. In his haste Goebeler removed the heavy steel cover, water gushing upwards, before tossing it into a corner of the control room, an action he would live to regret. Then, amid flying shrapnel and bullets, he joined his comrades in the water, passing the body of *Funker* Gottfried Fischer as he climbed outside, the only man killed during the action.

Meanwhile, American whaleboats chased the U-boat as it continued to circle, bow protruding from the choppy water as it slowly flooded. It was a whaler from USS *Chatelaine* that finally caught up with the elusive prize. Signalman Frank P. DeNardo was among them.

> "I jumped aboard and checked the conning tower. . . . I looked to my right and saw a whaleboat racing toward us from the other ships that had returned. When the other whaleboat [from USS *Pillsbury*] got to the sub, they entered and left their signalman

in the conning tower. I told him to go below and get me the decoding machine, which he did. I then told him to get me all the charts the he could find. He made two trips."

As the Americans tumbled into the flooding control room they raced to remove anything that they could find, also trying to stop the rising water. It was obvious that the main seawater filter was uncovered, water belching from it in torrents and the Americans hunted frantically for something to plug the hole. 'Luke' Lukosius miraculously found what looked like a large steel lid and ran with it to the filter that Goebeler had opened. He forced the lid onto its seating, later plugging small leaks caused by the loss of the gasket with another man's T shirt. Fortunately for the US Navy *U505* was now a captured prize, no longer destined to join so many of her sisters on the sea floor. As thick cables were slipped through the bull ring at the U-boat's nose she was taken in tow by USS *Guadalcanal*, the U-boat issuing one last defiance when a forward hydroplane sliced in the hull of USS *Pillsbury*, incautiously close.

Coupled with the capture of an intact U-boat, the intelligence haul was priceless. A working four-rotor Enigma, codes, charts and engineering manuals all proved of immense value to the Allied navies. The capture of *U505* also presented a copy of the *Addressbuch* – the codebook that provided keys for disguising grid references. It was the final piece of a large jigsaw nearly completed by ULTRA's Enigma decryption and from that point onwards Allied codebreakers were able to decipher messages as fast as the Germans could. *U505* was the last of a string of German intelligence disasters that had begun with *U110* three years before.

Among the German sailors there was dismay at the knowledge that they had failed to destroy their ship. Locked in a large iron cage below the flight deck on *Guadalcanal*, the incarcerated Germans could see their boat towed behind, the United States flag flying above a makeshift Kriegsmarine ensign.

On 19 June the Task Force, with *U505*, entered Bermuda's Port Royal Bay. Captain Gallery swore his 3,000 men to secrecy and the prisoners were taken away to seclusion apart from other Kriegsmarine men. They were also denied access to any Red Cross facilities for fear that they might communicate the boat's capture to BdU and lead to a change of codes. The secret remained unbroken until after the war, Dönitz unaware as to how *U505* ended its career.[169]

The same day that BdU reported *U505* lost *U802* sailed out of Lorient to the seas south of Newfoundland. Kaptlt. Schmoeckel had been delayed with a defective *schnorchel* but would spend nearly three months patrolling off Canada, harassed by aircraft of the escort carrier USS *Bogue*, even once inside the St Lawrence River. His hydrophone was put out of commission while creeping around the river mouth, where Schmoekel was hoping to control all shipping entering or leaving the St Lawrence. Lying at periscope depth with *Schnorchel* protruding, *U802* was aided in its bid to remain hidden by the increased density found in the saline waters at depth, pushed below by a layer of fresh river water. ASDIC waves bounced off the thick layer rendering the U-boat virtually invisible while dived.

---

[169] Of course the similarity with *U110* ends immediately after her capture. Unlike Lemp's boat, *U505* did not sink. It survived the war as USS *Nemo* and took part in a War Bonds tour of the United States. Eventually it was taken via the Great Lakes to Chicago (Gallery's home town) where it resides to this day as an exhibit at the Museum of Science and Industry.

However, the detection of a second U-boat in the area, *U541*, caused an escalation in Canadian air presence and Schmoeckel added no success to his score, a single T5 torpedo fired on 14 September at a range of only 500 metres towards HMCS *Stettler* resulting in premature explosion in the Canadian's wake. Diving to a safe depth of 170 metres after the attack in order to avoid the torpedo circling, *U802*'s crew heard what they thought were sinking noises following the detonation and Schmoeckel claimed victory. It was the sole 'success'. *U802* lurked around Halifax until early October before giving up the hunt and heading home.

18 July: *U129* crept towards Lorient, having been shadowed by aircraft offshore at the *Leben* rendezvous point with escort ships. Oblt.z.S. Richard von Harpe and his crew had endured nearly four months at sea, mostly spent cruising off Brazil, two British steamers all that they had to show for their exertions. Now, as he neared the safe haven of Lorient, the enemy would not give them an easy homecoming. Their path through the defensive minefields, route '*Eisleben*', was the standard approach route to Lorient and by mid-July was used also by all the Brest-based boats of the 1st and 9th U-Flotillas squeezed by constant enemy presence near Brest. Aircraft of *Fliegerkorps* 10 attacked the allied blockade whenever possible, but they too were fighting a losing battle of attrition, control of Biscay wrested from their grasp after battles over Normandy swallowed what meagre reserve the Luftwaffe had maintained in Brittany.

U129 stayed submerged as much as possible and was to have been picked up by escort craft during the following day until reports reached FdU West of enemy units sighted near *Leben*, von Harpe informed by radio that rendezvous was unlikely, lightly armed U-boat escorts 'endangered' by the renewed Allied attention of 'Operation Dredger'. So *U129* crept alone early the following morning into Lorient, Kriegsmarine coastal artillery engaging distant enemy warships skulking off shore, the fierce hour-long bombardment dissuading them from moving any closer. Once on terra firma *Obermaschinist* Heinrich Dammeier presented his list of mechanical defects and essential replacements needed. The most critical problem was the batteries, worn out after months of arduous service. They needed replacement urgently and, until spares could be fitted, *U129* would stay in dry dock within the Kéroman concrete pens.[170]

22 July: Kaptlt. Volker Simmermacher brought *U107* into Lorient once more, the boat's thirteenth war patrol dismally unsuccessful. It had been the first voyage undertaken since the fitting of the boat's *Schnorchel*, the supposed safety of being able to recharge batteries while running submerged replaced by new rigours peculiar to the device. Among problems faced by *Schnorchelling* U-boats were such mundane dilemmas as garbage disposal, U-boats no longer surfacing except in extreme emergencies. The days of slinging overboard a bucketful of waste were past and a special note was appended to BdU's War Diary and circulated to all flotilla commands. The techniques recommended included disposal through the *Bold* ejector of carefully stored garbage capsules, stowage of refuse in an empty torpedo tube to be later ejected (the so-called 'garbage shot') and the breaking up of refuse

---

[170] Dammeier was transferred to 6th U-Flotilla's *U270* in St Nazaire, engaged on a mission to rescue key personnel from Brest and return them to Germany. He was sunk on 12 August, seventy-one of the eighty-one men aboard rescued, including Dammeier. The day he became a POW he was awarded the Knight's Cross for his service, mainly aboard *U129*.

and jettisoning through the already overworked WC. Empty tin cans, on the other hand, were to be 'rinsed out, hammered flat and stored'. Nevertheless, Simmermacher had been content with the new *Schnorchel*, and, as he approached the Canadian coast, his was the first such-equipped U-boat to enter North American waters.

A T5 attack against an Allied destroyer rendered one claimed torpedo hit, although there is no record of this in Admiralty reports. For the last two weeks of May and early June *U107* patrolled the Canadian waters, finally sighting a worthy target on 13 June when the fishing schooner *Lark* crossed the U-boat's path. Simmermacher launched two torpedoes towards the small 237-ton American, both weapons missing. Surfacing, Simmermacher ordered the 3.7cm AA weapon manned and opened fire on the fishing boat. Fifteen rounds smashed through the wooden hull before the gun jammed – another legacy of prolonged *schnorchel* submersion. Unable to finish his attack, Simmermacher was forced to dive away from the area for fear of location by Allied aircraft. His last view of the schooner was as its crew rowed their lifeboat towards the heavily damaged ship, later successfully to sail her 300 miles home to Boston.

That same day a radio message from BdU received aboard Simmermacher's mouldy U-boat, stale with the stink of rotting refuse and unwashed men, as well as by seven others in the Western Atlantic, revealed the seriousness of the German position in France, Dönitz issued a triple enciphered 'Commanding Officer Only' message directing all eight U-boats to leave the United States and Canada with enough fuel to reach Lorient, or, if events warranted, Norway. The security of the Biscay bases could not be guaranteed with greater and greater Allied pressure on the Wehrmacht's front line in Normandy.

As *U107* entered Lorient, two 6th U-Flotilla Type VIICs, *U260* and *U608*, put to sea from Kéroman to attack Allied warships lying offshore. The small two-boat group was named *Marder*, designated a patrol area in BF6175 for two days. It was an identical technique to that already used off Brest where small two-boat groups, *Pirat*, lay on the sea floor or prowled at periscope depth hunting for blockading forces. Both groups failed to engage the enemy, the echoing thunder of distant depth-charging providing unsettling background music to their lonely vigils.

1 August: Off France's western shores the Royal Navy began a new offensive aimed at the complete destruction of the remaining Kriegsmarine presence. Named 'Operation Kinetic', the blistering assault was launched with blockading of ports stretching from Brest to Bordeaux, any German vessel fair game for naval forces with strong aerial support. Its goal was two-fold: eliminate the scanty German Kriegsmarine presence and support American attempts at invading Brittany. The storm on land broke the same day as American troops pierced the German lines at Avranches and General George S. Patton's 3rd Army cut deep into the German rear, a strong axis of advance tearing straight toward Lorient. While the American ground offensive had been building in Normandy, *Oberst* Karl Kaumann was replaced as *Festungkommandant Lorient* by *General der Artillerie* Wilhelm Fahrmbacher. Fahrmbacher had entered the army in 1907, serving during the First World War as an artillery officer. During the next war he had been decorated with the Knight's Cross as commander of 5th Infantry Division on 24 June 1940, before promotion to *General der Artillerie* in May 1942.

As the thin German line was shattered and American armoured units charged towards Brittany, Fahrmbacher took control of the Lorient pocket, reorganizing troops under his command to counter impending American or French assaults. To defend the bastion he had at his command 24,700 men, most of them infantry, including many Russian

Battalions belonging to the 265th Infantry Division. Infantry battlegroups (*Kampfgruppen*) 'Albrecht', 'Schaenske', 'Gutsche', 'Wachter', 'Esser', 'Huls' and 'Dontsch' were formed while Kriegsmarine men of the 2nd and 10th U-boat Flotillas, 14th *U-Jäger* and 8th Minesweeping flotillas and the dwindling *Hafenschutzflottille* bulked out the available naval troops. Fahrmbacher also controlled the formidable array of coastal artillery ranged around Lorient. The five batteries of *Marineartillerieabteilung* 264 and IV *Marineflakbrigade* mustered a fearsome collection of heavy guns. Offshore on Belle Isle protecting Lorient's harbour mouth the extra power of *Lechte Marineartillerieabteilungen* (Light Naval Artillery Detachments) 682 and 688 were entrenched, while on the smaller Ile de Groix were six batteries of *Lechte Marineartillerieabteilung* 681.

One day after taking post as Lorient's commandant Fahrmbacher was named as C-in-C Brittany and immediately ordered evacuation of outlying garrisons to easily defended fortress cities, a move that brought him immediately into conflict with the Kriegsmarine regional command.[171] The cities were soon isolated, frantically preparing for the American hammer to fall.

However, due to the rapid retreat of German forces into the Biscay fortresses and the subsequent confusion caused, Ernst Kals' snap judgement informed BdU that he doubted the ability of a prolonged defence of Lorient, Kals ordered all U-boats immediately to sea and dockyard labour cancelled, workers conscripted into the ground forces. Dönitz intervened to restore calm and soon restored 'normal' dockyard employment rather than waste the short time left to equip U-boats with *Schnorchel* and get them out of Brittany's harbours before hemmed in by Allied naval forces. The northern ports (Brest, Lorient and Saint Nazaire) were judged to be at greater risk than those to the south and U-boats ordered to transfer to La Pallice or Bordeaux if possible.

Those boats that could not be fitted with *Schnorchel* and made seaworthy were ordered paid off, their crews sent to Germany unless absolutely necessary. In Lorient this order marked the end of the two veterans *U123* and *U129*, neither able to move without replacement batteries. There remained crew elements, the 2nd U-Flotilla administrative structure and the pesonnel reserve pool stranded in Lorient, and they armed themselves for an impending ground siege as lead elements of the US 4th Armored Division reached the outskirts on 7 August. General Troy Middleton's VIII Corps of Patton's Third US Army had launched a huge two-pronged attack aimed at sealing off the Brittany peninsula. The 4th Armored Division had rolled south, capturing Rennes and Nantes before reaching Lorient, four divisions of Fahrmbacher's XXV Corps (7th Army) quickly trapped. Tanks of the US 6th Armored Division soon reached the edge of Brest while everywhere the French Resistance emerged from the shadows to block roads and attack isolated German outposts.

The day before the Americans hit Fahrmbacher's front line twelve Lancaster bombers returned once more to Lorient, this time from the specialist 617 Squadron guided by three Mosquito pathfinders. Each Lancaster carried one bomb, the 1,000lb 'Grand Slam', designed to penetrate the Kéroman bunkers after trials in Hampshire's New Forest on bunker mock-ups. Braving strong flak, two hits were scored on the bunker roofs before the bombers turned back for England without casualty. The explosions were cataclysmic, but ultimately futile, the massive concrete shelters shrugging off the renewed assault with barely a mark.

---

[171] See Lawrence Paterson, *First U-Boat Flotilla*, p. 253.

7 August: The opening clashes around *Festung* Lorient began. Men of US 94th Infantry Division with armoured support (CCA) attempted to take Lorient in an attack from the east and at Auray, on the road to Hennebont, fighting erupted as the confident Americans encountered resistance from German troops, artillery as well as White Russian cavalry. By sunset the battle was over, American infantry and tanks having passed over the river and taken up positions near Caudan and Lager Lemp. The barracks and lakeside dwellings that had housed the 2nd U-Flotilla were now empty and ruined, deserted in favour of the concrete shelters within besieged Lorient. The town's outer defences had been pierced and the following day, 8 August, a surrender ultimatum was sent to Fahrmbacher, unhesitatingly refused.

American artillery began to fire at targets of opportunity as the US lines reshuffled for the forthcoming siege of Lorient. A ring of steel now surrounded the fortress garrison and, amid counter-battery artillery fire and constant patrolling, the antagonists sparred relentlessly. In Lorient those U-boat men left behind took up their positions. Among them was Bernard Geismann, late of *U107* before transfer to Lorient's reserve pool.

> "Beside the maintenance of the combat U-boats, I was department leader of the naval radio post for the *U-Stützpunkt* Lorient. This was independent of the radio headquarters at Kernével, although this independence was ended after the invasion. The members of the 2nd U-Flotilla radio post were the personnel reserve for *Funker* on operations boats. After the enclosure of the fortress Lorient in August 1944 we had to obtain radio connection with the Fatherland. Consequently, I was duty news's officer with the flotilla staff. . . . After Lorient was surrounded, the bulk of the U-boat reservists were inserted into the front lines. These soldiers proved to be very brave. KzS Kals was the commander of these troops."[172]

11 August: At Bordeaux Oblt.z.S. Heinrich Niemeyer docked *U547*, carrying the captain of SS *Bodegraven* as prisoner. Niemeyer had returned from fifteen weeks in the Gulf of Guinea, claiming a single unconfirmed freighter hit and possibly sunk in late May and two steamers and an armed trawler confirmed sunk from a convoy off Liberia in mid-June. His was the last U-boat to enter the Gironde River and the comparative safety of Bordeaux's U-boat bunkers as chaos spread across France. Niemeyer's boat had suffered severe damage entering the Gironde, striking a British mine before docking in its concrete berth. Despite the fact that there was little that could be done to repair the injury sustained, Niemeyer was determined to get away from Bordeaux with his crew, the alternative to becoming stranded or having to fight their way back to Germany overland, not one that he or his men relished. Thus their stay was brief, the *Schnorchel*-equipped boat loading with ammunition and supplies before preparing to depart for Norway.

U548 put to sea that day from Lorient, bound for Norway as part of the base's evacuation. Temporary commander Kaptlt. Günther Pfeffer, whose own 10th U-Flotilla boat *U170* was transferred to the captaincy of her former Executive Officer, had been assigned to replace Kaptlt. Eberhard Zimmermann, unable to return to Lorient from leave in Germany due to the rapid Allied advance, many of her customary crew also on furlough. In the time that *U548* had spent in Kéroman she had received a *schnorchel* and Pfeffer cautiously departed Lorient's narrow entrance channel with a scratch crew and thirty key

---

[172] Personal correspondence with Herr Geismann, April 2002.

engineering personnel from the 2nd U-Flotilla. The overloaded boat, carrying eighty-four men, crept outward, Pfeffer determined to reach Norway. Once free of Biscay he elected to surface when possible in order to put distance between himself and the hovering 'Kinetic' forces. It was to spell tragedy for one member of the crew, *Mechanikergefreiter* Walter Heise, lost overboard on 30 August as *U548* crash-dived away from attacking aircraft. His was the only sacrifice, Pfeffer bringing *U548* into Bergen on 27 September after a gruelling voyage. Three days later the boat passed out of the ranks of the 2nd U-Flotilla into Flensburg's 33rd U-Flotilla.

13 August: *U534* put into Bordeaux at the end of its first war patrol. Her commander, Kaptlt. Herbert Nollau, had spent three months at sea, the majority spent weather reporting west of Greenland and the remainder unsuccessfully zigzagging across the North Atlantic. According to post-war accounts Nollau was not popular with his crew, remembered as stiff, formal and unapproachable.[173] But several stories of *U534* also relate that Nollau was among the few commanders who refused a *Wappen* on his conning tower, an assertion refuted by the fact that the *Wappen* in question, a shield sporting 'The Hunter from Kurpfalz' (Nollau was from the Pfalz region of Germany) leaping through a large 'U', now resides in a museum in Birkenhead, along with the remains of the salvaged boat itself. In the guest book of the 4th U-training Flotilla, *U534*'s entry sports both this particular design as well as the Olympic Rings of the 1936 class to which Nollau belonged. Whatever the facts of the matter, the young commander had kept his crew alive when odds were stacked heavily against them. Their stay in Bordeaux would be brief, Nollau moving heaven and earth to have a *Schnorchel* fitted to *U534*.

Meanwhile other boats were directed to bypass France altogether, BdU issuing orders on 14 August that:

> "All IXC boats on return passage are to proceed to Norway instead of Western France when their fighting strength is exhausted unless instructed otherwise."

16 August: *U107*, still sporting the four aces of Hessler's tenure as commander, sailed from Lorient for La Pallice, there to receive replacement batteries for its own worn banks. Two days from port her new commander Oblt.z.S. Karl-Heinz Fritz, ex Watch Officer aboard *U103*, was proceeding at periscope depth with *Schnorchel* deployed when tragedy struck.[174] Above them a 201 Squadron Sunderland, piloted by Flight Lieutenant E.H. Baveystock, was flying on station west of La Pallice when the nose gunner and 3rd pilot simultaneously sighted wake left by the boat's periscope and *Schnorchel* head. Within minutes six shallow-set depth charges landed astride the boat at an angle, detonating and sending *U107* straight to the bottom. There were no survivors from the fifty-nine crewmen, bubbles rising from two different spots indicating that *U107* had been blown completely in half. On 25 August Dönitz recorded:

> [*U107* must be] "considered lost . . . loss owing to mines probable".

[173] See Stern, *Battle Beneath the Waves*.
[174] Kaptlt. Volker Simmermacher had relinquished his command to Fritz at the end of *U107*'s last voyage, immediately transferred to Germany and assigned the new Type XXI *U3013*.

17 August: The evacuation continued, *U190* sailing from Lorient for Norway, her new *Schnorchel* allowing submerged passage all the way to safety in the 'Northern Redoubt'. As Reith departed, two smaller U-boats sailed inbound, *U445* and *U650* carrying nearly eighty tons of assorted ammunition and anti-tank weapons into Lorient from Army Group West's stores near Bordeaux.

Although not classified as operational at the time of her departure *U190* successfully reached her new base, transferring from Kals' flotilla to the 33rd U-Flotilla on the last day of September. Oblt.z.S. Hans-Edwin Reith had incurred the displeasure of Dönitz by reporting 'continuously' and for 'no apparent reason' during his voyage, running serious risk of Allied detection. Nonetheless he successfully brought the barely serviceable *U190* into port, in itself a minor distinction for the young commander.

23 August: *U547* sailed from Bordeaux for Norway. Running the gauntlet of mines and aircraft, *U547* reached Biscay and began a wretched thirty-five-day voyage to Bergen, loaded with extra passengers bound ultimately to Germany. Once in Norway *U547* passed out of the ranks of the 2nd U-Flotilla to the 33rd U-Flotilla based at Flensburg.

Kaptlt. Herbert Nollau's unblooded *U534* left Bordeaux on 25 August after a stay of only twelve days, the last 2nd U-Flotilla boat to leave France. Nollau's boat had in that brief time had a ring-valve *Schnorchel* installed, the large pipe unable to be hinged in the limited time available for installation, fixed rigidly to the conning tower instead. As *U534* edged downstream along the Gironde, the assembled crew knelt on deck with inflated life jackets, the threat of Allied mines very real. Several were detonated by noisemakers deployed by *U534* as it made its painfully slow passage to open water. There the danger continued, aerial attention immediately forcing the boat under. Without delay Nollau ordered the *Schnorchel* activated, but the crew had not received proper training in its use and it soon malfunctioned, flooding the boat with lethal carbon monoxide. Nollau and several of his men were rendered unconscious before *U534* could be brought to the surface and fresh air flushed through the interior. Almost at once *U534* was detected and came under attack by a several aircraft, her AA gunners managing to hit a 172 Squadron Wellington bomber and bring it down into the sea, three RAF survivors later picked up by a Sunderland flying boat.

Using the brief pause following the kill Nollau rushed his men below and put *U534* into a steep crash dive, the malfunctioning *Schnorchel* allowing nearly twenty-five tons of water to gush inside the U-boat before the deluge was stemmed and Oblt. (Ing.) Ludwig Schlumberger gained control of the boat's descent. Depth gauges showed the crew that they were well below their shipyard-rated maximum, waiting for the first telltale sound of their pressure hull buckling. Every frame groaning under the pressure, *U534* sailed stubbornly onward, gradually clawing its way towards the surface.

The remaining voyage was spent alternately submerged, learning to use the *Schnorchel* and sprinting surfaced with AA weapons manned. The *Schnorchel* continued to give trouble, Nollau's War Diary listing the head valve leaking, starboard diesel ventilation trunk broken off and no exhaust pressure among the woes that beset them. Further aircraft attacks were logged during the voyage but no serious damage sustained. Nollau was ordered to the familiar duty of weather boat during his transfer to Norway, where, sixty-one days later, *U534* arrived, transferring also to the 33rd U-Flotilla.

27 August: A final note on the fight in the Bay of Biscay was entered in the BdU War Diary.

"The area off the Biscay ports is no longer to be a field of operation owing to lack of counter-measures to the extensive mine and air danger and search groups."

It was a humiliating end to a fierce and prolonged battle, but still the war dragged on elsewhere. The next day Oblt.z.S. Albert Kneip took his new command the Type IXC-40 *U1223* from Bergen for its first war patrol, destined for Canada, the last day of the month seeing Oblt.z.S. Friedrich Altmeier depart Kiel on *U1227*'s initial war patrol. First he would sail to Horten, onwards to Norway and ultimately into the Atlantic, directed for a tour of duty west of Gibraltar. The huge odds against their survival caused no hesitation as they cast off from the Tirpitz Pier, little fanfare sending them on their way towards distant thunder.

13

TORPEDO TO PANZERFAUST:
SEPTEMBER 1944 TO MAY 1945

'Einer spinnt immer!'
"One of us is crazy!" –
inscribed on the interior wall of a Kriegsmarine artillery bunker, Etel, Lorient.

Lorient's German garrison faced a new and brutal war of fierce firefights and constant artillery fire. Sandbagged bunkers, roofed with corrugated iron filched from the remains of gutted houses, sprang up on both sides of the line as casualties from small actions, shrapnel and sniping slowly mounted. Battlefield ingenuity yielded frightening and often lethal results. During September German troops rolled an abandoned automobile chassis loaded with explosives along rail tracks into the American lines. The Americans retaliated in kind. Booby traps and snipers became a daily menace for those unwary enough to relax their vigilance. It had become a battle of small independent units and a struggle to survive. Meanwhile, at the end of September the BdU summary of western U-boat operations concluded:

> "The west is no longer available as a base for operations . . . operational possibilities are therefore limited. Type IXC boats can no longer operate in the Caribbean and along the Gold Coast without refuelling. For these the Newfoundland area and the American coast are of increased importance. The St. Lawrence River can be added to these, as it can be sailed again with *Schnorchel* boats."

At the beginning of September 1944 the 2nd U-Flotilla numbered sixteen U-boats, including those in the Far East. They were now due for transfer to the 33rd U-Flotilla at the end of their current assignments. Operational control continued to be exercised by BdU, as it always had during the course of the war, and 2nd U-Flotilla ceasing to exist in anything but name. In recognition of his length of service and stalwart conduct, Ernst Kals had received promotion to *Kapitän zur See* at the beginning of the month. He was present as the last boat to leave Lorient, 10th U-Flotilla's *U155*, passed out to sea on 9 September.

Of those boats still on flotilla strength *U1228* put out of Kristiansand on 12 September, returning two days later with damaged hydroplanes after running aground. The repair necessitated transfer to Bergen and it was not until 17 September that Oblt.z.S. Friedrich-Wilhelm Marienfeld took to sea once more. The day following his departure he, alongside flotilla mate *U858*, became embroiled in the remarkable struggle to rescue *U867*, suffering severe damage following Mosquito attack. BdU's War Diary recorded the drama:

> "*U218* and *U858* reported positions as intimation that they were going to the rescue of *U867*, which had made fresh report that she lay stopped with run–down battery,

surfaced between 1800 and 2000 in the evening and 0600 and 0800 in the morning. Requested tow. Towing however is quite out of the question due to weather conditions and enemy air activity. Rescue boats and *U1228* therefore received orders to take over crew of *U867* and to sink boat. The transfer will nevertheless be very difficult on account of the weather (SW6) and very heavy air activity, which picked up and attacked two boats (*U1228* – AF7962 – and *U667*) in AF."

On 19 September Allied aircraft found the helpless *U876* and sunk her, the crew taking to their dinghies. They were never found. But aboard *U1228* there were major problems, Marienfeld breaking off the search and heading back to Norway that same day. Dönitz recorded the reason for his curtailed mission as the "exhausted state of his crew . . . probably due to break-down of *Schnorchel*". In fact *U1228* had also been bombed, a 224 Squadron Liberator attacking by Leigh Light the previous night. The depth charges that followed *U1228* underwater caused heavy damage to the *Schnorchel*, the diesels also running erratically as the boat turned for home. The defective *Schnorchel* leaked a lethal amount of CO into *U1228*'s interior and minutes after restarting the engine the greater part of the crew were incapacitated, *Matrosenobergefreiter* Matthias Mittler dying from CO poisoning. The U-boat received constant air harassment on its approach to Norway, arriving bedraggled in Bergen on 20 September.

23 September: The last U-boat to leave France, *U267*, put to sea from St Nazaire. As the evacuation and redirection continued, boats belonging to the 2nd U-Flotilla were directed to Kristiansand South. The Type IXC boats were then to proceed to home waters in convoy as they could not be repaired in the Norwegian ports owing to an acute shortage of spare parts. The 'Sea Cows' had had their day.

Two days later *U548* put into Bergen, after being listed as lost in Biscay on 10 September following loss of communication. The U-boat had been destined originally for Bordeaux, not acknowledging its redirection order to Norway and presumed lost to mines or ASW patrols. After Kaptlt. Pfeffer's successful arrival he left the boat for a staff post in Kiel, Zimmermann returning to the helm from Germany and *U548* transferring to the Flensburg flotilla.

The remaining 2nd U-Flotilla boats began to reach Norway in dribs and drabs, all transferring to the 33rd U-Flotilla after their arrival; *U858* reached Farsund on 27 September, *U547* Marvikan two days later. *U1226* transferred to the Flensburg command on the eve of its first war patrol late in September, one from which she and her fifty-six crew would never return, listed missing in action some time after 28 October.[175]

1 October: In Lorient the expected American onslaught had not yet materialized. The besieged port's control structure had been reorganized, Lorient's naval shipyard commander VA Walther Matthiae becoming *Seekommandant* Lorient on 10 September, KzS Ernst Kals his Chief of Staff and head of Kriegsmarine security units. By the beginning of October Brest had fallen, the battle claiming the lives of thousands of men. Kals expected the same tornado of steel and remained on tenterhooks waiting for the bloodbath to begin.

"Group Command West's Most Secret 03007 AI of 1/10/44 on the subject of supplying the Atlantic fortresses:

[175] It was not until 1993 that the wreck of the U-boat was found four miles east of Cape Cod.

"Although the battle for Brest ended 12 days ago, the expected enemy reinforcements for a mass attack on Lorient have not yet been observed.

"The Lorient situation rather remains unchanged in the main since the first half of September. It is possible, therefore, that the enemy intends to abandon the idea of specific attacks on the Atlantic fortresses altogether . . .

"It is therefore possible that the enemy intends to starve the fortresses out."

Although Allied land operations in Brittany had originally intended to gain ports as points of entry for additional troops and supplies directly from the United States, the strong German defences at St Malo and Brest prompted a change in Allied plans. They decided not to rehabilitate the destroyed port cities and also not to begin construction of the planned harbour complex at Quiberon Bay, code-named 'Operation Chastity'. The need for a deep-water port was answered once wreckage from conquered Cherbourg could be cleared. Nor had the complete decimation of the German front line been anticipated, the Breton supply point being too distant as the Wehrmacht was thrown back towards Belgium.

Meanwhile 2nd U-Flotilla boats continued to return from the western Atlantic and be reassigned in Norway and Germany. Their successes were few, mere survival taken as proof of commander and crew's ability. By Christmas Eve 1944 there remained only two U-boats on paper strength of the 2nd U-Flotilla. One *U1223*, arrived in Kristiansand from a turbulent patrol off Nova Scotia and in the Gulf of St Lawrence. Oblt.z.S. Albert Kneip reported heavy shipping and claimed the successful torpedoing of a 'destroyer' on 14 October, frigate HMCS *Magog*'s stern severely damaged by a *Zaunkönig* torpedo, the wreck later towed to harbour and paid off. Freighter SS *Fort Thompson* was also hit in the St Lawrence River by two torpedoes, Kneip again mistakenly claiming a sinking. On 29 December *U1223* became the penultimate transfer from the 2nd U-Flotilla.

The final boat to leave Kals' unit was *U1227*, arriving in Bergen on 27 December without any prior radio arrival report. The U-boat's communications gear had been damaged by depth charges in fierce attacks west of Gibraltar. Like her sister ship, *U1227* had managed to damage a Canadian frigate, this time HMCS *Chebogue* on 4 October. When en route to Gibraltar Oblt.z.S. Friedrich Altmeier reported a fast convoy consisting of 'approximately twelve ships' and, continuously dogged by destroyers, fired a T5 before crash-diving away. The torpedo hit and caused serious damage, the German crew mistakenly claiming it sunk. Altmeier later reported sinking an Allied tanker near Gibraltar, which remains unconfirmed. Hounded by ASW patrols and severely depth-charged more than once, *U1227* left its operational area to transit by *Schnorchel* north of the British Isles to Norway.[176] On the last day of 1944 *U1227* was officially transferred from the 2nd U-Flotilla while moored in Marviken en route to Germany and the 2nd U-Flotilla was no more.

In Lorient they waited for an Allied attack that would never come. During November KzS Kals became one of the steady stream of casualties, injured in a landmine explosion as he toured the front line, but remaining in command. Decisions had been taken by the Allied High Command to let the Biscay garrisons wither on the vine, rather than undertake costly assaults to remove them. On 1 January 1945 the 66th US Infantry Division, the 'Black Panthers', arrived to take over the task of containment. Ironically, the torpedoing

---

[176] *U1227*'s marathon *Schnorchel* voyage to and from Gibraltar was later reflected in its chosen *Wappen* – an underwater elephant with raised trunk.

in the English Channel of their troopship SS *Leopoldville* by 11th U-Flotilla's *U486* during December had decimated their ranks. Depleted, they became the siege weapon that held the German defenders in their cage, joined in the line by irregular local militia units and French Infantry.

Months of continuous shelling and sporadic combat between raiding parties often numbering no more than a dozen men ensued as *Festung* Lorient staved off defeat. On the morning of 3 May 1945 a small group of surviving *Hafenschutzflottille* vessels carrying weary Kriegsmarine riflemen made simultaneous landings on the islands of Houat and Hoëdic, east of Belle Isle, that the Germans had abandoned during December 1944. Occupied immediately by French troops, they held a small element of strategic importance, positioned between Belle Isle and Quiberon. Overruning minor resistance, the Swastika flew over the tiny French outcroppings once again, captured food shuttled to Lorient under American artillery fire.

Finally on 7 May Bernard Geismann, still manning the radio for the 2nd U-Flotilla, reported an urgent radio message from Germany:

> "In the evening . . . I received the message from Germany, that a ceasefire would be in effect from 8 May on all fronts. I handed over this message personally to KzS Kals in the officer's bunker."

In the nearby fishing village of Étel a motor launch flying the unmistakeable Red Cross flag approached the quayside. It had crossed the currents of La Barre d'Étel from the tributary's western bank, watched by hundreds of men from both sides of the water. Heavily armed American troops stood on the quay, somewhat incongruously next to an immaculately uniformed 66th US Infantry Division Major. As the diesel motor of the launch spluttered and died, ropes were fastened through iron rings embedded in the stonework and two equally well uniformed officers climbed from the boat to salute the American. It was late afternoon on 7 May 1945 and *Oberst* Borst, sporting decorations from this war and the last, had arrived to offer the unconditional surrender of Lorient. By 2000hrs that evening he had signed the capitulation of *Festung* Lorient in the name of *General der Artillerie*, cessation of hostilities due to come into effect at one minute past mid-night the next morning.

On 10 May Fahrmbacher attended the ceremony of surrender in the field near Caudan where he symbolically handed his pistol to General Kramer, commander of the 'Black Panthers'. The war was officially over for Lorient and the remnants of the 2nd U-Flotilla. German and French casualties have never been accurately recorded, but combat records of the US 66th Infantry Division indicate total battle casualties for four and a half months of war amounted to seventy-eight officers and 2,170 enlisted men. Of these 728 perished in the sinking of the *Leopoldville*. Bernard Geismann was unwilling to give himself over to the French and Americans and a final defiance was left to him:

> "On the morning of 8 May, a sergeant I knew came and persuaded me to escape with another fourteen sailors in a boat that they had prepared within the fortress. So, on the day of the capitulation, we left Lorient. After thirty-two hours, we arrived in Santander. There, we were greeted kindly – later going to El Ferrol. In August, 1945 we delivered ourselves as German soldiers to the English, eventually arriving in Edinburgh as Prisoners of War."

His commander had also reached imprisonment. Taken prisoner by the FFI K.z.S. Ernst Kals would remain a captive of the French until January 1948.

The remains of Lorient passed into Allied hands along with its unbeaten garrison. The town was so badly smashed that thought was initially given to rebuilding it elsewhere, but the idea was later abandoned and construction began amongst the ruins. The châteaux that had been used by Dönitz to command his U-boat packs in the Atlantic were among the handful of buildings still intact and on 10 May 1945, as Americans of the 66th Infantry Division moved through the rooms and bunkers of the 'Château des Sardines', they used the building's captured transmitters to inform the scattered populace that their war was over, the ghostly shell of Lorient once more free from occupation.

APPENDIX: BOATS OF 2ND U-FLOTILLA

Pre-war (1936 to 31 August 1939)
U26 (Type IA) Commissioned 11/5/35 sunk 1/7/40
U27 (Type VII) Commissioned 12/8/36 Sunk 20/9/39
U28 (Type VII) Commissioned 12/9/36 Transferred 24.UF 9/11/40
U29 (Type VII) Commissioned 16/11/36 Transferred 24.UF 31/12/40
U30 (Type VII) Commissioned 8/10/36 Transferred 24.UF 30/11/40
U31 (Type VII) Commissioned 28/12/36 Sunk 11/3/40 and 2/11/40
U32 (Type VII) Commissioned 5/4/37 Sunk 30/10/40
U33 (Type VII) Commissioned 25/7/36 Sunk 12/2/40
U34 (Type VII) Commissioned 12/9/36 Transferred 21.UF 30/9/40
U35 (Type VII) Commissioned 3/11/36 Sunk 29/11/39

10 boats commissioned directly into 'Saltzwedel' Flotilla.

Tenders: *Syra, Saar, Mosel, Weichsel* and (escort/catch ship) *T158*.

September 1939 to December 1939
U25 (Type IA) Transferred from Neustadt US–FI 1/9/39 Sunk 3/8/40
U26 (Type IA) Commissioned 11/5/36 Sunk 1/7/40
U27 (Type VII) Commissioned 12/8/36 Sunk 20/9/39
U28 (Type VII) Commissioned 12/9/36 Transferred 24.UF 9/11/40
U29 (Type VII) Commissioned 16/11/36 Transferred 24.UF 31/12/40
U30 (Type VII) Commissioned 8/10/36 Transferred 24.UF 30/11/40
U31 (Type VII) Commissioned 28/12/36 Sunk 11/3/40 and 2/11/40
U32 (Type VII) Commissioned 5/4/37 Sunk 30/10/40
U33 (Type VII) Commissioned 25/7/36 Sunk 12/2/40
U34 (Type VII) Commissioned 12/9/36 Transferred 21.UF 30/9/40
U35 (Type VII) Commissioned 3/11/36 Sunk 29/11/39
U36 (Type VII) Transferred from Neustadt US–FI 1/9/39 Sunk 4/12/39

10 boats at 1/9/39
2 boats transferred into flotilla
3 boats sunk (25% flotilla operational strength 1939)

9 boats at 31/12/39

Tenders: *Saar* and escort/catch ship *T158*.

January 1940 to December 1940
U25 (Type IA) Commissioned 6/4/36 Sunk 3/8/40
U26 (Type IA) Commissioned 11/5/36 Sunk 1/7/40
U28 (Type VII) Commissioned 12/9/36 Transferred 24.UF 9/11/40
U29 (Type VII) Commissioned 16/11/36 Transferred 25.UF 31/12/40
U30 (Type VII) Commissioned 8/10/36 Transferred 24.UF 30/11/40
U31 (Type VII) Commissioned 28/12/36 Sunk 11/3/40 and 2/11/40
U32 (Type VII) Commissioned 5/4/37 Sunk 30/10/40

U33 (Type VII) Commissioned 25/7/36 Sunk 12/2/40
U34 (Type VII) Commissioned 12/9/36 Transferred 21.UF 30/9/40
U37 (Type IXA) Transferred from Hundius 1/1/40 Transferred 26.UF 30/4/41
U38 (Type IXA) Transferred from Hundius 1/1/40 Transferred 24.UF 30/11/41
U41 (Type IXA) Transferred from Hundius 1/1/40 Sunk 5/2/40
U43 (Type IXA) Transferred from Hundius 1/1/40 Sunk 30/7/43
U44 (Type IXA) Transferred from Hundius 1/1/40 Sunk 20/3/40
U64 (Type IXB) Commissioned 13/4/40 Sunk 13/4/40
U65 (Type IXB) Commissioned 15/2/40 Sunk 28/4/41
U103 (Type IXB) Commissioned 5/7/40 Transferred 2.ULD 1/1/44
U104 (Type IXB) Commissioned 19/8/40 Sunk 29/11/40
U105 (Type IXB) Commissioned 10/9/40 Sunk 2/6/43
U106 (Type IXB) Commissioned 24/9/40 Sunk 2/8/43
U107 (Type IXB) Commissioned 8/10/40 Sunk 18/8/44
U108 (Type IXB) Commissioned 22/10/40 Transferred 8.UF 31/8/43
U109 (Type IXB) Commissioned 5/12/40 Sunk 4/5/43
U110 (Type IXB) Commissioned 21/11/40 Sunk 21/11/40
U111 (Type IXB) Commissioned 19/12/40 Sunk 4/10/41
U122 (Type IXB) Commissioned 30/3/40 Sunk after 22/6/40
U123 (Type IXB) Commissioned 30/5/40 Decommissioned 19/8/44
U124 (Type IXB) Commissioned 11/6/40 Sunk 3/4/43

9 boats at 1/1/40
5 boats transferred into flotilla
14 boats commissioned into flotilla
4 boats transferred out of flotilla
11 boats sunk (39% flotilla operational strength 1940)

13 boats at 31/12/40

Tenders: *Isar* (January 1940 to March 1941).

January 1941 to December 1941
U37 (Type IXA) Transferred from Hundius 1/1/40 Transferred 26.UF 30/4/41
U38 (Type IXA) Transferred from Hundius 1/1/40 Transferred 24.UF 30/11/41
U43 (Type IXA) Transferred from Hundius 1/1/40 Sunk 30/7/43
U65 (Type IXB) Commissioned 15/2/40 Sunk 28/4/41
U66 (Type IXC) Commissioned 2/1/41 Sunk 6/5/44
U67 (Type IXC) Commissioned 22/1/41 Sunk 16/7/43
U68 (Type IXC) Commissioned 11/2/41 Sunk 10/4/44
U103 (Type IXB) Commissioned 5/7/40 Transferred 2.ULD 1/1/44
U105 (Type IXB) Commissioned 10/9/40 Sunk 2/6/43
U106 (Type IXB) Commissioned 24/9/40 Sunk 2/8/43
U107 (Type IXB) Commissioned 8/10/40 Sunk 18/8/44
U108 (Type IXB) Commissioned 22/10/40 Transferred 8.UF 31/8/43
U109 (Type IXB) Commissioned 5/12/40 Sunk 4/5/43
U111 (Type IXB) Commissioned 19/12/40 Sunk 4/10/41
U116 (Type XB) Commissioned 26/7/41 Transferred 1.UF 31/1/42
U117 (Type XB) Commissioned 35/10/41 Transferred 1.UF 31/1/42
U123 (Type IXB) Commissioned 30/5/40 Decommissioned 19/8/44
U124 (Type IXB) Commissioned 11/6/40 Sunk 3/4/43
U125 (Type IXC) Commissioned 3/3/41 Sunk 6/5/43
U126 (Type IXC) Commissioned 22/3/41 Sunk 3/7/43
U127 (Type IXC) Commissioned 24/4/41 Sunk 15/12/41
U128 (Type IXC) Commissioned 12/5/41 Sunk 17/5/43

U129 (Type IXC) Transferred from 4.UF 1/7/41 Scuttled 18/8/44
U130 (Type IXC) Transferred from 4.UF 1/9/41 Sunk 13/3/43
U131 (Type IXC) Transferred from 4/UF 1/11/41 Sunk 17/12/41
U501 (Type IXC) Commissioned 30/4/41 Sunk 10/9/41
U502 (Type IXC) Commissioned 31/5/41 Sunk 5/7/42
U503 (Type IXC) Commissioned 10/7/41 Sunk 15/3/42
UD3 (Ex-Netherlands 025) Transferred from 5.UF Aug 1941 Transferred 10.UF Sept 1942

13 boats at 1/1/41
4 boats transferred into flotilla
12 boats commissioned into flotilla
2 boats transferred from flotilla
5 boats sunk (17% flotilla operational strength 1941)

22 boats at 31/12/41

January 1942 to December 1942

U43 (Type IXA) Transferred from Hundius 1/1/40 Sunk 30/7/43
U66 (Type IXC) Commissioned 2/1/41 Sunk 6/5/44
U67 (Type IXC) Commissioned 22/1/41 Sunk 16/7/43
U68 (Type IXC) Commissioned 11/2/41 Sunk 10/4/44
U103 (Type IXB) Commissioned 5/7/40 Transferred 2.ULD 1/1/44
U105 (Type IXB) Commissioned 10/9/40 Sunk 2/6/43
U106 (Type IXB) Commissioned 24/9/40 Sunk 2/8/43
U107 (Type IXB) Commissioned 8/10/40 Sunk 18/8/44
U108 (Type IXB) Commissioned 22/10/40 Transferred 8.UF 31/8/43
U109 (Type IXB) Commissioned 5/12/40 Sunk 4/5/43
U116 (Type XB) Commissioned 26/7/41 Transferred 1/UF 31/1/42
U117 (Type XB) Commissioned 35/10/41 Transferred 1.UF 31/1/42
U123 (Type IXB) Commissioned 30/5/40 Decommissioned 19/8/44
U124 (Type IXB) Commissioned 11/6/40 Sunk 3/4/43
U125 (Type IXC) Commissioned 3/3/41 Sunk 6/5/43
U126 (Type IXC) Commissioned 22/3/41 Sunk 3/7/43
U128 (Type IXC) Commissioned 12/5/41 Sunk 17/5/43
U129 (Type IXC) Transferred from 4.UF 1/7/41 Scuttled 18/8/44
U130 (Type IXC) Transferred from 4.UF 1/9/41 Sunk 13/3/43
U153 (Type IXC) Transferred from 4.UF 1/6/42 Sunk 13/7/42
U154 (Type IXC) Transferred from 4.UF 1/2/42 Sunk 3/7/44
U156 (Type IXC) Transferred from 4.UF 1/1/42 Sunk 8/3/43
U157 (Type IXC) Transferred from 4.UF 1/6/42 Sunk 13/6/42
U161 (Type IXC) Transferred from 4.UF 1/1/42 Sunk 27/9/43
U162 (Type IXC) Transferred from 4.UF 1/2/42 Sunk 3/9/42
U173 (Type IXC) Transferred from 4.UF 1/7/42 Sunk 16/11/42
U183 (Type IXC-40) Transferred from 4.UF 1/10/42 Transferred 33.UF 30/9/44
U184 (Type IXC-40) Transferred from 4.UF 1/11/42 Sunk 20/11/42
U502 (Type IXC) Commissioned 31/5/41 Sunk 5/7/42
U503 (Type IXC) Commissioned 10/7/41 Sunk 15/3/42
U504 (Type IXC) Transferred from 4.UF 1/1/42 Sunk 30/7/43
U505 (Type IXC) Transferred from 4.UF 1/2/42 Captured 4/6/44
U507 (Type IXC) Transferred from 4.UF 1/3/42 Sunk 13/1/43
U518 (Type IXC) Transferred from 4.UF 1/10/42 Transferred 33.UF 31/10/44
U519 (Type IXC) Transferred from 4.UF 1/11/42 Sunk 10/2/43
U520 (Type IXC) Transferred from 4.UF 1/10/42 Sunk 30/10/42
U521 (Type IXC) Transferred from 4.UF 1/10/42 Sunk 2/6/43

U522 (Type IXC) Transferred from 4.UF 1/10/42 Sunk 23/2/43
UD3 (Ex-Netherlands O25) Transferred from 5.UF Aug 1941 Transferred 10.UF Sept 1942

22 boats at 1/1/42
17 boats transferred into flotilla
3 boats transferred from flotilla
8 boats sunk (21% flotilla operational strength 1942)

28 boats at 31/12/42

January 1943 to December 1943

U43 (Type IXA) Transferred from Hundius 1/1/40 Sunk 30/7/43
U66 (Type IXC) Commissioned 2/1/41 Sunk 6/5/44
U67 (Type IXC) Commissioned 22/1/41 Sunk 16/7/43
U68 (Type IXC) Commissioned 11/2/41 Sunk 10/4/44
U103 (Type IXB) Commissioned 5/7/40 Transferred 2.ULD 1/1/44
U105 (Type IXB) Commissioned 10/9/40 Sunk 2/6/43
U106 (Type IXB) Commissioned 24/9/40 Sunk 2/8/43
U107 (Type IXB) Commissioned 8/10/40 Sunk 18/8/44
U108 (Type IXB) Commissioned 22/10/40 Transferred 8.UF 31/8/43
U109 (Type IXB) Commissioned 5/12/40 Sunk 4/5/43
U123 (Type IXB) Commissioned 30/5/40 Decommissioned 19/8/44
U124 (Type IXB) Commissioned 11/6/40 Sunk 3/4/43
U125 (Type IXC) Commissioned 3/3/41 Sunk 6/5/43
U126 (Type IXC) Commissioned 22/3/41 Sunk 3/7/43
U128 (Type IXC) Commissioned 12/5/41 Sunk 17/5/43
U129 (Type IXC) Transferred from 4.UF 1/7/41 Scuttled 18/8/44
U130 (Type IXC) Transferred from 4/UF 1/9/41 Sunk 13/3/43
U154 (Type IXC) Transferred from 4/UF 1/2/42 Sunk 3/7/44
U156 (Type IXC) Transferred from 4.UF 1/1/42 Sunk 8/3/43
U161 (Type IXC) Transferred from 4.UF 1/1/42 Sunk 27/9/43
U168 (Type IXC-40) Transferred from 4.UF 1/3/43 Transferred 33.UF 30/9/44
U183 (Type IXC-40) Transferred from 4.UF 1/10/42 Transferred 33.UF 30/9/44
U189 (Type IXC-40) Transferred from 4.UF 1/4/43 Sunk 23/4/43
U190 (Type IXC-40) Transferred from 4.UF 1/3/43 Transferred 33.UF 30/9/44
U191 (Type IXC-40) Transferred from 4.UF 1/4/43 Sunk 23/4/43
U193 (Type IXC-40) Transferred from 4.UF 1/5/43 Transferred 10.UF 31/3/44
U504 (Type IXC) Transferred from 4.UF 1/1/42 Sunk 30/7/43
U505 (Type IXC) Transferred from 4.UF 1/2/42 Captured 4/6/44
U507 (Type IXC) Transferred from 4.UF 1/3/42 Sunk 13/1/43
U518 (Type IXC) Transferred from 4.UF 1/10/42 Transferred 33.UF 31/10/44
U519 (Type IXC) Transferred from 4.UF 1/11/42 Sunk 10/2/43
U521 (Type IXC) Transferred from 4.UF 1/10/42 Sunk 2/6/43
U522 (Type IXC) Transferred from 4.UF 1/10/42 Sunk 23/2/43
U531 (Type IXC-40) Transferred from 4.UF 1/4/43 Sunk 6/5/43
U532 (Type IXC-40) Transferred from 4.UF 1/4/43 Transferred 33.UF 30/9/44
U534 (Type IXC-40) Transferred from 4.UF 1/6/43 Transferred 33.UF 31/10/44
U536 (Type IXC-40) Transferred from 4.UF 1/6/43 Sunk 20/11/43
U538 (Type IXC-40) Transferred from 4.UF 1/11/43 Sunk 21/11/43
U545 (Type IXC-40) Transferred from 4.UF 1/12/43 Scuttled 11/2/44
U801 (Type IXC-40) Transferred from 4.UF 1/11/43 Sunk 17/3/44
U841 (Type IXC-40) Transferred from 4.UF 1/7/43 Sunk 17/10/43
U842 (Type IXC-40) Transferred from 4.UF 1/8/43 Sunk 6/11/43
U843 (Type IXC-40) Transferred from 4.UF 1/11/43 Transferred 33.UF 30/9/44

28 boats at 31/12/42
15 boats transferred into flotilla
1 boat transferred from flotilla
24 boats sunk (56% flotilla operational strength 1943)

18 boats at 31/12/43

January 1944 to December 1944

U66 (Type IXC) Commissioned 2/1/41 Sunk 6/5/44
U68 (Type IXC) Commissioned 11/2/41 Sunk 10/4/44
U103 (Type IXB) Commissioned 5/7/40 Transferred 2.ULD 1/1/44
U107 (Type IXB) Commissioned 8/10/40 Sunk 18/8/44
U123 (Type IXB) Commissioned 30/5/40 Decommissioned 19/8/44
U129 (Type IXC) Transferred from 4.UF 1/7/41 Scuttled 18/8/44
U154 (Type IXC) Transferred from 4.UF 1/2/42 Sunk 3/7/44
U168 (Type IXC-40) Transferred from 4.UF 1/3/43 Transferred 33.UF 30/9/44
U183 (Type IXC-40) Transferred from 4.UF 1/10/42 Transferred 33.UF 30/9/44
U190 (Type IXC-40) Transferred from 4.UF 1/3/43 Transferred 33.UF 30/9/44
U193 (Type IXC-40) Transferred from 4.UF 1/5/43 Transferred 10.UF 31/3/44
U505 (Type IXC) Transferred from 4.UF 1/2/42 Captured 4/6/44
U518 (Type IXC) Transferred from 4.UF 1/10/42 Transferred 33.UF 31/10/44
U532 (Type IXC-40) Transferred from 4.UF 1/4/43 Transferred 33.UF 30/9/44
U534 (Type IXC-40) Transferred from 4.UF 1/6/43 Transferred 33.UF 31/10/44
U545 (Type IXC-40) Transferred from 4.UF 1/12/43 Scuttled 11/2/44
U547 (Type IXC-40) Transferred from 4.UF 1/1/44 Transferred 33.UF 30/9/44
U548 (Type IXC-40) Transferred from 4.UF 1/4/44 Transferred 33.UF 30/9/44
U801 (Type IXC-40) Transferred from 4.UF 1/11/43 Sunk 17/3/44
U802 (Type IXC-40) Transferred from 4.UF 1/2/44 Transferred 33.UF 30/11/44
U843 (Type IXC-40) Transferred from 4.UF 1/11/43 Transferred 33.UF 30/9/44
U856 (Type IXC-40) Transferred from 4.UF 1/3/44 Sunk 7/4/44
U858 (Type IXC-40) Transferred from 4.UF 1/5/44 Transferred 33.UF 30/9/44
U868 (Type IXC-40) Transferred from 4.UF 1/8/44 Transferred 33.UF 30/9/44
U1223 (Type IXC-40) Transferred 4.UF 1/8/44 Transferred 33.UF 29/12/44
U1225 (Type IXC-40) Transferred from 31.UF 1/6/44 Sunk 24/6/44
U1226 (Type IXC-40) Transferred from 31.UF 1/8/44 Transferred 33.UF 30/9/44
U1227 (Type IXC-40) Transferred from 31.UF 1/8/44 Transferred 33.UF 31/12/44
U1228 (Type IXC-40) Transferred from 31.UF 1/8/44 Transferred 33.UF 31/10/44

18 boats at 1/1/44
11 boats transferred into flotilla
18 boats transferred from flotilla
1 boat decommissioned
1 boat captured
2 boats scuttled
7 boats sunk (24% flotilla operational strength 1944)

0 boats at 31/12/44 – operational flotilla disbanded completely.

From 90 operational U-boats 58 were sunk by enemy action, 64% of the total number of boats to pass through the flotilla's ranks.

BIBLIOGRAPHY

Bernard, Yves and Bergeron, Caroline, *Trop loin de Berlin. Des Prisonniers Allemands au Canada (1939–1946)*, Septentrion.

Blair, Clay, *Hitler's U-boat War*, Vols 1 & 2, Cassell, 1996.

Bohn, Roland, *Raids Aeriens Sur la Bretagne Durant La Seconde Guerre Mondiale*: Vols 1 & 2 self-published 1996.

Bowyer, Chaz, *Men of Coastal Command 1939–1945*, William Kimber, 1985.

Brendon, Piers, *The Dark Valley – A Panorama of the Thirties*, Jonathan Cape, 2000.

Brennecke, Jochen, *Jäger – Gejagte!*, Koehlers Verlagsgesellschaft, 1956.

Brown, David, *Warship Losses of World War Two*, Naval Institute Press, 1995.

Buffetaut, Yves, *Les Ports Francais: Les Ports de l'Atlantique 1939–1945*, Marines Edition.

Busch, Harald, *U-boats At War*, Putnam, 1955.

Caruthers, Bob, *Servants of Evil*, André Deutsch, 2001.

Chazette, Alain & Reberac, Fabian, *Kriegsmarine*, Editions Heimdel, 1997.

Churchill, Winston, *The Second World War*, Vols 1 to 6, Cassell, 1948.

Dönitz, Karl, *Memoirs – Ten Years and Twenty Days*, Lionel Leventhal, 1990.

Frank, Wolfgang, *Enemy Submarine*, William Kimber, 1954.

Franks, Norman, *Conflict Over The Bay*, William Kimber, 1986.

—— *Search, Find and Kill*, Grub Street, 1995.

Gannon, Michael, *Operation Drumbeat*, HarperCollins, 1990.

Gasaway, E.B., *Grey Wolf, Grey Sea*, Ballantine, 1970.

Gibbing, Peter, *Weep For Me Comrade*, Minerva Press, 1997.

Goebeler, Hans & Vanzo, John, *Steel Boats, Iron Hearts*, Self-Published, 1999.

Goss, Chris, *Bloody Biscay*, Crecy Books, 2001.

Grossmith, Frederick, *The Sinking of the Laconia*, Paul Watkins, 1994.

Hadley, Michael, *U-boats Against Canada*, McGill-Queen's University Press, 1985.

Hartmann, Werner, *Feind im Fadenkreuz*, Leipzig: Boreas, 1943.

Hague, Arnold, *The Allied Convoy System*, Chatham, 2000.

Hepke, Gerhard, *Der Radarkrieg* (unpublished).

Hessler, Günter, *The U-boat War in the Atlantic*, HMSO, 1989.

Hildebrand, Hans & Lohmann Werner, *Die Deutsche Kriegsmarine 1939–1945*, Podzun–Verlag, 1956.

Hirschfeld, Wolfgang, *The Secret Diary of a U-boat*, Leo Cooper, 1996.

Jones, Geoffrey, *U-Boat Aces*, William Kimber, 1988.

Kahn, David, *Seizing the Enigma*, Houghton Mifflin, 1991.

Kelshall, Gaylord T.M., *The U-boat War in the Caribbean*, United States Naval Institute, 1994.

Krug, Hans-Joachim; Hirama, Yōichi; Sander-Nagashima, Berthold; Niestlé, Axel, *Reluctant Allies*, Naval Institute Press, 2001.

Lane, Tony, *The Merchant Seaman's War*, Manchester University Press, 1990.

Le Berd, Jean, *Lorient sous l'occupation*, Éditions Ouest France, 1986.

Leroux, Roger, *Le Morbihan en Guerre*, Joseph Floch/Mayenne, 1978.

Lohmann, W. & Hildebrand, H., *Kriegsmarine 1939–1945*, Podzun-Verlag, 1956.

Macintyre, Donald, *Battle of the Atlantic*, Pan, 1961.

Martienssen, Anthony, *Hitler and his Admirals*, E.P. Dutton, 1949.

—— *Führer Conferences on Naval Affairs*, HMSO, 1948.

Middlebrook, Martin and Everitt, Chris, *The Bomber Command War Diaries*, Midland, 1995.

Nesbit, Roy Conyers, *The Strike Wings*, William Kimber, 1984.

Niestlé, Axel, *German U-boat Losses During World War Two*, Naval Institute Press, 1998.

Paterson, Lawrence, *First U-boat Flotilla*, Pen and Sword, 2002.

Peilard, Léonce, *U-boats to the Rescue*, Jonathan Cape Ltd, 1963.

Price, Alfred, *Aircraft Versus Submarine*, Naval Institute Press, 1974.

Rohwer, Jürgen, *Allied Submarine Attacks Of World War Two*, Naval Institute Press, 1997.

—— *Axis Submarine Successes*, Naval Institute Press, 1983.

—— *The Critical Convoy Battles of March 1943*, Naval Institute Press, 1977.

Romanowsk, Boleslaw, *Torpeda w Celu!*, Gdansk, 1997.

Ritschel, Herbert, *Kurzfassung Kriegstagesbücher Deutscher U-Boote 1939–1945, Band 1*, Korntal, 1996.

Rössler, Eberhard, *The U-Boat*, Arms & Armour Press, 1981.

—— *Vom Original zum Modell: Uboottyp IX*, Bernard & Graefe.

Rust, Eric C, *Naval Officers Under Hitler*, Praeger, 1991.

Runyan, Timothy and Copes, Jan M. (editors), *To Die Gallantly*, Westview Press, 1994.

Schaffer, Heinz, *U-Boat 977*, William Kimber, 1952.

Shirer, William, *The Rise And Fall of the Third Reich*, Simon & Schuster, 1960.

Showell, Jak P. Mallmann, *The German Navy In World War Two*, Arms & Armour Press, 1979.

—— *German Navy Handbook*, Sutton, 1999.

—— *U-Boat Command And The Battle Of The Atlantic*, Conway, 1989.

Steen, E.A., *The Norwegian Sea War 1940–1945*.

Stern, Robert, *Battle Beneath the Waves*, Arms & Armour Press, 1999.

Suhren, Reinhard and Brustat, Fritz, *Nasses Eichenlaub*, Berlin, 1983.

Terraine, John, *Business in Great Waters*, Leo Cooper, 1989.

—— *The Right of the Line: The Royal Air Force in the European War 1939–1945*, Wordsworth, 1997.

Thomas, Gwynne, *King Pawn or Black Knight?* Mainstream Publishing, 1995

Vause, Jordan, *Wolf*, Airlife, 1997.

—— *U-Boat Ace*, Airlife, 1992.

Whitley, M.J., *Destroyer*, Naval Institute Press, 1983.

Wiggins, Melanie, *Torpedoes in the Gulf*, Texas A&M University Press, 1995.

Williams, David, *Wartime Disasters At Sea*, Patrick Stephens, 1997.

Wynn, Kenneth, *U-boat Operations of the Second World War*, Vols. 1 & 2, Chatham Publishing, 1997.

1

INDEX

Army Units: German *(continued)*
  Kampfgruppe 'Schaenske', 246
  Kampfgruppe 'Wachter', 246
Athelprincess, SS, 194
Athenia, SS, 9–11, 13, 14
Atik, USS see *Carolyn*, SS.
Atlantis (Schiff 16), 42, 116, 117, 200
Aubretia, HMS, 93, 94
Audacity, HMS, 121, 123
Aurania, AMC, 113

Bahner, Rudolf, 165
Ballestrem, Johannes Graf von, 176
Balzac, SS, 69, 70
Baoulé, SS, 24
Barbara Robertson, HMT, 31
Bargsten, Klaus, 178, 179, 181, 182, 194, 197, 198, 206
Barham, HMS, 31
Barney, USS, 198
Baton Rouge, SS, 146
Bauer, Ernst, 98–100, 110, 116, 117, 138, 140, 159, 176, 177, 190
Baumann, Arend, 121, 122
Beaverburn, SS, 36
Beduhn, Heinz, 56, 59, 97
Beechwood, SS, 167
Behrens, Hans-Wilhelm, 41
Belchen, 91
Belpamela, SS, 41
Bender, Werner, 138, 218, 219
Benmohr, SS, 141
Bernbeck, Hinrich-Oskar, 82
Bessel, SS ('Bernardo'), 33, 53, 54
Bismarck, 88, 90, 91, 95, 108
Biter, HMS, 206
Bittersweet, HMCS, 153
Black Swan, HMS, 199
Blairlogie, SS, 12
Blankney, HMS, 121
Bleichrodt, Heinrich, 81, 90, 97, 99, 108, 111, 112, 118, 125, 129, 131, 142, 148, 149, 175, 187, 188
Block Island, USS, 232, 236
Blücher, 47
Blyskawica, 6
Bodegraven, SS, 247
Boehme, Hermann, 1, 2
Bogue, USS, 202, 243
Borkum, 28
Bourne, Dietrich von dem, 134, 135
Brachmann, Hans-Günther, 185
Brake, 211, 217
Brans, Hans-Joachim, 232
Brenas, MV, 167
Brinker, Rolf, 87, 100, 110, 114, 117, 118, 132
British Consul, SS, 136
British Mariner, SS, 116

British Statesman, SS, 79
British Zeal, MV, 78
Broadway, HMS, 93
Bronstein, USS, 232
Bruchhausen, Herbert von, 113
Brühl, Ewald, 113
Brüller, Ernst-Ulrich, 65
Brümmer-Patzig, Helmut, 53, 56
Buckingham, Thomas, 171
Buckley, US, 236–238
Büchel, Paul, 11, 29, 31, 32
Büchting, Hermann, 187
Büssinger, Heinrich, 134, 136
Buhl, Willi, 46n
Bulldog, HMS, 93–95
Bury, SS, 152
Burza, 6, 69
Byard, HMS, 219

C3, 3
Caddo, SS, 186
Calanda, SS, 148
Caldew, 19
Calgary, HMCS, 226
Campoamor, SS, 200
Canaris, SS, 151
Capellini, 169
Card, USS, 216
Carolyn, SS, 143, 144
Cassequel, SS, 115
Ceronia, SS, 36
Chambly, HMCS, 102, 103
Champlain, SS, 57n
Champlin, USS, 197, 232
Charles F. Meyer, MV, 74
Charlotte Schliemann, 33, 118, 211
Chebogue, HMCS, 253
Cheerio, 162
Cherry Valley, MV, 215
City of Cairo, SS, 175
City of Melbourne, SS, 156
Clausen, Nikolaus (Nicolai), 68, 78, 82, 83, 85, 100, 101, 108–110, 114, 127, 136, 140
Clematis, HMS, 202
Clyde, HMS, 105–106
Cockaponset, SS, 91
Coimbra, 129
Collegian, SS, 65
Columbia, HMCS, 178
Columbia, SS, 227
Core, USS, 211,
Corrientes, (*Culebra*), 33, 78, 83, 96, 99
Cory, USS, 232
Counsellor, SS, 41
Courageous, HMS, 14–16, 19, 49
Crane, HMS, 220
Cremer, Peter Erich 'Ali', 130n, 185
Crispin, SS, 81

264

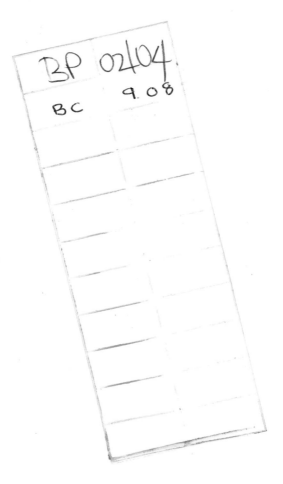

BP 02404

BC   9.08